Paul Bierley entered the field of music research through the back door. An aeronautical engineering graduate of Ohio State University in 1953, he was engaged in the complex world of aircraft and missile preliminary design for nearly two decades. Being gregarious by nature, totally unassuming and never too proud to ask for advice, he excelled in that work. Today he is still an aerospace engineer but involved in data management.

His first love, however, has always been music. For the greater part of his life he had been exceptionally fond of the music of Sousa and curious about the colorful titles of those famous marches. He supposed that some day there would be books telling all about Sousa and his music, but such books never appeared. The late Wilbur Crist of Capital University convinced him that he was better equipped to write such books than most musicians or music educators. With this bit of encouragement, he combined a veritable arsenal of skills and interests and commenced research. The rest is history.

Bierley has retired from the Columbus Symphony Orchestra but still performs with several groups, most notably the renowned Detroit Concert Band.

"Such a beautiful garden of memories I have cultivated!" he says. "My research has brought me in contact with some of the most interesting people in the world—musicians."

Henry Fillmore would probably go along with that.

HALLELUJAH TROMBONE!

HENRY FILLMORE
(JAMES HENRY FILLMORE, JR.)
b. Cincinnati, December 3, 1881
d. Miami, December 7, 1956

HALLELUJAH TROMBONE !

PAUL E. BIERLEY

INTEGRITY PRESS

HALLELUJAH TROMBONE!

INTEGRITY PRESS
3888 Morse Road
Columbus, Ohio 43219

Printed in the United States of America

10   9   8   7   6   5   4

**This book is respectfully dedicated to
George Stein, Jr.
of Cincinnati, Ohio
and
Richard Lambert Harris
of Columbus, Ohio**

Library of Congress Catalog Card Number 82-90686
ISBN 0-918048-05-2

CONTENTS

ILLUSTRATIONS AND CREDITS

INTRODUCTION AND BOUQUETS

THE REASONS FOR THIS BOOK

What does a so-called scholar do when he has researched a subject thoroughly for many years and has covered nearly all aspects of the subject through his writings?

He either rests on his laurels or picks another subject and begins a new study.

In my case, I commenced the study of the life and music of Henry Fillmore while my two books on John Philip Sousa were still being set into type.

The frantic pace I kept while completing my investigations of Sousa over the relatively short period of ten years had taken a rather cruel toll on me physically, so why did I not leave well enough alone? For two reasons.

First, I felt an obligation to the music world. I had gained expertise in this type of research, expanding upon and combining a wide variety of existing research tools. I was literally itching to flex my newly found curiosity-go-seek muscles.

Second, I learned that Henry Fillmore, one of my favorite composers, had not been the subject of any kind of definitive study. I knew I could do him justice. While it might seem immodest of me to say so, I knew I could do a better job than most others who might be inclined to try. While some might present the same findings in a more ingenious way than I, I was convinced that I could get straight to the heart of Fillmore's legacy in a more effective manner.

At first, I had entertained thoughts of writing about the American composer Karl L. King rather than Fillmore. In fact, I had spoken to Karl King about it personally. Shortly after that time, however, a tragic fire destroyed his manuscripts, and a few months later he passed away. Two others have since written on King, both living closer to his Iowa home than I.

As it turned out, Henry Fillmore was an extremely interesting subject. He was a fun person, and at every turn of my research I grew to love him more. When I became fully aware that he had a truly extraordinary sense of humor and also had great compassion for animals, I knew that the difficulties of my endeavor would somehow seem less strenuous; he was my kind of man!

Henry Fillmore was the epitome of American optimism, and the rags-to-riches story of his life was an endless series of interesting episodes. His music is happy music—the trombone "smears" in particular, which have become classics in their field. His lively marches—well, they speak for themselves. And his forgotten church music yielded many, many surprises!

Add to this the fact that he was one of the most flamboyant, entertaining conductors in the history of music, and you will see why I enjoyed putting this story together from thousands of bits and pieces of information.

Now let me tell you briefly about those bits and pieces; they lie scattered between the words of these pages. And if you don't mind, I'd like to toss a few bouquets along the way.

Fillmore's life centered around two cities: Cincinnati and Miami. Since I live in Columbus, Ohio, traveling to Cincinnati for research purposes was relatively convenient. Collecting information on the Miami period of his life posed more formidable problems, however, and was the most expensive part of my research.

WORKING PAPERS

As my research progressed, I developed several basic working papers which were referred to constantly. In fact, they were tacked all around my office or put in three-ring notebooks where I could see them at a glance. They were:

1. DAY-BY-DAY LOG OF FILLMORE'S LIFE. This was the most essential document; how could I write about a man's life if I did not know what he was doing—and why—at any given time?

2. NOTEBOOKS OF FILLMORE'S MUSIC (nine fat ones), complete with copyright and publishing data.

3. CHRONOLOGICAL LIST OF FILLMORE'S MUSIC. This list was constantly changing and was not possible to compile until a copyright search was complete. Of all my tasks, this was by far the most difficult. Consider the fact that Fillmore wrote under eight different names, and you'll begin to understand why!

4. PHOTOGRAPH FILE. I accumulated an extensive file of photographs, approximately one third of which were used in this book. These I studied by the hour. I attempted to put myself inside each picture and look outward—asking questions about what was going on at that time and place. And why.

5. FILLMORE FAMILY TREE. This covers eight generations and is four feet long. The entries contain vital statistics data and other scribblings, all written with an ultra-fine engineering pen.

6. DOSSIERS OF FILLMORE FAMILY MEMBERS. Isn't it obvious that a biographer must know as much as possible about his subject's family?

7. LIST OF HENRY FILLMORE'S ADDRESSES. (See Appendix II.)

8. INTERVIEW NOTES. I interviewed nearly two hundred people who were associated with or related to Fillmore.

9. LETTER FILE. I corresponded with several dozen people whom I could not interview personally.

10. CLIPPINGS FILE. Many clippings and articles were copied from the career scrapbooks at the Fillmore Museum; others were gathered from sources too numerous to attempt to list here.

11. FILLMORE CORRESPONDENCE FILE. An accumulation of letters between Fillmore and his closest friends provided insights into his professional and private life which would have been impossible to gain through any other method of study.

12. MASONIC FILE. Fillmore was affiliated with many Masonic organizations. Since I am a Freemason myself, I have an appreciation of the importance of these affiliations.

13. CIRCUS FILE. Fillmore was associated with five different circuses in his lifetime, and these circuses had a profound influence on both his career and his personal life. Indeed, even in his twilight years.

14. RECORDINGS OF FILLMORE'S MUSIC. The study of recordings—and even listening for pleasure—greatly facilitated the understanding of my subject's creative output.

15. FILE ON THE FILLMORE BROTHERS PUBLISHING OPERATIONS. This included as many copies of their music and periodicals as I could locate.

16. WILL HUFF DOSSIER AND LIST OF MUSIC. Momentarily, you will see the importance of this. Will Huff was an important man in Fillmore's life.

I must emphasize a point which I always try to drive home when asked about the process of doing research on a composer: It is futile to attempt to write intelligently about a composer's life unless one knows all his music thoroughly. It is also futile to attempt to write intelligently about a composer's music unless one knows the composer intimately. I mean intimately, not merely gaining an acquaintance by reading a short summary of his life.

Perhaps you are beginning to see why this book was over nine years in the making. I absolutely refused to write the first paragraph until I felt I was well enough acquainted with Henry Fillmore to know how he would react in any given situation.

THE DELIGHTFUL FILLMORE FAMILY

Early in my research, I discovered that Henry Fillmore was not one of a kind when it came to plain old-fashioned pleasantness. Every member of the Fillmore family I contacted was a chip off the same old block. I approached cousins, nieces and nephews (in the absence of direct descendants) and was amazed to learn that one was not a Fillmore unless he or she was agreeable and hospitable. And I could write volumes about the Fillmore sense of humor, which I shall never forget.

It would take a separate chapter to tell about Annette Fillmore Manning, Henry's second cousin, whose help and encouragement was of inestimable value. She recalled countless memories, documented family affairs, supplied photographs and identifications, educated me on Cincinnati history (that figures; she's a retired schoolteacher) and checked the entire manuscript for accuracy.

Being a gifted musician, Annette also helped locate and evaluate Henry's little known church music—which we joyfully played together on the piano. What a lovely person to be with! (She makes good coffee cake, too.)

Annette's sister, Hildegarde Fillmore Smith, also added to the Fillmore saga. Since she was a former editor, her critique of parts of the manuscript was valued.

Southern hospitality abounded in Lawrenceburg, Kentucky, where I was privileged to meet with Henry's niece, Nancy Smith. From the collection of family stories, memorabilia, old hymnals, photographs, diaries and other documents handed down from her mother (Henry's sister, Fred Toll), I was able to extract much information without which the overview of Henry Fillmore would be sadly lacking. I also learned of the wonders of "sock-it-to-'em" cake at Nancy's home.

Nancy's sister, Leslie Hollingsworth, also provided a wealth of useful information, and she too possesses the typical Fillmore charm and warmth.

Leslie and Nancy's cousin, Annie Emily Ramsdell, who also extended that Southern hospitality, recounted numerous interesting accounts of Fillmore's early life as handed down from her mother (Henry's sister Mary). Annie Emily also permitted me to study other family documents and photographs, and it is with her kind permission that the song "Roses" (written expressly for her by her Uncle Henry) is reproduced in Chapter 38.

Other Fillmore family members who helped in various ways were Mabel Bradley, Katherine Lemons, Ruth Ella Lentz, Carol McMasters, William Millard Fillmore and Joshua Everett.

A distant relative, Charles L. Fillmore of Nova Scotia, helped more than I can begin to say. I am truly indebted to him for sharing his fabulously detailed family genealogy. Using this as a guide, I drew the family tree mentioned above, and it became one of my most valuable reference tools.

KEEPING UP WITH THE JONESES

Hospitality was the watchword not only on Henry's side of the family, but also on Henry's wife Mabel's side of the family. Thelma Bernum, Mabel's niece, as well as Thelma's son Bill and his wife Bea, provided valuable information on the Jones family. Before having the pleasure of meeting with them at Port Huron, Michigan, it appeared that I had reached a dead end on Mabel Jones' immediate family, most of whom had moved away from Michigan decades ago. The Bernums put me in touch with Clarence A. Jones, Jr., of Hawaii, who also provided several missing links.

Others whom I wish to thank for information on Mabel Jones' family include Ranea J. Scott and Roger Mendel of the Alpena (Michigan) Public Library, Kathleen S. Schoene of the Missouri Historical Society, Frances A. Marshall of the St. Clair (Michigan) Public Library and T. Wilson Sparks of the International Association of Fairs and Expositions.

MMI'S COLD TRAILS

Gathering data on the Miami Military Institute, for the years Fillmore attended, at first seemed hopeless. The main MMI building (now part of Camp Miami, owned and operated by the United Methodist Church) was partially destroyed by a 1903 fire in which most records were lost. The Germantown (Ohio) newspaper building had also had a tragic fire, destroying back issues of the paper. The Germantown Public Library and the Germantown Historical Society are the repositories of a few surviving documents, and I made maximum use of these. Other newspapers of the period, at the Ohio Historical Center in Columbus, were in a ruinous condition.

If it had not been for Alice Kepler of the Germantown Historical Society, Carl Becker of Wright State University, Paul F. Erwin of the University of Cincinnati and Thurston E. Manning of the North Central Association of Colleges and Schools, I would have been in a dilemma. Each of these people came forth with bits of data on MMI, and I eventually completed the picture.

A breakthrough on the MMI situation came by an incredible coincidence. My daughter, Lois Walker, who was doing graduate work in archival science at Wright State University, notified me (at the peak of my period of frustration) that the school archives had just received a cache of old photographs and that among them were two albums of MMI photographs. As it turned out, these albums covered the years I was looking for—and I found several photographs in which Henry Fillmore could clearly be identified! These photographs enabled me to learn the year of his graduation—a date which had, until that time, been questionable.

EARLY RELATIONSHIP WITH BILLY KOPP

Fillmore's association with the First Regiment Band of the Ohio National Guard and with Kopp's Military Band of Cincinnati was another gray area until Kopp's daughter, Jane Jensen, came to my rescue with old photographs, programs and other information. For other data on the First Regiment Band, I am indebted to Arthur Terry and John P. Seimer of the Ohio Adjutant General's Department.

EARLY RELATIONSHIP WITH HOMER RODEHEAVER

Collecting data on Fillmore's association with songleader Homer Rodeheaver was another difficult task. For verifying details obtained from various interviews, the following people must be given proper credit: Mrs. J.H. Rodeheaver; Mrs. Hobart H. Bell; Don W. Berg, Editor of the Ohio Wesleyan University alumni magazine; and William Darr of the Grace Theological Seminary.

PLACE OF MARRIAGE

To be sure, attempting to learn when and where Henry and Mabel Fillmore were married was an adventure. Henry mentioned the date in a 1953 interview with the noted bandmaster Jack Mahan, and I am exceedingly grateful to Mahan for making the text of this invaluable interview available to me.

I knew when the marriage took place, but not where, and this was critical to other areas of my study. Fillmore ran away from home, was married, and joined a circus. Thinking he was married while trouping with the circus, I traced the path of the circus and systematically wrote lengthy letters to thirty-four county clerks along the route. O. Williams, Recorder of Deeds of the City of St. Louis, came up with the actual marriage license and certificate, and further details on that period of Fillmore's life came thanks to Kathleen S. Schoene of the Missouri Historical Society.

CIRCUS AFFILIATIONS

To understand Henry's early circus affiliations, I immersed myself in circus history and lore for several months. It is with considerable pleasure that I acknowledge the help of Bob Parkinson of the Circus World Museum at Baraboo, Wisconsin, who gave me much needed direction in this endeavor and furnished many books and other materials for study. In a rather lengthy exchange of letters and phone calls, I am sure I tried Bob's patience many times.

Merle Evans, the legendary circus bandmaster, was another store of information. After several interviews, I was convinced that the "Toscanini of the Big Top" knew every circus bandsman who ever lived! Accounts of his long-time personal friendship with Fillmore were fascinating, and he put me in touch with numerous other circus authorities. One of these was Bill Pruyn, Evans' successor as Ringling Brothers and Barnum & Bailey's bandmaster, who provided much insight on circus band operations and Fillmore's music in particular.

Merle Evans also pointed me in the direction of the co-editor of *Bandwagon*, the circus buff's neat little journal. By a fantastic stroke of luck, this was Fred Pfening III, who lives just twelve miles from me! Since Fred is one of the world's leading circus historians, it goes without saying that I benefitted tremendously from what little time I was privileged to spend with him. His critique of the circus chapters of my manuscript is very much appreciated.

I must also thank John Hurdle, formerly of the Ringling Museum of the Circus in Sarasota, Florida, Elaine L. Strand of the Grand Forks (North Dakota) Public Library, and Albert Conover for their help in giving me a rounded picture of circus operations at the turn of the century.

MASONIC AFFILIATIONS

Masonic affiliations were extremely important to the understanding of Henry Fillmore, because many of his activities were aligned with Freemasonry. I began my probe of this area by consulting several Masonic brothers here in Columbus. Dick Gowdy, Recorder of Aladdin Temple Shrine, provided much useful information and put me in touch with many others. Harry Fuller, with whom I worked in the aerospace industry for many years, also increased my knowledge of Masonic orders about which I knew little, as did Bob Hinshaw, Secretary of the Grand Lodge of Ohio.

Much knowledge of Henry's involvement with the Syrian Temple Shrine of Cincinnati came from their Recorder, Charles Settle. William J. Guentter, Jr., of Syrian Temple and Impressario of their Jesters auxiliary unit, was also most helpful. I must also thank George G. Smith, who now leads the band which Henry Fillmore brought to national prominence, for permitting me to "sit in" one night at a band rehearsal and to view memorabilia at the hall.

Also in Cincinnati, I learned quite a bit about Henry's Shrine Band and Grotto Band activities from Jack Rahm (and his daughter, Ruth Gram), Ralph Van Wye, Earl Behrman, James R. Croswell, Eugene Mulhauser, Dorothy Rixie, Eppa Rixie III, Eddie Zeuch and Irwin H. Bollinger.

The most detailed stories of Fillmore's Shrine Band years came not from a Shriner but from a Shriner's widow. It was indeed a pleasure to visit and correspond with Marie Grau, who was eighty-seven years of age when I met her. The George Graus and the Henry Fillmores were very close personal friends, so I learned much from this alert young lady.

Shrine officials from other cities also provided Masonic data, enabling me to compile Appendix III. This included James C. Hathaway, Recorder of Mahi Temple in Miami; John Paul Koitzsch, Recorder of Lu Lu Temple in Philadelphia; and William P. Jacobs, Recorder of Almas Temple in Washington, D.C.

HENRY'S TREASURED TIMEPIECE

Who says big companies don't have a heart? One which does is the Herschede Hall Clock Company of Starkville, Mississippi. After I had written for information on Fillmore's prized grandfather's clock, their president, Richard Herschede, became interested in the history of the clock and arranged to have it completely restored at their expense. It may now be seen at the Fillmore Museum.

THE CINCINNATI YEARS

Of all those in Cincinnati with whom I came in contact, I learned most about the personal side of Henry Fillmore from Luise Reszke, former clarinetist of the Fillmore Band and one of Henry and Mabel's most admired friends. Luise not only located an abundance of old programs; she also assisted in the cataloging of Fillmore's music and gave my manuscript a thorough critique.

Phil Gates, a pioneer music educator, also provided many keen insights into the Cincinnati period of Fillmore's life. I must also acknowledge the help of his son Robert of Columbus and his daughter, Elizabeth Benton, whose published articles about Henry Fillmore are interesting and informative.

Frances Jones Poetker, the internationally acclaimed floral arranger, author and lecturer, helped me understand Henry's personal life. Her father, Charles B. Jones, was regarded as Henry's alter ego. I am greatly indebted to this brilliant woman for her insights and her hospitality.

Herbert Tiemeyer and Corwin Taylor also contributed much information on Fillmore's life, as well as insights into his conducting and the rank of his musical works. In talking with them numerous times, I learned more of Fillmore's philosophy of entertainment than I had anticipated.

Eugene Frey, President of the Cincinnati Musicians Association (Local 1), enabled me to expand my base of information on Fillmore's relationship with the musicians' union and with his fellow musicians. He permitted me to study all the old records of his organization. Joyce Van Wye and Wilbert Little of that office were also most helpful.

I would also like to thank James and John Yeager of Harrison, Ohio, who provided interesting stories about Fillmore's many visits with their uncle and aunt, Harry and Norma Schott—and for making it possible for me to photograph the grave of Mike, the "radio hound," Fillmore's celebrated canine companion.

For information on other aspects of Henry Fillmore's Cincinnati years, I am indebted to the following: Ruth Young; Elmer Seibert; Jean Buck; Tillie Hahn; Carl E. Martin; Matthew Joseph Kuhn; Leo Hirtl and Jack Klumpe of the *Cincinnati Post;* Luke Feck of the *Cincinnati Enquirer;* Charles F. Hardy of Delco Remy; Pat Brewer of the Middletown (Ohio) Public Library; Jordan Zimmerman of the Otto Zimmerman & Son Printing Company; David Shepherd, Principal of Walnut Hills High School; Major Charles P. Erwin of the United States Marine Band; Betty Burnet of the Lexington (Kentucky) Public Library; Janet Ross of the Cincinnati Zoological Society; Jim Ferguson of the Cincinnati Reds; Robert Herbert and Maxine Hughes of the Cincinnati Board of Education; Maxine W. Shank and Marie S. Ludeke of the University of Cincinnati; and Sandy Tietjen of the Cincinnati Symphony Orchestra.

Things were so informal in the early days of commercial

radio broadcasting that about the only reliable way to learn what actually went on is to study old newspapers. This I did until I reached the point where I never wanted to see another microfilm reader.

I was also able to pick up little pieces of information about Fillmore's early association with radio stations WLW and WSAI from the following: Waite Hoyt, the veteran Reds baseball game announcer and Hall of Fame pitcher; Milt Wiener; Charles M. Williams; Don Becker; Minabelle Hutchings; Charles K. Murdock and Terry Edwards of WLW; John Bruning of the Gray Wireless Museum; William L. Utter of the Miami University Telecommunications Center; Louis H. Krems of the National League of Professional Baseball Clubs; C.C. Johnson Spink of the *Sporting News;* and John Whiteman of the General Foods Corporation.

THE FLORIDA YEARS

Data on the last years of Fillmore's life in Florida was easier to obtain, because more of the friends and associates of this era were available for interviewing.

Chief among these were John and Margaret Heney. They told me of the interesting visits by the Fillmores over the years, and I spent many long hours listening to the tape recordings they made in response to questions I had sent them. My numerous visits with the Heneys were rewarding in many ways —we "snowbirds" are not often treated to grapefruit fresh from the tree in the winter.

I was greatly dismayed when John passed away suddenly, because above all others I had wanted him to read this book. Since he was a former member of Sousa's Band, I had previously spent much time with him while working on my biography of John Philip Sousa. The Sousa book passed his test with flying colors, and I was eager to see if this one would also meet his approval.

If this book has any degree of excellence, it is partly because of the help received from another former Sousa man, Otto Kraushaar. It pains me that Otto, like John Heney, did not live to read it. Otto's dear wife Fern, however, provided much vital information after Otto passed away.

Fillmore had lived with the Kraushaars for nearly two years, and their recollections were paramount to the study of his personal likes and dislikes. I am particularly grateful to Fern, who carefully read the manuscript of all the chapters of the Florida period of Fillmore's life and offered excellent suggestions for improvements. And I shall always remember Otto for generously sharing his painstakingly compiled list of Fillmore's music and the concert tapes of his Lake Wales High School Band, which Fillmore guest-conducted many times.

Fred McCall was still another man whom I am extremely sorry to say did not live long enough to read these words. Fred had become Henry Fillmore's dearest friend, and he painted a beautiful picture of Fillmore's last eighteen years in Florida. I am most grateful for the many accounts of Fillmore's professional and personal pursuits which were passed on to me by Fred and Betty McCall. In particular, I am grateful to Betty for reviewing large portions of my manuscript, offering timely suggestions and being helpful in so many ways. And I can confirm what Henry Fillmore used to say about her cooking!

Another of Henry Fillmore's close friends and associates was Al G. Wright who, like Henry, became a giant in the band world. I was overwhelmed by his willingness to help me in every possible way. Most assuredly I benefitted from his knowledge of Fillmore's career and the meaning of his music. I loved the countless anecdotes which he recalled with delight.

Al graciously supplied several of the photographs used in this book, and I also wish to acknowledge his considerable help in critiquing parts of the manuscript and for making available recordings of Fillmore's performance with both the Purdue University Band and the Miami Senior High School Band.

To Stan Dulimba, I am grateful for the story of why Fillmore settled in the Miami area and for data on their personal and professional relationships. I am also grateful to Logan Turrentine for his recollections of Fillmore's early Florida activities and for a better understanding of Fillmore's amazing rapport with students.

The personal recollections of Bob Lampi are also gratefully acknowledged. Bob's long association with the Florida Bandmasters Association served to make him a fine source of information on FBA history and Fillmore's role in its development. Bob generously consented to read several chapters of the manuscript for accuracy. Incidentally, one of the stories he told me across the breakfast table at an FBA meeting in Tampa became the topic of Chapter 52.

Paul Yoder, who knew Fillmore as a fellow composer and arranger, was kind enough to spend several hours with me explaining why the Fillmore music has stood the test of time. I considered it a rare privilege to have been in the company of this world renowned creative artist and performer, and I discovered that both he and Henry Fillmore had many things in common, not the least of which was modesty.

For other personal recollections of Henry Fillmore during the Florida era, I wish to thank William Foster, bandmaster at Florida A & M; Manley R. Whitcomb of Florida State University; Colonel George S. Howard, formerly of the United States Air Force Band; Paul Lavalle, formerly of the Cities Service Band of America; author Glenn D. Bridges; FBA President Joe Courson; Milburn Carey of Phillips University; Fred Humphries; Amado Del Grado; Alton Rine; Lester Thayer; Bennett Vance; and Ernie Siler.

For other help in gathering information on Fillmore's Florida life, I wish to acknowledge the help of Colonel Arnald Gabriel of the United States Air Force Band; John S. Knight, Editor of the *Miami Herald;* Bea Moss of the *Coral Gables Times/Guide;* Norman Gillespie of the Miami Public Library; Rebecca S. Smith of the Historical Society of Southern Florida; Richard Gosselen; and Robert C. Zimmer.

ASSOCIATION WITH THE UNIVERSITY OF MIAMI

Since Henry Fillmore was Permanent Guest Conductor of the University of Miami "Band of the Hour," I had no trouble locating former members of the band who were willing to share many vivid memories of playing under his direction.

Many of these people went out of their way to recount to me these memories. Jerry and Allene (Bushong) Capley, for example. Jerry's exposure to Uncle Henry extended back to Miami Edison High School during Fillmore's early relationship with Fred McCall, who was bandmaster at Edison. Allene was one of those gorgeous majorettes Fillmore always bragged about. I shall be forever grateful for the charming tapes they made in which they poured out their recollections of those happy days. These tapes were returned so their children and grandchildren will have a wonderful record of an unforgettable era.

The Capleys had a lovely buffet dinner on the occasion of my visit to Melbourne, and at this dinner I had the pleasure of meeting several members of the Melbourne Municipal Band who had known Fillmore. Their esteemed conductor, Chick Catterton, had earlier named me to the band's Board of Advisors, and he insisted that I conduct the band in a few numbers at the rehearsal that night. Let me tell you. . .researching Henry Fillmore's life and music had its rewarding moments!

President of the Melbourne Municipal Band was Althea Krasney, and hearing of her long association with Henry Fillmore was truly delightful. Her incredibly detailed and interesting personal accounts of the days when she was a member of the University of Miami Band or enrolled at the summer band camps helped me tremendously.

The sincerity of Ed Caughran of Savannah, another of Henry Fillmore's favorite students who was present at many of the student gatherings at the Fillmore home and elsewhere, is impressive. Ed graciously spent many hours preparing tapes to answer what must have seemed like a million questions I had sent him. His carefully considered answers were revealing indeed.

Others who helped paint the picture of Fillmore's relationship with the University of Miami were Coach Andy Gustafson, former twirler Bill Allen and Harold Supank. (I hope Harold will forgive me for the egg I have him laying in Chapter 64.)

THE FILLMORE MUSEUM

The Fillmore Museum at the University of Miami was, of course, a focal point of my research. Bandmaster Bill Russell graciously granted me permission to study the materials and to copy photographs. On my last visit, he assigned student assistant Deborah Richey to help with the photographic work, and for this assistance I am thankful.

The assistance of Ken Moses, Assistant Band Director, is also gratefully acknowledged; he helped immeasurably in locating music, identification of items in the museum, explaining how Fillmore conducted his music with the University of Miami Band, and in many other ways.

Jackie Pepper, former Band Department Secretary, was a specialist in cutting red tape. She also provided much information on Fillmore's relationship with the band, particularly on the trips to South America.

I also wish to acknowledge the help of University of Miami President Henry King Stanford. Also Leyla Arner of the University of Miami Band, who copied numerous photographs which I had missed at the museum.

LOCATING MUSIC AND RECORDINGS

Without the help of Robert Hoe of Poughkeepsie, New York, producer of the *Heritage of the March* series of recordings, my cataloging of Fillmore's music would have taken much longer and would have been less complete. Indeed, there would have been several pieces of music I might never have seen if he had not located them in his intensive worldwide search for rare music of band composers. All lovers of military band music have Bob Hoe to thank for producing a record of the lesser known Fillmore music as performed by the Morehead State University Band.

Another gentleman whom I wish to thank profusely for locating both music and recordings is Robert P. Hills, Jr., of Delaware, Ohio. One of his favorite pastimes is getting together his "Nuts in a Bandshell" group of local musicians for the purpose of playing through old music which is seldom heard. Fillmore figured in several of these sessions. Bob, Bandmaster of Windjammers Unlimited and a noted composer himself, also made valuable comments on this music and its performance.

For helping locate still other music, I wish to thank band historian/author/composer Loren D. Geiger, Walker Thorsby, and Bob Seifert. Bob is organizer and director of a unique Cincinnati musical aggregation known as the Charter-oak Stationary Marching Concert Band, which usually plays at least five Fillmore pieces at each of its concerts.

I also wish to acknowledge the help of Jon Newsom, Bill Parsons and other staff members of the Music Division of The Library of Congress for helping locate some of Henry Fillmore's all-but-extinct church music. Several of the juvenile cantatas completely escaped them in their searches, however, because it was believed that this music had been transferred to a remote warehouse many years ago and had probably been destroyed.

I then sent an S.O.S. to a master sleuth, William Lichtenwanger, former Head of the Reference Section (Music Division) of The Library of Congress. Bill donned his Sherlock Holmes cap, came charging out of retirement and headed straight for the warehouses where the music might be found. He found every last page! It is a matter of fact that if it had not been for Bill's memory, I would have been totally unable to catalog a significant segment of Fillmore's music.

I am also indebted to Gary Tirey of Otterbein College for making available old Fillmore music and publishers' catalogs for study; to Oliver R. Graham of the Cameron-Graham Music Museum at Altoona, Florida, and Thomas C. Bardwell for recordings of Fillmore's music; to James Perkins of the Chatfield Brass Band Lending Library for the loan of much music; and to William Quimby of the Ohio State University Library for publishing data on the Fillmore music.

For their efforts in locating other Fillmore church music, I also thank Dr. Floyd Faust, Judd McClevey, John Stanton, Henry Crespi, Flora Tehiman, Reverend David L. DeBow, Reverend David F. Brown and Reverend Larry H. Pigg.

COPYRIGHT DATA

It was necessary to spend a total of three weeks at the Copyright Division of The Library of Congress to ascertain the titles and dates of Fillmore's compositions and arrangements—plus the same on the music of his father, grandfather and uncles. This process was greatly complicated, of course, by the fact that Henry Fillmore wrote under eight different names. I must admit that my first reaction was, "This is impossible!" But, armed with the knowledge that I had solved an even greater problem when undertaking a similar study on the music of John Philip Sousa several years earlier, I trudged onward.

There are millions of card entries in the Library's files, arranged by groups of years. All musical compositions are supposed to be listed by (a) composer, (b) title and (c) copyright holder. They are not, however, and because of these omissions one must go back and forth among the cards of these three classifications to complete a search.

It is also necessary to document the copyright renewals, thus doubling the work. I soon developed an appreciation for those individuals who maintain this massive file, and I wish to thank the staff for their helpfulness and patience.

MILITARY ESCORT

For many years, there has been a rumor to the effect that one of Fillmore's most popular marches, "Military Escort," was actually composed by a rather obscure Indiana composer by the name of Will Nicholson. Hopefully I have successfully laid this rumor to rest in Chapter 28, and for vital information on the subject I wish to thank Irvin H. Weber, Frank B. Neal and William K. Braun.

THE FOOTLIFTER

Another of Fillmore's popular marches is "The Footlifter," the story of which is found in Chapter 39. Despite an intensive search, however, I was never able to determine the name of the small organization which asked him to compose it. In addition to perhaps twenty-five persons mentioned elsewhere in this introduction, I wish to thank the following people for their help in narrowing down the search: Jean E. Coleman of the Prudential Insurance Company of America; Charles Barrett of Western-Southern Life; John A. Lloyd and David F. Westerbeck of the Union Central Life Insurance Company; and Malcolm Mackay of the New York Life Insurance Company.

APPRAISALS OF FILLMORE'S MUSIC

To appraise a composer's music, it is best to consult several authorities. This I did, and the names of most have already been mentioned. There are others I must also thank, including several Central Ohio musicians. Among them are John Mitchell, Glenn Harriman and Jack O. Evans. I have Jack Evans to thank for kindly reading several revisions of Chapter 1 with a critical eye; he played a prominent role in the concert described therein.

I also wish to thank arranger Dave Wheeler and the very talented Terry Waldo. Terry is the renowned ragtime pianist and composer, and since the Fillmore trombone "smears" are actually rags set to march tempo, Terry was able to provide insight into their history and their place in today's popular music repertoire.

By far the most significant contribution to my effort in this regard came through the efforts of pianist Anne Droste, the artistically gifted wife of Paul Droste, Director of the famed Ohio State University Marching Band. Anne loves a challenge, and she helped immeasureably with my cataloging and assessment of Henry Fillmore's church music.

Fillmore wrote numerous juvenile cantatas, gospel hymns and other pieces of vocal music. The juvenile cantatas (playlets) included as many as fifteen songs each. Cataloging was tedious because several of the short cantata pieces were later re-published as gospel hymns—some several times, with different sets of words. The music was almost identical in all cases. I thought of an expedient and asked Anne for her help.

She played all these unfamiliar pieces on the piano and recorded them on individual cassette tapes according to category. I then took the tapes and armloads of music and sat back in my rocking chair. After many long hours of study, I had spotted all the duplications, at which time the cataloging process was begun. This was the least documented part of Fillmore's creative output, and it was a thrill to have made the first comprehensive listing.

THE ELUSIVE WILL HUFF

As you will see in Chapters 13, 22 and 23, Fillmore's use of the name Will Huff caused considerable confusion—because there really was an Ohio composer by that name! What's more, most of the Huff music was published by the Fillmore Brothers Company. Despite what most musicians have believed for decades, Will Huff was not just another of Fillmore's pseudonyms. It is the writer's earnest hope that this book will settle the matter once and for all.

The duplicate use of the Huff name brought me no end of trouble, because in order to set the record straight I found myself doing research on two composers rather than one! I hadn't counted on this, but it was fascinating.

The most difficult task was cataloging all the music published under the name Will Huff. The problem was compounded almost beyond belief in 1916 when Fillmore engaged the real Will Huff to compose a set of sixteen pieces for a collection. Huff did not finish the job, so Fillmore completed the collection himself. The name Huff appeared on all sixteen pieces, and Henry never revealed which pieces were his and which were Huff's!

The only way to solve the mystery, as I saw it, was to have a band record all the questionable pieces so I could study the tapes. The Gahanna (Ohio) Lincoln High School Band, conducted by my old friend Bob Kessler and Jim Singer, his worthy assistant, graciously did that. Their theory and harmony class then adopted the project as their final class project of the year, and after a period of four weeks we had the puzzle solved.

I must make it clear that these wonderful young ladies and gentlemen are not to be held responsible in the event that technical cataloging errors are discovered in the future. If errors are ever found, I shall take the blame and beg the indulgence of the sharp scholar who finds them—on the grounds that my errors were honest errors. Final judgments on who wrote which pieces were based upon a comparative study of stylistic, harmonic and melodic content.

The name Will Huff is unfamiliar to most musicians today. His name is so little known that it was not until 1973 that I learned of his existence—despite the fact that I had lived all my life less than fifty miles from where he spent most of his.

Upon learning of the real Will Huff's existence, I located several of his relatives. I am greatly indebted to three of his children: William Huff, Jr., Marjorie Huff and Beulah Clark, for biographical information and for permission to study family documents. For much other information on Huff's career, I am indebted to Charles M. Crow and Walter Howard Tinker, both of whom had many personal recollections. Charles Crow, in particular, was able to document the history of most of the bands in the Chillicothe, Ohio, area with which Will Huff was associated.

I am also grateful to the following people for information on the life and music of Will Huff: Lloyd Savage of Chillicothe High School; Amelia Hydell of the *Chillicothe Gazette;* Mildred and Margaret Hart; Carl F. Nolze; Tom Paridon; Dave Pontius; Herman and Bill Hinton; Jim Bonners; Ray Connett; Oscar Leach; Boyd G. McFall; Wallace J. Williamson of the Boyd County (Kentucky) Historical Society; Catherine Preston of the Tobacco Merchants Association of the United States; Barbara Greer of the Fiveco Regional Library of Louisa, Kentucky; Jane H. Kobelski of the Suffolk (Virginia) Public Library; Mary E. Winter of the Kentucky Historical Society; Frances L. Sellers of the Wellston (Ohio) Public Library; Karen Potter of the Owensboro (Kentucky) Public Library; and Mrs. E. McKenna of the Ironton (Ohio) Public Library.

A.B.A. ASSOCIATES

Lynn L. Sams, of the American Bandmasters Association, is a most unselfish man. He put aside the manuscript of his forthcoming history of bands, now in preparation, to answer—in amazing detail—dozens of questions about A.B.A. history and the part Fillmore played in it. Lynn, now eighty-seven years young, had edited the A.B.A. newsletter for thirty-five years and was the logical man to approach with such questions. I could scarcely begin to thank him enough for all his help, so this acknowledgment is a rather feeble try.

Numerous other A.B.A. members, in addition to those already mentioned, were generous with their time in relating stories of the happy, lovable Henry Fillmore they once knew. This was especially true of H.E. Nutt of the Vander Cook School of Music; Lieutenant Colonel William F. Santelmann, formerly of the United States Marine Band; and Forrest L. McAllister, Consulting Editor of the *School Musician/Director & Teacher.* All went out of their way to bring me their vital messages. The same was true of Raymond and Florence Dvorak and Albertus L. Meyers.

Other A.B.A. members and wives to whom I am also indebted for sharing their memories are Mrs. Karl L. King, Mrs. Howard Bronson, Mrs. Harold Bachman, William D. Revelli, Frederick Fennell, Everett Kissenger and Herbert N. Johnston.

FILLMORE THESIS PROBLEMS

I also wish to acknowledge the assistance of two men who were simultaneously working on doctoral dissertations about Henry Fillmore: Leon Bly and William Higgins. It was discovered that both were writing in nearly identical areas, and since Bill's had been declared first, Leon deferred.

Leon then turned the bulk of his data over to me, and I immediately expanded upon it. He subsequently published a remarkable treatise on the military march and received his doctorate. Meanwhile, Bill has encountered difficulties but is still pursuing his degree; we have exchanged numerous research items.

ILLUSTRATIONS

For the attractive frontispiece and the illustration in Chapter 66 of Fillmore receiving an honorary doctorate, I am deeply indebted to the ambitious young bandmaster-artist Thomas J. Trimborn of Palatine, Illinois. For much of the photographic work, I wish to thank Carel Cadot of Chroma Studios in Columbus.

COMPOSER'S VIEWPOINT

I also gratefully acknowledge the help of Leonard B. Smith, conductor of the peerless Detroit Concert Band, for innumerable insights into Henry Fillmore's composing processes. Smith is a remarkable composer and conductor in his own right, and I learned that his methods for producing memorable music are, in many instances, much like Fillmore's.

Since Fillmore had known Smith for many years and had conducted his Moslem Temple Shrine Band on several occasions, I learned much about Fillmore's personal and professional life. To put it mildly, my discussions with Leonard Smith were enlightening.

LIBRARIANS

Where would biographers be without the help of our country's librarians? Elsewhere in this introduction, I have thanked many librarians for their help on specific problems. I wish now to acknowledge the assistance of others who helped in ways literally too numerous to mention.

First and foremost, I am most grateful to Olga Buth, formerly of the Ohio State University Music Library, and to Bob Jones of the University of Illinois Main Library, for their assistance in gathering data on Fillmore Brothers Company publishing operations. Next, hearty thanks to Conrad Weitzel of the Ohio Historical Center and Richard Fisher of the State Library of Ohio, both of whom I kept busy searching for countless bits of historical data.

Others, whose help I gratefully acknowledge, are: Major Judson E. Bennett of the United States Marine Corps Museum Branch; Matilda V. Sparenblek of the Indianapolis Public Library; Richard Abell, R. Jayne Crave, Yeatman Anderson III and Patrice Callaghan of the Cincinnati Public Library; Frances Forman, Ed Rider, Alden Monroe and Edward Malloy of the Cincinnati Historical Society; Elmer Geers, Librarian of the *Cincinnati Post;* Ronald K. Huff, Kitty Huff and Marvin D. Williams of the Disciples of Christ Historical Society; Suzanne Fisher, Samuel Roshon, Dougal Pendergast and Gay Banks of the Columbus Public Library; Arlene Peterson and Ed Lentz of the Ohio Historical Center; and Mrs. Lee Ketham of the Samford University Main Library.

HELP FROM MANY OTHERS

In addition to all those mentioned thus far who helped in specific ways, there were many who helped in a variety of similar ways—or in a multiplicity of ways. To name just a few: Arthur Lehman, former euphonium soloist of the United States Marine Band; Norrie H. Wake; Robert N. Hance; Robert Campbell; Katherine A. Ling, Editorial Assistant of *The Instrumentalist;* Mike Roche, Sports Information Director of Fordham University; Heather D. Conner of the National Music Publishers Association; and Howard Zettervalle, Executive Editor of Lorenz Industries.

FRIENDS AND RELATIVES

Veteran Ohio music educator Richard L. Harris was, in many respects, my right arm. His willingness to share his vast knowledge of music with me has been a tremendous help in years past, particularly while my biography of John Philip Sousa was in work, and he lived up to all expectations during the Fillmore research.

He did a considerable amount of library research, and when the manuscript was finished he gave it a thorough reading and offered many truly outstanding suggestions. Had it not been for his expertise and keen sense of balance, I would likely have stumbled numerous times.

It's often very handy for a man to have a daughter and son who are brighter than he is. My daughter, Lois Walker, took upon herself the onerous task of transcribing some two reams of handwritten letters from Fillmore to his friends, thus saving me many hours of valuable study time. Since she is a professional historian and editor, it is needless to say that her editing of the entire manuscript helped make this a better book.

My son, John E. Bierley, read segments of the manuscript and also offered appropriate comments. His specialty seemed to be catching me in ambiguities of speech. Better this way than to be embarrassed by an editor!

It's also handy to have an English teacher in the family. After all the editing was complete, my nephew, Blaine S. Bierley, had his turn at the manuscript. He read it more carefully than anyone else, and his suggestions for improvement were both erudite and clever. This is a much better book by his having a hand in it.

I have a habit of imposing on friends and colleagues when I have isolated chapters in need of outside opinions. I would like to acknowledge the help of the following victims: Homer L. Horst, James E. Stauffer, Charles F. Hyde, Ralph J. Simms, Daniel P. Brown, Hallie Brotherton, John Jenkins, Robert C. Raugh and David B. Legger. Most of all, I am indebted to Paul E. Spencer for proof-reading the entire manuscript.

I have saved the best until last, of course.

On television detective shows, there is often a "leg man" who is an underpaid fact-finder. In Cincinnati, I found a Fillmore buff by the name of George Stein, Jr., who became a "leg man" of the first magnitude. My many trips to Cincinnati were really for the purpose of delighting in George's latest findings, not for the purpose of indulging in his charming wife Betty's fantastic cooking—despite what the bathroom scales registered immediately after each trip.

Whereas most people use their spare time for self-serving pursuits, George used his in constructive endeavors such as: collecting photographs and clippings; writing letters and conducting interviews in my behalf; collecting and assimilating recordings of Fillmore's music; studying Cincinnati history, with emphasis on the neighborhoods where Fillmore lived; doing detailed research in libraries, museums and public archives; extracting vital statistics data on members of the Fillmore family; and much more.

It was George who, in the course of his investigations, learned the location of the grave of Mike, the "radio hound." If it had not been for this, I might not have had occasion to get to the bottom of this poignant story (as reported in Chapter 42).

All things considered, the timely efforts of the totally unselfish George Stein have made this a much better book.

To my wife, Pauline, the biggest bouquet of all.

She served as consultant, interviewer, sounding board, answering service, first reader, second reader, third reader (etc.), editor, proof reader, and God only knows what all else. For nine years, she put up with my multitudinous idiosyncrasies. As you might well imagine, her patience is endless.

Pauline also put up with my escapades and panics during the

previous ten-year period I was working on John Philip Sousa. That, combined with the trials of my Fillmore research, is surely the cause of the gray hairs which dot her sweet little head. If some day there is a reward for all my frantic efforts, I shall direct it all to her.

A CLOSING THOUGHT

While some have said that Henry Fillmore was egotistical about his music, I must counter this by saying emphatically that down deep inside he was truly a man of great humility. Obvious humility, when you look at his life as a whole. He even burned most of his manuscripts, thinking they would never be the subject of serious study.

Although he could have lived sumptuously in the last half of his life, he was exceptionally conscious of his humble beginnings and lived modestly. In my estimation, this is wisdom.

Henry Fillmore was generous in the extreme, even designing his will in such a way that the monies from his estate would be used for the benefit of unknown future generations of young musicians.

Henry Fillmore's music will never be forgotten. Neither will Henry Fillmore, so long as anyone who ever knew him is still living. As for the perpetuation of his memory, it is sincerely hoped that this book will be a small step in that direction.

The saga of the late Henry Fillmore, a classic example of the American rags-to-riches phenomenon, is the lighthearted tale of a man with an amazing gift for lifting the spirits of multitudes of people through music. *Happy* music.

Composer, bandmaster, teacher, publisher, benefactor, sportsman—Henry Fillmore was this and more. But foremost, he was an entertainer of the first magnitude, and things began to happen the instant he walked onto a stage. For example, take an evening back in 1952. . .

The scene is the campus of the Ohio State University in Columbus. The occasion is a college band concert at a convention of the prestigious American Bandmasters Association. The program is featuring many celebrities of the music world, and the audience eagerly awaits the appearance of the famous bandmaster who will no doubt provide the climax of the evening.

The kindly, flamboyant Henry Fillmore, "father of the trombone smear," was an entertainer of the first magnitude. "Lassus Trombone" and several other of his short pieces have become popular classics. He composed under eight different names.

A portly, aging figure, dressed in a white Palm Beach suit and white shoes, steps up on the stage. It is the legendary Henry Fillmore.

As he is being introduced, he makes his way toward the podium with short steps, smiling broadly and looking directly into the audience. He nods and waves at three elderly ladies seated in the front row. It is as if he is telling us that he will do everything in his power to please us, and we cannot help but believe that we will love what we are about to see and hear.

He stops short of the podium, turns to the audience and begins a slow, deliberate bow. But he doesn't come back up! Does he have a hitch in his back? He continues to dip lower and lower, and the applause grows louder and louder. He bends so low it appears that he will surely bump his head on the floor! By this time the applause has reached a feverish pitch, and gradually he straightens up, grinning from ear to ear. Such a ham!

We have enjoyed Henry's flamboyant entry as much as anything on the concert thus far, though not one note of his music has been heard! Meanwhile, the members of the band he is to lead are enjoying this too. They are eager to launch into the scheduled number, the popular "Men of Ohio" march which Henry composed for President Harding back in 1921. Henry steps to the podium, and down comes the baton.

The musicians perform with great enthusiasm, and the effect is absolutely electrifying. Henry is looking into their faces rather than at a sheet of music on the conductor's stand, urging them on. He is applying a zany type of body English which is hard to describe. The baton he is using is very long, and his rhythmic beat—plus the outlandish motions—are obviously easy to follow. He is also requesting accents and dynamics that are not on the printed music, much to the pleasure of everyone. This is exciting!

We sense that the end is nearing, and immediately after the final note sounds there is a deafening applause. Henry steps down from the podium, gestures with outstretched arms to the musicians to indicate that *they* deserve the reward, not he. He then takes a shallow bow and heads for the edge of the stage.

He descends the steps of the stage, walks over to the center aisle, out to his seat in the middle of the fifteenth row, and sits down. All the while there is no reduction whatever in the applause! It is intermission time, but no one wants an intermission just yet; we want more of Henry Fillmore.

So Henry arises, makes his way down the aisle, around to the steps and up on the stage. He strolls leisurely back to the podium and raises his hand for quiet so he can make an announcement.

"My, but it's warm in here," he says. "Would you folks mind if I removed my coat?" The answer comes with a ripple of applause. As he peels off his white suit coat, the audience roars with laughter—he is wearing what must be the widest, brightest fire engine red suspenders in existence! He lays his jacket across the conductor's music stand.

After the laughter dies down, he announces the title

of his encore: "We'd like to play a trombone specialty of mine. It's called 'Shoutin' Liza Trombone.' " With that he mounts the podium, and one can tell by the smiles on the faces of the band members that whatever is coming will be very interesting indeed.

By offering an encore, he is breaking a rule. Because of the length of their concerts, the ABA has a policy for their convention programs: NO ENCORES. However, they have learned over the years that when Henry Fillmore appears on a program, something has to give. So their policy has, for all practical purposes, been altered to: NO ENCORES—EXCEPT FOR HENRY FILLMORE.

"Shoutin' Liza Trombone" had originally been entitled "Hallelujah Trombone," but we'll discuss that later. It is a paraphrase of the familiar opening of the "Hallelujah Chorus" from Handel's *Messiah* and is one of Henry's fifteen trombone rags, or "smears" which feature glissandos on that instrument. It begins very slowly with the trombones glissandoing—smearing, if you wish—upward. This is followed by a short musical statement of the "Hallelujah Chorus" theme and then a long, long pause.

That was the introduction. Henry stands motionless through the pause and finally raises his clenched fist high and shouts "Ho!!!" so that he can easily be heard in the back rows. And away they go at a furious pace— loud, fast and spirited! The band members lean forward to be closer to their music, because those little black notes are really going by in a hurry.

Henry is bouncing up and down ever so gently in time with the music, but with his feet firmly planted on the podium. He is heavier than at any other time during his life, and it is rather obvious that he is not all muscle. His midsection and posterior are floating around completely unrestricted, and we are much amused.

A lady near us comments that if he were on the football field he would surely be penalized for *backfield in motion*. A section calling for solo trombone smears comes up, and he turns sideways on the podium so that everyone can see his stomach dancing around in a most happy manner. When he gives an extra motion for an accent, it is hilarious. He leans over to one side and quickly to the other, and his excess baggage follows— slightly later.

Then comes a short staccato passage, and he leans over backwards—all but his stomach, that is—and makes a motion like horses prancing. It is as though he is actually conducting with his stomach! It fits the music perfectly. Then he looks out into the audience and gives a big grin reminiscent of vaudeville days. He has been there, you can tell. There is a roar of laughter. Some of those around us are laughing so hard the tears are streaming down their faces.

When the trombones do more smears, Henry rocks over and back parallel to the motion of the trombones and makes other exaggerated gestures accompanied by quaint little flicks of his baton. And all his extra poundage. . .well, use your imagination. He likes what he is hearing and shouts out "Good!" and "All right!" This has an obvious effect on the players, and they seem to play with even more vitality than before and are enjoying every second of it. They come to a repeated section,

SOUVENIR PROGRAM

18th ANNUAL CONVENTION

AMERICAN BANDMASTERS ASSOCIATION

THE OHIO STATE UNIVERSITY
MARCH 7-10, 1952

When the prestigious A.B.A. held its annual conventions, it attempted to advance the cause of serious band music. But when the master showman Henry Fillmore conducted at one of their concerts, he turned their world upside down. Audiences loved him.

and he yells, "Let's go, now!" They certainly do!

The piece ends in a flourish with one final fortissimo smear and a cymbal crash which must have been intended to wake the dead. Henry shouts, "Good enough!" Then it is bedlam. There are ear-shattering cheers, whistles, foot-stomping and the most vigorous applause one could ever hope to hear. Henry gestures for the band to rise, takes a little bow and mops his sweaty brow with a huge red polkadot handkerchief from a hip pocket. Then he waves several directions to the audience, picks up his white coat and walks toward the edge of the stage.

The narrator, Prof. Jack Evans of Ohio State, arises from his seat and starts onstage to announce the intermission, not knowing that Henry and the students have conspired to disrupt the dignity of the evening still more. Evans extends his hand to Henry as he had done to the conductors preceding him. But with a mischievous grin, Henry waves him aside, dances a circle around him and says, "Just a minute, Sonny; I'm not finished yet!" Evans is visibly taken back, but he politely retraces his steps.

On the way back to the podium, Henry gives some verbal instructions to the band, and they begin to repeat the last section of "Shoutin' Liza Trombone." Meanwhile, some of the brass players come to the front, and

2

Henry leads them around the edge of the stage in a sprightly little cakewalk dance. What a show! Just as they finish, Henry again shouts, "Good enough!"

Another thunderous applause. This time, Henry again gestures to the band, bows, walks off the stage and back to his seat. The applause has died down very little, but there is to be no more from Henry; the chubby seventy-year old man is apparently exhausted. He slowly pulls himself up out of his seat, turns around and waves his red polkadot handkerchief above his head, then sits down.

Good enough!

The twelve-minute scene described above, a factual account of a concert held in Columbus on March 8, 1952, gives you a personal glimpse of James Henry Fillmore, Jr., one of President Millard Fillmore's illustrious cousins. It was the only time this writer was ever privileged to see Henry Fillmore perform, and I shall never forget those twelve minutes—it was the funniest thing I have ever seen.

I had waited many years to see this kindly old gentleman. I was a student at Ohio State at the time, and the ABA convention provided the opportunity to see not only Henry but many other famous bandmasters and composers as well.

The band Henry conducted was an all-star aggregation selected from twenty Ohio colleges and universities. It was called the Ohio Intercollegiate Festival Band and was organized by Jack Evans, narrator of the part of the concert at which Henry appeared.

I was not the only one left with vivid impressions of "Uncle Henry." I have recently talked to numerous Columbus residents who attended the same concert, and *none* had any trouble remembering details. Does this tell you something about Henry Fillmore?

Henry Fillmore was not a musician's musician; he was the people's musician. Most emphatically. He cared little for Bach and Beethoven, and his genius manifested itself in the entertainment field.

His claim to fame comes principally through grass roots music creations which live on and on. The title "father of the trombone smear" is often used to identify him, and several generations of student musicians have had liberal exposure to those "smears" and to his other music—which was composed under not one, but *eight* different names.

It might seem incongruous that such a man could achieve wealth and international fame in several fields of endeavor and remain so uncommonly common as to be totally indifferent to his social standing—and so modest and unassuming that even his closest friends did not know he was related to a President of the United States.

It is also unusual that a man with no children of his own would have the ability to shatter age barriers so thoroughly as to be universally loved by thousands of youth one quarter his age and be known to all as "Uncle Henry."

But such a man was Henry Fillmore, and this is his story.

2 THOSE ADVENTURESOME FILLMORES, PART ONE

Here is a multiple choice question for non-genealogists: The name Fillmore was originally spelled in which manner?

(a) Fillmore
(b) Filmer
(c) Phillmore
(d) Fillamore
(e) Phillemore
(f) Filmore
(g) All of the above
(h) None of the above

The answer is (g). It depends upon which documents are consulted.

The majority of the American Fillmores descended from a family living near East Sutton, Kent, England. This family immigrated to the United States in the late 1600's and settled in the small coastal town of Beverly, Massachusetts, just north of Boston.

Little is known of this family except for John, who was born about 1676 and married Abigail Tilton from the village of Ipswitch, eight miles up the wagon trail from Beverly. From the time of John and Abigail hence, the Fillmore descendants are pretty much accounted for.

If you are ever in Beverly and come across Fillmore Street, you may impress your friends by stating that it was named after the great-great-great-great-grandfather of Henry Fillmore.

John purchased land in Beverly, but he spent little time at his home except during the harsh winter months. He was a seafaring man. The proud owner of one ship, John was engaged in trade with the West Indies but met an untimely end while returning with a cargo in 1710. His ship was commandeered by a French frigate. After being treated most cruelly for several months, he reportedly died of poisoning.

John and Abigail had three children: John, named after his father; Abigail, named after her mother; and Ebeneezer. Son John and his second wife, Dorcas Day, are the common ancestors to all the Fillmores of interest to us here. To avoid confusion in the identity of the two Johns, let us call the son *Captain* John. He was an interesting character indeed.

Of all the stories handed down through the various branches of the Fillmore clan, perhaps none is so dramatic as an adventure which befell Captain John. This gripping but gory tale took place in the year 1721 or 1722.

Captain John did not have the rank of Captain at that time; this was acquired later in military service. He was a young man of about nineteen who, like many other New England lads, had a burning desire to take to the sea. After petitioning his widowed mother for several years, she finally relented, and he found work aboard the sloop *Dolphin* which departed on a fishing trip to the West Indies.

Once in fishing territory, the *Dolphin* was overtaken by a pirate ship commanded by a most bloodthirsty and dishonorable cuss, Captain Phillips. John was a robust youth, and Phillips took him into slavery. He offered words of resistance, but the pirate crew made it clear that he was coming with them dead or alive. The *Dolphin* had no valuable cargo, so the pirates released it and the crew to go about their business.

With John a guarded captive aboard the pirate ship, numerous ships were raided. Additional prisoners were taken. A few of them eventually "signed the articles" of the pirates and became members of the notorious crew.

There was very little opportunity for companionship among the newly taken prisoners, and to prevent their conspiring to escape, their conduct was monitored constantly.

Some months later, when one particularly desirable ship was captured, the pirate crew was split up so that both ships could become pirate vessels under the control of Phillips. But the crew manning the second ship plotted to break away from him and strike off on their own.

A fierce battle ensued, and Phillips' forces prevailed. The ringleader surrendered upon promise that he would be pardoned, but after surrendering Phillips ran him through with his sword and then blew his brains out!

Phillips reasoned that the prisoners, too, were plotting some kind of rebellion. After one prisoner was confronted and professed his innocence, Phillips jammed his sword into his belly with such force that it broke his backbone—and Phillips' sword. For good measure, he shot him in the head. Fillmore was next, he declared.

Phillips summoned John, put the pistol to his chest and pulled the trigger. Miraculously, it misfired, and he let John off with a warning and a few menacing swishes of his broken sword.

The pirates proceeded to put more pressure on John to join their ranks, and he came to the realization that he would soon be slaughtered if he continued to refuse. Therefore, there was little to lose by planning a do-or-die escape.

An opportunity soon presented itself. The pirate crew indulged in heavy drinking one evening, and the two men assigned to guard John and some of the other prisoners passed out. John convinced two of the other prisoners, a chap named Cheesman and an Indian, that freedom was possible only if they acted immediately.

The first step was to disable the two pirates guarding them. This they did by removing their shoes and burning off the bottoms of their feet with coals from the stove as they lay helplessly unconscious. No doubt they were dreaming of walking on the fires of hell.

Early the next morning, four of the pirates were methodically isolated and set up for a quick but bloody execution. John was armed with only an axe; Cheesman and the Indian had hammers.

John struck first. With a mighty blow of the axe upon the top of the pirate's head, he parted not only his hair but his entire head! The pirate dropped to the deck in a pool of blood and scrambled brains. Meanwhile, Cheesman bashed in the second pirate's head and heaved him overboard.

One of those targeted was the abominable Captain Phillips, who was conveniently nearby. Before he could draw his sword or pistol, John swung the broad side of his axe around to his skull, stunning him. Cheesman rushed to John's aid and planted his hammer deep into the back of Phillips' head, putting an end to his mortal existence. Three down and one to go.

The fourth pirate charged at Cheesman from behind, but the Indian intercepted him and held him as John closed in. With a swift diagonal stroke, John's axe cut into the side of the pirate's head and through most of his neck, leaving his head dangling as he crumpled to the deck.

The prisoners now had a commanding position. With the remaining pirates below deck and unprepared to do battle, John and the others demanded and received surrender of the vessel.

The ship sailed into Boston Harbor, some nine months after John had left home. As they approached the harbor, one of the pirates committed suicide by throwing himself in front of a cannon as a signal shot was being fired. The others were turned over to the authorities, tried, convicted and sentenced. Two were hanged. The court presented John with the personal belongings of the infamous Captain Phillips.

Many years later, the firsthand account of Captain John's adventure was published. Several versions appeared, the most significant edition being printed in 1849 by his own great-grandson, Augustus Dameron Fillmore—Henry's grandfather. The not-so-short title was *A Narrative of the Sufferings of John Fillmore and Others On Board Capt. Phillips' Pirate Vessel: With an Account of Their Daring Enterprise.*

Captain John was the common ancestor to both Henry Fillmore and President Millard Fillmore, and an explanation of the relationship between Henry and Millard is in order.

Let us put this explanation in semi-Biblical language. Captain John begat Nathaniel and eleven others. Nathaniel begat Nathaniel, Junior. Junior begat Millard Fillmore, the thirteenth President of the United States of America.

From Captain John again, this time let us descend the family tree through the elder Nathaniel's next younger brother, Comfort Fillmore, one of the other eleven offspring of Captain John.

Comfort begat Adan. Adan begat Augustus Dameron, the itinerant singing school teacher. Augustus Dameron begat James Henry, the hymn writer. James Henry begat James Henry, Junior—Henry, if you will—the subject of this book.

Captain John was thus the great-grandfather of President Millard Fillmore and the great-great-great-grandfather of Henry Fillmore. Therefore, as genealogists would put it, Henry and the President were second cousins, twice removed. Were they close? Hardly; Millard died seven years before Henry was born.

Augustus Dameron Fillmore, Henry's grandfather, always went by his initials, A.D. In fact, if you would ask most Fillmores today if they had ever heard of an Augustus Dameron Fillmore, they would probably have to give it considerable thought.

A.D. was a righteous man who is remembered for doing three things very well. He was a minister, a hymn writer and a singing school teacher. He was born in the southern Ohio town of Gallipolis (some say Pine Grove, a few miles away) on September 7, 1823. His boyhood ambition was to be a physician, and he entered medical school in Cincinnati. Religion took a stronghold on him, however, and he studied for the ministry instead.

He was eventually ordained, but as a young man he had a longing to travel as a singing school teacher. He was gifted with a magnificently powerful voice which made him a convincing figure in this humble but gratifying profession. This, of course, made his students remember his original hymns all the more.

Although perhaps not utilized as widely as in the New England States, singing schools were important to the cultural heritage of the Midwest. A singing school was as much of an event as it was a school. The itinerant teacher would visit a community for a week or so and hold classes, usually in a schoolhouse or church. Sometimes, classes were held in town halls or even taverns. This was the way most rural folks learned music in those days. First came the fundamentals, followed by simple songs sung in unison and then in two-part and four-part harmony. It was a rewarding experience for all concerned.

These do, re, mi classes were also social affairs. Youngsters of varying ages, and quite often older people too, came for many miles around to "get some learning" as well as to be brought up to date with the doings of their neighbors. New romances were in order, too. Classes were usually held for the children after school and for adults in the evenings. The evening classes were bring-your-own-candle affairs.

Being a singing school teacher was no occupation for one who fancied living in style. It called for unusual dedication. Some, like A.D., collected and published their own hymnals and instruction books in order to subsist. Tuition was typically a dollar a week, and the results were bared to the public at a concert held at the conclusion of the instruction period, admission being ten cents per head.

Thus A.D. was a sort of dignified traveling salesman whose product was put to the test at a public hearing before he left town. He was good at it and made a name for himself in Kentucky, Ohio, Indiana and Illinois. When he nailed his notices to barns and fenceposts in a community, he had little trouble attracting a crowd because his reputation had usually paved the way for him. Still, he was not well off financially. If he broke even and got free lodging and meals, however, he considered it a success. He traveled light, his only instrument being a tuning fork. Not all his classrooms had pianos or pump organs, even the churches.

The musical tradition of the Fillmore family began with Henry's grandfather, Augustus Dameron Fillmore, a pioneer teacher of the old singing schools. A.D. endured the hardships of the wilds for many years while helping enrich the cultural heritage of the Midwest. He was also an ordained minister in two denominations and composed several dozen gospel hymns.

Life was difficult for a singing school teacher, and when the bloom of his youth had passed, A.D. settled down to the ministry. He was ordained first as a Baptist minister and then as a minister in the Disciples of Christ Church. The latter was and is frequently referred to as the *Christian* Church. This might seem confusing, because all churches founded on the teachings of Jesus of Nazareth are *Christian* churches, not just this one denomination.

As a minister, A.D. served parishes in Illinois and Ohio and was a compelling, intense pulpit man. His specialty was temperance. With his booming voice he could move masses of people, and when the hymns were sung, his beautiful baritone voice could be heard above an entire congregation. On Sunday afternoons, he would sing in the parlor of his home just for the benefit of his family. At least it started out this way, but it was usually only a matter of minutes before the entire neighborhood would gather around.

Lest one should think Henry Fillmore inherited the

gift of song solely from his grandfather, A.D., it is well to consider the talent of A.D.'s devoted wife Hannah, daughter of a Cincinnati boatbuilder, Ezekial Lockwood. She was considered a fine soprano in her day. Henry got something other than a musical inheritance from Grandmother Hannah; he also got his name, as did his father. One of Hannah's brothers was a minister named James Henry Lockwood.

The extent of A.D.'s musical compositions is subject to debate, but it is safe to assume that they number less than two hundred. Many are very short. He was a self-publisher, too, issuing ten or twelve books of songs for church and temperance work. His most successful publications were *Songs of Zion* and *The Christian Psalmist,* the latter carrying through eighteen printings.

A.D.'s older brother, Comfort Lavius Fillmore, was also a creative musician. He invented a numerical-phonetic system for writing music. With this, he assigned the numbers 1 through 8 to musical notes, as opposed to representing the notes on a staff. His book, *Fillmore's Phonetic Singer,* was published in 1854. Fortunately for C.L., he had another means of making a living, that of being a boatbuilder, because his marvelous phonetic music system ended up on the rocks, so to speak.

We now know that Henry Fillmore came from a musical family. But this was only the beginning, for of A.D. and Hannah's seven children, six were in the music profession at one time or another. The oldest and by far the most famous of these was Henry's father, James Henry Fillmore.

James Henry was known by most simply as J.H., but his closest friends and most of his relatives called him Jim. To Henry, it was always *Papa.* Jim was born at A.D.'s east side Cincinnati home, 1208 East Front Street, which overlooked the Ohio River. It was a modest home just east of the general area known as the Shipyards. He grew up loving the river. He was a frail boy but became an excellent swimmer, spending many hours in the river.

Jim exhibited talent for music early in life, both as a vocalist and on the piano. While yet in school he studied theory and harmony and practiced the piano long hours every day. Through extraordinary discipline, he was largely self-taught.

He probably would not have become such a zealous prohibitionist in later life except for a frightening experience he had when a lad of twelve. He and one of his chums were hanging around a wharf one day where barrels of whiskey were being loaded aboard a steamboat. They noticed a small opening in the top of one of the barrels and reasoned that if they would stick a straw through the opening they could learn why whiskey was so attractive to the riverboat men in that rather rough section of town. There must have been something wondrous about it, they reasoned, because it was all those burly riverboat men seemed to be interested in when they came ashore for any length of time.

Their straw-in-the-hole scheme worked. But not previously having been acquainted with spirits and the potency thereof, they overindulged. Before half an hour elapsed, they passed out. Some dockworkers discovered

them, revived them sufficiently to learn their names and addresses, and fetched their fathers. Jim was so perilously intoxicated that he might not have lived through the ordeal if it had not been for the perseverance of A.D. and Hannah, who forced him to walk around most of the night to work off the effects. He learned a valuable lesson, however, and vowed never to touch a drop of alcohol for the remainder of his life. He never talked about this much in later years, but you may be certain that his relatives did! He was the last Fillmore known to be inebriated before Henry came upon the scene.

As adolescence came on, two strong forces were acting upon Jim. One was a love of music, and the other was the desire to be a printer. He and A.D. discussed this freely, and it was concluded that there was really no conflict because at such an early age he could involve himself with both until such time he would be able to decide which career would be more to his liking.

Shortly after Jim reached the age of fourteen, A.D. made arrangements with the Western Book Company in Cincinnati to take him on as an apprentice printer. During the next seven years he learned practically all there was to know about printing, binding and other bookmaking practices. Best of all, he became skilled in both regular and music typesetting. And during the evenings and on Sundays he continued to learn all he could about music, singing at every opportunity. He was one of the mainstays in the choir at the Central Christian Church in downtown Cincinnati.

A.D.'s final years were spent on the east side of Cincinnati, but he also owned a small farm in the area known as Terrace Park. His estate was modest, consisting of the farm and a meager income from the two hymnals mentioned above.

On June 5, 1870, A.D. died of typhoid fever, complicated by pneumonia. Upon his passing, another hymn writer, Knowles Shaw, paid him a lasting tribute by composing a hymn in his memory. He called it "Bringing in the Sheaves," and the touching reference to A.D. is clearly seen in the second verse:

> By and by the harvest,
> And our labor ended,
> We shall come rejoicing,
> Bringing in the sheaves.

A.D. was always predisposed toward humility and dedication. Just as this beautiful old hymn also states, he sowed his seeds of kindness, fearing not the hardships of the seasons.

It was just a few days after Jim's twenty-first birthday when A.D. passed away. As the man of the house, Jim was then obligated to support his widowed mother and the younger sisters and brothers. The next oldest was Minerva, eighteen, who was helping around the house. Frank was seventeen and working in town. The others were still in school. Fred had just turned fourteen, Kate was twelve, Charles nine and Aden seven.

With Frank's help, Jim could make ends meet, but barely. A better way, he reasoned, was to follow in his father's footsteps as an itinerant singing school teacher. Conditions were better now than when A.D. was trekking the wild country of the Midwest, and he could possibly augment his income by selling the musical compositions he had begun to write. His diligent study of music was beginning to bear fruit. He was still an amateur but was a man of many inspirations and was full of what is called the Christian spirit. With such faith, how could he possibly fail?

Jim bade a fond farewell to his family and headed south. For the next four years he traveled throughout Kentucky, Tennessee and Missouri. Hymnals, especially those of his father's, sold more briskly than they had in years past, even in the new territories he visited. He was also able to sell a few of his own original hymns. He earned his success by plain old fashioned hard work and enthusiasm, using what free moments he had to compose new hymns and songs.

By the spring of 1872, he had written a sufficient number of hymns which, when put with established pieces, would make a complete hymnal. On one of his infrequent trips back home, he offered the proposed hymnal to the Methodist Book Concern. He called it *The New Harp of Zion*. They liked it so much that they not only published it but gave him two hundred copies as an advance against his royalties. It was a wise decision on their part, because in the next two years *The New Harp of Zion* sold nearly a hundred thousand copies. Jim—from now on it was to be *J.H.*—actually had a best seller on his hands. He was far from wealthy, however, because the royalties were very low. He had agreed to a low rate just to get himself established as a published composer.

By the time he reached the age of twenty-five, J.H. had a fine reputation both as a singing school teacher and as a composer. He was somewhat of a celebrity and drew bigger and bigger crowds. This made the pay better, and his fine selection of hymnals was an inducement to prospective attendees for the classes.

He had a dream whereby he could captitalize on all this and also make use of the trade he had learned earlier. He wanted to form his own music publishing company. He was full of genuine inspirations and was confident he could write more and better hymns for many years to come.

Heading home from Missouri in the early summer of 1874, J.H. engaged in some heavy thinking. If he could utilize his several talents and experiences and be the proprietor of his own publishing house, another publisher would not reap the profits of his creations. He would form a company built on Christian idealism. Honesty, sincerity and service would be the new company's credo.

By the time he crossed the Ohio River, his plans were formulated in detail. As soon as he had greeted all the members of his family, he told his younger brother Frank of his grand idea. He would need his help. Frank was twenty and was gainfully employed. J.H. was so optimistic and eager, however, Frank could not help but believe in his proposition. Thus the Fillmore Brothers Company came into being.

Frank went to work as a music teacher, arranging his schedule so that he could assume the duties of manager of the new company. Since he did all the paperwork, this left J.H. free to compose and to teach Fred, who joined the company shortly thereafter, the various printing and binding skills. They rented a storeroom in a building at 8 East Fourth Street and purchased enough second-hand printing equipment to get started. All of their printing was done by the old wood block method. The storeroom had adequate storage space, so this was to be their place of business for the next eight years. A motto came easily: "A music store in '74." This was later modified to "A music store since '74."

Thanks to the success of *The New Harp of Zion*, J.H. had been hard at work on new hymns, and now that he had his own company, he wasted no time issuing the company's first hymnal. It was called *Songs of Glory*, and the most popular hymn included was "Bringing In the Sheaves." Once the book was in print, the burden shifted to Frank, who was not only the manager but the entire sales force. He spent many long, tiresome evenings and weekends traveling to churches throughout the area extolling the virtues of the grand new hymnal. It sold reasonably well. This was soon followed by an even better seller, *Hours of Song*. Next came several instruction books for singing schools, these containing some "fun" songs. J.H.'s sense of humor had finally come through.

With another good seller in 1878, *Songs of Gratitude*, the Fillmore Brothers company was well on its way to becoming a pillar of the religious music publishing field. For the most part, J.H. was now writing just the music for most of his new hymns, because he had attracted several experienced verse writers as collaborators. These included such writers as Elben Rexford, Lina H. Barton and W.T. Tibbs.

At the Central Christian Church where the family had been attending, J.H. was a decidedly popular man. Besides being the central figure of the choir, he also taught a Sunday School class of teenagers. He was a handsome young man, and the unattached ladies of the church went out of their way to make his acquaintance. He was a widely read, congenial, mild mannered fellow, and Christian benevolence seemed to radiate from him. He would have been an ideal husband for any of the young ladies who always seemed to be surrounding him in church.

But his attention was drawn to a quiet, dignified farm girl who was not chasing him. Instead, he chased her. She was a pretty young Sunday School teacher, Anna Eliza McKrell, who had a class of small children. She was known to all as Annie. Her widowed mother, Nancy Ryan McKrell, ran a boarding house at 105 Broadway near the steamboat dock, or Public Landing.

Nancy Ryan McKrell was a very interesting woman who had been through hard times since the days of the Civil War. Her husband was a farmer of Mays Lick, Kentucky, some ninety miles southeast of Cincinnati. The farm was called Absolom, Absolom supposedly being an acronym for Abraham and Solomon McKrell, two settlers of that area. It was in a two-story log cabin on this farm that Annie Eliza McKrell was born on March 5, 1852, one of a family of twelve girls and one boy.

Annie's father had slaves but treated them with exceptional fairness and was a sympathizer of the North

The mother of Henry Fillmore was Anna (Annie) Eliza McKrell, a Kentucky farm girl and schoolmarm. She carried an air of aristocratic dignity about her but was a gentle, kindly Sunday School teacher and church worker who was an inspiration to all who came in contact with her.

during the Civil War. This caused him to fall into disfavor with the Confederacy. Since the farm was on a north-south route frequented by Confederate troops, it was stripped of its livestock, crops and supplies, and Annie's father fled to a cave in the hills. He became seriously ill and died of consumption shortly after the war.

This left Mother McKrell in precarious circumstances. Annie became a schoolteacher, but it was soon apparent that Mother McKrell, one son and the girls could not manage the farm. She was an enterprising and self-sufficient woman, however. She sold the farm and moved six of her children and one of the former slaves to Cincinnati. She purchased a three-story home at 105 Broadway and established a boarding house.

J.H. liked everything about Annie—and also Annie's hardy mother. When he would call upon Annie at the parlor of the boarding house, he would always swap stories of the wilds of Kentucky with both Annie and her mother. The courtship blossomed into a fullblown love affair, and James Henry Fillmore and Annie Eliza McKrell were married in Mother McKrell's boarding house parlor on Thanksgiving Day, November 25, 1880. He was thirty-one, and she was twenty-eight. A blizzard raged outside all during the ceremony, but this made it even more memorable. Looking back on this twenty years later, verse writer Palmer Hartsough put it this way:

> Pure the snow
> Drifting so
> In a blizzard madness,
> Now 'tis done
> Two are one
> In Thanksgiving's gladness.

After a short honeymoon of three days across the river in Kentucky, J.H. and Annie returned to the boarding house to live.

Over the years, J.H.'s infectious manner had an astonishing effect on all of his younger brothers and sisters, with the exception of Frank and Minerva. Minerva was never involved with the company and did not carry her music into later life, and Frank became more interested in business than in music.

Fred, however, had been writing songs and hymns all along. His first noteworthy effort was written for his high school graduating class and was sung at the commencement ceremony. He was a reserved lad, perhaps the only one of the Fillmores who could not be classified as an extrovert. Eventually he bought his brothers' interests in A.D.'s old farm and lived there. He continued to contribute pieces for hymnals and other publications and was often referred to as the "musician farmer."

Kate was not old enough to be a part of the Fillmore Brothers business in the beginning, but she was an intelligent and aggressive girl and was to make her contribution to the business before another ten years were to pass.

Charles was the next-to-youngest, J.H. being eleven years his senior. He lived with zest and was by far the most humorous and colorful of all the Fillmores. Until Henry came along, that is. Both verse and music came to him easily. To illustrate this, here is a poem for which he was reprimanded for circulating in the third grade:

> Johnny had a billygoat,
> A Number One old butter,
> And everybody that he met
> He knocked into the gutter.

When Charles discovered he could put his poetry to music, he was thereby incurably afflicted. But composing was only a sideline with him. He became a well known minister in the Christian Church, yet with his sideline he played an important part in the development of the Fillmore Brothers Company.

Aden was the baby of A.D.'s family. He worked in the business for only a year and then launched out on his own, first as a carpenter and then as an evangelical singer. Later, he taught music in public schools and directed choirs and choruses in the suburbs of Pittsburgh.

Most all of Henry Fillmore's illustrious relatives have now been accounted for, the offspring of Augustus Dameron Fillmore in particular. Since most of the latter influenced the life and career of Henry Fillmore, they will be discussed in later chapters.

Among the many things introduced to the bustling Ohio River metropolis of Cincinnati in the year 1881 were electric lights and Henry Fillmore.

Just before dawn on Saturday, December 3, Annie Fillmore was experiencing labor pains. J.H. rushed five blocks to the west and two blocks north to awaken Dr. T.C. Bradford at his 315 Race Street home. At approximately 9:30 a.m., James Henry Fillmore, Jr., was brought into the world, the first of five children of James Henry Fillmore, Sr., and Annie Eliza McKrell. From the beginning, he was called Henry.

Henry's first home was some fourteen hundred feet from the banks of the Ohio River, due north of where Riverfront Coliseum now stands. It was not a pretentious home, consisting only of a large bedroom on the second floor of Mother McKrell's boarding house at 105 Broadway between Third and Fourth Streets. At the foot of Broadway was the Public Landing, where the steamboats docked.

Thirty years earlier, this had been a fashionable residential area, and Mother McKrell's house was a remnant of that period. But by 1881 it was in the heart of an industrial area, with horse-drawn trolleys passing a scant twenty feet from their front entrance. Behind the house was the Spence Bros. & Co. Tobacco Works, and next to that a shoemaker's shop. Within a stone's throw were such establishments as the Diamond Distillery, the Queen Cigar Mfg. Co., a boiler factory, an ink works, a coffee and spice mill and a trolley stable.

The origin of Henry's name is clear. In the previous chapter, it was mentioned that his paternal grandmother had a brother, James Henry Lockwood, and that both Henry and J.H. had been named for him. On the maternal side, the name appears again; Mother McKrell's father was James Henry McKrell, and her brother was James Henry McKrell, Jr.

Annie had not been well since Henry's birth. She was diabetic, but it is not known whether it was this or another malady which brought about their change of residence. Another factor was J.H. and Annie's realization that a one room boarding house apartment in a noisy end of town was not the ideal place to raise a baby. So when Henry was seven months old they moved to A.D.'s old farm. J.H.'s mother, his sister Kate, and brothers Fred and Adan were still living there most of the year. Once in the country, Annie's condition improved. The farm was thirteen miles east of town, high enough to be unaffected by the great floods of 1883 and 1884.

J.H. and Fred had quite a distance to commute to and from the Fillmore Brothers establishment, but the trip was a quick one by train, with a station not far from the farm. The business was moved to a new location at Fifth and Race Streets and was there only during 1881 and part of 1882, at which time the move was made down the street to larger quarters at 185 Race Street in what was then known as the Glenn Building. This location was sufficient to contain the company's expansion for another nine years.

Frank, or George Franklin, was no longer with the company. Shortly before Henry was born, he had seen better business opportunities in the West and had moved to Oklahoma. There he entered the newspaper publishing business while living on farm land, and later he became a Federal Indian agent. Some time after this he moved to Arkansas.

Up until this time, the Fillmore Brothers Company had been a family institution. But expansion brought about the hiring of non-relatives. It should be noted that the business did not have total family endorsement. Most of the Cincinnati Fillmores approved of its operation, but there were some who did not. The religious beliefs of one branch of the family were such that they did not approve of music in the church, either vocal or instrumental. J.H. firmly believed that music should be a vital part of any worship service, and the matter of having some of his distant relatives looking down their noses at him was more than a little annoying to him.

The *New Christian Hymn and Tune Book* of 1882 was another financial success for the company, and in 1883 Charles M. Fillmore's collection *Songs of Gratitude* also saw a sizable distribution. This contained twelve of Charlie's own compositions and was his first major contribution to the company's growing catalog.

Also in 1883, the *Children's Glee Book* was printed. The moderate sales of this led to the issuance of juvenile playlets and song continuities, sometimes called "kiddie cantatas," for Sunday School use. These were even-

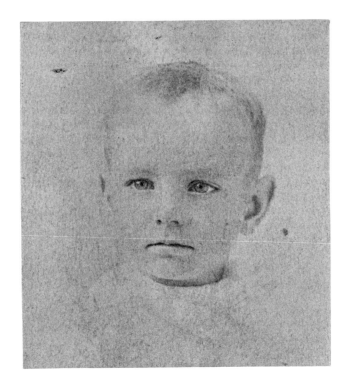

A faded, unmarked portrait in the Fillmore Museum at the University of Miami in Coral Gables, Fla., is the earliest known photograph of Henry Fillmore. His age is approximately four.

tually to become one of their staples, with new ones printed seasonally for Christmas, Thanksgiving, Children's Day or Easter.

Henry's sister, Mary Hannah, was born on August 14, 1884, when farm boy Henry was two-and-a-half years old. He was four-and-a-half when the next member of the family, Fred, was born.

How Fred came to be so named bears out the sense of humor which has always distinguished the Cincinnati Fillmores. J.H. had been engaged to lead the singing at an organizational meeting of the newly formed Cincinnati Sunday School Commission on Thursday, May 22, 1886. Annie was expecting a baby just about this time and was uneasy about him going into town. But he told her not to worry and promised to let her spend his five dollar fee any way she wished when he returned.

As luck would have it, Annie went into labor shortly after the train left the station. Fred was working on the farm this day, rather than being in the shop, since this was the middle of the planting season. She rang the dinner bell to summon him. He came quickly, realizing that it was not dinner time and that something was wrong. She told him the baby was on its way and that he should fetch the doctor as quickly as possible.

Fred teased her, saying he would do so only if she would name the boy after him. Annie was in no condition to argue, and since she and J.H. had already discussed this very thing, she assured him that the new boy would indeed be named Fred. As Fred hitched up the horse and buggy, he gave Henry instructions to stay close to his mother and to do anything she asked. The doctor's office was over four miles away, so Fred took the liberty of stopping at the next farm house to ask a neighbor lady to go look after Annie until he returned with the doctor.

They did not make it back in time, however, and the neighbor lady was obligated to play the part of a midwife. When Fred and the doctor came into the bedroom, Annie introduced Fred to Fred. Fred Evans, to be exact. She explained that the name had come from two of her brothers-in-law, the Evans part of the name having come from the husband of one of her sisters.

Imagine Fred's surprise when Annie then told him that Fred Evans was a girl! It was not Freda, Fredericka, Freddie or anything like that. Fred, just as she had promised! He was speechless but much pleased. Little Fred Evans had no say in the matter, but there were to be many times during her lifetime when she wished she could have been given a girl's name.

Fred, the "farmer musician," was about to start a family of his own. For some time, he had been courting Laura Ferris Moore, a Cincinnati girl, and they were married on November 25th, 1886. The marriage was performed right there on the farm by his younger brother Charlie, now a minister. Like his older brother J.H., he was married on Thanksgiving Day. The old farm house would not be adequate for two families, so J.H. and Annie made plans to move back into the city. This they did the following March, taking up residence in the near northwest section of town at 66 Betts Street.

Fred lived there on the farm for the rest of his life, even though he maintained an office in town for his teaching. He was regarded as one of the finest gospel singers in that part of the country. Because of his remarkably sweet, clear, baritone-tenor voice and exceptional range, he was in demand as a teacher. His professional standing had been furthered in 1885 with the publication of his first book, *Banner of Beauty*. This was not a hymnal but a book of instruction, used widely by singing school teachers. It contained forty-two of his original songs plus two of Charlie's. Oddly, none of J.H.'s were included.

Fred was a great lover of hymns and played both the piano and pump organ very well, but he was also a lover of band music. He would travel miles to hear a band play. When a band was formed in nearby Milford, he took up the tuba. In less than a month he was able to play all the parts in a recognizable manner and then took up the euphonium.

It was Fred who introduced the young Henry to band music while he still lived on the farm. Henry was never the same after this! A good band selection, to Henry, was more exciting than all the hymns in the world put together. Fred also introduced him to the circus. The winter quarters of the John Robinson circus were right there in the Terrace Park area a short distance from the farm. Several times Fred and Henry drove past the site for a glimpse of the brightly colored wagons, the animals and the many other sights unique to this holding area at the end of Robinson's sawdust trail.

Had J.H. been able to foresee the heartaches he and Annie were to suffer later because of the indelible impression which bands and circuses made on the youthful Henry, he would never have permitted Fred to take Henry off the farm.

5   CITY BOY

Number 66 Betts Street, and two other residences of J.H. and his family during the next seven years, were in a quiet residential section of town called "Over the Rhine." This was the German sector, with both English and German being spoken, even in some of the schools. "Over the Rhine" was a quaint name applied to the general area west of the Miami-Erie Canal as though the canal itself was a miniature Rhine.

With the move to the city came a change in church membership. The Richmond Street Church was only a few blocks closer to 66 Betts than the Central Christian Church, but J.H. thought it more progressive, even though Central Christian was a larger church. He was welcomed into numerous church activities, being appointed choir director and named an elder. Among the elder's duties were serving the weekly communion, and this meant the family had to be in attendance every Sunday.

More than most children, Henry disliked sitting in church. The Fillmores always occupied the third pew, and since J.H. sat nearby in the choir facing the congregation he could keep a watchful eye on the sometimes errant Henry. Henry's only escape was to sleep in the cushioned pews. Sunday School was not distasteful to him, but he despised sitting through long, boring sermons and rituals which he didn't understand. He was a restless boy, full of energy and craving excitement.

Henry's acquaintance with music in those days was mostly limited to what he heard at church and at home. For all practical purposes, this was one and the same; Papa composed his hymns at home, and more of the same were heard in church. At first Henry welcomed the opportunity to take piano lessons, but the novelty soon wore off. The lessons began at age six and continued through age twelve, off and on. Mostly off, for one teacher after another tired of his indifference and rebellious attitude. One teacher said plainly to Annie, "Why bother, Mrs. Fillmore? I'm just taking your money." Another, whose house faced the river, said, "He's far more interested in the steamboats going up and down the river than in taking piano lessons." Nevertheless, he learned the basics.

The family was at the Betts Street address for slightly over a year. They moved a block away to a nicer home at 52 Clinton Street in the fall of 1891, in time for Henry to be enrolled in the first grade at the 11th District School. School was dull for him. He was a very bright boy in all respects but simply refused to apply himself. Arithmetic was the only subject which held his attention, and the teachers were astonished with his mathematical ability in the three years he spent at this school.

Excitement was not permissible in class, so Henry created his own going to and from school. He was continually making detours from the recommended path between school and home, dissipating his excess energy one way or another. Quite often he would wrestle with the other boys or pick fistfights. He arrived at school dirty so often that his teachers pegged him as a "rowdy"—despite the family's social standing. They questioned whether he ever bathed.

He was devious enough to conceal his identity from a new third grade teacher, who somehow got the mistaken information that his name was George. He did not correct her, answering only to "George." This way, he reasoned, his mischief would not reflect on his kindly mother and father. The scheme came to an abrupt end one day when Annie was called to school to account for some of her son's misdeeds which neighbors had reported. When she knocked at the door of the classroom, the teacher informed her there was no Henry Fillmore in her class—just a George Fillmore.

Henry's younger sister Mary started the first grade as he started the third, and his shenanigans on the school route were cut to a minimum because he was instructed to escort her. He was afraid that talk of his misbehavior would reach home by way of Mary, so he informed her that she was not to mention any of his school activities,

The first family portrait of J.H. Fillmore's family was taken in January, 1888. Henry, age six, is standing behind his father and mother. Sister Mary was not yet four, and sister Fred was a year-and-a-half old.

good or bad, when she got home. Gentle little Mary did not understand this.

One day his teacher sent a note home to report some of his bad conduct. She knew the chances of his mother getting the note would be remote if it were given to Henry, so she sent it via Mary. He reacted to this by taking the note away from Mary as soon as they were out of sight of the school and threatened to beat her up if she uttered a word about it. He wouldn't have, but she was sufficiently intimidated and kept her silence until later when his day of reckoning came. History has not recorded how many whippings he got in school, but the chances are they were numerous. Nothing broke his spirit of rebelliousness for long, however, and he was a constant source of embarrassment to his parents.

Henry was the ringleader among neighborhood boys of his age. This came about naturally; many of them were of German extraction and were somewhat shy because of the difference between the language spoken in family circles and that spoken at school. He exhibited his ability to organize one day when Uncle Fred brought him a fancy walking stick with a gold colored knob. It resembled a drum major's baton, so a baton it became. Henry rounded up eight of his friends and furnished them with toy instruments, dish pans, washbuckets and other noisemakers. They marched right down the middle of Clinton Street, making a terrible clatter and arousing the entire neighborhood. Drum major Fillmore strutted his stuff at the head of his first "band."

The third of Henry's younger sisters was born on April 24, 1890. At this time, a noted educator and temperance worker was making national news: Frances E. Willard. She was in the prime of her career as a prohibi-

Only one of Henry Fillmore's school pictures has survived. This was probably taken in the spring of 1893 when he was in the fifth grade at the 8th District School. It was not uncommon then for students to start school at an older age, thus accounting for the variation in ages. Too, this was probably a multi-grade class.

tionist and was largely responsible for the prominence of the Women's Christian Temperance Union, which she founded. In her popular lectures, she shocked everyone with her vivid descriptions of the abuses of alcohol. Her stand on the alcohol issue met with J.H.'s wholehearted approval, and since she was also an out-spoken advocate of women's suffrage, Annie also held her in great esteem. So the new young lady of the family was christened Frances Willard Fillmore.

The fall of 1891 saw J.H. and his family moving to another residence closer to the downtown district, 368 West Seventh Street. J.H.'s travel time to work was cut in half, and the Richmond Street Church was now only three blocks away. This was primarily a neighborhood of larger homes. Henry started the fourth grade and Mary the second, at the 8th District School. Here, Henry wasted no time convincing his new teacher that he did not intend to apply himself unless forced to. And the new neighborhood was not particularly a rough one, so Henry helped make it a little rougher.

Annie Louise, the fourth and last of Henry's four sisters, was born on June 1, 1892. Having four younger sisters and no brothers tended to make him a little domi-

neering around the house when Papa was away. He fancied himself king of the roost and felt he was assigned more than his share of household chores and was a bit sassy. But he was able to let off steam by roughhousing with his pals around the neighborhood, so there was very little friction between him and the girls. Besides, he enjoyed being their protector.

Thanksgiving was normally a time of rejoicing and merrymaking around the Fillmore household, but in 1892 the house was very still and faces were long. Little Frances, now two-and-a-half, lay desperately ill with bronchitis, and the doctor had soberly told the family she might not live. The next day, Friday, November 25, was J.H. and Annie's twelfth wedding anniversary, but it was not mentioned the entire day. Their sick child had become unusually quiet during the night, and when Annie looked into the tiny bed, she burst into tears, waking all. Little Frances had drawn her final breath. Palmer Hartsough, now a fast friend of the family, put it best:

...To November's solemn tune
Was Frances borne to realms of light.

12

The skies were often gray above Cincinnati in the mid-1890's. Gray because of smoke puffing from thousands of steamboats which docked at the Public Landing each year and from the smokestacks of a multitude of factories and mills. The city was built on two plateaus, bounded by what Cincinnatians called their Seven Hills, much the same as Rome. The two levels were connected by numerous very steep streets and five picturesque inclined plane railroads ("inclines"). Most all the smoke-belching factories and mills were on the lower level. This, combined with the smoke issuing from as many as a dozen steamboats lined up at the landing at any one time, often made the sun all but invisible, especially on days when there was no breeze to dissipate the pollution—the Queen City's number one by-product.

Some of just about everything manufactured in the United States at that time was being manufactured in Cincinnati: any kind of American alcoholic beverage that could be named, textiles of all sorts, steamboats, steam engines, machinery, machined parts, foundry parts, tobacco products, farm equipment, furniture, flour, plus many other consumer and service items. It was also a meat packing center, giving rise to the nickname "Porkopolis." The world's largest playing card factory was also located there.

Cincinnati's pride and joy was the first professional baseball team anywhere, the Red Stockings. Henry loved baseball and could be found playing in the streets or vacant lots or anywhere else it was possible to get a game together. The old baseball park was within walking distance of all three of Henry's "Over the Rhine" homes, and the thrills of the games he saw there were engraved on his memory. He idolized the Red Stockings' players, not dreaming that some day he would know many of them personally.

Cincinnati was also noted for its rich musical heritage, especially strong in the German sector with its many choruses, orchestras and bands. Henry loved them all. At times, it would appear that he was surrounded with music.

It became obvious that by the age of eleven Henry had an outstanding singing voice, and J.H. encouraged him to sing solos in Sunday School. He might not have been inclined to do so, but there was often a reward of as much as fifty cents per performance. He sang in all the juvenile playlets or cantatas, often being joined by his sister Mary in duets.

Henry was also beginning to exhibit unusual musical talent on several instruments—any one he chose to try, in fact. He had almost completely lost interest in the piano, but with amazing ease he learned to play the violin, flute and guitar. With Mary as accompanist on the piano, he performed solos at every opportunity and was developing into a regular young showman.

The astonishing thing about his solo performances was that he was writing much of his own music. J.H. was amazed at this and dreamed of Henry someday outgrowing his social wildness and becoming a great

composer of church music. It is most unfortunate that none of the manuscripts of these youthful compositions have ever been found.

His vocal abilities caught most of the attention, however, with his clear, resonant voice, and his pitch was faultless. He even received an invitation to appear as soloist with the choir of the big Episcopal church downtown. This would have brought him a stipend of a dollar per performance, but J.H. would not permit it. He did not have as much control over Henry as he would have liked and was actually apprehensive of Henry being converted to the Episcopalian faith.

The flute, violin and guitar were interesting to him, but the instrument which fascinated him most was forbidden. J.H. would not approve of the slide trombone—or any other brass instrument, for that matter. He had a queer notion about bands and band instruments, associating these things with evil. Henry wanted to play the trombone more than anything else in the world and pleaded with his mother for several months to buy him one. A retired teacher down the street had a good used one he was willing to sell for eight dollars.

Annie was not quite in agreement with J.H. about brass instruments being associated with evil. If this were the case, his brother Fred would not be so enthusiastic about bands. Besides, she reasoned that a trombone might just be the thing to keep Henry out of mischief. Secretly, she saved the money from household operating money and bought the second-hand trombone.

The trombone did indeed keep Henry out of mischief, at least for an hour or so when he came home from school each afternoon. With the coming of summer vacation, the practice sessions were much longer. After every practice session, he hid the horn in the barn. One day J.H. came home from work earlier than usual and followed the sound of trombone and piano right into his own parlor. There was Henry, accompanied by Mary at the piano. He knew that Henry had great music talent, but he could not have acquired such a degree of proficiency overnight and demanded to know what was going on.

Annie stepped in and explained. She told him of purchasing the instrument six months before and then stated her reasons. By a stroke of good fortune, the piece Henry had been playing when J.H. walked in was a hymn. But he didn't recognize it and asked what it was. "I wrote it myself, Papa," Henry replied. J.H. then asked who had taught him all this, and Henry said he had acquired a book and had taught himself.

This came as such a complete surprise to J.H. that he sat down to think it over. Soon he got up, walked over to Henry and said, "Well, son, if you must learn how to play that thing, let's do it right." He arranged for lessons the next day. Henry did not continue the lessons for long, but he continued to practice diligently. He also began to compose solos for himself, but these, like his other early compositions, have not survived.

Henry narrowly missed hearing the most celebrated trombone soloist of all time, Arthur Pryor, in 1893. The family attended the Columbia Exposition, or World's Fair, in Chicago for a week in July. Pryor was playing with John Philip Sousa's band, which had performed there for several weeks, and their final concert took place three days before the Fillmores arrived. Henry was to be associated with both Sousa and Pryor in later years.

7 THE BUSINESS FLOURISHES

J.H. and his family were living comfortably now, because the Fillmore Brothers Company was doing well. Still, there were very few family extravagances, because J.H. was a generous man who was constantly giving money away to those he thought to be needy. He was a soft touch for any charitable cause. The Richmond Street Church, for instance, relied heavily on his giving, for their special collections in particular. He once made a loan of five hundred dollars to the *Christian Century* when this time-honored Chicago journal was in financial straits and later learned that this enabled them to avoid bankruptcy.

Business expansion had made it necessary for the company to acquire additional printing facilities. J.H. formed a partnership with George A. Armstrong, a Cincinnati printer, and the Armstrong and Fillmore Printing House was established in 1890. Their business was located in a big building at 117 West Sixth Street. In 1891, J.H. moved the Fillmore Brothers Company nearby, to 161 West Sixth Street, and when some offices were vacated in the building adjacent to Armstrong and Fillmore in 1895, he moved there, to 119 West Sixth Street. This was a convenient arrangement.

J.H. was not satisfied with the publishing of hymnals and other music on a periodic basis; he wanted to start a regular monthly music journal featuring church music. There were numerous secular music periodicals in print, and he thought church music should be similarly represented. In January, 1891, he launched out on a most ambitious undertaking with a monthly, the *Musical Messenger*. This was published in three periods over the next thirty-three years.

In the first period, totalling six years, the *Musical Messenger* consisted of news items, inspirational messages, book and music reviews, poetry, business "cards" and, of course, a liberal sampling of the latest Fillmore Brothers publications. At this time no band or orchestra music, or advertising thereof, was included. There was a substantial amount of advertising from competitive publishers, but not enough to make it highly profitable. The expense of printing could not have been justified had the paper not served as a promotional platform for Fillmore Brothers' music. Precious few of the early issues of the *Musical Messenger* have weathered the times, and today they are treasured collectors' items.

Another bold step for the business came in 1891, with the opening of a retail store in New York City. The address was appropriate, and so was the name of the owner. The store's location was 40 Bible House, and the owner was Cash Worth. Cash Worth's wife was J.H.'s younger sister Kate, who conceived and promoted the operation. The opening day was also appropriate—November 25, the eleventh anniversary of J.H. and Annie's wedding.

In 1893, J.H. made another wise move by adding the venerable Palmer Hartsough to his staff. Brother Charlie had met Hartsough ten years earlier at the National Prohibition Convention in Chicago, and this had led to the association with the company. Hartsough had been collaborating with J.H. with increasing regularity, so it was merely a matter of time until he became a full time employee. In addition to his verse, he also did quite a bit of editing and wrote articles and poetry for the *Musical Messenger*.

Hartsough and J.H. made a marvelous team, for they had much in common. Hartsough was five years older, having been born in Redford, Michigan, on May 7, 1844. He had studied for the ministry at Michigan State Normal College and Kalamazoo College, but song leading was his calling. Like J.H., he too had been an itinerant singing school teacher. He traveled widely in Michigan, Ohio, Kentucky, Indiana and Illinois. This was his life for twenty-five years, and he became one of the most highly regarded men ever to grace this profession. And also like J.H., he was a devout, tenderhearted man who loved children. He was very emotional, a quality seen in his writings.

The collaborating procedure which these two tireless workers evolved was often frustrating for Hartsough, but he always rose to the challenge. He did not write verse and give it to J.H. for musical treatment; their practice was just the opposite. J.H. wrote the music and then turned it over to Hartsough to match with verse. This was a difficult process, and he could not be rushed. His best work came when he was given plenty of time to smooth things out by many revisions.

Another thing Hartsough and J.H. had in common was that they were both prohibitionists. But put together, their effectiveness would not be the equal of Charlie, who not only had his say in the *Musical Messenger* and in his music but also through the pulpit as well. One matter of much interest to all was the passage of the Owen Law in 1888 which was intended to close the saloons on Sunday.

As one might expect, this law was difficult to enforce in Cincinnati, where alcoholic beverages were not only manufactured in large quantities but consumed in like manner. The people of the German sector were not convinced of the necessity of such a law and had beer and wine in their homes whether it was available elsewhere or not, regardless of the day of the week.

Henry was puzzled by the prohibition movement. He heard plenty about the scourge of alcohol, both at

The *Musical Messenger*, founded in 1891, grew into one of the most venerated music journals and was published, with two interruptions, until 1924. Palmer Hartsough, J.H. Fillmore's esteemed collaborator on hundreds of hymns, is upper right.

home and at church. But on the other hand, the German people of his neighborhood drank their beer regularly and seemed to be very nice people. He wasn't exposed to the drinking practices of riverboat workers who inhabited the riverfront docking area, because J.H. had moved the family away from this section of town shortly after Henry was born. In the German households of some of the boys he played with, one would find a container of beer almost anytime, and these people seemed to have moral standards as high as anyone else. So what was the problem? He carried this philosophy with him into later life, as we will see in later chapters.

8   GROWING PAINS

With adolescence came a change in Henry's voice. He was relieved of his duties as soprano in the children's cantatas at church, but a new job opened up for him. He was growing stronger and had energy to burn, so he was put to work behind the organ pumping the hand bellows. Whenever the service called for organ music, Henry left his seat in the third pew and pumped away.

This was boring, to be sure, but it was a slightly more desirable pastime than listening to poorly sung hymns. It was quite a sight to see him pumping furiously to fill the bellows for the closing measures of the final hymn so he could dart out the back door and race home to pump a marvellous contraption of quite a different nature—an ingenious device he had constructed himself.

This device was something he had put together to speed up the process of freezing homemade ice cream, which it was the family's custom to enjoy each Sunday after dinner. The family used a hand-crank freezer, powered by Henry, until Henry thought of an expedient. He propped his bicycle up on blocks, attached an old rear wheel sprocket to the freezer, fastened the freezer to the back porch floor and connected the freezer to the bicycle with the bicycle chain. He could then sit on the bicycle and crank the freezer. By the time the family had walked home and dinner was on the table, the ice cream would be ready.

Late in the summer of 1894, the Fillmores headed for the suburbs. Their new 647 Forest Avenue address in Avondale was forty-five minutes away from the old Richmond Street Church by trolley. Henry considered the hour and a half spent on the trolley going to and from church a total waste of time, especially since attending church was not his favorite pastime anyway. This also fouled up his ice cream making process, which he had down to a science.

The new neighborhood was less crowded and therefore more quiet, and this was something else which did not please Henry in the least. Too, he had been kingpin in the old neighborhood and now had to start anew. All things considered, the move to Avondale was not to his liking.

One of the few things Henry liked about the change of address was that he now had two grandmothers to spoil him. His grandmother Hannah Fillmore had lived with the family for years, and now Grandmother McKrell joined them. She was a woman of much fortitude and determination, and Henry was very fond of her. The feeling was mutual, and she thought Henry's streak of independence was an admirable trait which would get him somewhere in the world. It is a pity that she lived there for only a year-and-a-half before moving to California to live with another of her daughters, because her practical ways made sense to Henry and he was actually in the process of softening his attitude in numerous areas of disagreement with his father. When Grandmother McKrell moved away, Annie's sister Molly moved in. While Aunt Molly was a sweet lady, she could in no way fill the shoes of Grandmother McKrell.

Grandmother McKrell's former slave, Sarah, was still with her. Sarah did all the cooking. Henry was enamored of her and was impressed by the way Grandmother McKrell treated this Negro lady with respect and kindness. He could not understand why Sarah chose to walk a step behind them when they went out in public, however.

Sarah was a jolly soul, always joking with Henry, There were times when he stuck to her like glue, as if he were attempting to absorb her mannerisms and her philosophy of life. She would hum or sing catchy old spirituals while she was working, much to Henry's delight. Sarah had friends who worked for other white folks in the neighborhood, and when they visited her, Henry was fascinated by their conversations. The influence of this association with Sarah and her friends manifested itself in a spectacular and happy manner before another two decades passed, in the form of Henry's famous trombone "smears."

Henry had completed the sixth grade at the Eighth District School and now entered the seventh at the Avondale Public School. Mary entered the fifth grade and Fred the third. He spent two years in this school, in the grades now called junior high. By Avondale's classification, these grades were part of intermediate school. After finishing the eighth grade, Henry entered the Walnut Hills High School at its old location at Burdette and Ashland Avenues.

J.H. was still a very active man. Although in his late forties, there was plenty of spring in his quick, short steps. One of the things he and Henry enjoyed together was an occasional swim. At many other times, though, Henry was a trial to him. J.H. dearly loved all his family, including his wayward son, despite his pranks, protests and general air of rebelliousness.

Home life was joyous and pleasant, especially around the dinner table. Petty bickering was almost unheard of. Instead, one tried to outdo another in telling funny stories. They all made the most of every situation and saw the lighter side of things. Although very proper—ex-

J.H. (center, back row) was proud of his modern Avondale home. This photograph was made in the fall of 1895, the family's second year there. To J.H.'s left is his cousin Lavius Challen Fillmore, secretary/bookkeeper of the Fillmore Brothers Co. Henry, age thirteen, is on the porch with his mother and three sisters.

cept for Henry, sometimes—they were an informal lot. It was Papa and Mama, not Mother and Father, and Henry was Hen.

After Grandmother McKrell left with Sarah, a white cook was hired. This was Elizabeth, a most unusual and highly organized domestic worker. She was French-German and was artistic not only in the culinary arts but in other ways as well. Portrait painting was her avocation, and she would work long hours in her third floor room striving to perfect her art. She was with the Fillmores for only two years, leaving to study art more seriously. Eventually she established her own studio.

Elizabeth's replacement was another Negro cook, Molly. She was remembered affectionately for one of her specialties, Southern style biscuits and gravy. This endeared her to Henry, and those biscuits and gravy were the subject of Henry's reminiscing fifty years later. That and the homemade ice cream.

The Avondale home had been the first house built on Forest Avenue, but it was quite modern. It was solidly constructed and was the first house owned by the Fillmores which had a cement-floored basement and a furnace. It was a big house, facing south, with a bay window on the west side. The front room, or parlor, was used for entertaining, and the door opened up onto a large porch which extended the width of the house. Annie's delicate touch was evident in the parlor, with its white wall-to-wall rug, lovely lace curtains and fine furniture. And for the first time, J.H. had his own library.

J.H. was generous with his entertaining of church people, most of which he did on Sundays. He enjoyed this immensely and was of the belief that showing kindness to someone doing the Lord's work would bring blessings in return. He was continually making loans to a minister or missionary. Sometimes these loans were repaid and sometimes not, but he was never heard to complain if not. Rather, he felt needy persons were somehow directed to him by Providence and that his many blessings were to be shared with them. He was not a man of great wealth, but he managed to be a benevolent, gracious and unselfish man. Henry's philanthropic nature, as evidenced half a century later, is directly attributable to the impression his kindly father made upon him at this period of his life.

J.H.'s gifts, loans, entertaining and the like were made possible by the continued success of the business which he had openly founded upon Christian principles. The Fillmore Brothers' latest book, the *New Praise Hymnal,* was released in 1896 and sold extremely well. It became so popular it had to be updated several times and was kept in print for over thirty years. The *Musical Messenger* was being phased out to make way for another journal which J.H. thought would better serve the purposes of the company. This was the *Concert Quarterly for Sunday Schools.* It was centered around new anthems and had less advertising—a mistake which was soon to be realized.

The welcome mat at the Fillmore home was always

17

out for workers and officials of the Disciples of Christ Church. Almost every Sunday of the year one or more guests would be seated at their dinner table, feeling perfectly at ease in the home of such a happy family. J.H. entertained many distinguished visitors—missionary workers, church officials, authors, college professors and numerous others. If guests were to be in town for any length of time, their home away from home was 647 Forest Avenue. The Fillmore children were accustomed to doubling up in their beds or sleeping on cots. Annie would often invite the guests to give lectures for church-affiliated or civic groups with which she was associated.

It cramped his style, but Henry behaved reasonably well with guests in the home. Except for one time, when J.H. was hosting one particular minister Henry thought to be a long-winded bore. He sneaked into the dining room and put salt in the minister's water. He also slit his bread and stuffed it with salt. The minister did not show up, however, and the doctored items were given to little Annie Louise. She did not keep her silence, as the minister might have, and everyone looked at Henry. Who else?

The Fillmores, and Molly, saw the West for the first time in the summer of 1897. They were away from home for over three months to attend the World Christian Endeavor Convention in San Francisco. J.H. wrote the official convention song and led the singing of the huge crowds. With fourteen trainloads of people from Ohio, the state was well represented.

On this trip, the Fillmores also went down to Los Angeles for a visit with two of Annie's sisters, Nan and Ida, and once again Henry got to be with his Grandmother McKrell. The Ohioans camped out in the foothills of Pomona, and Annie was afflicted with such a severe case of poison ivy that she could not travel. Henry made use of the extra time by shooting a great number of the pesty jackrabbits which annoyed the farmers in the area.

Because of the trip to California, 1897 was the only year in which the Fillmore clan did not have their annual reunion. The reunions were traditionally held at the Terrace Park farm each Fourth of July and were happy events indeed. Fred's home was often crowded because it was open to friends and relatives all year long, but during these reunions the place would be bursting at the seams. The meals resembled feasts, with every family group bringing more than enough foodstuffs. One of the family traditions was the Fillmore sing-along, with Fred and J.H. taking turns playing the old pump organ. Most all of the songs were composed by the three Fillmore brothers or A.D.

The highlight of the sing-along was usually Uncle Charlie's rendition of his own "Tell Mother I'll Be There." This he sang in all seriousness. Of all the music he composed in his lifetime, this song was the most popular, and the story behind it is very interesting.

Late in 1896, Presidential candidate William McKinley received a telegram informing him that his mother was deathly ill. He wired back "Tell Mother I'll Be There," and this reply had such a ring to it that the press picked it up and made it into a celebrated news item. Charlie read of this in the newspaper and said to his wife, "There's a beautiful idea for a song." Ironically, J.H. paid him only five dollars for it and then declined to publish it because it was "too sickily sentimental." He did put it into print the following year, however.

After being published, the song did not sell well. But two years later, evangelist Charles Alexander sang it at the opening of a convention in Newton, Kansas, as he put it, "to get the audience awake." The pianist at that convention, incidentally, was Henry's aunt, Kate Fillmore Worth. Alexander was surprised at the audience's enthusiastic reception to the song, making somewhat of a discovery about the psychology of revival songs. He bought limited rights to the song, published it himself, and for two decades sold it at revivals for ten cents a copy. "Tell Mother I'll Be There (in answer to her prayer. . .")", Charlie's tearjerker, sold over a quarter of a million copies and was published in French, German, Spanish, Rumanian, Armenian, Turkish, Siamese, Japanese, Chinese and approximately forty other languages.

In those days, there were no school bands for Henry to join. Neither could he blow his trombone for people in church. He played solos for an occasional guest at home, and while they might have acknowledged that it was pretty, they sometimes also acknowledged that he was not another Arthur Pryor. He loved the sound of the trombone and wished all the world could appreciate it as much as he.

He tried to impress a girlfriend with his trombone playing one night, but it got him in trouble. His concert stage was the horse and buggy he used for the date. He pulled up in front of the young lady's home and asked if she would like to hear a trombone solo. That would be nice, she said, so he took his trombone out of the case and proceeded to serenade her with a song he had written himself. Neighbors' windows flew open; they were curious to see what kind of an idiot would be blowing a horn out in the street after dark. The girl's father bolted out his front door, practically dragged her into the house, invited Henry to leave immediately, and suggested that he might receive bodily harm if he did not!

Henry's two years in high school were spent at Walnut Hills. In his freshman year he studied algebra, English, physiology, German and elocution, but the record of his sophomore year is lost, as well as any record of the grades he received for either year. Neither is there a record of his participation in sports.

In August of 1898, the summer after his sophomore year, the family took a vacation in Michigan to escape the hot, muggy Cincinnati weather. Henry had had an earlier "vacation" in June, however, by doing something which shocked the entire family beyond belief. He ran away from home and joined a circus.

This happened after an argument with J.H. and was such an unspeakable act that thereafter the family seldom made mention of it. Details of what actually transpired are vague, but a brief account has been reconstructed from numerous sources.

Henry's running away from home was inevitable. His running away with a circus might also have been predicted. Still, it was a terrible blow to the entire family. J.H. was mortified, and Annie nearly lost her mind. This was really only the first of many serious differences between father and son, and Henry was to do exactly the same thing seven years later. J.H. could handle just about any situation with his seemingly endless patience, but he was not ready for this.

Ever since Uncle Fred had shown him around the John Robinson winter quarters atop the hill in Terrace Park many years earlier, Henry had been intrigued with the circus. He attended one whenever possible, but what he saw from the public's viewpoint was the glamour, not the everyday drudgery behind the scenes.

He had seen various circuses at Norwood, the little town next to Avondale; Norwood had its own circus grounds and was a regular stop. He also had seen numerous circus bandwagons, cages and transport gear manufactured there in Cincinnati. Anything associated with the circus appealed to him. He was one of the "lot lice," as circus people call those who hang around a circus operation seeing all they can see without paying.

How Henry caught up with the Robinson show while it was on the road is a complete mystery. Neither is it known exactly where he traveled; just that this tour covered Midwest states west of Ohio. He was sixteen and old enough to be taken on as a laborer, with very low pay. The Robinson circus of this year was called the John Robinson 10 Big Shows, but this year it was actually under lease to the Ringlings.

Circuses had graduated from the horse-drawn wagons of bygone years and were now transported by rail. But it was still long before the days of power driven stake drivers, tractors, tent erection machinery and electrical generators. Everything had to be done by hand, and nighttime operations were carried out by the light of torch lamps. Henry was one of those who did the dirty work. He cleaned up after horses, watered elephants, helped erect and tear down tents, assisted in the loading and unloading and so forth. Only once was he permitted to sit in for a trombone player at part of a performance. Here he learned quickly that he was much too inexperienced to "cut the mustard."

The stint with the Robinson circus lasted perhaps three weeks or less. He was broke and homesick. He wrote home admitting this and asking for money to catch a train home. J.H. wanted his wandering son home, especially for the sake of his heartbroken wife, and would have paid any price to get him back. By the

Henry displayed an outstanding musical talent by age sixteen, but church music was not his forte and under no circumstances would he follow in the footsteps of his father and grandfather. Shortly after this picture was taken, he ran off with a circus, the John Robinson 10 Big Shows.

time he received Henry's letter, however, he had recovered from the shock and decided to teach him a lesson. Instead of sending money for the train fare home, he wrote to Henry saying that if he would compose a nice Thanksgiving hymn, both words and music, he would *then* send the money. Henry complied immediately. This piece of music disappeared many years ago, but it would be interesting indeed to be able to study the words!

In Henry's sixteen years, J.H. had seen one dream after another disintegrate. At first, he had wanted Henry to become a minister. Then he had hoped he would become a composer of church music, but this too seemed extremely unlikely. What was he to do about his son's wildness? What *could* he do? He had been praying for guidance all along, and little by little a solution became apparent. He would send Henry to a military school.

9   TURNING POINT

When Henry's train pulled into the downtown Cincinnati depot, J.H. was there to meet him. As he approached his father he saw a benign look of forgiveness on his face, not the look of stern vindictiveness he expected. Tears filled his eyes, and he put down the small battered cloth carrying case which contained his few belongings. J.H. too was full of emotion, and they embraced. It was all Henry could do to utter three words:

"I'm sorry, Papa."

As they walked through the depot and up the street toward the trolley stop, J.H. tried to cheer him up. He asked how long it had been since he had eaten, and Henry said it had been about a day and a half. "Molly, the cook, will take care of that," he said. "She's fixing your favorite." That could only mean biscuits and gravy.

On the streetcar, J.H. did not ask about the hardships of Henry's adventure. By the appearance of his clothing, it was obvious that he had seen difficult times. He looked tired, but physically he looked stronger and healthier than he had ever looked before. He had evidently been fed well up until the time he left camp, and the hardy circus life had toughened him.

J.H. said that the family had been through an ordeal in his absence and that they all needed a change of scenery. They would take a vacation up in Michigan. After that, Henry would not have to return to high school, since public schools were not to his liking. Instead, application had been made for registration at Miami Military Institute, just fifty miles north of Cincinnati. There he would not be restricted to the study of the academic subjects he had found so dull in the past. Some outdoor military training would surely appeal to him, and he would get plenty of exercise and have the opportunity to participate in team sports such as baseball and football. Henry had no knowledge of this kind of school, and it all sounded just wonderful.

They stepped off the trolley and walked down Forest Avenue toward number 647. J.H. relieved Henry of his bag and motioned for him to enter the front door first, because Annie, the three girls and Aunt Molly were waiting for him.

Annie had kept her composure until she saw Henry's shaggy clothes as he approached the house. She managed a smile, but when Henry came through the door she threw her arms around him and wept uncontrollably. Then one by one the girls and Aunt Molly hugged and kissed him, with tears streaming down their faces. Mary told the whole story for all when she said simply that they had missed him.

When little Annie Louise loosened her grip on him, he looked up and saw Molly, the cook, standing in the dining room doorway and made his way toward her. She put her big arms around him and squeezed him until he nearly smothered, offering a few words of encouragement in her own inimitable way and saying something about biscuits and gravy.

He was home again, and all was well.

A letter having considerable bearing on Henry's future awaited them when they came home from the vacation in Michigan. It was from Orvon Graff Brown, President of the Miami Military Institute. Henry had tentively been accepted at MMI for the 1898-99 school year, and he and J.H. were invited to come look over the campus and to discuss policies and procedures. They were asked to bring a deposit which would apply toward tuition if enrollment was mutually acceptable.

Because of its small size, MMI's enrollment was limited to thirty students. Accordingly, the school kept a low profile and advertised very little. It was an exclusive school, and their brochures gave assurance that the student body would be made up of young men "from the best families." Tuition for the year was three hundred and fifty dollars. The faculty, consisting of Col. Brown, his two sons and a commandant, expected problems with the students brought there. Incorrigibles, however, were not admitted.

Col. Brown greeted J.H. and Henry cordially, and in the informal briefing he promised that Henry would be developed mentally, physically and socially. MMI was a junior college, and it would prepare him well for higher colleges, universities, West Point or Annapolis. If he did not choose to continue his education elsewhere, he would be adequately prepared for the general business of life and could serve his country in many capacities.

Both J.H. and Henry had numerous questions about the rules and regulations. Col. Brown answered these satisfactorily and then emphasized the fact that every effort was made to instill in each student the elements of self discipline and subordination. He then explained their honor system. It was simple and direct, the purpose being to impress upon the student that honesty and integrity were of more worth than money or social position. It was the school's hope to make a boy ashamed of any misconduct and thus endow him with grace, poise and restraint.

With the preliminaries out of the way, Henry was asked to look around the grounds and to get acquainted with other boys who were also there that Sunday afternoon, while arrangements were made with his father. The main reason for the closed door meeting was to discuss Henry and his problems in detail. Col. Brown wanted to know exactly what to expect. The staff came in, and J.H. bared all. They appreciated his frankness, because it would enable them to exercise a positive approach. By knowing the shortcomings of students, they could use the proper psychology and tailor the course of instruction to the student's best advantage.

Henry liked the school, and J.H. was impressed. A deposit was made, and they left. The entire family was invited to visit the school on Labor Day, when Henry was to report.

Miami Military Institute had an interesting history. In 1874, the school was founded as an Evangelical Lutheran synodical school and chartered as the Germantown Institute. The Lutherans abandoned it in 1877, however, selling the one and only building to the town. Orvon Graff Brown purchased it in 1885 at a bargain price and established a school known as the Twin Valley College and Ohio Conservatory of Music. Music was dropped after a series of financial difficulties, and the school was then called simply Twin Valley College. Gradually the concept of a military college began to look more attractive, and it became the Miami Military Institute in 1894.

Germantown was easily accessible from Cincinnati by the Cincinnati, Jackson and Mackinaw Railroad, so Henry would be just two hours away from home. German was the predominant language spoken among the retired farmers and their families who were, for the most part, the inhabitants of this quiet little residential town of some two thousand. The town was almost completely surrounded by forest lands.

The meticulously clean and tidy MMI campus was located on a scenic ten-acre plot of ground at the northwestern edge of Germantown, on what was called Stump's Hill. It was a one-building campus, that building being a large three-story brick and stone structure which blended with nature because the foliage around it had not been cleared away during construction. It had hot and cold water and a steam furnace to provide comfortable quarters and classrooms.

The townspeople referred to the cadets as the "Browns." Col. Brown, although a very sociable man, maintained a kind of condescending attitude toward the community. The residents overlooked this implied superiority because Brown had married a local girl of no particular social prominence who was pleasantly unaware of class distinctions.

In huge letters inside the vestibule of the campus building, and also in the classrooms were painted the MMI motto: COGITATIONES ET INDUSTRIA CLAVES FACTORUM (Study and diligence are the way to success). These words meant little to Henry at first, but before three years were to pass, the wisdom thereof was to descend upon him with startling reality.

More to his immediate application were the words of Col. Brown about honesty and integrity being of more value than wealth and social status. Generally speaking, Henry would fit into this scheme of things. He might have been naughty and unmanageable at times, but he was completely honest and was not the least bit concerned about wealth or status. He was a plain American boy, rough around the edges. The only part of the honor system that worried him was the practice of cadets reporting their own misbehavior. This would be difficult.

Based upon the brochures of the day, it is likely that Henry studied the following subjects in his three years at MMI:

First Year	Second Year	Third Year
Geometry	Trigonometry	Calculus
Ancient History	Bookeeping	Astronomy
English	Modern History	English
Zoology	English	Literature
Biology	Elocution	Political Economy
Geography	Chemistry	Physics
Theology	Psychology	Mythology
Civil Government		

Classes were usually very small, often a single student studying a subject at any one given time and progressing at his own rate. Class periods were shorter than those of public schools, allowing time for the daily calisthenics, drills, dress parades and sports. Weapons of the U.S. Army were used for firearms training and for the drills. Much of the other equipment, too, such as camping gear, was the same as that used by the Army. The field uniforms also were very similar to those of the Army, and the dress uniforms were patterned after those of West Point. Their insignia had the general appearance of West Point's but were not quite the same; a second lieutenant had one chevron, a first lieutenant two, a captain three, and so forth.

Shortly after arriving, Henry's civilian clothing was sent home and the regimentation began. It was not as strenuous as that he had experienced with the circus, but it kept him very, very busy. For the first few days he followed regulations down to the letter and felt rewarded when the sports period came late in the afternoon. The recommended sports were baseball, football, tennis, track and boxing, most of which he excelled in.

A typical day in the life of an MMI cadet was controlled, down to the minute, and was arranged like this:

6:00	Reveille	3:10	Drill
6:30	Inspection	4:15	Sports
6:45	Breakfast	5:30	Call to quarters
7:50	Chapel	5:45	Dress parade
8:00-11:30	Classes	6:00	Supper
11:35	Calisthenics	7:00	Call to quarters
12:00	Dinner	7:00-9:00	Reading and study
1:00-3:00	Classes	9:30	Taps

There were other regularly scheduled activities, such as the monthly social gatherings, which were receptions when the cadets were strongly urged to invite young lady friends from home or from the town. On Saturday evenings, each cadet was required to write a letter to his family. On Sunday mornings, the cadets would march as a unit through town to attend one of the five churches in Germantown. They got a broad view of Protestant theology, there being no Catholic or Jewish houses of worship there. The five churches were Lutheran, Reformed, Methodist, United Brethren and Constitutional (Radical) United Brethren.

The cadets were kept on the straight and narrow, each having to perform his own duties. They were not allowed to receive extra spending money from home; such funds were channeled through the President's office, and allowances of five cents per day or slightly more were dispersed according to the satisfactory performance of duties.

Henry had withstood the regimen without incident for three weeks, but he ran afoul of the rules one day and did not comply with the code of conduct requiring that he report the infraction himself. Another cadet took it upon himself to do the informing, and Henry threatened to push his face in if it led to a reprimand. This was overheard and duly passed on to the commandant, and Henry was summoned before Col. Brown.

Henry did not know what to expect. Punishment, according to the posted notices, consisted of restriction to the grounds, loss of spending money, walking tours, arrest, suspension, or dishonorable discharge. Col. Brown lectured to Henry and put him under arrest. The arrest in this case was solitary confinement. He was confined not to a darkened cell but to a large room on the ground floor. As a test of his honesty, the windows were not guarded, and the door was left unlocked.

The solitary confinement was short but was actually the turning point in Henry's life. This was not because his spirit of independence was destroyed but because it accidentally provided an opportunity for self expression. In the room was an old piano which was in a sad state of disrepair. Instead of quietly contemplating his misdeeds, as he was supposed to do, Henry chose to disassemble the piano, find the source of trouble, and reassemble it. When this was accomplished, he tested it.

Down the hall, Col. Brown was startled to hear the dilapidated old piano being played. Henry was cunning enough to be playing hymns when Brown approached the room. He listened outside, then entered, saying nothing because he was puzzled. He had heard music in all the Germantown churches for several years, had a broad music background and was experienced as head of a conservatory, but the pieces he heard were totally unfamiliar to him. When he asked what they were, Henry gave the same answer he had given some five

21

years earlier when his father had caught him playing the trombone: he had composed the pieces himself.

"Your period of confinement is over, Cadet Fillmore," Col. Brown said. "Follow me to my office." There, he played the role of a master psychologist and did precisely the thing Henry's father would have hoped for. He told Henry that he recognized an unusual talent for music and that he respected him for this. Henry could not believe what he was hearing—imagine the head of the school respecting *him!*

Col. Brown then told Henry he had noted signs of leadership in his participation in sports and asked if he would like to apply this leadership to music. Henry did not know quite how to answer this but said he supposed he would like it. Then Brown told him of the period in the school's history when it was known as the Twin Valley College and Ohio Conservatory of *Music.* He said that he missed music on the campus and that it would be nice if Henry would organize some sort of orchestra as a recreational activity.

This effected a complete turnaround for Henry, and as he walked out of the office his head reeled with ideas for the orchestra he had been challenged to form. No doubt Brown was pleased that he had, by coincidence, been tipped off to his errant student's prime motivation and had been able to apply positive thinking so easily. And the errant student's father would surely be elated if this experiment worked out.

By the time of the next Saturday evening write-home period, Henry had polled all of the cadets and found nine willing to be members of an orchestra. He excitedly told his father of Col. Brown's suggestion and asked that he send some music and possibly some instruments as soon as possible. J.H. was delighted with this development and wasted no time in supplying both. Some of the boys had very little by way of music background, but Henry promised to instruct them as best he could. Two of the boys were "day students" from Germantown, living at home rather than at the quarters, and through their families they helped locate additional instruments.

Henry's orchestra, such as it was, was not destined to be a competitor of the Cincinnati Symphony Orchestra, the small civic orchestra in nearby Dayton, or any other serious group. It was informal, and it was fun. The instrumentation was two violins, two ukuleles, two guitars, a flute, a banjo and a snare drum. Henry played one of the guitars. The significance of Henry's little orchestra was that it was the only musical unit the MMI student body had up until that time.

It is a well known fact that to accomplish anything at all in group music, one must exercise considerable self-discipline and practice the most refined sort of teamwork, so Col. Brown approved of the orchestra. The biggest benefit to Brown was that one of his problem students was solving his own problems and even directing the efforts of upperclassmen!

In team sports, Henry tried hard. He was competing with bigger boys, but nevertheless he made his mark. He placed on the reserve football team that first autumn,

Three weeks after enrolling at the Miami Military Institute, Cadet Henry Fillmore was placed in solitary confinement for a misdemeanor. The school president then learned of Henry's unusual musical talent and challenged him to organize this orchestra, the first such group at MMI.

22

At the end of his freshman year at MMI, Cadet Henry was catcher and equipment manager of the reserve baseball team. MMI founder Col. Orvon Graff Brown (extreme right) took a personal interest in Henry.

but what position he played is not known. In the spring he was catcher and equipment manager of the reserve baseball team.

As the school year came to an end, J.H. was proud of his son's achievements and told family members privately that the steep tuition fee was the best investment he could possibly have made. Whereas Henry might have become an even bigger problem than before, Col.

Brown was adroit enough to recognize Henry's potential and quickly made the most of it. By employing psychology such as this, Brown's small school became a springboard for several famous men. One of Henry's classmates that year, for example, was Andrew Nicholas Jergens, Jr., who later headed the Cincinnati toileteries company best known for such products as Jergen's lotion and Woodbury soap.

10   A MAN EMERGES

In August of 1899, after Henry's first year at MMI, a big event for the Fillmore family took place. The family reunion at Uncle Fred's farm on the Fourth of July was nothing compared to the gathering of the clan in August. The occasion was a national convention of the Christian Church, held in Cincinnati's Music Hall. The Avondale home was literally packed with relatives from many states, as well as prominent church leaders and missionaries.

There were three reasons for the Christian Church's celebration. First, it was the fiftieth anniversary of the first national convention of the Disciples of Christ

Church. Second, it was the fiftieth anniversary of the American Christian Missionary Society. Third, it was the twenty-fifth anniversary of the Christian Women's Board of Missions.

J.H. was in the thick of things. He trained a massive choir of nearly five hundred voices and published a special paperback volume of anthems. Annie, too, was heavily involved. She was in charge of a tea at which perhaps as many as two thousand were served. She organized workers from all the Christian Churches around Cincinnati and arranged to buy wholesale lots of a new product, Nabisco crackers, which came in three flavors.

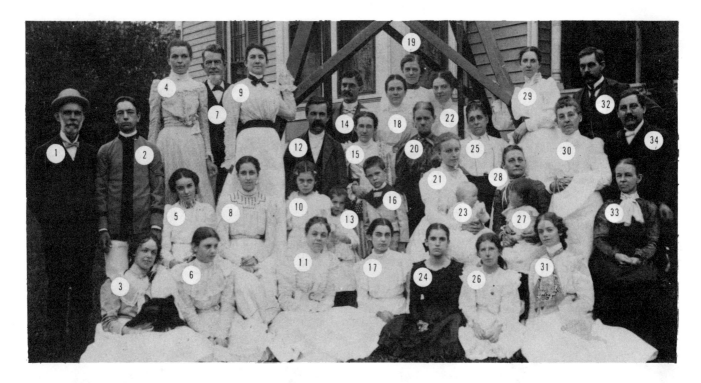

The best existing photograph of Henry Fillmore with his relatives was taken on August 11, 1899, at the Avondale home. The occasion was the Disciples of Christ Jubilee, held in Cincinnati at Music Hall. Those pictured are: 1—James Henry Fillmore, father; 2—Henry Fillmore, age 17, soon to start his second year at MMI; 3—Margaret Vickers, first cousin (daughter of 33); 4—Maggie Fillmore, aunt by marriage (wife of 12); 5—?; 6—Mary Hanna Fillmore, sister; 7—James Henry Lockwood, great-uncle (brother of Mrs. A.D. Fillmore); 8—?; 9—Annie McKrell Fillmore, mother; 10—Annie Louise Fillmore, sister; 11—Jennie Vickers, first cousin (daughter of 33); 12—Charles Millard Fillmore, uncle (father's brother); 13—Georgia Fillmore, first cousin (daughter of 12); 14—Aden L. Fillmore, uncle (father's brother); 15—?; 16—Herbert Worth Fillmore, first cousin (son of 32); 17—Fred Evans Fillmore, sister; 18—Ella Hall Fillmore, aunt by marriage (wife of 14); 19—?; 20—Sarah Lockwood, great-aunt (sister of Mrs. A.D. Fillmore); 21—Emma Wulke Fillmore, first cousin once removed, by marriage (wife of 34); 22—Anna Lockwood, first cousin once removed (daughter of 7); 23—Hildegarde Maria Fillmore, second cousin (daughter of 34); 24—Maude Trowbridge (related through Maria Trowbridge, wife of Comfort Lavius Fillmore, uncle of Henry's father); 25—Addie Trowbridge (same relationship as 24); 26—Frances Trowbridge (same relationship as 24); 27—Mabel Frances Fillmore, first cousin (daughter of 32); 28—Annie Fillmore, first cousin once removed (daughter of Comfort Lavius Fillmore); 29—Laura Moore Fillmore, aunt by marriage (wife of 32); 30—Nettie Fillmore, first cousin once removed (daughter of Comfort Lavius Fillmore); 31—Annabell Vickers, first cousin (daughter of 33); 32—Frederick A. Fillmore, uncle (father's brother); 33—Minerva Fillmore Vickers, aunt (father's sister); 34—Lavius Challen Fillmore, first cousin once removed (son of Comfort Lavius Fillmore).

To accommodate the crowd at the Avondale home, extra bedding was borrowed from neighbors. J.H. jokingly complained that the pillows around the house, which had been sent out to a pillowmaker for thinning, had been stretched so far he was sleeping on six feathers. The Fillmore children gave up their bedrooms so that four or five people could sleep in every room. Henry slept in J.H.'s study, doubling up in a borrowed bed with a bearded church official. At first he balked at sleeping with a bearded man, saying he would rather sleep on the piano.

J.H. was extremely busy that entire summer. Just before the big event he had led the singing at the Kentucky state convention of Christian Churches at Mt. Sterling. Also, he found time to help organize the Protestant Home for Working Boys in Cincinnati and was named treasurer. As might be expected, he was a heavy contributor. He was also just launching a new monthly paper of the Fillmore Brothers Company, *The Choir,* which dealt with church vocal music and was intended to supplement the *Concert Quarterly for Sunday Schools.* Additionally, he was making preparations to reinstate the *Musical Messenger.*

Henry started his second year at MMI in September, and the second year went much better than the first. A contributing factor was his passion for sports. The quarterback of the varsity football team had graduated, and Henry was elected to replace him. The MMI team was not in a regular league but played games with such teams as those from Dayton Steele High School and the Miami Business College (of Dayton). In the spring he played on the varsity baseball team, becoming one of only two cadets who played both varsity football and baseball. He also participated in rowing and was a member of the equestrian team.

The summer of 1900 proved to be quite adventuresome for Henry; he was finally allowed to perform on his trombone. Professionally, no less. The famous song leader, Homer Rodeheaver, was just beginning his illustrious career and needed an assistant on a revival circuit. Since J.H. was doing business with Rodeheaver, he made arrangements for Henry to tour with the evangelical troupe. His job was to sell hymnals and help "Rody" with the music.

The colorful Rodeheaver had a flashy and exciting way of presenting his music, particularly the opening

The 1899 MMI team in offensive formation. The one with the big nose is Henry Fillmore.

Henry is holding the football in this MMI varsity team portrait taken in the fall of 1899. He was quarterback of the team for two years.

hymn. Henry enjoyed this tremendously, taking a lesson in showmanship. This was the way hymns *should* be sung, he thought. He also reveled in Rodeheaver's sense of humor.

Rodeheaver was also a native of Southern Ohio, just a year older than Henry, and had been a cheerleader at Ohio Wesleyan University. His enthusiasm carried into the music field. He was also a trombone player and had been a member of the 4th Tennessee Regimental Band in Cuba during the Spanish-American War. He created quite a bit of attention by playing his trombone along with the singing and invited Henry to join him. After this, Henry would go about selling the hymnals. These were paperback volumes published by the Fillmore Brothers Company, and they sold so well that Henry had to telegraph several times for additional copies.

The area where this troupe traveled is not clear, but it is believed that it proceeded generally in a northwesterly direction. The tour probably extended into South Dakota because of a story Henry told many times in his twilight years. According to this story, a South Dakota cowboy approached him outside the tent and asked if he could play the trombone and dance at the same time. The cowboy then drew his six-shooter and fired several shots at Henry's feet. In Henry's version of the story, this was "the most vigorous exhibition of a trombone-dance ever seen this side of the Rockies."

The revival tour probably lasted about two-and-a-half months, after which Rodeheaver returned to Ohio Wesleyan. He had only occasional contact with Henry after this time but maintained business relations with the Fillmore Brothers Company for many years. He composed numerous hymns and other pieces of church music, but his greatest fame came in his twenty-year association with Billy Sunday as Sunday's song leader. Later, he established his own publishing house at Winona Lake, Indiana.

In the first week of September, 1900, the Fillmore family moved to a new home in Norwood, not far from the Avondale home. It was difficult for them to leave their beautiful home and neighborhood in Avondale, but the Norwood home at 4228 Floral Avenue was even nicer. They did not move because of any dissatisfaction; Annie realized that the three girls were missing most of the Richmond Street Church's social activities because of the distance from the Avondale home. In Norwood, they would be much closer to a church of the same denomination, even though it was having financial difficulties.

The Norwood Christian Church was in its infancy, having been founded in 1897. The congregation was meeting temporarily in a Presbyterian church while the old Lutheran church they were buying was being remodeled. The minister was the Rev. Alvin Taylor, an old friend of J.H.'s, and J.H. went the second mile in providing financial support. He pledged seven hundred and fifty dollars to the building fund, payable within a year. His business associates advised against this, pointing out that the burden would surely be too great because of the purchase of his new home and the sums he was paying to keep Henry in a select military school. His answer to this was that he would pray about it a lot. For the record: J.H. Fillmore paid his pledge in full in the specified time.

Henry's third and final year at MMI began with a flourish, with his being elected quarterback of the football team for the second time. The team did not set the world on fire this year, but Col. Brown and his staff monitored Henry's performance closely and were impressed by the leadership he exhibited. He was promoted to the rank of captain just prior to the Thanksgiving weekend. Brown chose that time for the promotion so that Henry could have his stripes sewed on when he went home for Thanksgiving, at which time a very special event took place in the new Norwood home.

The special event was J.H. and Annie's twentieth wedding anniversary. The anniversary date was actually four days earlier, because Thanksgiving fell on the 29th of the month in 1900. But since they had been married on Thanksgiving Day in 1880, a Thanksgiving party would have added meaning.

An extravagant affair was planned, with the intent that it could also serve as a housewarming. Over three hundred invitations were sent out. The party began in the late afternoon and continued until almost midnight. Annie was dressed in a beautiful white China silk gown with a long train, generously trimmed with ruffles and lace, and wore a corsage of pink and blue flowers. J.H. was fitted in a specially tailored Prince Albert cut tuxedo and ruffled shirt. Even Henry dressed up in a dark suit and took his place in the receiving line with his sisters, who were dressed in attractive white gowns.

Caterers served a lavish evening meal to sixty-five guests, and soon thereafter the remainder of the guests began to arrive. A total of over two hundred visitors were served refreshments during the evening. When the crowd had peaked, the Rev. A.M. Harvuot, pastor of the Central Christian Church where J.H. and Annie had attended at the time of their marriage, called for attention. He climbed part of the way up the stairway and pulled a handsome new book out of his pocket. It was called *Twenty Years* and was a surprise gift from the staff of the Armstrong and Fillmore Printing House.

From the book, Rev. Harvuot read aloud a poignant and thoughtful poem of twenty-one verses by Palmer Hartsough. There was a verse describing their wedding plus a verse describing events for each year of their marriage. He then read several other poems which had been contributed by authors of Fillmore Brothers publications, as well as numerous telegrams and congratulatory messages.

One touching poem, written by brother Charlie, eventually came to be considered as one of his better pieces of writing:

THE STREAM AND THE BROOK

Upon a western prairie,
Not many years ago,
Sprang up a little streamlet,
And east began to flow.

Soon after in the southland,
Sprang up a little brook,
And toward the colder northland,
Its cheerful way it took.

MMI cadets on bivouac. 1899-1900 school year.

MMI cadets in rifle drill. 1899-1900 school year.

Cadet Fillmore blows the bugle as the evening dress parade is about to begin. The cadets are shown here in their blue and white dress uniforms, blue and white being the school colors. Germantown people nicknamed the students the ''Browns,'' however, as a tribute to the school's founder.

27

MMI's horse-drawn excursion wagon was used mostly for extracurricular activities, such as fishing trips and picnics. School brochures described the wagon as "large enough to carry all our cadets." In Henry's three years there, the total enrollment probably did not exceed thirty. This photograph was taken in the spring of 1900.

Shortly after this photograph was taken, in November, 1900, Henry (holding ball) was promoted to the rank of captain in recognition of the leadership he displayed. He graduated from MMI in the spring of 1901 with the degree of Bachelor of Arts.

Anon, the brook and streamlet,
Approached—then became one;
And now for twenty summers,
Together they have run.

God grant that many seasons
May for them come, and go,
While they in blessed union,
Continue still to flow.

Also included in the book was an appendix listing J.H.'s significant musical works of the past twenty years, listed chronologically. Without his knowledge, the entire book had been conceived, planned, printed and bound with ribbon and bow. He remarked humorously about this, saying that if such an ambitious project could be consummated secretly right under his nose, what else might these sneaky employees be up to?

The Sunday after Thanksgiving, Henry reported back to MMI with a renewed appreciation for his father and his accomplishments. Who wouldn't be duly impressed after such a mass of testimonials as those printed in *Twenty Years?* Not only did the son respect the father; the father was also proud of the son for his record of achievement at MMI. Henry finished the school year in good standing. What a contrast this was to his record at the time of his enrollment!

On Thursday, June 6, 1901, Henry's proud family sat in folding chairs on the north side of the solitary MMI campus building as Col. Orvon Graff Brown presented a diploma reading "Bachelor of Arts" to Captain James Henry Fillmore, Jr.

11　　　　　PREPARATION

The Miami Military Institute was a junior college, and a degree conferred by this school was not quite the equivalent of a degree from a college or university. Rather, it was equivalent to one-and-a-half or two years. The training received at MMI prepared students very well for most any institution of higher learning, however, and Henry was definitely of a mind to continue his education.

He had given much thought to his future and was determined that his career would be in music. Music or nothing; he would go on to college only if he could study music. At first he was uncertain about which curriculum would be the most suitable, but after studying a catalog of the College of Music of Cincinnati and talking to several of the faculty members there, he decided that his majors would be performance and composition. For the performance studies, his instrument would of course be the trombone. As for the composition, he was uncertain about which direction this would take him except that light classics appealed to him.

The summer of 1901 was young; it was nearly three months until the fall semester was to commence at the College of Music. Annie kept him exceptionally busy for over two weeks by volunteering his services to help in the remodeling of a parsonage for Rev. Alva Taylor of the Norwood Christian Church. She was chairman of a committee to select a suitable home, and the house they settled upon needed considerable work. Annie, Henry and two others cleaned, painted and varnished the interior of the house while other church volunteers worked on the exterior.

For the remainder of the summer, Henry was employed at the Fillmore Brothers Company. J.H. wanted him to learn all aspects of the business, so he worked at everything from typesetting, printing and binding to editing music and verse. He also made vocal and choral arrangements for some of the hymns and other pieces being published. Since he had studied bookkeeping at MMI and was very quick with figures, he also worked on the record books.

Two things bothered him about the business. First, he was beginning to like hymns less and less. Second, the pay was pitifully low. J.H. did not have to remind him that he had paid dearly for those three years at MMI and that he would also be footing the bill for college. But still, Henry would have appreciated something more than just spending money. After all, he was working as a full-time employee, six days a week. Papa was generous with others; why not him?

Henry felt he was at least entitled to make a few criticisms of the business. These fell on deaf ears, for the most part, but nevertheless he had some valid arguments. In working with the record books, he noted that the business had stabilized; that is, it was not growing as it had in previous years. Henry thought they should diversify in some way because of increasing competition in the religious music field.

He had the audacity to suggest that the Fillmore Brothers Company enter the band music publishing field. This did not set too well with the staff, but Henry was merely trying in a sincere way to pass on the benefit of what business training he had had at MMI. J.H. was measuring Henry's words; he himself had not had a high school education, much less three years in a junior college, so he listened very carefully.

Another thing which Henry thought should be considered was the opening of a retail store of some sort where not only music could be purchased but musical instruments as well, particularly band instruments. This idea was much too revolutionary for the older employees of the shop who had shared J.H.'s earlier views about band musicians being a class of people who were, as a whole, not among the pious. Henry asked J.H. to conduct an experiment by running an advertisement for a reputable musical instrument shop in the *Musical Messenger* and then monitoring the response. J.H. agreed, so Henry approached A. Squire, a nearby dealer who was highly regarded. Squire could not see the necessity of advertising in a religious journal, but Henry had planned to run the ad at no cost to Squire except for the engraving. Squire consented and was pleased to receive numerous inquiries and visits to his store. Henry had

Bicycle racing was another of Henry's loves, and he was a daredevil. He won a medal for a half mile race at the Lexington (Kentucky) Fair in the summer of 1901. The fellow behind him is believed to be his future brother-in-law, Sylvanus Carlyle Shipley, also an excellent racer. The two had met in the Norwood Christian Church.

made his point.

Sports seemed to be in Henry's blood, and he kept physically active. He took one day off to try out for a professional baseball team (probably not the Cincinnati team) but was not selected. He had also been intrigued by bicycle racing for several years, and during evenings and on Sundays he could be seen whizzing down roads and streets around the northern suburbs of Cincinnati and beyond.

There is no record of his participation in distance racing, but it is said that he took part in a six-day race that summer. Sprinting was his specialty. He was good enough at it to win at least one half-mile race at the Lexington (Kentucky) Fair, and the tiny medal presented to him is now in the Fillmore Museum.

Henry's time for this race was 1 minute 15 seconds, which converts to an average of 24 miles per hour. This was a pretty good average for those days, before the advent of specialized bicycles like those used in the Olympics. By way of comparison, the Olympic record for 1,000 meters (0.62 mile) set twenty-seven years later was 1 minute 14.2 seconds, or an average of 30.14 miles per hour.

The College of Music of Cincinnati, founded in 1878, is not to be confused with the Cincinnati Conservatory of Music, although the two did merge in 1955 and became part of the University of Cincinnati in 1962. At the time of Henry's enrollment at the College of Music, there were numerous professional musicians on the faculty. Two of these, Prof. Charles Kohlman and Mr. John A. Broekhoven, had the most influence on Henry. In addition to his duties there, Broekhoven was also on the faculty of a new school which was eventually called the Ohio Conservatory of Music.

Henry attended for only one semester, at the end of which he left because he had learned all he wanted to know about serious music. He came to the realization that a career in any kind of classical music was definitely not for him. The mainstream of his interest was entertainment, and he could see no reason to continue studying at a conservatory where music for entertainment was of secondary importance.

Kohlman was the highest ranking trombone mentor at the school. He taught Henry as many basics as he could but sensed that Henry did not have his heart in studying classical music excerpts or in refined exercises. Although Henry loved the trombone, he was obviously much more interested in composition than in performance, and Kohlman did the best he could to raise his level of proficiency in the limited time he had to work with him.

Broekhoven's experience with Henry was much different. He was astonished at Henry's grasp of theory, harmony and orchestration and immediately separated him from the rest of the class. He went out of his way to prescribe advanced studies whereby Henry could orchestrate music in his own "commercial" manner. He recognized Henry's creative talent in the popular field and wisely let him progress in his own direction. Henry's days at the conservatory were definitely numbered, so Broekhoven tried to make it possible for him to use his time in the most profitable manner.

A month before the semester's end, Broekhoven had a heart-to-heart talk with Henry. He said that in his career thus far he had not had a student with so much natural talent. Henry had acquired so much practical knowledge on his own, he said, that he had taught him all he was capable of teaching him and that further study would therefore be a waste of time. This little chat was one of Henry's most treasured memories, because he had not often been so flattered in his youthful life. Broekhoven then announced that he had a special project for him.

Each year in Cincinnati there was an extravaganza known as the Fall Festival. It was mostly an outdoor event held in and around Music Hall, with merchants and civic groups presenting what amounted to a gigantic street carnival, complete with parades. Even the Miami-Erie Canal was decorated—with gondolas. Broekhoven was to be in charge of three band concerts for the Fall Festival the following year. His special project for Henry would be to make band arrangements for several of the pieces to be performed.

Henry felt honored to be asked to make such a contribution and eagerly went to work on his rather unusual term paper. To the amazement of Broekhoven, he finished the pieces long before they were due, and they were letter perfect. It is sad that Henry's manuscripts, like virtually all other pieces of his early unpublished music, are not accounted for. It was hoped that some of these early pieces would turn up in a relative's attic or in a music library someplace during the course of research for this book, but they apparently are lost forever.

After dropping out of college, Henry turned once again to Papa for a job. The opportunity for composing and arranging band music did not exist, at least not for the time being. But he was not giving up on the idea of having the company publish band music. To him, this was where the money was. Bands, such as those of John Philip Sousa, were drawing capacity crowds all over the country; it was actually the golden age of bands.

Not long after Henry had gone back to work, the business hit its first serious stumbling block. The trusted relationship with George Armstrong came to an abrupt end. Exactly what happened is not clear, but J.H. hinted that either Armstrong or employees under his control had engaged in improprieties. He never elaborated on this publicly; perhaps it was something he could not prove. Whatever, J.H. and Armstrong agreed rather hurriedly to call it quits.

The Fillmore Brothers business moved from 119 West Sixth Street to 421 Elm Street and re-incorporated under the Fillmore Brothers Company name with new stockholders, Armstrong not being one of them. Thereafter, the majority of the printing was done by the Otto Zimmerman Company, later known as the Otto Zimmerman and Son Company.

J.H. had to think of something to keep Henry occupied and happy. Henry simply was not cut out to be an office man who worked exclusively on religious music. The business was therefore expanded in two new directions. First, in September of 1902, J.H. acquired the musical instrument holdings and music publishing facilities of A. Squire and rented first floor space at 528 Elm Street for a retail store. Since this was Henry's idea, he worked at the retail store most of the time in the capacity of junior clerk.

Second, a few pieces of band music were published. A major problem arose, however: distribution. Advertising in the company journals brought very little return because these journals were aimed strictly at religious institutions.

Because of the acquisition of A. Squire's facilities, money lost in the split with Armstrong, and high rental on the new store, the business was clearly in a crisis. With the December, 1902 issue, publication of the *Musical Messenger* ceased for the second time. The older employees of the company, who thought band business would bring disrepute to and eventual collapse of the company, were saying "we told you so." It appeared that they might possibly be right. For the first time, J.H. had to borrow money, obtaining a sizable loan from the Fifth-Third Bank in Cincinnati.

The situation became so bad that drastic changes had to be made. At a meeting of company officers and stockholders, Palmer Hartsough made a surprise move by volunteering to retire. It would be an early retirement, because he was not yet fifty-nine years old. J.H. was overcome with a feeling of guilt, thinking he alone was responsible for injudicious business decisions which were, in effect, forcing his very best friend out of the business. It was indeed a sad day for all when this

saintly old gentleman walked out the front door with his belongings. He agreed to continue his versewriting for the company, however, as needed.

Hartsough, like J.H., had been a generous and benevolent man and had not saved up much for old age. He really did not consider himself old, though. He left the Fillmore Brothers premises in the spring of 1903 and immediately returned to the profession of choral directing. The word had gotten around that he was to be at liberty, and his services were much sought after. He served as music director on several revival tours and also did private teaching.

Palmer Hartsough was certainly a young man mentally, if not physically. Four years after he left the Fillmore Brothers, at the age of sixty-two, he entered the ministry! He was ordained a Baptist minister and went back to his home state of Michigan, where he preached until the age of eighty-three. Looking back on his lengthy career, perhaps the best example of his writing was "I Am Resolved No Longer to Linger," in which he collaborated with J.H. He wrote verse for over fifteen hundred hymns, anthems, recitations, children's cantatas and other pieces of church music. Last, but not least, he composed fifty-nine prohibition songs.

The prohibition issue was still another reason the company was in financial trouble. Much more prohibition-oriented music was being published than was selling. J.H. refused to regard this as a loss, however, because he had an axe to grind and believed he was merely doing his Christian duty. But the fact remained that the business was evidently headed for martyrdom. Their offerings were not what would be considered high class music. Consider this song, called "The Saloonatic," by brother Charlie:

> Who drinks just a little of lager or rum?
> He is the saloonatic.
> Who thinks that he never will turn out a bum?
> He is the saloonatic.
>
> Saloonatic, saloonatic, he is a saloonatic,
> Saloonatic, saloonatic, he is a saloonatic.

And consider this literary gem, also by Charlie, who was answering politicians who were of the opinion that the prohibitionists were fighting a losing battle. He called this one "Cranks":

> . . .Well, perhaps they may be right—and then, again—
>   They might be wrong.
> And perhaps we are a set of cranks
>   This conflict to prolong.
> But until this mighty question has been settled
>   In the right,
> We propose to still continue cranks,
>   And carry on the fight.
>
> To be real frank, I'd rather be a crank,
> And stand right square on the Prohibition plank,
> Than to be in the rank of the blankety, blank, blank,
> Who votes the self-same ticket as the montebank.

The prohibitionists enlisted all the help they could get, minority groups included. "I Draws de Lin Right

Dar," with words by T.C. Johnson and music by Charles H. Gabriel, is a good example:

I'se a 'Publican Niggay, yes I is,
And I votes dat ticket ebry time;
But de Mastah, he say, I am his,
And my 'legiance in de heb'nly clime.
So I votes fo' de man, ef he's all right,
An' takes no likker at de bar;
But ef fo' de whiskey side he'll fight,
Den I draws de line right dar.

Yah! Yah! I draws de line right dar, right dar,
Yes, I draws de line right dar, right dar.
I votes fo' no pahty an' I votes fo' no man,
Who gives deir support to de bar.
I puts dem all right under the ban,
For I draws de line right dar.

These three songs were included in a collection of over two hundred tunes, edited by Charles M. Fillmore, called *Fillmore's Prohibition Songs*. It was published as a hardback volume in 1903, having been preceded by a less extensive paperback issue three years earlier. The stated reason for its existence was to "assist in the Prohibition [Party] campaign, patriotic services and all meetings in the interest of reform." Charlie contributed nineteen of the pieces, J.H. eleven and Fred three.

In addition to original pieces, prohibition words were added to such well known tunes as "Old Kentucky Home," "Battle Hymn of the Republic" and "Yankee Doodle." The front section of the book was devoted to many Biblical references dealing with drinking, although it might be argued that some of the Biblical passages quoted were indirect or taken out of context.

Henry was not asked to add to *Fillmore's Prohibition Songs,* and it is very unlikely that he would have had the desire. He made himself unpopular by remarking that this sort of publication, even though it had its humorous side, would not be a moneymaker for the company. The entire collection bordered on the mediocre, and since the company was family owned and operated, outside editing was not solicited.

Perhaps the most interesting tune in *Fillmore's Prohibition Songs* was "Bibles and Beer." J.H. wrote the music, and the verse was by Ida M. Budd:

Over the sea in their ignorant blindness,
Dwell the poor heathen 'mid darkness and night.
We in the homeland with brotherly kindness,
Reach out with longing to send them the light.

So o'er the ocean our good ships are speeding,
Gladly to bear them the tidings of cheer;
But side by side with the Word of God, think of it!
Travels its foe—our American beer.

Bibles and beer! What a strange combination!
Who ever heard of the like in creation?
Mustn't the heathen consider us queer,
Sending them cargoes of Bibles and beer?

It must be admitted that they had a point.

The business was in serious straits when the final fifteen hundred dollar payment of the bank loan came due. Two days before the deadline, the treasurer announced that liquid assets were such that the payment could not be made and that no immediate solution was evident. J.H. stood to lose credibility and be embarrassed, and it was entirely possible that he could go bankrupt. He called upon a Higher Authority; that night he went to bed with an earnest prayer for guidance.

The following morning, when he opened his mail at the office, he received one of the most profound surprises of his entire life. Enclosed in a letter from Australia was a check for exactly fifteen hundred dollars!

Many years earlier, J.H. had befriended an Australian prohibitionist worker who was penniless and stranded in the United States. J.H. loaned him fifteen hundred dollars so he could return home. None of the loan had ever been repaid, and he had forgotten about it. Then, on the very day of his life when he needed it most, it was returned to him. A coincidence?

13   THE CASE OF THE DUPLICATE COMPOSER

The early spring of 1903 was another period of Henry's life about which very little is known. It was an important period, however, because this was the only time he was ever in Europe. From the recollections of friends and associates, however, it has been learned that J.H. sent him abroad to make a brief study of the European church music situation and to learn if there was significant market potential for Fillmore Brothers publications.

Henry sized things up rather quickly, learning that the situation was worse in the two or three countries he visited than in America. Apparently he went alone, because if someone would have accompanied him his travel itinerary would surely have been different.

When he realized that sales possibilities were nil, he decided to enjoy himself. But he did not go about seeing the sights as most others would have done. One of the first things he did was attend a circus performance. In talking with the bandmaster he learned that one of the trombone players had just left the troupe. So he volunteered his services!

He played with the circus for several days, and when he ran out of money he came home. Of course, J.H. was more than a little disgusted when Henry told him of this. The entire trip had been a waste of time and money as far as J.H. was concerned, but he had no choice other than to consider it a market research expense and forget about it.

The story about what happened right after Henry's return from Europe became one of the favorites among those who today love to tell about the antics of the Henry Fillmore they once knew. Henry finally persuaded Papa to publish a march he had written himself. But Papa said that he would consider publishing it only if the name Fillmore did not appear on the music as the composer.

Henry thought this was a bit absurd and downright funny, so he handled the problem in a humorous manner. He remembered how he had longed to play the trombone as a boy and had to do it secretly because Papa did not approve of bands and band instruments. He also remembered saying to one of his chums at the time, "I will huff and puff and play my trombone whether Papa likes it or not." "I will huff and puff. . . will huff. . ." That was it! His pseudonym would be *Will Huff*.

Henry's first published march, "Higham March," was therefore published under the name Will Huff in September, 1903, and it was many moons before J.H. learned the origin of the title and realized that he had been duped by his conniving son. The name Higham came from a line of imported English brass instruments which the new Fillmore store was carrying. Joseph Higham was the inventor of an improved valve design, and his instruments were fairly popular around the turn of the century. He called his system "clear bore" because they were easier to blow than many other brands. The musical instrument industry eventually made numerous other substantial advances, however, which overshadowed Higham's improvements, and he went out of business. Today, Higham instruments are collectors' items.

Two local events in the fall of 1903 helped shape Henry's future—the appearance of two great bands, John Philip Sousa's and Frederick Innis'. Hearing these superb organizations is probably what inspired Henry to press his father on the matter of publishing more band music. J.H. attended these concerts too, out of curiosity, and came away convinced that bands and band music had come a long way since the days of the Civil War. Henry went to work on five more marches, all of which were published early in 1904.

The first was called "Vashti," and J.H. let him put his own name on this one because Vashti was a Biblical character. The reason for this choice of titles, as on many other of his early compositions, is not clear. But Vashti (Book of Esther, Chapter I) was a nonconformist, just like Henry. If she were living today she would be classified a womans' libber.

Two of the other marches were called "Gary Owen" and "Lord Baltimore," and these titles were neutral enough to have the Fillmore name on them. But for "Under Arms" and "March of the Blue Brigade," pseudonyms were used again. For the former, Henry chose a new penname, Al Hayes, and for the latter he again used the name Will Huff. These were inspired by national guard units in the Cincinnati area. The "March of the Blue Brigade" was so named because some of Henry's personal friends were soldiers in one of the maneuvering units called the "blue army," which was in mock battle with the "brown army."

The innocent use of the name Will Huff turned out to be not so innocent after all. In fact, it brought about a monumental complication in the world of band music. Shortly after the "March of the Blue Brigade" was published, one of the Fillmore Brothers employees brought Henry a piece of sheet music called "Howard March" which, according to the notation on the music, was composed by Will Huff. He asked Henry if he was writing music for another publisher, because this piece was published by the Rudolph Wurlitzer Company, also of Cincinnati. Henry took a look at the music and was dumbfounded. Someone was stealing his name!. . .he thought.

He visited Wurlitzer's place of business and inquired about this Will Huff and was told that Will Huff was a composer from Southern Ohio. Well, so was Henry! They explained that Huff had been writing music for them for five years, although not on a regular basis. Henry was not the only one surprised at this development, because the Wurlitzer people had seen Huff's name on the two Fillmore publications and had assumed that Huff was publishing with two different publishers to gain wider publicity!

It was not long before Henry arranged to meet this Will Huff fellow, who was living in Williamson, West Virginia, at the time. They had a good laugh over the dual use of the name. Henry apologized for any inconvenience he might have caused and promised not to use the name again.

Henry's two "Huff" marches were selling well, because the Fillmore Brothers Company was now working out the distribution problem effectively. On the other hand, Huff's marches published by Wurlitzer had not had the benefit of much promotion because Wurlitzer was primarily a piano manufacturer. Therefore, Henry made him a business offer. Since the Fillmores could promote Huff marches better than Wurlitzer, he offered to publish them. Very few knew that Henry had written two "Huff" pieces, and he reasoned that if the real Will Huff would thereafter be publishing with the Fillmore Brothers, no one would ever know the difference. This made sense to Huff, because their styles were actually similar, and he agreed.

Thus began one of the most effective cover-ups in modern music. And the fact that two composers from the same part of the country were writing the same type of music which was published by two different publishers in the same town at the same time—with neither composer having knowledge of the other—is one of the most amazing coincidences in the history of music.

We shall learn more of the real Will Huff in later chapters.

By the year 1904, Henry had made numerous acquaintances among Cincinnati musicians, both amateur and professional, and with the publishing of his marches he was all the more eager to play with organized bands. There were a few amateur bands around town he was able to play with occasionally, but his proficiency on the trombone was now such that he was ready for bigger things.

Friends urged him to join the band of the First Regiment, Ohio National Guard. After three years of military style living at MMI, however, he had no desire to join the National Guard. But when he learned it was not necessary to enlist to play with the First Regiment Band, he decided to give it a try. There were not enough musicians among the regular ranks to form a band, so they were obliged to recruit civilian musicians. Henry auditioned for William J. (Billy) Kopp, the director of the band, and was accepted.

Billy Kopp was one of Cincinnati's finer musicians. A skilled trumpet player, he was a charter member of the Cincinnait Symphony Orchestra when it was founded in 1895 and was manager at one time. He also played viola. His versatility was evident in both the classical and popular music fields. The bands and orchestras he formed and conducted over the years were actually civilian organizations, but many of the players were also members of his National Guard band. Sometimes his civilian bands were billed under the name Kopp's Military Band.

It was Kopp who gave Henry his first professional job as a musician. He saw in Henry the potential for becoming a prominent composer and took pride in playing his music. Henry respected him and learned quite a bit about conducting from him over the years. He played for Kopp as much as he possibly could until 1910, at which time Kopp temporarily moved to Florida. Their association was to continue for many years after that.

Trouble was brewing between father and son at the Fillmore Brothers Company. The religious music business was merely marking time, and Henry believed they should plunge into the band music business in a big way. But J.H. pointed out that the company was founded as a church music publishing house, that it was currently a church music publishing house and that it would always be that way. *He* was the boss, and band music would have to remain a sideline.

Henry envisioned the business dwindling away to nothing after a few years. He was eager to write and arrange more band music and was frustrated because the company his own father headed did not provide the opportunity. The record shows that in 1904 only five of Henry's pieces were printed, and there were no plans for stepping up the rate. He was capable of turning out many times that amount.

During the summer of 1904, the Fillmores cast their worries aside and went to St. Louis for a three-week vacation. The occasion was the Louisiana Purchase Exposition, otherwise known as the St. Louis World's Fair.

Henry played trombone with the First Regiment Band of the Ohio National Guard, shown here at the Lexington Fair of 1904. He did not actually enlist in the National Guard; at that time the band was a special unit, and members were not required to be in military service. The conductor, Billy Kopp (extreme right) was primarily a symphony musician but was also a popular conductor of both civilian and military musical organizations in the Cincinnati area. This was Henry's first professional job as trombonist.

Visiting this great exposition was the fashionable thing to do, because it was heralded as the largest international exposition of all time and the latest of just about everything imaginable would be on display. While there, J.H. and Henry took turns manning a display of the Fillmore Brothers Company.

The exposition, which commemorated the centenary of the purchase of the Louisiana Territory from France, was indeed magnificent. In size, it covered almost as much ground as all previous World's Fairs put together. To see all the displays in the agricultural pavilion alone, for instance, one had to walk nine miles. The buildings were constructed of white plaster and were richly ornamented. In all, over nineteen million visitors were attracted in its seven months of operation.

Those in attendance were certainly brought up to date with progress at this exposition. Teleprinters and wireless telegraphy devices were demonstrated; the latest in gasoline and electric powered carriages were shown; modern telephones, machinery, balloons and even dirigibles were on display. And, of course, the crowds flocked to see the flying machines, because the Wright brothers had just recently demonstrated the feasibility of powered, heavier-than-air flight. We were on the verge of a revolution in transportation. It would seem that the most important technological advances in history were demonstrated at this colossal fair.

There was art galore, plus monuments and displays from all the states and thirty-four foreign countries. Music was heard in abundance too, with performances by such great bands as Sousa's, the British Grenadiers and the Garde Republicaine, and such renowned orchestras as the Berlin Philharmonic. There were amusements everywhere, and even the Olympic games were held nearby. A new culinary delight, introduced at this fair, made a big hit with the crowd and one young man from Cincinnati in particular—the ice cream cone.

The Fillmores stayed with relatives out on the west edge of town, and to get to the fair they rode the trolley. On one of the first trips in, Henry sat beside a very pretty young girl with big blue eyes and a warm, friendly smile. She was exceptionally quiet, but he learned that her name was Mabel May Jones and that she was a dancer in one of the shows at the fair. The next morning he saw her waiting at the trolley stop, struck up a conversation and managed to sit by her again on the long ride into town.

Mabel was a year younger than Henry and had come from Michigan. In subsequent trips, he learned more of her background. Her parents, Jesse and Mary Jones, had lived very modestly with their children in a houseboat, or "shantyboat," off the shore of Alpena, Michigan, on Lake Huron. Jesse owned three small schooners which he leased for shipping lumber. Mabel was the seventh in a family of twelve and had been born on this houseboat on November 2, 1882. She had grown weary of the austere life and had left the family a year earlier to go live with her oldest sister Hanna Whitford. Hannah—who went by the name of Toots, or Tootsie—and her husband Ned were living two blocks away from where the Fillmore relatives lived.

Henry promised to come see the show Mabel was in.

She gave him directions for finding the theater and then added that it might be a good idea if he came without his family. He did not understand this but said he could come alone.

He excused himself from the family at the fair and went to see the show. Not just once but several times, and he met with Mabel often between shows. He also visited her at Toots and Ned's house during the evenings, and before he realized it, he and Mabel had a full fledged romance going.

Since Henry had absented himself from the family so much while in St. Louis, and since he was usually in the presence of the Jones girl when absent, the family reasoned that for the first time in his life Henry was in love. They did not press him for details until they were on the train headed back for Cincinnati and Henry appeared to be preoccupied. It was a long trip for him. When they asked about Mabel's dancing, Henry decided to let them have it all at once: she was a hoochie-coochie dancer in a vaudeville show.

A hoochie-coochie dancer!

"Oh, my God, Henry! How could you?" He never forgot those words of his mother's and seldom told of the unpleasant scene he had created until years after she was dead—and then only to his closest friends. Annie, J.H. and the girls were petrified. Mabel was such a neat looking girl and seemed so nice! She *was* nice, he insisted. Very nice.

They were not convinced. After J.H. and Annie recovered from the shock, they told Henry that this relationship was clearly beneath his dignity and that it would be to his best interest if he would forget the whole affair. That was the worst possible thing they could have said.

Mabel had come from a poor family and did not finish her high school education before going to work. She was demure, humble, sincere and totally unpretentious. Henry had not found this combination of qualities in even the most cultured young ladies of his acquaintance. More importantly, she seemed to understand him. None of the girls he had ever dated, and indeed no one in his family except for Uncle Fred, had ever seemed to understand him. He was incurably lovestruck.

Once home, Henry's romance with Mabel did not diminish; rather, it intensified—through the mail. He was greatly perturbed over the family's flat rejection of her. Every time he received a letter from her, things got very tense at home. The frustration of not being allowed to compose and arrange more band music added to the tension.

In the fall of 1904, some additional floor space at 528 Elm Street became available, and everything was moved from 421 Elm so that all of the Fillmore Brothers Company could be under one roof. This became the company's permanent home, and when the financial situation improved a few years later, J.H. purchased the building. It had five floors.

Four Henry Fillmore compositions published in 1905 were processed before April, and they were all marches. For the first one, Henry tried to appease Papa by naming it "Tell Mother I'll Be There." It consisted of Uncle

35

Charlie's hymn of the same name, the hymn "Brighter Days Are Coming," a few measures of "Home Sweet Home," and some original material thrown in, all set to march tempo. He was allowed to put his name on that one.

The others were "Honor and Glory," "Troopers Tribunal" and "Cradle of Liberty," the pseudonym Al Hayes being used for the latter. The "Troopers Tribunal" title was another joke on Papa. It was a circus march, and Henry intentionally misspelled "Troupers" so that it would appear as a military parade title, the equivalent of "Troopers on Review." It had an unmistakable circus flavor, but Papa did not know the difference. His conniving son was at it again.

Henry was confident that his marches were good and that if the Fillmore Brothers did not publish them, some other company would. J.H. said frankly that he did not believe this and that he was actually doing Henry a favor by publishing them for him. In making this remark, he grossly underestimated Henry's determination. That evening, Henry took music paper home with him, and a week later he sent a march called "In Uniform" to the Philadelphia music publishing house of Harry Coleman.

The last week of March, when J.H. and Henry came home from work, there was a letter for Henry from Harry Coleman. They had accepted "In Uniform," and when Henry showed the letter to J.H. they engaged in a bitter argument. After they had fought over the matter of publishing band music, Henry opened up the old wound of the family's refusal to accept Mabel. He said he was tired of the family looking down their noses at her, because he intended to marry her!

That brought stares of disbelief, and both J.H. and Annie told him they were unalterably opposed to such a marriage. He was their firstborn and the only boy, and they let him know they expected him to choose a girl who was higher on the social ladder.

Henry was emotionally crushed. An impasse had been reached, and he saw only one way out. He leaped up the stairs, slammed shut the door of his room, packed as many of his belongings as possible in his suitcase, grabbed his trombone and left. They asked where he was going as he rushed through the front door, but he said nothing and disappeared into the night.

He took the trolley downtown and headed east on the electric interurban car to Uncle Fred's farm in Terrace Park. His favorite uncle was the only one he felt he could confide in under such circumstances, even though Fred was Papa's younger brother. Uncle Fred and Aunt Laura were surprised to see him and inquired as to the reason for the visit so late in the evening. He said that after the four children were in bed he would elaborate.

The relationship with Papa was absolutely intolerable, Henry explained, and the fact that both his parents appeared to have a low opinion of the only girl he ever really cared for only made matters worse. He was deeply hurt and felt the family was treating him like the proverbial black sheep, so the only answer was to start life anew elsewhere. Since Mabel was in St. Louis, that would be a good place to begin. In a recent letter he had asked Mabel to marry him, and she had accepted. They had not set a definite date, however.

He sat down and wrote a letter to Mabel to see if she was now ready for marriage, saying that if she was he would be on the next train to St. Louis. Four days later, Mabel's affirmative answer came. Uncle Fred loaned him some money and bade him farewell.

The tie had been broken.

15   TWO BECOME ONE

One thing Henry and Mabel had in common, though for different reasons, was that they had both left home. When Mabel had struck out on her own, she joined Toots and Ned while they were on the road performing with a circus. At the end of the season, they took up residence in St. Louis.

Toots, whose stage name was Tootsie Jones, had quite a name as an exotic dancer and had no trouble finding work in a burlesque show in downtown St. Louis. Ned, the first of her two husbands, was quite versatile. In addition to his other talents he was a comedian and was taken on by the same theater. Toots taught Mabel the basics of theater dancing and through various contacts was able to secure a job for her at the St. Louis World's Fair. Mabel found a job in another St. Louis theater after the fair closed and was still working there when Henry arrived.

In his brief visits with Toots and Ned the preceding summer, Henry had been fascinated by their accounts of show business life, particularly with the circus. He was thinking about circuses a great deal, and now that he was unemployed he reasoned that it would be exciting if he could earn a living as a trombonist with a circus band. Numerous shows had their winter quarters in Missouri and the neighboring states. Since Toots and Ned knew many circus people, they promised to write letters inquiring about job openings for Henry and Mabel. Toots and Ned had themselves contracted with the Lemon Brothers Circus for the upcoming season. But first there was the matter of getting Henry and Mabel married.

James Henry Fillmore, Jr., age twenty-three, and Mabel May Jones, age twenty-two, were united in marriage on Monday, April 10, 1905. Mabel, Toots and Ned were not affiliated with a church there in St. Louis, so they called upon the Rev. John H. Flower, a minister of their acquaintance, to perform the ceremony in the parlor of his home at 1910 Olive Street. Rev. Flower was Superintendent of the Lighthouse Mission in St. Louis.

The full story of when and where Henry and Mabel spent their honeymoon is not to be found on the pages of recorded history. But from stories Henry told down through the years, they had precious little money between them to spend for travel.

The simple, poignant ceremony they reenacted on their wedding anniversaries in future years provides a vital clue to the manner in which this humble, devoted couple coped with adversity and found happiness. Each year, they would open a can of baked beans and eat alone by the light of a single candle. Theirs was always to be a true love; and even in their final years, when they could afford any cuisine imaginable, they would go off to themselves and have their beans by candlelight.

Such was the beginning of Henry and Mabel Fillmore's married life. For the next forty-nine years, their dedication to one another was a perfect example of the old adage that love conquers all.

16   THE SAWDUST RING, PART ONE

The results of Toots and Ned's inquiries were not encouraging, but a job was open to Henry with the Lemon Brothers Circus. There would be work for Mabel, too, not as a performer but as a nursemaid and tutor for the children of a family of performers.

Both accepted the jobs. Together with Toots and Ned, they reported to the Lemon Brothers' winter quarters at Argentine, Kansas (now part of Kansas City), approximately a week-and-a-half before the start of the season, which was April 29. Toots was to be billed as "Tootsie Jones, Oriental dancer." Ned's name does not appear in accounts of the 1905 Lemon Brothers' show, so it must be assumed that he used an assumed name.

A month earlier, the circus camp had been inactive except for a few members of the staff and some mechanics, painters and animal trainers. All the performers and laborers had been released at the end of the preceding season. During the winter months, many of the rolling vehicles were reconditioned and decked out with new paint. Meanwhile, the management had worked diligently making plans for the 1905 tour. This included scheduling the railway passages, preparing advertising, securing local permits and so forth.

By the time the Fillmores and Whitfords came upon the scene, many of the performers had reported and were practicing their acts. Band rehearsals were about to commence. Henry met the leader, Ed Lemon, and the other band members. Ed Lemon, incidentally, was not related to the brothers who operated the circus. Ed's brother, Fay, also played in the band.

Frank Lemon, the owner, needed a calliope player, and Henry volunteered. He had never played a calliope before, but he was eager, even though this would mean double duty because he would also be playing trombone in the band. The calliope was in a sad state of repair. Henry managed to fix the whistles, but it was necessary to hire a railroad engineer to get the remainder of this steam monster operating properly. Together, the engineer and Henry got it operating, whereupon Henry tuned it and started his noisy rehearsing. First he learned a few simple tunes and then graduated to ragtime. The circus people liked that.

Mabel's job was to care for four children of the Cooke sisters, who had an equestrian act. They reportedly were descendants of the Scottish family which founded Cooke's Royal Circus and New Equestrian Arena and brought it to this country in 1836. The sisters (and in-laws) had been with Frank Lemon for several years, and he had developed their talent. Little Edna Cooke, as she was billed, was the youngest and was a skillful trick bareback rider. The others were Anna Cooke Somers and Theresa Sommers.

Mabel not only cared for the Cooke children; she gave them their schooling until the second week of June. But this was not all she was required to do—she appeared with the entire family in the grand entree, or "spec." This was the opening parade around the arena. For this, her costume was a fancy long white dress and a large embroidered white hat. She rode various animals. Usually it was a white horse, but sometimes she rode a camel or an elephant.

The circus put its best foot forward in the "spec," or "walk-around," as it was often called, starting things off in grand style. Actually, it was a pageant in motion. Practically everyone with the circus participated, whether they were performers or not. Even the roustabouts were dressed as clowns. This part of the show was exciting for Mabel, because she loved to dress up and seldom had ever been able to afford it. She definitely added something to the show, being attractive and physically well endowed. She was sometimes referred to as "Mabel Fillmore, the Circassian beauty," as though she was a native of Circassia (Soviet Union).

To begin the "spec," in came the mounted riders with great majesty in their colorful, silky costumes. Then came the Zouaves, or girl drill corps. Next were the elephants, the clowns, a variety of animals, other performers, more animals, and then the remainder of the elephants. Meanwhile, the band furnished music for all the pageantry. As the last of the parade disappeared through the exit, the ringmaster blew his whistle to begin the show.

Henry was now a bona fide windjammer, or circus musician. He performed with his trombone, the instrument often referred to as the backbone of a circus band, but on several occasions Ed Lemon let him conduct. Either as an ordinary windjammer or as the leader, he was at the height of his glory. The pay was not so glorious, however. He received eight dollars a week, plus cakes (meals) and was given a berth on the train. Payday was Saturday between the matinee and evening performances, with two weeks' pay always held back to encourage good behavior and to minimize desertions. Tips were an added expense; it was customary to tip the train porters, mail clerks and many others who received only

Henry and Mabel trouped with the Lemon Brothers Circus on the
1905 tour, which lasted five months. The advertising promised more
than was actually produced. Although claiming two hundred performers, there were many less than that.

token pay from the circus.

Circus bands were not unionized at that time, and the
windjammers often had to help erect tents and seats and
do other chores too. The stamina required for playing
was incredible because of the number of performances
in a day's time. It was a well known fact that circus
band jobs in those days were the most difficult of all
musicians' jobs. The first order of the day was usually
the parade, which was followed by a pre-show concert.
Sometimes the players moved around before the concert, ballyhooing the show from various places on the
grounds. After the show came the sideshow and other
post-show functions. With all this activity, it is little
wonder that their uniforms usually looked a little
shabby.

Henry learned that a windjammer must remain alert
at all times. The music was usually difficult, and great
flexibility was required because of the constantly changing texture of the show. No two performances were
alike—something to be expected with moving acts, each
with split-second timing. Despite the fact that it was
necessary to play loudly most of the time, circus bandsmen were generally known for their ability to play with
sensitivity. Henry's musicianship improved greatly over
a short period of time.

The Lemon Brothers Circus was organized in 1887 in
Clinton, Illinois, and went through lean and trouble-
some years in their tours of the Great Plain States. Because it at first toured exclusively in that area, it was
known among circus people as a "high grass" show.
The turning point came with the association of the well-
known circus figure Martin S. Downs, of Toronto, who
was responsible for the acquisition of numerous elephants, camels and draught horses. Downs knew Canadian territory well because he had toured there with several other shows, and the Lemon show made Canadian
tours thereafter because of his influence. He was not an
employee of the Lemons; he purchased "working privi-
leges," i.e., he paid the Lemons for the privilege of
operating various concessions.

The Lemon Brothers Circus went by several names
over the years, as was commonly done by small circuses
so townspeople who felt they had been gypped would
think they were getting a different show the next time
around. Sometimes it was Lemon, sometimes Lemen.
Initially, it had been called the Great New York and
New Orleans Combined Shows, a name used earlier by
the W.W. Cole Circus, which the Lemon show succeeded. In 1901, it was the Lemen Brothers World's Monster
Shows." The year before Henry and Mabel toured, it
was called the Great Pan American Show.

Henry and Mabel were not with the show the following year, when it went bankrupt. This again was a
Canadian tour, but the tour was not completed. An itinerant "white slaver" followed the show, running a
brothel close to the circus grounds and thriving on trade
from circus workers. Several difficulties arose, and
eventually a scuff in Roberval, Quebec, resulted in the
jailing of numerous circus workers and in the cancellation of the remainder of the tour.

In general, the Lemon Brothers Circus did not have a
good reputation. According to their advertising there
were two hundred performers; but to reach that total,
several performers had to function in multiple roles.
Counting all performers, their families, the
management and workers, there were probably less than
one hundred and twenty-five touring with the show.

The bad name came from several things. First, it was
known as a "gaming show," or "grift show"; gamblers
paid for the privilege of traveling with the circus. The

three-shell (pea-under-the-pod, or "old army") game, three-card monte men, roulette wheels and other gambling devices were almost always right out in the open.

It is said that pickpockets, dishonest ticket sellers and short-change artists followed the show and that sometimes thieves ransacked houses during the parades. If gambling was not permitted in a town, an unwritten gambling permit could often be obtained by graft. Henry did not participate in any of this, but he knew what was going on. This is one of the reasons he seldom talked about his tour with the Lemon Brothers.

Despite the ugly aspects, it cannot be denied that underneath their huge white tents with the colorful streamers and flags, the Lemon Brothers Circus was entertaining. One of the most exciting acts was the hippodrome chariot race, in which danger always lurked because the ground was not the same in any two successive towns. The Cooke Sisters' equestrian act was not outstanding, and they were often upstaged by the bareback horse racers.

The tumblers were very good, but the trapeze artists and other stunt men were apparently just average performers. If the stunts were not "death-defying," as advertised, they were at least serious injury-defying. The clowns were, according to reviews of the day, hackneyed. Perhaps the high spot of the Lemon Brothers Circus was its side show, which was bright and attractive. There was a snake charmer, a tall man, an "electric woman" and twenty other freaks of nature.

One of the show's greatest assets was its menagerie, the elephants in particular. All the elephants, or "bulls," worked hard in moving the wagons and cages into place. Then these formidible creatures would appear at various times during the course of the show. One terrifying monster, Rajah, reportedly killed nine men during his stormy lifetime. He was succeeded by the gentle Albert, who never harmed a soul. Albert was with the show the year Henry and Mabel were there, as was Jennie. Jennie was another huge elephant, and her constant companion was a female goat. The goat once disappeared for several days, and Jennie would perform absolutely no work in the goat's absence.

Among other animals in the Lemon menagerie were "giant, racing, fighting" camels, four lions, three tigers, two leopards, two hyenas, two jaguars and numerous monkeys, horses and ponies.

The primary reason for the abundance of animals was that Frank Lemon was a lover of animals. He might have had his shortcomings in other ways, but he was a fanatic when it came to kindness to animals. To him, it was unthinkable to abuse any dumb animal. Once he kicked one of his hostlers in the shin because the hostler had kicked one of the horses.

Lemon's first love was horses. He was a shrewd trader and an expert hostler and rider and had gotten his start in the circus business by tending horses. He loved to drive the ten-horse hitch of the bandwagon and would occasionally relieve the head hostler of this duty.

Although Frank Lemon's ethics were sometimes questionable in his dealings with the public, his circus people were like family to him. He wore an old raincoat and to outsiders was indistinguishable from the rest of

Frank V. Lemon (also Lemen), the oldest of the three Lemon brothers and proprietor of the circus, had a profound influence on Henry. He taught him organizational skills which were useful for the remainder of his life. He also taught him great compassion for animals. Lemon was square with his own people, but his show had a bad reputation because he permitted outside gambling concessions to operate on circus grounds.

the crew. He ate in the cookhouse with everyone else, not in a separate dining room. When it was necessary to eat away from the cookhouse, he often picked up the tabs of those around him. His word was good, and he always paid the employees' salaries, even if sometimes several weeks late.

Frank Lemon's nickname was Joe Hepp. Circus people called him that because he was always hep, or wise, to a given situation. He was a very alert person—a keen observer who always seemed to know what was going on and where. When a member of the crew needed fatherly advice, Joe Hepp was the man to see. He was very perceptive on medical matters, too, his father having been a doctor. He had followed his father around on calls for several years and acquired a considerable knowledge of medicine. There was always a store of drugs in a locker above the desk in the ticket wagon, and Joe Hepp acted as both the circus doctor and pharmacist.

There were three of the Lemon brothers, but Frank owned and operated the show. James (Frost, or Frosty), was business manager and treasurer, and Colvin was the purchasing agent. Frost had once been a circus bandmaster and would often leave the confines of the ticket wagon to sit in with the band. There were other relatives in the show, all hard working, honest people. Frank knew they were above suspicion but often quipped, "If there are any leaks in money matters, at least we keep it in the family."

One might say that Frank Lemon was a molder of young men. He watched his people carefully, always seeking signs of potential so he could better utilize their talents. He took a liking to Henry immediately and saw in him the ability to become a great man some day. Henry did not hesitate to approach him for advice, and his influence on Henry was obvious for the remainder of his life.

17 THE SAWDUST RING, PART TWO

The circus of the turn of the century was a city unto itself. Although many joined the circus to see the world, they seldom ventured from the show grounds except on off-days, which, for almost all circuses, were Sundays. Most of the scenery was seen from the window of a train, but this was impractical because most of the traveling was done by night.

The car Henry and Mabel traveled in was a double-decker passenger car, while the laborers rode in triple-deckers. Either type was stuffy on hot nights, but the luxuries were not expected by circus people. There were probably twenty-four cars in the Lemon Brothers train: twelve flatbed cars, six stock cars and six coaches.

Any successful circus is a marvel of efficiency, and the Lemon circus was no exception. Loading and unloading the train, for example, was an ultra-methodical operation, carried out in an exact, unvarying sequence. There was a set routine for moving each vehicle: the stake and chain wagon, the canvas wagons, the pole wagons, the side show wagons, the stable wagons, the water tank wagons, the cookhouse wagon, the blacksmith wagon, the animal wagons and the ticket wagon. If the prescribed sequence was not followed, there was chaos. Once each vehicle was in place, its assorted brackets, hangers and other items of equipment were bolted into place.

At times, the story of circus people was mud, mud, mud. But entertainment was their business no matter what the obstacles, and these hardy individuals took handicaps in stride. Each did his duty, with no excuses allowed. They passed through many remote towns where they were providing the only entertainment available, and disappointing the public was simply out of the question. Besides, this would be bad for business. Promptness was encouraged at every turn, even at the cookhouse; if one did not get there before the flag went down, he did not eat.

The performers, or "the acts," as they were called, were a breed apart from the rest of the circus. The hangers-on such as gamblers and crooked ticket sellers were the ones who gave the circus a bad name, not the performers. The performers were a courageous lot, generally possessing an integrity which grew from combating many hardships together. They were proud people.

The performers' standard of morality was high primarily because there was no time to get into mischief. Most of the women were married and rarely mixed with the public except in the execution of their duties. Drunkenness was not tolerated; one of the laws of the circus was that no alcohol was permitted in the tents. Because of the nature of the business, with its extreme demands on both mind and body, there was little desire for excesses of any kind. So circus performers led regular lives.

Although in some circuses the band members did not fraternize with "the acts," Henry made friends easily. Since Mabel was working for one of "the acts," he was accepted as one of them. He got along well with the roustabouts, too, finding them interesting because of their diversified backgrounds. The roustabouts came from all walks of life; they were with the circus for a host of reasons and often used assumed names. A circus was a good place to take refuge from one's past, and the roustabouts have sometimes been referred to as the "Foreign Legion of the labor army."

There were many Negro workers with the circus, usually working in segregated crews. They were happy-go-lucky individuals, but they were reliable and virtually indispensible. Henry loved them. He sympathized with them and even identified with them at times, so they felt at ease around him. He studied them carefully, learning as much about their personal lives as possible. He was intrigued by their informal, simple music, and the orientation he acquired in this association had a direct bearing on the trombone "smears" which he was to start composing three years later.

The 1905 season lasted five months, beginning on April 29 in Salisbury, Missouri, and ending on September 9 in Camp Point, Illinois. In the first nine days of the tour, they passed hurriedly through Missouri, Illinois, Indiana and Michigan and then settled down to the main part of the tour in Canada. This lasted until July 20 and took them through the provinces of Ontario, New Brunswick and Quebec. The remainder of the tour was spent weaving its way back through Michigan, Ohio, Indiana and Illinois. Throughout, it was a tour of small towns.

Circuses of that era were not always met with open arms. In fact, many towns would rather not have had them. The "towners" felt that circuses took too much money away from their communities, especially the "grifting shows." There was often trouble.

As a whole, circus people are quiet, never looking for trouble. But they were prepared for it. The Lemon Brothers clan had the reputation of being able to hold its own in a brawl, or "clem." Their canvasmen were often hired strictly for their ability to fight. Anyone could learn to string up tents, but not all could be victorious in a brawl, so scrappers were hired first. The Lemon crew was impossible to intimidate, even without local police protection. And since Henry had previously been with the John Robinson circus, the toughest of all circuses, he knew what was expected of him.

Circus people might have had their differences and a caste system of their own, but they stuck together like glue when in the face of peril. The circus was their home, and they protected it accordingly. They had to be "with it and for it," and their sense of fraternity transcended the caste system. The canvasmen, for instance, guarded their tents as if they had paid for them themselves. When the universal distress call of "Hey Rube!" was heard, every available hand descended upon the scene. There was never sufficient time to conduct orderly, fair fights, so they didn't fool around. They grabbed hammers, axe handles, stakes, various implements or anything else resembling a club and started swinging away.

On show day, people came for miles around, and the atmosphere was charged. With liquor usually being sold freely, there were often booze-crazed ruffians seeking the excitement of a fight. This was the situation a circus encountered in town after town. Then, too, there were college students who usually came in groups, parading and making whoopee and often attempting to kidnap a circus person just for the sake of adventure.

More often than not, circuses received practically no help from local law enforcement officers, because the police forces in small towns were seldom equipped to handle bands of hoodlums who ripped tents, shot out lights, cut ropes, started fires and so forth. Quite often, they were obliged to take matters into their own hands. Any circus person who did not enter into the fray was immediately branded a coward.

Henry was certainly not one of those cowards, but after this 1905 tour he had had enough fighting for a lifetime. This was one part of circus life he rarely mentioned; and if asked about it, he changed the subject. He had been a scrapper from the time he was a small boy, so it is safe to assume that he did his share of head-bashing. But he simply did not talk about such matters. In fact, he was in his seventies before he let it be known that he was with the Lemon Brothers Circus.

Despite the Lemon Brothers' reputation as a "grifting show" and their being known for the ability to come out on top in a brawl, the public looked the other way when parade time came. Their parade was not the finest, but it was more than adequate for a circus of its class. The parade caught everyone's attention, and the business community took a holiday when it came up the street.

In those days there were few autos and little traffic, so the parade proceeded unimpeded down the main street of a town. The bandwagon came first, with its team of eight or ten horses. Behind the band came the prancing ponies, the costumed cast waving to the crowd, the clowns and the caged animals. Most of the performers rode horses, camels, elephants, or the brightly colored wagons and chariots bedecked with gold leaf and ornate carvings. A bagpipe band, placed in the center of the procession, added to the excitement.

The calliope brought up the rear, with Henry sometimes a bit behind the rest. There was a good reason for his tardiness, however. As soon as the bandwagon would get through the main part of town, he would jump off, mount a horse, race toward the tail end of the parade on back streets and jump into the awaiting calliope wagon.

By 1905, circuses were tapering off what is generally regarded as their golden age. The parades presented by the Lemon Brothers were not as sumptuous of those of some of the bigger shows; but such as it was, the daily parade was made come rain or shine. There were numerous times when the crew got back to camp wringing wet, just in time to change into dry uniforms and grab a bite to eat before starting the afternoon show.

It is interesting to note how the Lemon Brothers Circus was received in some of the towns it visited. One critic of the *London* (Ohio) *Times,* who wrote under the name "Wooden Man," was not so kind in his column of August 3, 1905. He said this, for example, of the female Zouaves:

> [There were]. . .some soldier girls in tights who thought they could drill; but they seemed to be going two directions at the same time and were in a hopeless tangle when doing the simplest marches. The drill was too long and like Polonius' beard "should to the barber."

He was highly critical of the parade, being especially unsympathetic toward the band. Apparently he did not account for the difficulties of playing atop a swaying wagon which did not have the benefit of pneumatic tires and shock absorbers:

> . . .And even the horns and trombones were out of joint and ran away into melodies that made one think he had been taking Iron Brew.

And what he said about Henry's calliope playing!

> . . .And the steam calliope! Mercy! Bill Bailey never would come home if he could hear that jangling steam-puffer. It was a Chinese puzzle to discover what tune it was playing at all. The Wooden Man thought once it was playing "Yankee Doodle," but it turned out that the thing was only practicing "Home Sweet Home." No wonder the horses pricked up their ears and wondered what kind of a new automobile was in town.

The "Wooden Man's" scathing windup was thus:

> All in all, the only word that will describe the Lemon Brothers' show is "bum." The public is entitled to something for their money and such a cheap and clap-trap performance as was presented Wednesday is not worthy of the patronage it received.

The "Wooden Man" obviously had very little appreciation for the extreme hardships which the personnel of a small circus had to endure day after day to bring their show to towns such as his. Their lives were difficult every step of the way, and it must be considered that they were doing their best under the circumstances. If he could have followed a trouper like Henry Fillmore around for a week, his attitude would undoubtedly have softened.

As if Henry's life was not already complicated enough, he was called upon to use his cycling skill in addition to his musician's duties. The circus had a performer, H.R. Cooper, who was billed as the "chasm-

41

The Lemon Brothers musicians rode atop this ornamented band-wagon drawn by six white horses. The life of a circus band musician, or "windjammer," was difficult indeed, because they had many other chores. Henry, for example, was the show's calliope player and also substituted for an ailing acrobat in the dangerous "leaping the gap" act. At times he was also a clown.

After riding on the bandwagon at the head of the daily parade, Henry looped around on horseback via backstreets and brought up the rear playing ragtime music and other popular tunes on this calliope.

vaulting Coopero." Coopero had two acts. In the early part of the show, he rode his bike across a tightrope. His big act, however, came near the end of the show when he roared down a long, steep ramp which curved up at the lower end, vaulting him over five elephants, through a slit in the tent wall, and into a haystack beyond. This was called "leaping the gap."

One day when Coopero was doing his tightrope act he lost his balance and crashed to the ground, spraining one of his ankles so badly he could not perform for approximately two months. During this period he was replaced by a novice, the "chasm-vaulting Fillmore!" The *New York Clipper,* a show business newspaper, reported it thusly in its August 5 issue:

. . .Since H.R. Cooper left the show at St. John, N.B.

[June 6] on account of illness, Henry Fillmore has been successfully leaping the gap at every performance.

Henry did not have the skill for the tightrope act, but he was daring enough to do the treacherous ramp act. Mabel watched nervously every day as her daredevil husband flew down the ramp, over the elephants and into the haystack. Henry considered it a challenge, but Mable did not relish the idea of becoming a widow at such an early age and was greatly relieved when Coopero was able to return.

Another time Henry replaced one of the clowns who was ill, and on another occasion he helped with one of the lion and tiger acts. These things meant a few extra dollars, but still Henry and Mabel's combined pay was scarcely enough to make ends meet. During the first part of the tour, they were actually so hard pressed for cash that Henry walked around with extremely sore feet, using pieces of stiff cardboard in the bottoms of his shoes to cover up the holes.

Henry's five-month experience with the Lemon Brothers Circus of 1905 was actually the most trying period of his life. He worked unbelievably hard all during this time, not because he had to but because he wanted to prove to his family back home that he could be a success at anything he undertook.

He learned many lessons during these difficult months. Most important was the advisability of organizing any activity with extreme care, right down to the last little detail. Any army on earth could take a lesson in logistics from a successful circus (some actually did), and Henry was to apply their principles of organization very effectively in his show business career. He also learned that great obstacles could be overcome by the proper combination of determination, patience and common sense.

The importance of punctuality to the success of show business was also impressed upon him. Too, he developed the ability to make himself at home wherever his feet were planted and to pull up stakes and move on without regret.

The personal influence of Frank Lemon was considerable. By example, he taught Henry how to live harmoniously with people from all walks of life by remaining humble and treating everyone fairly and with equality. Also from Lemon he learned great compassion for animals.

The lessons he learned from the sawdust ring were to serve him well for the next half century. He was now a finely tempered young man, ready for anything life would offer.

If the story of Henry Fillmore could be referred to as a rags-to-riches story, the rags era continued for several months after his 1905 tour with the circus.

When he had stormed out of the Norwood home in April, he had left the family in a state of anxiety and turmoil. He did not write home until final arrangements had been made with the Lemon Brothers Circus, and for a period of approximately three weeks the family did not know of his whereabouts. Uncle Fred volunteered the information that he was headed for St. Louis to be married, but this was all he knew.

Henry had not left in anger. Rather, he was deeply hurt. Very deeply hurt. He was an uncommon person in that throughout his entire lifetime he seemed not to have the capacity to be angry or harbor a grudge. And it was most unusual to hear him speak ill of another person, particularly those of his own family, regardless of the circumstances. His mother had always told him (and his sisters) that if he could not say anything good about a person to say nothing at all.

When hurt, he suffered in silence and could never understand why intimate friends or family members would want to gossip about or intentionally hurt one another's feelings. It was beyond his comprehension why his parents had not accepted Mabel with open arms, and he was so completely crushed that his reaction was to remove himself from their presence. The impact of his absence was so great that J.H. and Annie came to appreciate his agony, and they reassessed their position.

In his first letter home, Henry politely informed them that he was happily married to Mabel Jones, that he hoped they would treat her as a member of the family if he ever returned to Cincinnati, and that he and Mabel would be making a long tour, mostly in Canada, with the Lemon Brothers Circus.

The family was so embarrassed by his sudden disappearance, marriage and the circus association that they made no formal announcements of his marriage. Consequently, Cincinnati newspapers carried no mentions. When asked about their son, they merely said he had moved west, was married and was playing with a band.

J.H. and Annie were pleased to receive letters from him as the tour wended its way toward and into Canada, and they responded with concern. Under no conditions would they ignore their only son; this would have been against the teachings of Christianity, and they were incapable of such action.

As for the situation with Mabel, they spent many long hours deliberating and then acted in a most proper and intelligent manner. Despite the fact that Henry had taken a wife who was not of their choosing, they would accept her for what she was and not ridicule her or make her feel unwanted.

Once communication had been reestablished, Henry's letters home were more detailed. He told of his many accomplishments with the circus and carefully worded his letters in such a way as to create a favorable image of Mabel. According to these letters, she was thoughtful,

considerate, understanding, faithful, comforting and in possession of all the virtues of a loving wife. He did such a good job of selling Mabel to the family that they insisted he come back to Cincinnati to live when the circus season was over. Above all, this was the thing he had hoped for. He assured them that he and Mabel would return to Cincinnati.

J.H. had done some soul-searching on his own. Henry was obviously going to carve his career in band music and had shown creative talent in both composing and arranging. If the Fillmore Brothers did not publish his music, another company most certainly would. Why shouldn't the Fillmore Brothers reap the benefits thereof? Besides, the sale of Henry's music had been increasing. Now that he had become a full-time professional musician in the band field, there would be no stopping him. J.H. wrote to Henry to explain his plans. This was something else Henry had hoped for. It was settled; he would work for his father upon his return.

Several members of Mabel's family had a brief opportunity to meet her circus jack-of-all-trades husband when the show came back to the United States through Port Huron, Michigan, where they were living. The Jones relatives were common, unpretentious folks, and Henry fit right into the family.

Unfortunately, Henry's family did not see the Lemon Brothers Circus, even though it passed very close to the Cincinnati area as it zigzagged its way through the western part of Ohio. There were performances in nearby Miamisburg on August 9 and in Oxford on August 10. The train actually passed within twenty miles of Norwood on the C.H. & D.R.R. line between those two towns, but in the middle of the night. The family had wanted to go see the circus when it was in the area, but Annie had taken ill and was not able to make even a short trip. She was diabetic and at times unable to function normally.

After a tour of over seven thousand miles, the final stop of the circus was at Camp Point, Illinois, one hundred and thirty miles northwest of St. Louis. Once back in St. Louis, Henry and Mabel bade farewell to Toots and Ned and caught a train for Cincinnati.

It was a wonderful feeling for Henry to be home again, all the much nicer now that his family was more understanding. The Norwood home had been big enough to accommodate entire families in the past, so there was no problem accommodating Henry and Mabel for a few days until they could find an apartment of their own. They preferred to live alone and found a second-floor two-room apartment in downtown Cincinnati at 631 West Fourth Street. It was just three blocks from the Fillmore Brothers establishment at 528 Elm.

The apartment was adequate, although only partly furnished. They had no money to buy furniture, so they did without temporarily. Mabel was resourceful, having been brought up in a poor family, so she went to a grocer and asked for old orange crates. From these she made a table and chairs and covered them with calico cloth. It was far from an elegant dining room set, but it was a start.

A piano was also beyond their means, and this was something Henry would need occasionally for his composing and arranging. It is rather poignant that one of their first pieces of furniture was a toy piano. The man who was some day to be referred to as Sousa's successor as "March King" composed most of his music for the first two years of his married life using that toy piano as his only reference instrument!

Henry and Mabel lived in this apartment for a year-and-a-half, after which they moved to 2 View Court in the suburb of Mt. Auburn. It was here that Henry bought his first piano. He did not sit at the piano fingering out his music by a trial and error method, as composers are often depicted. He had perfect pitch and would commit his ideas directly to music paper and try them out on the piano afterward.

Henry did not spend much time in the store or in the offices upstairs. The atmosphere there was not conducive to composing, arranging or editing, so with J.H.'s approval he did much of this at home. Most of the time spent at the office was during afternoons.

Another of Henry's responsibilities was the acquisition and evaluation of new music by other composers. The word got around quickly that the Fillmore Brothers Company was in the market for new band manuscripts, so Henry was kept quite busy. He hired several wind

instrument players from the Cincinnati Symphony Orchestra, plus a few theater musicians, to play through the manuscripts and expedite the evaluation.

Once the acquisition process was going well, Henry spent more time composing original pieces and arranging the works of others. During 1906, he published more music of his own than in the three previous years combined, some under his own name and some bearing the Al Hayes pseudonym. The titles of his marches for the year were still on safe ground for a religious publishing house: "Shall We Gather at the River". . ."Safe in the Arms of Jesus". . ."The Old Oaken Bucket." This applied to the Hayes pieces as well as to the Fillmore pieces, just in case someone would discover that Al Hayes was actually one of the Fillmores. The purely secular music titles published were, for the most part, those written by outside composers.

The primary reason for Henry and Mabel's move to Mt. Auburn was because the apartment downtown was in a business district with few neighbors and no relatives. Henry constantly met people in his work, but there was no social life for Mabel. She was not intellectually inclined and did very little reading, so she needed people. There was no radio or television in those days; and with Henry gone most evenings, she was lonely and bored—a sorry life for one who had traveled over seven thousand miles within the last year. For hours she

The Fillmore Brothers retail store at 528 Elm Street looked like this in 1906. Henry is far right, and J.H. is third from right. The publishing offices, repair shop and storage areas were on upper floors.

would sit looking out the window, watching people walk by and hoping to see an automobile racing down the street faster than the seven miles per hour speed limit so she could tell Henry about all the excitement.

Henry's salary was low, because J.H. had agreed to pay him royalties on his music in addition to his salary. The problem was that it took from two to three months for the music to get into print, even longer to get into circulation, and longer yet to have an accounting for the number of copies sold. At that time, the Fillmore Brothers were paying royalties only once a year.

To augment his income, Henry did three things. First, he found nighttime work as a musician. Second, he gave trombone lessons. Third, during the fall, he played semiprofessional football. The Spaulding Sporting Goods Company opened up a retail store on Fountain Square in 1906, and they sponsored a football team under the name Reliance Athletic Club. For three seasons, Henry played in their backfield. Since the games were played on Sunday mornings, when people were supposed to be in church, he played under an assumed name. This way he did not discredit the good name of Fillmore. It is believed that he used the name Gus Curtis. Often the Reliance Athletic Club played double headers; the first game would be football, and the second rugby.

Football was not the big thing in 1906 that it is today. Professional football was not yet an organized sport, and most of the interest in the game was generated by college teams. Bowling was coming on strong as baseball season ended. Baseball was clearly the national game, and the season did not end with the World Series. For example, members of the Cincinnati Redlegs team often went out barnstorming after the regular season, playing semipro teams in the area. Semipro and amateur teams were still battling it out well into October.

Henry played his trombone in numerous theaters, minstrels, dance halls and the like. On weekends he would "jam" from 8:00 p.m. until 4:00 a.m. for the grand sum of four dollars, the going union rate. In the summer of 1906, he played in an Ohio River showboat minstrel band.

He moved around from theater to theater until finding steady work at the People's Theater, where he played for several years. During this period he made many arrangements for theater pit orchestras, but these were never published. The People's Theater was a glorified burlesque and vaudeville theater. The management found this type of entertainment more profitable than the legitimate theater which once was its fare. Many famous burlesque and vaudeville figures appeared there, such as Sam Rice and former heavyweight champion boxer John L. Sullivan.

The years Henry spent working in theater orchestras were hard years, but they were enjoyable. He made many lifetime friends in this work. Among these were the noted march composer John Klohr, who influenced Henry's music as much in those early years as Henry was to influence his in later years. Klohr became famous for just one of his many compositions, the familiar "The Billboard" march, the trio of which was one of the most popular show tunes ever written.

In the winter of 1906, at age 24, Henry had been toughened by the circus and was leading a very busy life. He worked at his composing by day, played trombone in theater orchestras by night and also gave trombone lessons. On Sunday mornings, he played semiprofessional football under an assumed name.

Henry was a good theater trombonist, but he never aspired to greater things. He did some symphony work, possibly substituting for one of the trombonists in the Cincinnati Symphony Orchestra occasionally. But he was not interested in the type of music they played, because it was not what he would call entertainment. Those who assessed Henry's contribution to music fifty years later often remarked that he never had a "serious" musical thought in his life. They were probably right; he liked *happy* music.

Between 1907 and 1911, Henry Fillmore established himself as a composer and arranger, even though these were not his most productive years. Nearly half of his published output in this period consisted of marches.

He invited the 1st Regiment Band of the Ohio National Guard, in which he was playing, to practice in the store. "The Victorious First," another march, was the result of his continued association with this unit. Henry insisted that the march was good enough to bear the Fillmore name, but J.H. still did not like the idea of the family name appearing on non-church music. Rather than start another monumental argument, Henry sold it to Harry Coleman, the Philadelphia publisher, and it was released in May, 1907.

"The Victorious First" sold so well that J.H. could no longer soft-pedal the fact that his son was composing secular band music. People were asking why his son's music was being published in Philadelphia rather than in Cincinnati. He finally gave up and allowed Henry to put his name on whatever he wished, because everyone seemed to know about it anyway.

At the same time, Henry had evidently considered offering more of his music to other publishers. He arranged one piece called "Silver Bell Waltz," by T.L. Eells, for the Rudolf Wurlitzer Company of Cincinnati. This was published in April, 1907, but there is no evidence that Henry did any other moonlighting for Wurlitzer.

The license to put his own name on all his music was a breakthrough of sorts, and Henry celebrated in grand style by composing a very fine circus march, "The Circus Bee." It was published in February, 1908, and was the most lively and difficult piece he had written thus far. When asked about the unusual title, he explained that he had concocted it for an imaginary circus newspaper. There were many papers bearing the name *Bee,* such as the *Ripley Bee,* the *Batavia Bee* and so forth, so why not a *Circus Bee?* He pointed out that his good friend John Klohr's most famous piece was named "The Billboard" after a show business newspaper, and if circuses did not have a *Bee* of their own he would give them one. "The Circus Bee" became one of his most popular pieces and is today a staple of better bands.

In 1908 he also made his first contribution to one of the Fillmore Brothers' specialties, the children's Sunday School song. This was a humorous Christmas "motion song" called "Better Be Good," with instructions for the performers to point with their index fingers while singing "Better be good, better be good." On this and other songs and cantatas to follow, he collaborated with lyricists. J.H. was pleased to have him work on this type of music because his melodies were unusually pretty and would no doubt be pleasing to choral directors.

Also in 1908, he composed the first of his famous trombone "smears," or trombone "characteristics," "Miss Trombone." This lighthearted piece, more than any of his other early compositions, put him on the musical map. It put the spotlight squarely on the trombone, featuring the technique which can be demonstrated on no other brass instrument in general use—the glissando (Italian, meaning "in a gliding manner"). The comical potential of the slide trombone was brought out, and "Miss Trombone" announced that the trombone was a lady. A *happy* lady.

J.H. was reluctant to issue "Miss Trombone" because it was a rag. After all, ragtime music was associated with brothels, where its roots were firmly planted, and some clergymen preached that ragtime music was the work of the devil. But it was being played everywhere, even on the steamboat calliopes and by such prestigious organizations as the band of John Philip Sousa. J.H. could not resist issuing "Miss Trombone," however, because everyone in the shop thought it was catchy, and he liked the tune very much himself. At first, he had thought it was merely an imitation of other pieces, but Henry convinced him that it was different. History has proved him right.

The ragtime style of writing came naturally to Henry, because he was playing so much of it in theater orchestras. Cincinnati, like other American riverboat cities, played an important part in the development of ragtime. One of the biggest influences on ragtime was the itinerant Negro musicians who came up the inland waterways from New Orleans. It is obvious in listening to "Miss Trombone" and other of Henry's pieces written in that idiom that he understood these people and their music.

Although Henry Fillmore is today called the "father of the trombone smear" because his contribution to this style of writing was greater than any other composer's, this is a cognomen of respect rather than a cognomen reflecting historical accuracy. He did not originate the form.

Trombone novelty pieces had been around for quite some time before Henry began to write them. Arthur Pryor (1870-1942), the famed trombone soloist of Sousa's Band and later himself a very popular bandmaster, had used slide effects in some of his novelty compositions as early as 1902. His band had played ragtime and cakewalk music several years before Henry came upon the scene. Several other composers had also used trombone smears in their pieces of this period, including Frank Losey (1872-1931) and Fred Jewell (1875-1936).

Henry combined ragtime with march elements and trombone glissandos, molding them into something the public could identify with. The vehicle of identification was the minstrel style. This inferred humor, which was his strong suit. He loved minstrels, where the trombone was sometimes used in comedy routines.

Professional minstrel companies were responsible for the discovery of "Miss Trombone." It was a tricky piece of music to play, but these musicians could handle it, and they liked it. When performed in theaters, musicians in attendance wanted it for their own bands and orchestras. There was no doubt; Henry had written a happy, catchy tune.

The only drawback of "Miss Trombone" was its difficulty to the average musician, especially trombone

Among the many musical organizations with which Henry performed was Kopp's Military Band. Billy Kopp was also leader of the First Regiment Band of the Ohio National Guard, for which Henry composed "The Victorious First" in 1907. This photograph of Kopp's Military Band, which was really a civilian band in military style uniforms, was taken at the Lexington Fair of 1909.

players. The next time Henry would do it differently—if there was a next time. J.H. made the final decision on what to publish, not Henry.

Two-and-a-half years passed before the Fillmore Brothers issued another trombone smear. This was "Teddy Trombone," printed in March, 1911. Henry dedicated this to a good friend, Theodore Hahn, who was a popular theater orchestra conductor and also professor at the College of Music of Cincinnati.

Also that year, another one of Henry's novelty pieces made a little ripple on the waters of band music. This was called "The Only Tune the Band Could Play Was Auld Lang Syne," in which it was suggested there was a band that could play just that one tune, disguised several ways.

The period between 1907 and 1911 was clearly the period in which Henry made his initial splash in the music world. In addition to the pieces mentioned above and many others of less consequence, he also composed a march he always considered one of his best: "His Excellency." Another one which sold well took its name from the new motto of the Fillmore Brothers Company: "Fraternity."

Henry Fillmore, the composer and arranger, had arrived.

NOT REALLY SLOWING DOWN

A change in the lifestyle of Henry Fillmore came at the beginning of the year 1912. He had worked exceedingly hard since leaving the Lemon Brothers Circus some six-and-a-half years earlier. Not just at one job, but several, and burning the candle at both ends was beginning to take its toll. Although he was only thirty years old, he felt and looked older.

He had grown weary of writing music by day and performing in theater orchestras at night. Mabel also disliked this arrangement, so he promised her he would give up the theater work. It was a difficult decision, be-

cause he was now well established in popular music circles and in his position at the People's Theater.

His decision to abandon the theater work allowed him to spend more time on company business, and this came at a most opportune time. The church music business was declining, and the Fillmore Brothers' board of directors made a decision to publish more instrumental music. Henry had become a remarkably skilled arranger by now and was the only one in the company who was in a position to make this possible.

At times he appeared troubled, and his associates

These portraits were made on April 10, 1915, Henry and Mabel's tenth wedding anniversary. Henry was thirty-three, and Mabel thirty-two. Her hair was still brown, but before another two years passed it turned snow white.

could not understand why the usually effervescent Henry Fillmore looked so preoccupied. Only his closest friends knew the reason, because it was a highly personal family matter. His dear mother had been behaving strangely at times, and the family was obliged to have her committed to Longview Hospital in July of 1911. Longview was a mental hospital.

It was a delicate situation for all concerned. To make matters worse, she had also been stricken with tuberculosis. Annie passed away quietly a year-and-a-half later at Longview, on Sunday, February 23, 1913. On her death certificate, the cause of her demise was given as pulmonary tuberculosis, with no other contributory causes. J.H. was so grieved by her death that he stayed a widower for the remaining twenty-three years of his life.

During the time of Annie's illness, it was often very difficult for Henry to put himself in a frame of mind to create the happy music for which he was known. But he managed. In 1912, his output was greater than in any other year of his life, partly because much of his music was being published for orchestra as well as for band. Off and on during the year, he worked on a special edition of the *Songs of Praise* hymnal. This was a collection of one hundred and twenty-nine church pieces arranged for small orchestra, and it was released in December.

Also in 1912, the first two of his eight children's cantatas, or playlets, were issued: *Easter Joy-Bells* and *Hail! Joyful Morning.* It is a pity that all eight were short-lived, because they reveal an intimate side of Henry Fillmore totally unknown to music audiences today. They are full of colorful melodies and have modern (for the time) harmonies which made them palatable to youthful performers.

Most of the individual pieces in the cantatas had a pleasant, lighthearted swing to them, although some were downright pensive. "A Meditation," for example, which appeared in *Hail! Joyful Morning,* could hardly be more perfect for meditation and reflection; it is possibly the most beautiful thing he ever composed. Since these minor works had limited usefulness, J.H. salvaged some of the individual pieces and re-issued them as hymns, usually with new words.

Encouraged by the reception of the two children's cantatas of 1912, Henry let out all the stops on the three he composed in 1913. For *Easter Bells,* he utilized melodies and harmonies similar to those being heard in Tin Pan Alley, raising the eyebrows of staid choral directors. *Happy Children's Day* had humor in the text, and Henry responded accordingly by supplying music reminiscent of the popular parlor songs. A Christmas offering, *The Star-Lit Way,* was another "swinger."

In "Sweet Thoughts of Gratitude," one of the pieces in *The Star-Lit Way,* one can see the mischievous Henry Fillmore at his best. When this piece is performed faster than the indicated tempo, it does justice to the cream of gay nineties waltzes. It was re-introduced seven years later as a hymn, "Sweet Are the Songs of the Wild Birds," but it did not become a standard. Too progressive.

Several other short pieces of *The Star-Lit Way* were written in the same vein. Henry was obviously trying to take the stuffiness out of church music; it was his way of letting church people, including his father, know that their music needed a little livening up. Why not start with the children? The final selection of *The Star-Lit Way* was called "Closing Song," and it is as majestic and bold as anything Henry ever wrote.

The five children's cantatas Henry wrote in 1912 and 1913 were quite a contrast to most of the Fillmore Brothers offerings of the time, especially *Comforting Melodies,* a book of hymns for use at funerals.

Also in 1913, Henry wrote eight hymns for a compilation called *Quartets and Choruses for Men.* No doubt this was drudgery for him, because the format (close four-part harmony for male voices) did not lend itself to his free spirit style of composing. He did, however, slip in a sly bit of humor in "The Wireless S.O.S." Where the words read "List, o list! Far away where the bright waters wave. . ." his music is suggestive of *Les Preludes,* by the Hungarian composer Franz Liszt. Liszt. . .list. . .it is unlikely that many recognized this subtle little prank.

The volume of music from Henry's pen was becoming so great that he was concerned about flooding the market with music by one composer. He therefore used several pseudonyms. He did this methodically, assigning classifications to these phantom composers. Harry Hartley wrote and arranged twelve solos for use by music teachers. Al Hayes continued to write for average bands, while the newcomer Harold Bennett wrote non-progressive pieces ("Play one and you can play 'em all," he explained) for beginning bands. Ray Hall, also a newcomer, composed only three pieces, all of medium difficulty. All the Hartley and Hall pieces appeared between 1911 and 1914. Henry reserved the use of his own name for those pieces which were the most difficult, or were not "watered down."

By using pseudonyms, Henry successfully kept the company from gathering the image of a one-composer publishing house. He did not want directors and teachers thinking that the name Fillmore was dominating the market served by his company. In actuality, however, it turned out that most all the best selling pieces issued by the company were the ones Henry had composed himself. He enjoyed this immensely, and it bolstered his self-confidence. Also his pocketbook.

Several humorous situations arose from Henry's use of multiple names. One of his favorite stories of later years was about a letter which Harold Bennett received, wherein an admirer said he liked Bennett's marches much better than Fillmore's. And just for the fun of it, he would often register at hotels with Mabel as "Mr. Henry Fillmore and Mrs. Harold Bennett." In his office he had a framed picture of himself autographed "To Henry Fillmore from his friend Al Hayes."

21 SOUSA, MOLASSES AND BEANS

Henry's idol in the music world was, of course, John Philip Sousa. Sousa appeared in Cincinnati approximately fifteen times in the course of his career, and Henry saw him on numerous occasions. In addition, Henry spent his summer vacation of 1913 in the East just so he could see and hear the peerless Sousa Band perform. The band was presenting four concerts per day, seven days a week, at the pavilion in Willow Grove Park, the beautiful Philadelphia amusement park which was regarded as the summer music capitol of America.

During the two days Henry was there, he attended every concert, marvelling at Sousa's double-edged effectiveness as both a composer and an entertainer. He was beside himself with pride when "Miss Trombone" appeared on one of the programs as an encore. He held Sousa in such awe that he could not muster the courage to go backstage and introduce himself. He should have, however, for Sousa was truly a magnanimous person, ever eager to meet and encourage young composers.

Henry's rewarding association with Sousa was to come at a later date. He did make the acquaintance of a few of the Sousa Band players while at Willow Grove, however. These acquaintances were renewed in 1915 when the same musicians visited his store in Cincinnati. They remarked about how "Miss Trombone" had pleased audiences everywhere it was used, and this was probably what inspired Henry to compose his most famous piece of music—"Lassus Trombone."

The trombone smear "Lassus Trombone," published on June 14, 1915, is the one piece of Henry Fillmore's music known by the man on the street. Even if a person is not familiar with the name Henry Fillmore, he will surely recognize its cheerful strains.

For all practical purposes, "Lassus Trombone" is a classic. The structure is solid. The melody, harmony and rhythm are combined in a glorious, near perfect manner. It is highly listenable, clever and snappy. Because it literally exudes happiness, it is little wonder that Henry lived to see sales of the sheet music surpass the two million mark. "Lassus Trombone" quickly took a place among the world's toe-tappers, and it still falls in that category.

When asked about the origin of the title, Henry had a standard answer: "Why, molasses, of course. I really don't know why except I thought of molasses on bread for breakfast, dinner and supper." It did not take the astute Sousa long to discover the magic of "Lassus," and he performed it almost daily for several years.

According to a story handed down by musicians of Sousa's Band, Sousa had actually believed Henry Fillmore was a black man! When Henry heard this, he was greatly flattered; he had imitated the Negro's music style so well that even the great Sousa thought "Lassus" could have been composed only by a Negro!

One of the most talked-about incidents of Henry's career, which had some significance in the music publishing business, took place late in the fall of 1915. It began one Saturday afternoon when the Fillmore Brothers' "tryout band" was playing through manuscripts being considered for publication. At this time, there were several employees of the company in this small band; it was not made up of just professional musicians as it had been ten years earlier when this manuscript evaluation process had been initiated.

Henry was somewhat perturbed because an elderly Kentucky bandmaster had been submitting marches on a regular basis, none of which had been found worthy of publication. He remarked that he wished the old gentleman would send his works elsewhere so it would not be necessary to hurt his feelings with so many rejection slips.

It so happened that one of the musicians in the band that Saturday was Henry's friend and colleague John Klohr. At that time, John was a salesman and advertising consultant for the John Church Company, a rival Cincinnati publisher. John expressed the belief that one or two of the pieces should be published, but Henry insisted they would not sell well. A lively discussion ensued.

Henry said that both he and John could, with minimum effort, write better marches than those submitted. John's reply was that anything Henry published under his own name automatically sold well because of his reputation. Henry disagreed, saying that music sold because of its excellence, regardless of whose name was on it.

John and Henry could not agree, and John challenged him to prove his point. Henry wanted to be fair, so he devised a scheme which would settle the argument. He asked John to select one of the manuscripts and write three advertisements for it. Henry would sit down and compose a brand new march right on the spot and write three advertisements at a later date. He would publish both marches at the same time and give both advertisements equal prominence.

For the sake of propriety, Henry never revealed the identity of the elderly Kentucky bandmaster or the title of the piece he had submitted. He called his own march "Mt. Healthy"—by Gus Beans. With a twinkle in his eye, he selected the title at random from a list of suburbs in the Cincinnati area. Gus Beans was a fictitious name, but before using it he checked several directories to ascertain there was no one by that name in the Cincinnati area. In one of his advertisements he intentionally clouded the issue by adding "Gus Beans of Lima," knowing full well that there were several cities by that name.

Henry won the argument hands down. "Mt.

'S all Right, Gus!

To prove that music sold because of its merit rather than because of the composer's popularity, Henry wrote a march under a fictitious composer's name, Gus Beans. He called it "Mt. Healthy," selecting the title at random from a list of Cincinnati suburbs. This comical advertisement heralded its publication.

Healthy" and the other march were released in January, 1916. "Mt. Healthy" quickly went through three printings, while the other piece sold less than five dozen copies and was gathering dust on the Fillmore Brothers' shelves some twenty years later.

22   WILL THE REAL WILL HUFF PLEASE STAND UP?

Henry Fillmore was Will Huff. But then again, Will Huff was Will Huff too.

Many musicians have believed that the name Will Huff was just another of Henry Fillmore's pseudonymns. It *was* one of his pseudonyms, but the *real* Will Huff lived a life of his own and made a noteworthy contribution to band music in the early part of the twentieth century.

The humorous manner in which Henry Fillmore chose his "Huff" penname was explained in Chapter 13. When later he met the honest-to-goodness Will Huff face to face, he promised not to use the name again.

Twelve years later, however, he was obliged to break this promise.

Had Will Huff gone on to become a great composer, there would probably be no confusion today. Unfortunately, his music has practically passed into oblivion while Henry Fillmore's has lived on. Since so many legends have surrounded Henry because of his colorful personal life and his liberal use of pseudonyms—while Huff has all but been forgotten in music circles—many labor under the mistaken impression that "Will Huff" was just another of Henry's many names. Add to this the fact that the only Huff music found in most libraries today is that which was published by the Fillmore Brothers Company, it is understandable that the false story has persisted.

Henry was not one to squelch a good story, but during his last years he hinted that there really was a man named Will Huff. He did not offer many details, however, and this is most unfortunate indeed. All of those who knew the true story are now dead, so the erroneous legend lives on. The real Will Huff deserves a better fate, and it is earnestly hoped that the information presented between these covers will set the record

"A fine old fellow"—this was how the real Will Huff (1875-1942) was described by the bandsmen he led. Several generations of musicians believed that "Will Huff" was just another of Henry Fillmore's pseudonyms, but nothing could be further from the truth. Huff was a part-time itinerant bandmaster and composer who organized bands in five states but spent most of his life in the Chillicothe, Ohio, area.

straight once and for all.

Huff did not switch over to the Fillmore Brothers immediately after he met Henry, probably because he felt an obligation to Wurlitzer, the company which gave him his start as a published composer. Although he evidently met Henry in the summer of 1904, he did not submit his first manuscript to the Fillmore Brothers until late in 1907. This was a march called "Salute to Uncle Sam," and it was published on February 28, 1908.

Huff was not a prolific composer by any means. A study of his writing activities during his productive years shows that in the periods he published with companies other than Fillmore he averaged only two pieces per year. Fillmore expected many more, especially since the burden of the final arranging and editing was assumed by Henry himself.

It must be emphasized that Huff was not an inferior arranger in any way or that he was incapable of planning instrumentation for his own music. He was obviously a proficient arranger, because the bands he led before and after his association with the Fillmore Brothers were performing his music regularly with no difficulty.

Music published with the Fillmore Brothers, however, was released to the public only after Henry Fillmore's personal touch was added. He was a genius at preparing music which would sound full whether played by small or large ensembles—and which would appeal to the musicians who were buying it. He was a "commercial" writer, as they say in the trade, not a musical purist. He knew how to write and prepare music which would sell.

In 1908, four of Huff's pieces were published by Fillmore, and there were two in each of the years 1909, 1911 and 1912. "The Show Boy" (1911) sold briskly, and some of the others did better than average. The themes of "The Show Boy," incidentally, had come to Huff in a dream one night; he arose and committed them to paper. The company was pleased to have another writer whose music was received well, so they asked Huff to compose a set of sixteen pieces to be published in booklet form.

With considerable effort, Huff complied, and the *Will Huff Band Book* was published in April, 1913, arranged by Henry Fillmore. Henry also arranged the same sixteen pieces for orchestra, and this book was released the following January as the *Will Huff Orchestra Folio*. Initial sales were very encouraging, so Huff was asked to prepare a second set of sixteen pieces. This created a serious problem.

The congenial Will Huff agreed to compose the second set, but the deadline was unrealistic. The pieces were wanted for publication in the spring of 1916. Huff did the best he could, but when the submittal deadline rolled around he had written only ten of the sixteen pieces. Since advance publicity had been sent out and had generated no little amount of anticipation among potential buyers, Henry had a problem on his hands.

There was only one solution: Henry would have to compose the remaining pieces himself. He did this in secrecy and went to his grave forty years later without ever revealing which pieces in the book were his and which were Huff's! (The mystery was eventually solved, and the story behind this is given in the introductory section of this book.) The second set of pieces, called the *Huff Par-Excel Band Book,* was released in June, 1916. It was later "arranged for orchestra by Al Hayes" and issued as the *Huff Par-Excel Orchestra Folio* in December, 1918.

The demands which the Fillmore Brothers put upon Will Huff to produce the second book were too much for a part-time composer. He worked hard at his trade, usually six days a week, and the only times left for his music activities were evenings and Sundays. He was an interior decorator, specializing in wallpaper hanging and painting.

Huff was a small man and not especially strong, owing to a severe bout with scarlet fever in his youth. He is remembered as a good natured fellow, but sometimes sullen, and those who played in the bands he directed often got the impression that there was a degree of sadness in his life. He was not a forcible person; rather, he was a retiring man who did not have grandiose ambitions. His wife, Eleanor, a fine pianist, was more aggressive than he.

The *Huff Par-Excel Orchestra Folio* was the last music of Huff's published by the Fillmore Brothers except for the reissue, in 1942, of a march called "Salute to the Stars and Stripes." (This had originally been published by Wurlitzer in 1903.) Huff submitted numerous pieces to Fillmore in the early 1920's. None were published, however, perhaps because of the situation arising from the second Huff book.

A total of thirty-eight of Will Huff's compositions were published by the Fillmore Brothers. All but "Salute to the Stars and Stripes" were purchased outright, but as the copyright on each piece came up for renewal, it was put on a royalty basis. After the latter arrangement, the royalties usually amounted to between one hundred and three hundred dollars per year. It is interesting to note that Huff was also paid royalties on the six pieces in the *Par-Excel* books which Henry wrote!

It is possible that Huff also sold musical sketches to the Fillmore Brothers which Henry re-wrote and published under the Harold Bennett name, but this has not been definitely established.

One thing which *has* been established, however, is that Will Huff enriched the Fillmore Brothers' catalog for quite a few years.

23   THE REAL WILL HUFF STANDS UP

Now let us take a brief look at the life of this kindly gentleman whose memory has undeservedly fallen into the shadow of the man who borrowed his name.

William L. Huff was born in Massieville, Ohio, a small town five miles due south of Chillicothe, on January 16, 1875. While he was a small boy, his family moved to the Jackson-Wellston-Coalton area of Ohio, living in several different homes. For a short period, his father was postmaster at Glen Roy, but he was primarily a photographer. Will also worked at this profession in his youth.

At the age of fifteen, in Coalton, Will and several other boys organized what came to be known as the "Kid's Band," raising money for instruments and music by subscription and by giving charity dinners and the like. He played cornet most of the time but eventually learned to play almost all band instruments.

From 1896 until 1901, Huff lived in the Ironton, Ohio and Catlettsburg, Kentucky area. While playing in the Catlettsburg town band, Will met a sister of the euphonium player. She was Eleanor Hastings, and she became Mrs. Will Huff on February 17, 1897. She bore him six children, all talented musically, two of whom became professional musicians. Will eventually was named conductor of the Catlettsburg band.

The 17th Regiment Band of the Ohio National Guard was stationed in Ironton, and Will played cornet with this band until the unit marched off to serve in the Spanish-American War. He was not actually enlisted in military service, however. Will had been harboring the desire to become a composer of band music. He read much on the subject and studied every piece of band music he could get his hands on in an effort to learn the techniques of successful writers. His eventual successes are a credit to his persistance and industry; he did very well indeed as a self-taught composer.

His first composition was called the "17th Regt. Band March." The band members liked it, so he sent it off to the Rudolph Wurlitzer Company of Cincinnati. He thought his chances of getting it published were slim, because Wurlitzer printed very little band music. But patriotism was at a high pitch at this time, and they offered him five dollars for it. He not only accepted it but immediately composed "Battleship Maine March" and "Canadian Club March," both of which were accepted by Wurlitzer. He was now a celebrity of sorts in the Ironton-Catlettsburg area.

The next residence for Will Huff was Wellston, Ohio, where he directed the newly formed Florodora Band. It succeeded an older organization, the Manhattan Band, and took its name on a lark—from one of the leading ladies in a popular musical comedy, *The Bloomer Girl.*

Between 1903 and 1917, Will Huff resided in Holden, West Virginia; Williamson, West Virginia; Chillicothe, Ohio; Williamson, West Virginia (second time); Suffolk, Virginia; Decatur, Illinois; Owensburg, Kentucky; and Stearns, Kentucky, probably in that order. Sometime during this period he also made a tour as cornetist with a circus band. It is believed that this tour was made in 1912 when "The Squealer" march was published by Fillmore. His "card," giving notice of his availability at the end of the circus season, was printed in the October, 1912, issue of the *Musical Messenger* and read as follows:

WANTED TO LOCATE: Composer and arranger, instructor and director. Bands desiring a director, or in need of cornet, baritone, trombone or tuba would do well to answer this and receive particulars. Will Huff, Mingo County, Williamson, W. Va.

Huff was founder of the bands in most of the towns mentioned above. All were amateur groups, and he not only served as bandmaster but also as mentor for the players. After a band would get itself established—or if it folded—he would move on to another town. Some of the towns were coal mining towns, like Stearns, where a coal company would hire him to organize and train bands as a recreational activity. He often joked that he had to write the titles of pieces on the top of each page so the players would know which end was up!

Huff made a permanent move back to Chillicothe in 1917, where he became assistant conductor, and later conductor, of the Odd Fellows (I.O.O.F.) Band. He led this band up until the time he died twenty-five years later. The band was made up of both professional and amateur musicians and had been primarily a marching band until Huff assumed leadership. He increased the level of musicianship by obtaining permission to have the membership extended to non-I.O.O.F. men.

In the winter of 1921, the Mead Pulp and Paper Company of Chillicothe prevailed upon Huff to organize an industrial band bearing its name. This might have developed into a fine band over a period of years, but too much was expected in too short a time. Mead was the city's dominant industry, and the management was community-oriented. The company had its own park and sponsored a comprehensive recreational program. There was much excitement when the formation of a company band was announced, but it was doomed from the start.

The band was a beginner's band at best, because any employee could join whether he had musical talent or not. Another complication was that the bandsmen worked different shifts. Nevertheless, Huff did the best he could as both director and teacher. Questionnaires were circulated, employees responded, and twenty-eight men showed up for rehearsals, which started in the first week of June, 1921.

The expected progress did not take place as rapidly as

The mild-mannered redhead Will Huff was a loner—a quiet man who seldom conversed with his musicians or those attending his concerts. If his bandsmen downed a few beers after a performance, he did not indulge, owing to his Methodist background. One of the first bands he conducted was the Florodora Band of Wellston, Ohio. The band is shown here in 1901, the year it was organized. This photograph appeared on boxes of Florodora cigars, but there was no tie between the tobacco company and the band.

Will Huff organized and trained numerous industrial bands, the best documented being the Mead Pulp and Paper Co. Band of Chillicothe, Ohio. The band was beset with serious problems, however, and did not survive long enough to be fitted with uniforms.

The popular Odd Fellows Band of Chillicothe was Will Huff's finest band. He was conductor from 1919 until his death in 1942. The library of the band, containing manuscripts of numerous unpublished pieces, mysteriously disappeared.

was hoped, but in a Mead paper (undated, mid-June) the following note of optimism was sounded:

> The band can now play about four pieces very well, without anyone making any serious discords and without someone getting hopelessly lost.

The four pieces referred to were no doubt some elementary pieces Huff had written for the band: "Meaco Overture," "Meaco Waltz," "E-Z Waltz" and "Scioto Waltz." At rehearsals, he first coached small groups of players in separate rooms before getting them all together.

The band made its debut at the annual company picnic on the Fourth of July, 1921. It was quite an accomplishment—a new experience for the listeners but, unfortunately, for all too many of the performers as well. A few months later the band fell apart, victim of insurmountable problems.

Meanwhile, Huff's I.O.O.F. band was becoming very popular in the Chillicothe area. It played concerts each summer in Yoctangee Park and for all the festivals, fairs, parades and civic events. Most of the concerts were sponsored by either the city or merchants. He was a surprisingly good conductor, demanding but pleasant, and well liked because he was a man of unquestioned personal integrity. His vigorous style of conducting was similar to that of the famed circus director Merle Evans. For a time in the mid-1920's, he conducted the Adelphi Band (formerly the Hallsville Band) just east of Chillicothe.

The end came suddenly for Will Huff at the age of sixty-seven. On November 5, 1942, while doing interior decorating work on the Knights of Columbus Hall in Chillicothe, he was stricken by a fatal heart attack. He was laid to rest at Greenlawn Cemetery. His death went almost unnoticed outside the Chillicothe area, because he had the extreme misfortune of dying on the same day as one of the greats of American show business—George M. Cohan.

Fillmore Brothers' Treasurer William Jung, upon learning of Huff's passing, wrote Eleanor Huff to express regret and to assure her that future royalties of her husband's music would be assigned to her. Two-and-a-half years later, a lump sum settlement of one thousand dollars was agreed upon, but there is conflicting evidence about who initiated this. Papers of the Fillmore Brothers indicate that Mrs. Huff requested it, but the Huff family has suggested that it was the company's idea. The royalty cancellation contract was drawn up on August 22, 1945.

From the scratchy old pen Will Huff always used came an estimated total of ninety compositions. Sixty-six have been catalogued by the author and are presented in another book. Thirty-eight of these were published by the Fillmore Brothers, and seventeen others were published by three small publishers. The remainder went unpublished.

Several people around the Chillicothe area who played for Huff were of the opinion that his best music was that which was never published. It is tragic, therefore, that this music cannot be found. The library of the defunct Odd Fellows Band was reportedly donated to the local high school, but efforts to locate it proved to be in vain.

The titles of most of Huff's compositions, with the exception of those the Fillmore company changed or revised, have to do with his personal life. "Wireless Despatch" was so named because of his association with the family of Gugliemo Marconi, developer of the wireless telegraph; "Florodora March" was dedicated to the band he once directed; "Fort Gay" was a historic site in Virginia he often visited; "Night Riders" was inspired by constabulatory friends sent into the tobacco country of Kentucky to quell a disturbance; "Lincoln" was inspired by the President of the United States whose ideals were much the same as his own; "Salute to Yoctangee 1925" was a tribute to crowds he pleased at Yoctangee Park that summer; "Screamer," one of his most interesting marches, was named for the solo cornetist of the circus band he toured with; "A Rural Celebration" is a descriptive piece which recreates the sounds of his boyhood farm; and so forth.

Several of his titles were inspired by members of his immediate family. "Cotton Top" was actually his white-headed son Bill; "Margaret" was dedicated to the memory of a daughter who died at age three; "Eyes of Brown" was named for his wife, as was "Eleanor," which is perhaps his most beautiful work. His sense of humor shows in "Ironclad," which was nothing more than the brand name of some ribbed stockings his children wore!

If a detailed study of all the titles of Huff's music were made, the collective stories would document the interesting life of this modest, unassuming all-American bandmaster who was loved and respected by all who were ever privileged to be associated with him.

He was no Beethoven, but he provided useful, entertaining, grass roots music for one brief period in American history. Will Huff *was* Americana, and he is deserving of a spot in American folklore.

24   THE BIG TIME AND A GOOD TIME

The *Musical Messenger,* which had begun its third period of publication late in 1905, had gradually changed its scope of interest to include coverage of band and orchestra matters. By 1912, it was almost completely band-and-orchestra-oriented, and it stayed that way; everyone in the company realized that the religious music publications were merely going along for the ride. This was a complete turnaround but was the only way the company could exist. Without the band and orchestra trade, it is probable that J.H. would have taken early retirement and dissolved the company. J.H. was founder and President, but Henry was in the driver's seat, so to speak.

In 1916, the *Musical Messenger* was expanded from sixteen to thirty-two pages to include more news from all around the music world. School bands and orchestras were just beginning to be organized, so most younger musicians depended upon periodicals such as this for useful information. The retail store was now called the Fillmore Music House to distinguish it from the publishing end of the business, which retained the Fillmore Brothers Company name.

Musicians of all levels benefited from the improved *Musical Messenger*. The most popular articles were those written by well-known performers and composers, telling of their experiences and giving advice on performing techniques and the proper use of instruments. It was a practical magazine, almost completely devoid of theory and musicological treatises.

It had a high interest level because there was always something for everyone—instructional courses, questions and answers, reviews of new music and books, letters-to-the-editor, an abundance of advertisements, and even jokes and an occasional cartoon. Uncle Charlie contributed witticisms in a column called "Fillmore Filosofics." His proverbs were somewhat commonplace and trite and were not destined to make people forget the Holy Bible or Confucius, but now and

then he would hit upon a profound thought. Here are some of his better ones:

"Success has its office in the 10th floor of a building that has no elevators."
"Gossip is a human buzzard."
"It is just as sinful to overwork as to overrest."
"A wise man will learn from the biggest fool, but a fool will not learn from the wisest man."

Quality advertising helped defray the considerable cost of publication. The ads came from many sources but mostly from music publishers and instrument manufacturers. Fillmore advertising did not dominate. Attractive engravings of the latest instruments were a boon to business, as were printed excerpts of new music publications. Schools of music and dealers also found the *Musical Messenger* to be helpful. "Cards" were also a regular feature, whereby performers and teachers gave notices of their availability.

As might be expected, J.H. kept the journal on a high pitch of optimism, writing editorials on such subjects as fraternity and brotherhood. At times he got carried away, and his editorials resembled sermons. Those readers not of the Christian faith had to overlook this.

On the matter of brotherhood among musicians, he changed the company motto from "Fraternity" to "More Fraternity." Special pins bearing the new motto were manufactured and given as premiums to new subscribers. Henry wrote a march called "More Fraternity," dedicating it to the national convention of the

For several summers, starting in 1917, J.H. and his immediate family vacationed at Crooked Lake in the northern part of Michigan. J.H. (left) is seen here next to his daughter Mary (Mrs. Carlyle Shipley), Mary's daughter Annie Emily and his daughter Fred. Mabel and Henry are third and fifth from right. Those in the car are not identified, and the others are not related.

American Federation of Musicians, held in Cincinnati in May, 1916. On opening day, a huge band of two hundred started things off by playing Henry's new march, which was designated the official march of the convention.

The Fillmore Music House was now doing a booming business, thanks to the advertising in the *Musical Messenger* and the general popularity of bands at that time. The store carried Buescher instruments, a prestige line. Just a step down from the Bueschers was a *Fillmore* line. Perhaps not a step down at all, according to advertisements, which proclaimed the Fillmore "Contesting" model cornet as "the greatest business cornet ever designed. . .in use in every state by top professionals." A brass finished model was available for $42.50, a silver plated model for $50.00, and a gold plated model for $80.00. They were endorsed by August H. Schaefer, and if anyone did not know who Augie was they had not been around Cincinnati much; he was a popular local figure and a close friend of Henry's since childhood.

Numerous imported instruments were sold, too. Gras clarinets, for example, which were endorsed by members of Sousa's Band. For a while, a line of Japanese violins were carried, but these turned out to be so bad the last shipment was sold directly to a vaudeville company. There they were used nightly in an act where one fellow bashed another over the head with his violin. Henry thought this was hilarious, and he was relieved because it helped keep these inferior instruments out of circulation, thus minimizing the damage done to the reputation of the Fillmore Music House.

The store also carried a complete line of accessories. Al Hayes got into the act via the Al Hayes brand of trombone slide oil. Few knew that this superior (?) brand of slide oil, which was endorsed by Ralph Corey, trombone soloist of Sousa's Band, was tapped from the same tank as another brand of oil selling at a much lower price. There was Al Hayes valve oil, too.

Quite a few of Henry's musician friends were members of Masonic orders, and Masonic bands around the country were regular purchasers of Fillmore Brothers publications. Also, Masonic musicians in the Cincinnati area were loyal customers of the Fillmore Music House. This probably was the reason Henry had gone into Masonry back in 1912, and he took a much broader interest in Masonry when a group of Cincinnati theatrical men formed their own lodge in 1916. This was the High Noon Lodge, chartered for the convenience of those who worked evenings in the theater. Henry demitted from the E.T. Carson Lodge, where he had been "raised" back in 1912, and was enrolled at High Noon in November, 1916.

High Noon had its own small orchestra which was used for lodge ceremonial work. Henry conducted this orchestra and made numerous arrangements for the ceremonials. Several influential men belonged to High Noon, and they liked Henry's flamboyant and enthusiastic conducting. This led to his being appointed conductor of a newly formed training band of the union (Local 1, Cincinnati Musicians Association). This informal organization met weekly for the benefit of new union members who wished to improve their professional skills.

The year 1916 was a memorable year as far as Henry's composition was concerned. It was not only the year of the Will Huff and "Mt. Healthy" challenges; it was also the year of another of his slam-bang circus marches, "Rolling Thunder," and "Pahson Trombone," one of his wildest smears.

Also this year, he arranged a medley of hymns which was later credited to John Philip Sousa. It was called "Billy Sunday's Successful Songs," and when Sousa heard of it he began to use it on his Sunday concerts—in preference to two such medleys he had compiled himself. On one occasion, evangelist Billy Sunday shared the platform with the Sousa Band and was so impressed when they played Henry's arrangement he jumped up and excitedly proclaimed that only the great Sousa could have masterminded such an artistic work! Sousa was dumbfounded. He did not want to contradict Sunday publicly, but he was highly embarrassed and wished the incident could have been forgotten by all. He later complimented Henry on the arrangement and personally apologized for Sunday's misunderstanding.

J.H. decided that both he and Henry had been working too hard and that they needed a vacation at a place where they could get away from civilization. In August of 1917, he rented a cottage at Crooked Lake, in the wilderness of Upper Michigan. He invited two of his daughters to come enjoy nature with them for a month. Mary and her husband joined them, as did Fred. Annie Louise could not come because she was in China doing missionary work for the United Christian Missionary Society.

A good time was had by all, and Crooked Lake became the family retreat for many summers to come. Eventually, several of Henry's musician friends from Cincinnati, such as Louis Hahn and "Teddy" Baer, joined them there. Crooked Lake was not a resort area; recreation was left entirely to the individuals. Cottages were the only buildings, and these were equipped just for summer living.

At the age of 68, J.H. was still an excellent swimmer and could do front and back somersaults off a diving board. A picture similar to this was published without his knowledge in the October, 1917, issue of the *Musical Messenger*, ". . .to show readers that with all his seriousness he can turn kid again." The heading read "PUTTING ONE OVER ON THE BOSS—The Genial Chief Exponent of 'More Fraternity.' "

Henry was not an expert swimmer like his father, but he was an expert floater. He could even sleep while floating on his back and spent many hours this way at Crooked Lake.

Henry and Mabel are in the canoe on the right. Several of his musician friends from Cincinnati also took their vacations at Crooked Lake.

Henry had this picture taken of a 16-pound muskie he caught so he could show his friends back in Cincinnati what was needed in the Ohio River to make fishing more interesting.

During the years in which the United States was involved in World War I, Fillmore Brothers publications took on many forms. One of the most interesting pieces was a dreamy reverie, with words by Eleanor Allen Schroll and music by Henrietta Moore. It was called "Twilight Song" and was not specifically religious music but neutral enough to be used in churches. It was arranged as a cornet solo by that noted rival of Henry Fillmore's, Al Hayes. As for Henrietta Moore. . .Henrietta Fill-*Moore*—Henry was up to his old tricks again.

Another interesting twist was a march called "Joyful Greeting" by Al Hayes and John Littleton. Littleton was a long-time employee of the Fillmore Brothers, and "Joyful Greeting" is the only one of Henry's original compositions in which he collaborated with someone (his collaborators always wrote verse, not music). Another rarity was the only published article known to have been written by Henry, entitled "Frank Simon." This was a brief biography in the July, 1917, *Musical Messenger.* Simon, from nearby Middletown, was cornet soloist with Sousa's Band at the time.

During the war years, Al Hayes and Henry Fillmore were busy creating arrangements and original music of a nationalistic nature. Practically all of the published titles had a patriotic flavor, and like his patriotic cousin, Millard Fillmore, Henry was doing his thing. Many Hayes arrangements of the Allied countries' national airs were in print before the war had ended. These were very useful to bands of the armed forces and were also popular with community bands because they were easy to play and were arranged in such a way that a small band would sound bigger.

Henry Fillmore, like John Philip Sousa, felt that any march he had just finished was better than anything he had written previously. When the next one would be written, he would feel the same way about that one. When the "136th U.S.A. Field Artillery" march came out, the *Musical Messenger* quoted Henry as saying it was the best piece he had ever composed. While this might not have been an accurate assessment, the march was a dandy. The military unit of the title had formerly been the 3rd Field Artillery of the Ohio National Guard and was fighting in France near Verdun when the piece was published.

Henry's most stirring piece of music of the war years was a song called "Our Own Red, White and Blue," with lyrics by Eleanor Allen Schroll. It is one of the most tuneful melodies to come out of World War I, and if Henry had known the right people on Tin Pan Alley to help in a promotion, it might have become one of the great war songs.

The piece was played around Cincinnati, at least, because the Fillmore Brothers printed words and distributed them gratis whenever it was played in public. Henry surprised the company employees with it during a Red Cross drive parade in July, 1917. A two hundred-piece band of volunteers from Local 1 led the way, and Henry arranged to have the parade routed right up Elm Street past the Fillmore Building. A huge flag was stretched out horizontally by the marchers so that the occupants of tall buildings in downtown Cincinnati could toss their coins into it. The parade stopped right in front of the Fillmore establishment, and the band struck up "Our Own Red, White and Blue." An unusually heavy shower of coins came from all the surrounding buildings, because there was the popular and much admired Henry Fillmore leading the band!

Toward the end of the war, the Fillmore Brothers went all out on patriotism. J.H. and Palmer Hartsough composed "Hymn to the Dawn of Peace" and distributed it free. Henry did his part, too. He was nearly thirty-nine years old but took steps to enlist as a U.S. Army bandmaster. He wanted to take a band of his own off to war with him and ran the following notice

HENRY FILLMORE

Henry was cover boy for the May, 1917, issue of the *Musical Messenger.* Few knew that when they looked at this picture they were also seeing Al Hayes, Harold Bennett, Harry Hartley, Gus Beans, Ray Hall, Will Huff (partly) and Henrietta Moore. Note the "More Fraternity" emblem at the top.

in the November, 1918, issue of the *Musical Messenger:*

COME ON! LET'S GO TO FRANCE!
THE ARMY NEEDS MUSICIANS!

Our fighters—the boys who are out there mopping the ground with those barbarous Huns, and the boys who are in training to help finish the job—are begging, yes, and more than that, they are pleading for bands. We—all of us who play band instruments and can arrange to absent ourselves from home and business duties for the period of the war—should answer their plea. We owe it to our country, to those boys and to ourselves.

The physical requirements for musicians consist principally of a good heart and good feet. Those in the draft age can be specially inducted into the Army as musicians.

COME ON! LET'S HELP FINISH IT UP!

I'm going, and if YOU want to go in the same crowd, write me telling your age, instrument, experience, etc. Good positions for the deserving still open.

HENRY FILLMORE
528 Elm Street
Cincinnati, Ohio

His intentions were good, but the grand volunteer band never materialized because the war ended a few days after this issue was printed.

Henry's trombone smears were quality merchandise and were now very much in demand, especially with minstrel shows. Each smear was dedicated to a stereotyped minstrel type person, and on the sheet music covers were caricatures of minstrel people—not real Negroes. Henry would never have permitted this type of display if he thought anyone would be offended. The smears were even called "niggah smears" because this terminology was in common use at the time. A good example of the advertising was the following, printed on the back page of "Sally Trombone" (1917):

> SALLY TROMBONE, "niggah" jazzer,
> Came to town equipped with a razzor,
> Said if she no job could get,
> There'd be one less town, you bet!
>
> Course the folks were kind o' scared,
> 'Cause but few were Heaven-fared,
> And a job for SAL' was found,
> Jazzing trombone in this town.
>
> As a jazzer she's "some bird,"
> Greatest at it ever heard;
> If the proof you want to know,
> Try her on your P-I-A-N-O.

In February of 1918, Henry met a man who was to become a lifelong friend simply because this friend, Merle Evans, was making wide use of the smears. Evans was later to become the most celebrated circus bandmaster in history. In 1918, he was musical director of the Gus Hill Minstrels which were playing in Cincinnati. Each evening, he would form his band in a semicircle on the sidewalk in front of the theater to draw attention to the show. He found that Henry's trombone smears drew big crowds with happy smiles. One figure in the crowd every night without fail, grinning broadly, was Henry Fillmore! He was so delighted and flattered that he reminisced about this whenever his path crossed Evans' from that time on.

During the Sousa Band's off-season in the spring of 1919, Frank Simon conducted the Armco Minstrels in nearby Middletown. Two guest conductors were featured: Sam Harris, also of the Sousa Band, and Henry. Since Henry's trombone smears were the latest craze and seemed to be made to order for minstrels, Frank asked Henry to lead the band through "Sally Trombone." It was so enthusiastically received he conducted "Lassus Trombone" as an encore. This literally took the house by storm, and he was obliged to repeat it and then do "Pahson Trombone" and "Miss Trombone." Over the objections of the audience, Henry lay down the baton and announced that the show must go on.

In the spring of 1919, Henry became affiliated with the Masonic organization that would soon place him in a position of national prominence—the Syrian Temple of the Ancient and Arabic Order of the Nobles of the Mystic Shrine. Syrian Temple, for short. Prior to his becoming a Shriner, however, there was much Masonic work which had to be accomplished. To reach the Thirty-second Degree in Masonry, a prerequisite of the Shrine, there are two paths of elevation: York Rite and Scottish Rite. Henry chose the Scottish Rite work,

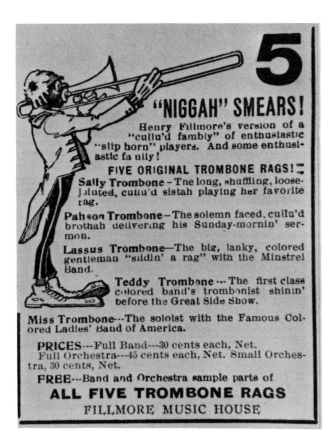

Advertisements of this nature, unthinkable in today's society, were commonplace in the early 1900's. The minstrel character was the logo of the Fillmore Brothers Company and depicted a White comedian with make-up, in typical minstrel attire. *Henry Fillmore's Jazz Trombonist,* an instruction book, was published in 1919, explaining how to play the smears and other popular music.

which is much the shorter of the two. He took his various degrees in April and May, and on May 22 he became a Thirty-Second Degree Mason. Two days later, on May 24, he went "across the burning sands" at Syrian Temple. He was now a Shriner, and his life would never be the same again.

26   GRAY MICE

The trombone smear Henry wrote in 1920, which was described in Chapter 1, gave J.H. one of the greatest shocks of his life. It was a paraphrase of the familiar theme of the "Hallelujah Chorus" from Handel's *Messiah,* and Henry called it "Hallelujah Trombone." It was set into type under that title, and two proof sets were sent to the Library of Congress for copyright registration. When J.H. reviewed a set of the company's proofs, he nearly went through the ceiling. This was sacrilege!

He gave Henry a lecture he would never forget and ordered the recall of all parts. It is not known how many copies were circulated under that name. The title was changed to "Shoutin' Liza Trombone" and was described in the advertising as "The latest member of Henry Fillmore's cullu'd fambly—a jazz barber-shopped, camp meetin' style tune."

This was one of the few times J.H. was ever known to have asserted himself in such a vehement manner. Henry might have been a famous man, but he was still learning from Papa. J.H. eventually cooled down, however, and at the next meeting of the Fillmore Brothers stockholders he gave his blessing to the motion that Henry be elevated to Superintendent and Manager.

J.H. published his last hymnal in 1920, *Hymns for Today.* Henry played an important part in its development, starting his preparation early the preceding year. There were three hundred and thirty-two hymns and gospel songs in all, and it was Henry's responsibility to arrange them all for small orchestra. He also wrote three of the hymns, all unmistakably martial in nature. He came through at his "swinging" best, reflecting the usual undertow of mild rebellion found in his other church works. He was still trying to tell Christian Church leaders that the church was unduly inflexible, but they were still not listening.

Unfortunately, the *Hymns for Today* books did not stand up under constant use because of faulty construction materials. Before the war, the Fillmore Brothers had used sturdy binding materials imported from Germany. During and after World War I, however, these materials were not available, and the substitute bindings disintegrated. *Hymns for Today* was reissued several years later, and many of these volumes are still in use.

When Henry became a Shriner in 1919, he played trombone in the Syrian Temple Band. At that time, the band was under the direction of the renowned Herman Bellstedt, former cornet soloist and staff arranger for Sousa's Band. Bellstedt was a brilliant musician and a remarkable conductor, and he accomplished as much with the band as could be accomplished. But there was a handicap which seriously limited his effectiveness: any Shriner who could play an instrument could become a member of the band, whether he was a good musician or not. Bellstedt directed the band in 1919 and 1920 and then relinquished leadership to Charles Eisen, who resigned after only one year.

At this time, fraternal bands in the United States were becoming very popular. It was a matter of pride for a fraternal organization such as the Elks, Eagles, Moose, Odd Fellows and various Masonic affiliates, to have an outstanding band which could act as a showpiece for the city it represented. With numerous rank amateurs in the Syrian Temple Band, its level of competency was restricted. They needed an ambitious leader who would whip the band into shape and perhaps bring it into prominence.

The qualifications of Henry Fillmore were carefully considered, and he was appointed the sixth leader of the Syrian Temple Shrine Band on January 8, 1921. Thus began an association which Cincinnatians would long remember.

In the next five-and-a-half years, Henry brought the band to national fame and to such a level of excellence that it was recognized as the finest fraternal band in the world. Henry benefitted too; the band was the vehicle for his own professional growth. Those who played in the band during this period took pride in relating that Henry "made" the band and the band "made" Henry.

This was Henry's first big conducting opportunity, and he pulled no punches. He immediately lost some friends by personally auditioning every player to determine where the weaknesses were. Some who obviously could not meet his standards dropped out of the band right away. Others, however, did not quit until they were embarrassed at rehearsals. He would ask sections of the band to play difficult passages alone, then narrow it down to individual players whose lack of musicianship was readily seen. One by one, the "chair warmers" realized that they did not belong and resigned from this elite new musical unit.

The band promptly shrank in size, but it was considerably better than ever before. Some of the older members who had been with the band for several years were hurt, but it soon was apparent to all concerned that the revitalized band was going places. They not only had the prestige of having a director who would not compromise on musical matters, but who was also a nationally known composer as well. The Syrian Temple Shrine Band was clearly going to be a band to be reckoned with in fraternal circles.

Henry inspired the band, and the band inspired Henry. He composed a march which he wanted more than anything in the world to be the finest he had ever written and which would be something his band could be proud of. He worked very hard on it, revising some sections over and over until he felt he had his most perfect march. When it was finished, he gave it the name "Men of Ohio" and was so pleased with it he wanted a very special dedication. Would a President of the United States be special enough?

Warren G. Harding had just taken office as President. Henry knew that Harding had become affiliated with Masonry while serving as Senator from Ohio, and in checking Masonic records he learned that Harding was a musician himself and had played with the Aladdin Temple Shrine Band up in Columbus.

He wrote to President Harding and asked permission to dedicate the new march to him. It so happened that the President was familiar with quite a bit of Henry's music and did not hesitate to grant permission. "Men of Ohio" was published on April 28, 1921, with the sheet music bearing the inscription "To the President, Warren G. Harding, and his staunch loyalists." Henry had been eminently successful in composing his finest march up until that time; "Men of Ohio" has, over the years, come to be regarded as one of the finest of all parade marches and has been used widely.

During the spring months of 1921, Henry and his Shrine Band prepared in earnest for their first big splash— the Shrine convention, or Imperial Council, at Des Moines, Iowa. They rehearsed indoors, and when the weather permitted Henry had them parading up and down the streets of Cincinnati to sharpen their marching skills. He wanted to be sure they had the proper military bearing plus that extra flash of showmanship associated with Shrine parades.

The Imperial Council at Des Moines took place June 14-17, and the band got in an extra practice by parading for members of the Medina Temple Shrine in Chicago. Once in Des Moines they strutted their stuff, with Henry at the helm, and achieved their goal by being voted the best band at the convention, both in quality of music and in marching.

The fine showing at Des Moines was just the beginning of Henry's grand plan for the Shrine Band. He realized that such trips cost a great deal of money and that they would probably have to raise their own. Giving concerts would be a step in the right direction, but this would not be sufficient. Why not a circus—an *indoor* circus? He had read of a Shrine-sponsored circus in Dallas back in 1918, so why not Cincinnati? John Robinson—Mr. Circus himself—was a member of Syrian Temple and could book the acts very easily because circuses were not active during the winter months. And Cincinnati's huge Music Hall would be an ideal facility.

Henry talked it over with Shrine officials, the band, and John Robinson, and they all thought it would be a splendid way to raise money for their charitable causes and have enough left over for trip expenses. A date was set. Robinson was given a free hand to engage the performers, and Shrine officials handled all other arrangements. Henry and the band went to work on circus music with the realization that this would be their most difficult assignment ever.

The first Shrine Circus, held the week of Monday, February 27 through Saturday, March 4, 1922, was a grandiose affair. It began with a flourish on Monday night with a parade from the Scottish Rite Cathedral to Music Hall. Henry knew exactly what he wanted, since he had been with the Robinson circus for a brief period in his youth. John Robinson noted his suggestions and took it from there. As booking agent he acquired twenty acts, some rated as the best in the world. A special bonus was the appearance of Tillie, his famous elephant, who was a hundred and five years old at the time. Six evening performances and five matinees were given, with all seats reserved, and it proved to be a huge success both artistically and financially.

The circus was a success because of the efforts of many individuals. Shriners sold tickets for weeks in advance and then donated their time to sell hot dogs, peanuts, pop corn and soda pop at every performance. Many underprivileged children were admitted free and given treats; to Shriners, this was the most enjoyable part of the whole week. Some have poked fun at Shrine organizations because of some of their carefree antics and general playfulness, but charity is a serious business with them and none can question their sincerity.

Not all services were donated. Those members of the band who were professional musicians had to be paid union scale because of an agreement with the Cincinnati Musicians Association (Local 1), dating back to 1917, wherein the Shrine Band agreed not to play competitive engagements unless union members were paid. A competitive engagement, generally speaking, is one in which admission is charged or which would otherwise prevent professional musicians from being gainfully employed. This was not a problem with the circus, however, because the Shrine made a substantial profit.

Since the original purpose of the circus was to raise money for the trips of the Shrine Band, and since a good bit of money was now at their disposal, no expense was spared when the band went to San Francisco for the convention which took place June 13-15, 1922. Expenses were covered all the way, and the union members were paid an additional ten dollars per day. There were few complaints about the professional musicians being paid, because they were the ones who were primarily responsible for the overall excellence of the band. Some were members of the Cincinnati Symphony Orchestra, and Henry even "borrowed" a few professionals from Dayton and Columbus to make the trip.

The happy troupers made whoopee all the way to San Francisco and back. Whenever there was a stop of any duration, they piled out of the train with their instruments and played "California, Here I Come." If there was time, they paraded around a town just to create excitement.

Henry wrote another fine march for the occasion, "Noble Men," and dedicated it to Ralph A. Tingle, Potentate of Syrian Temple. In San Francisco, the band again won top honors. This time, they did not come straight home; they took a detour up through several provinces of Canada. Henry made sure the men got enough to eat and drink. Everything was "on the house," and the liquor flowed freely. Henry himself, it is said, got gloriously drunk after the San Francisco parade.

These were the "roaring 20's" to be sure, and one Henry Fillmore of Cincinnati helped make them roar.

Cincinnati's ambassadors to San Francisco in 1922 were Henry Fillmore and the Shrine Band of Syrian Temple, A.A.O.N.M.S., the occasion being the Imperial Council of the Shrine. This band was considered the world's finest fraternal band in its time, thanks to Henry's emphasis on quality musicianship. The band is shown here wearing suits, but they also had gray uniforms with black trim and were humorously referred to as the "gray mice." Henry is far left, front row.

27   CIRCUMNAVIGATORS

While Henry was blazing a path of glory with his Shrine Band in 1921, Papa and sister Fred were blazing a path too. They took a ten-month trip around the world, starting in Cincinnati on October 24, 1921, and ending there on August 10, 1922.

Circling the globe was not their original plan; at first, they were planning to travel only to China. Annie Louise, now Mrs. Charles Clark Shedd, was back in the United States with her family. They were returning to China with their baby boy, James Nelson. Annie Louise had married Charles in China in 1918, where he was a YMCA secretary. She was obliged to give up her missionary work when she married, because the church forbade women missionaries to be married to non-missionaries. The Shedds had come back so their baby could be born in the United States. (He might want to be President some day, you see!)

The Shedds invited J.H. and Fred to go back with them and visit for several months. If things went well, J.H. and Fred might elect to take the long way home and thus travel around the world. Their passports were arranged so they could return home either way.

J.H. was now seventy-two years old and was not eager to embark on such an ambitious journey, but Fred thought that since he had worked so diligently all his life he needed an extended vacation. He was in good health, had been a widower for eight years, and was not otherwise tied down. He deserved to see more of the world he had helped make a better place. Besides, this would be an ideal opportunity to visit with many friends and correspondents of long standing.

Fred was thirty-five and still single, but she was about to be married to James Leslie Toll, a widowed physician of Lawrenceburg, Kentucky. When the trip came up, however, she told the good doctor he would have to wait until she returned because Papa should not travel back from China alone. Dr. Toll had not yet presented her with an engagement ring and joked that it was better that way because she might find another man while abroad—adding that he, too, would be free to find someone else! Actually, they agreed to be married immediately upon her return.

J.H.'s oldest daughter, Mary, also figured in this trip. She had become Mrs. Sylvanus Carlyle (Carl) Shipley in 1909. Carl was a professor of engineering at the University of Minnesota and was teaching at Robert College in Constantinople on an exchange program. Mary and their two daughters, Annie Emily and Mary, were with him. They were scheduled to return to the United States the following summer, and if J.H. and Fred decided to come home the long way they could come through Constantinople and accompany them from there.

The employees of the shop encouraged J.H. to make the trip. Henry encouraged the encouragers, of course, because if J.H. went, Henry could run the business his own way for a while! With Papa thousands of miles away, there could be no arguments over business matters or publishing priorities.

Henry gave Fred his Shriner's pin, saying this would

protect her no matter where she traveled. After a farewell party at Papa's church, he, Fred and the three Shedds headed westward. They sailed from San Francisco to the Hawaiian Islands, and while aboard the ship J.H. won a trophy in a diving contest. At the age of seventy-two, he could still do his back flip and other fancy dives!

J.H. felt strangely at ease in Japan, which had been a severely isolated island until the 1850's. Commodore Perry, who made the treaty which opened up commerce between Japan and the United States, had been sent there by President Millard Fillmore, J.H.'s illustrious distant cousin.

In Tokyo, J.H. received a pleasant surprise. He was approached by a musician from Canada who mistook him for the Fillmore who had composed the fine marches which his army band had played in France during World War I. Henry's fame was more widespread than Papa had realized.

From Japan, the Fillmores and Shedds traveled to China. J.H. and Fred were in China for four months seeing the sights and visiting missionary friends and others in numerous cities. Fred was keeping a diary, as was Papa, and she noticed that Papa seemed to be making unusually long entries. When she inquired, he said friends had suggested that he write a series of travel articles for the *Musical Messenger* upon his return. As Editor-in-Chief it was his duty, he explained.

The articles J.H. eventually wrote gave a vivid account of the state of religion in China and, to a certain extent, Japan. Emphasis was placed on missionary work, and he was somewhat amazed to learn that although there were one hundred and thirty different missionary groups in China there were still only eight Christians for every ten thousand Chinese in most of the provinces. He commented on moral, social and government interfaces and expressed his sorrow at such things as child labor, the cheapness of human life and the lack of sanitary facilities.

At Manchu, he was deeply shocked at the sight of the devastation and plunder of the Tai Ping rebellion and the horrors brought upon innocent persons, especially women. In eloquent language he gave the following description (in the *Musical Messenger* of June, 1923):

. . .The contemplation of such atrocities makes one wonder how the great Creator and Father of mankind looks upon such scenes; and what He will do as a compensation for those who suffer innocently, as well as what will be the rewards He will mete out to those who so wantonly force upon mankind such conditions.

J.H. was much pleased to find his *Hymns for Today* being used by missionaries of several denominations in China. It had been highly recommended by the Missionary Publishing House in Shanghai. He was also pleased that Charlie's song, "Tell Mother I'll Be There," was well known there. Meeting with so many notable missionaries, and finding them using the hymns he had written many years earlier, was one of the most gratifying experiences of his life.

J.H. and Fred bade farewell to the Shedds in Han-

kow, the location of their new YMCA post. The decision had been made to return to America by continuing in a westerly direction so as to be able to meet with the Shipleys in Constantinople. Traveling over the Indian Ocean and stopping briefly in India, they proceeded up through the Red Sea to Ethiopia and then spent several days in Israel. Visiting the Holy Land had been a lifelong dream for J.H. Fred described the famous Biblical locations in considerable detail in her diary and made note of the fact that the areas around them had been overtaken by commercialization.

After J.H. and Fred visited with Mary and her family in Constantinople and had seen the sights of Turkey, they all packed their trunks and set sail for America. In a rather roundabout way, it should be noted. Stops were made in Malta, Italy, Germany, Austria, Switzerland, France and Britain.

While in Paris, J.H. visited the clarinet manufacturer who was making the "Fillmore Model" clarinet and placed a large order for more. Meanwhile, Fred was shopping for her wedding trousseau. On July 29 they sailed from Liverpool, England, and docked in New York on August 7, 1922.

Just as the missionaries whom they admired so much, J.H. and Fred traveled mostly third class. This way their money (gold coin, acceptable almost anyplace) lasted longer. They also saved considerably on accommodations by being hosted by YMCA and YWCA workers in nearly every city they visited, remarking that these organizations were the finest of any worldwide organizations.

J.H.'s article for the *Musical Messenger* appeared in thirteen installments running from January through December, 1923, and January, 1924. When one considers J.H.'s stand on band music twenty years earlier, these issues provide an interesting contrast in philosophies—with J.H.'s sermonizing articles printed alongside advertisements for Henry's band music.

The large order of clarinets which J.H. had placed in Paris arrived in Cincinnati just days after he did. This was earlier than expected, and the company found itself financially embarrassed. They wished to pay the bill in full but were short exactly one thousand dollars. Once again J.H. prayed for guidance, this time for help in finding a way to raise the money. The next morning, Lavius Challen Fillmore, the Fillmore Brothers' Treasurer, came across a distant relative on the street. In the course of their conversation, the relative asked Challen if the company had any preferred stock for sale. When Challen asked how much he would like to invest, he said, "About a thousand dollars' worth." Another coincidence?

Fred wasted no time in picking up her romance where she had left off. Dr. Toll had waited faithfully for her, and eleven days after her return she became Mrs. James Leslie Toll. They lived happily ever after, as the saying goes. Fred had become quite a well-known evangelistic singer, especially around Kentucky. Dr. Toll had a marvelous sense of humor, and he told friends he was marrying a famous singer so he could retire and live a life of luxury.

28 IN IT WITH BENNETT

With J.H. out of the country, Fillmore Brothers operations were left to Henry and the other employees. Although Henry did nothing overtly to discourage the religious music business, he did little to promote it either. He merely let this end of the business follow its natural course, which could best be described as a steep decline. His own compositions and arrangements were carrying the business more than ever before.

Henry was not surprised with this turn of events. He was strongly of the opinion that churches needed a shot in the arm as far as their music was concerned. He stood ready to help liven things up and assist in a break from tradition, but his happy tunes failed to start a new trend.

His last attempt in this regard was a juvenile cantata called *Crowned With Light,* published in February, 1922. Most of its individual pieces were pleasantly martial or waltz-like in nature. Some had such a lilt that if divorced from the words and speeded up a bit they might even be suitable for dancing or parades. Henry's one-man reformation did not gather impetus, and so he washed his hands of it. The only other piece of church music he wrote after that was a rather dull hymn called "Paths of Pleasantness and Peace" (1927).

Another Fillmore Brothers periodical bit the dust in 1922. This was *The Choir,* which had been published without interruption for twenty-three years. Henry had been trying to convince J.H. for some time that it was a liability, and after his trip around the world J.H. was not too keen on the idea of continuing the hassle of a monthly deadline. With sales of choir music slacking off badly, continuing publication of *The Choir* was not worth the effort. J.H. and Henry also took another long, hard look at the *Musical Messenger* which, too, was precariously near the chopping block. But since it was the best medium for advertising their own products, they decided to hold on a while longer. Its days were numbered, however.

During the latter part of 1922, Henry was working diligently to fill a gap in the publication of "training," or "primary" band and orchestra music. The Hayes and Huff music was fine for most organized bands and orchestras, but there was very little quality music available for beginning ensembles. These were school groups, mostly; more and more schools were initiating instrumental music programs. Henry had previously published a few "easy grade" pieces under the Harold Bennett pseudonym, and they were in such demand he decided to write more.

Sixteen new Harold Bennett pieces were published in January, 1923. These were later put into a collection called the *Bennett Band Book No. 1,* and several million copies were sold. This collection became the most widely used of all beginning band or orchestra books, and three other *Bennett Band Books* eventually were published.

Although the Bennett pieces were easy to play, they were very hard to compose. This might seem odd, but Henry maintained that it was many times easier to write a difficult piece than something of the Bennett class.

With a difficult piece, he worried less about the individual parts because they would probably be in the hands of competent musicians. Bennett music, however, would be in the hands of learners. Keeping each individual part on the same performance level required considerable skill and patience.

His method for composing the Bennett music was to write a piece in the normal manner and then alter each individual part so that a young musician could handle it, while at the same time attempting to maintain acceptable musical integrity. This is a tricky bit of artistry which can be appreciated only by one who has tried it.

Henry said this composing-uncomposing-recomposing process was by far the most tedious activity of his entire career. He complained that even his composer friends did not know of the agony he went through in constructing the Harold Bennett pieces. Often a whole day's work would seem to fall apart, and he would have to start over.

Mabel used to tell friends that when Henry was working on a Bennett piece he would often become so frustrated he would work until late at night and then go off by himself in his car and drive around endlessly until a solution would come to him. She had no idea where he was going but knew that when he got things straightened

"Keep your eye on that Fillmore boy," said John Philip Sousa, the man called "march king" and the most celebrated bandmaster of all time. Henry's "Military Escort" became so popular that Sousa told him, "I wish that march had *my* name on it!"

65

out in his mind he would be back. Hours later he would amble in and hurriedly commit his thoughts to music paper. The next day he would feel spent and would tell his friends, "I had another one of those crazy nights last night!"

The loving care which Henry gave the Bennett pieces explains why they became standards in their field. Music educators have recognized their quality and outstanding educational value, and several generations of budding young musicians have cut their teeth on the *Bennett Band Books.*

One of the Harold Bennett tunes struck gold. It was called "Military Escort," and even though it was intended for beginning bands and orchestras it had all the essentials of a great march. When Henry finished his manuscripts, he had his Shrine Band try it out. Much to his astonishment, they proclaimed it one of his very best marches. Being easy to play, it was ideal for parade use and was a popular favorite of all types of bands until long after the World War II era. For a period of about four years, "Military Escort" even outsold Sousa's "The Stars and Stripes Forever." Some time later, Sousa himself said to Henry, "I wish that march had *my* name on it!"

Interestingly, "Military Escort" grew from an idea which was not Henry's. Will Nicholson, a musician of Vallonia, Indiana, sold Henry a march for thirty-five dollars. Henry elected not to publish it. Instead, he took the basic concept of two of the short sections (believed to be the first forty measures), revised the melody and harmony, and then added his own material (an additional ninety-six measures). By the time he had put it all through the gamut of the Bennett-type shredding and revising, there was so little left of the original march that he did not add Nicholson's name to it. (This is in contrast to "Joyful Greeting," on which Henry collaborated with John Littleton four years earlier.)

Nicholson noted that there was not enough of the piece he had submitted to be readily identifiable, so he never made an issue of it. Rather, he had the satisfaction of saying that he had sold Henry Fillmore the idea from which one of the most famous of all Fillmore marches was developed. Will (William J.) Nicholson, incidentally was the composer of several other band pieces, mostly unpublished. He was a fine trumpet player and was conductor of the Vallonia Concert Band for forty years.

A few words about Henry's composing process are in order here. Unlike some composers—Sousa, for instance, who wrote only when an inspiration hit him— Henry could compose anytime and anywhere. He preferred complete silence; but if he could not have it that way, he created his own silence by mentally slipping off into another world. He had extraordinary powers of concentration. He would simply shut everything else out of his mind and sit staring for such long periods of time that people would think something was wrong with him. After ignoring everyone around him and being seemingly oblivious to whatever was going on, he would suddenly start writing or play his new creation on a piano.

Henry seldom ever used a piano; nearly always he conceived and worked out every detail in his head. As mentioned in Chapter 18, he did not even own a piano

in the early period of his married life, and when he did buy his first one it was a toy piano. Right after J.H. returned home from his world trip, Henry acquired a special piano with a shifting keyboard. The entire keyboard could be shifted to the right or left, and he could thus play in any key he wished while he fingered everything in the key of C. A lazy man's piano? Perhaps not; it was the same type of piano used by Irving Berlin, who played only in the key of F-sharp.

If asked about when he did his composing and arranging, Henry usually answered "While others sleep," or "While you were asleep." He did sometimes work late at night, but usually he would get up at 5:00 or 5:30 in the morning and work until just before noon. Mabel would either stay in bed or work quietly so as not to disturb him. His routine was to do most of his work at home before noon and then go to the office. During

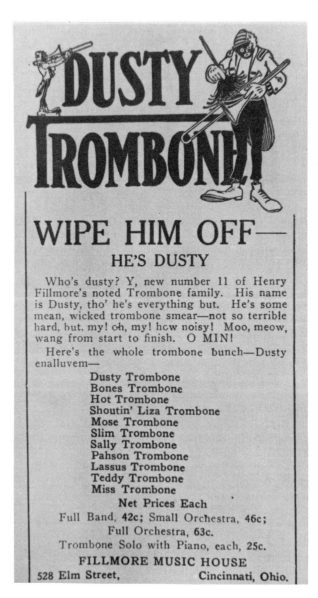

Eleven of Henry's trombone smears had hit the stands by 1923, and they were all given interesting sendoffs by whimsical advertisements such as this. Musicians eagerly awaited his latest one, hoping it would be the equal of "Lassus Trombone." "Lassus" was never topped, however, by Henry or anyone else.

baseball season, things worked out fine; he would usually find an excuse for leaving the office and head for Redland Field (later Crosley Field) to take in a Reds game.

When obsessed with a musical idea, he would work tirelessly until it was completed. He worked with great speed and could write music almost as fast as he could write a letter. Despite his haste, the manuscripts he produced were remarkably free of errors and were relatively easy to read.

He did not construct full conductor's scores, but he often wrote "vertically," i.e., write out all the harmony along with the melody, as opposed to writing the melody and filling in the harmony afterward. He often elected to write out the solo cornet part for an entire piece and then do likewise for all the other instruments. After this he could condense it all to a piano score, if needed.

Very seldom would he make a condensed piano score for his marches, because this might encourage people to play them on a piano, and he did not care for this. "My marches do not sound right on a piano!" he often said most emphatically. "I wrote them for bands, and they should be played by bands! How the dickens can you play all those countermelodies, obligatos and percussion parts and all the other stuff too with only two hands?"

Like most other composers, Henry was not content to let his music go straight from the pen to the printing press. He would always have a band try out the manuscripts first. He used his Shrine Band for this, and later his professional band. Afterward, he would walk around from section to section and ask such questions as "Does it lie right?" or "Any clinkers?" or "How does it project?" If things were not just right, he would make appropriate changes.

Since he put himself in the shoes of each musician, Henry Fillmore's music was a pleasure to play. His music has always been a pleasure to hear, too, because he was a showman and first put himself in the shoes of the listener. These are two of the many reasons why his music has stood the test of time.

29   MEN OF OHIO

Encouraged by the overwhelming success of their first Shrine circus in 1922, Syrian Temple officials sponsored another one in 1923. This was held February 26 through March 3, again in the vast expanse of beautiful Music Hall. There was another grand parade on opening night, this time with Mayor George P. Carrel officially opening the first show. Once again John Robinson and the five thousand Shriners of Cincinnati spared no expense to bring a fine array of veteran performers from the big top. As in 1922, there were twenty acts.

William J. Howard, Past Potentate of Syrian Temple and a close friend of Henry's, was one of the band's most enthusiastic supporters. He promoted the circuses, and his influence was also felt when the band's budget for the trip to the 1923 Imperial Council in Washington, D.C., was discussed. He was most generous and urged Henry to enlist the help of several non-Shriner professional musicians to make the trip.

That year's Imperial Council was to be an important event for Ohio Shriners, because an Ohio Shriner was now President of the United States. Howard wanted the whole world to see that Ohio had the best fraternal band anywhere. Henry thanked him for his efforts by dedicating a new march to him, "The Man Among Men."

The band's trip to Washington, during the week of June 4-8, lived up to all expectations. Over fifty thousand Shriners from all over the United States were in attendance, and members of the host Shrine (Almas Temple) extended a welcome which was impressive indeed. They opened their homes to visiting brethren, made automobiles available for sightseeing, and extended hospitality that the visitors would never forget. There was no doubt about that week being "Shrine week" in Washington.

The grand review parade, with Noble Warren G. Harding on the review stand, was truly a spectacle. There were one hundred and twenty-four bands in the parade! So many flags went past that the President was seen to salute over a thousand times. Sixty-one of the bands were playing Henry Fillmore's "Men of Ohio" as they paraded past the President!

When Henry's professional-sounding Shrine band marched down Pennsylvania Avenue, they were met with solid applause from one end to the other. As they marched by the review stand, they played "Men of Ohio" as they had never played before. The President, recognizing Henry, first waved and then applauded vigorously. Henry Fillmore never had a prouder moment.

As soon as the Syrian Temple band had passed the review stand, President Harding instructed one of his aides to go catch up with the band and invite them to the White House. They were elated, of course, and accepted.

Gathering on the White House lawn, they formed a huge semicircle. President Harding came out and asked Henry if the band would play "Men of Ohio" once more, just for him. He said he was delighted to have heard it performed by so many bands in the parade, but the rendition by the composer's own band had thrilled him so much that he wanted to hear them play it again.

Henry mounted a platform, and the band launched into "Men of Ohio" with an enthusiasm that can come only through profound inspiration. Henry directed with a spirit his men had never seen before, and when they were finished there were tears of joy trickling down many cheeks. Other members of Syrian Temple, as well as many family members present, broke into a mighty cheer. President Harding walked over to Henry, and a hush fell over the crowd. He expressed his sincere gratitude and spoke words Henry remembered until his

At a Shrine convention in Washington on Tuesday, June 5, 1923, Henry and his Syrian Temple Band played a "command" performance for President Warren G. Harding. They are shown here on the White House lawn. Earlier, sixty-one bands had played Henry's "Men of Ohio" as they marched past the President's review stand! This picture, owned by nephews of Harry B. Schott of the band, yielded a surprise when removed from its dust-covered frame for copying; Schott's membership card fell out, and it bore the autographs of two Presidents of the United States—Warren G. Harding and William Howard Taft.

dying day: "Henry, that is a great march. It is one of the snappiest pieces I have ever heard, and bands will be playing it long after you and I are gone."

Henry told the President that the band wished to dedicate a solo to Mrs. Harding. He motioned to August Schaefer, principal trumpet of the Cincinnati Symphony Orchestra, who stepped to the front of the band and played "A Perfect Day." Mrs. Harding was visibly moved and shouted excitedly that she had never heard the song played more beautifully.

After this, the President made a short address to the band and asked if he might shake the hands of every member. All the entourage from Cincinnati cued up at the end of the line, and the President graciously shook their hands and gave autographs.

The grand review was just one of several parades given before the convention was over. The big evening parade was a sight to behold, with every visiting band trying to outdo the rest. One band, from El Paso, Texas, was costumed as "Forty-niner" prospectors and miners; each member of the band from Muskogee, Oklahoma, had forty tiny electric lights strung over his uniform; the band from Butte, Montana, even had a white piano on wheels. The "gray mice" from Cincinnati were no longer gray; they now had attractive white uniforms with long white capes, plus something no other band could boast: Henry Fillmore.

Henry and the band performed twice in Washington's Griffith Stadium. The first time, the Washington Senators were playing the New York Yankees. When Yankee manager Miller Huggins heard the band, he was so impressed that he invited them to come over to Yankee Stadium in New York the following Sunday. They accepted, making as much of an impression there as in Washington.

The second appearance of the band in Griffith Stadium was on the morning of Thursday, June 7. It was a special day for all, because the massed bands were directed by a very famous new Shriner: Noble John Philip Sousa. Sousa had been a Mason since 1881 but had not gone into the Shrine until 1922. Shortly thereafter, he wrote a march for Almas Temple, "Nobles of the Mystic Shrine." It was to be the highlight of that morning's gathering.

Sousa had a special request when the lineup of the bands was being deliberated; he insisted that the best of all Shrine bands be situated directly in front of his podium. "You mean the Cincinnati band?" someone asked. "Yes," he said boldly, "the one directed by my colleague, Henry Fillmore!" Thus it was.

At 10:05 a.m., there was deafening applause as Sousa ascended the podium. He looked out into a colorful sea of Shrine bands—six thousand, two hundred musicians in all! Down came his baton, and "Nobles of the Mystic

Henry had dedicated his march "Men of Ohio" to President Harding in 1921. When the President (left) heard Henry's own interpretation on the White House lawn he said, "Henry, that is a great march. . . bands will be playing it long after you and I are gone." Harding once played French horn in the Aladdin Temple Shrine Band of Columbus, Ohio, and before his college days was drum major of the Caledonian Brass Band.

Shrine'' rattled the rafters. The reception was so great that he had to repeat it. As an encore, the bands played "The Thunderer," another of Sousa's Masonic marches. This, too, had to be repeated.

When Henry and his men returned to Cincinnati after this, the forty-ninth annual Imperial Council of the Shrine, they could hold their heads high. They had played for a president and a king. A "march king," that is. They had also played for a sultan—a "sultan of swat"—Babe Ruth thought they were pretty good too!

30   GOOD OLD HERMAN

Henry and Mabel had been living in a second-floor apartment at 2900 Vine Street since the summer of 1915. This was in Coreyville, a northern suburb near what is now the University of Cincinnati. Even though they lived alone, they wanted a home to call their own—a larger home which could accommodate a greater number of guests. Several of their friends had suggested the Westwood section of town. This area provided the surroundings they liked, and they purchased a two-story Cape Cod style house at the intersection of Harrison and McHenry Avenues in September, 1923.

The home at 2458 Harrison Avenue was large enough for the parties Henry often had for his musician friends. It was a white frame house with green trim, situated on a deep lot with a long driveway and a garage for his new Ford touring car. It also had a screened-in back porch which they found very pleasant, spending many hours there on hot summer evenings.

Henry would not have had this home had it not been for the wise counsel of Herman Ritter, the Fillmore Brothers' Business Manager. Ritter was a good personal friend of Henry's and knew him like a book. He knew, for example, that Henry had never been successful at handling his own money. He had been advising Henry on overall financial planning for some time and had made several investments for him which enabled him to purchase the house.

Ritter was given a free rein in company business matters. It was he who influenced J.H. and Henry to replace the *Musical Messenger* with an advertising circular issued on a non-regular basis, the *Fillmore Advertiser*. Although the *Musical Messenger* had been of great service to musicians, teachers and students, it was not paying for itself. The February, 1924, issue carried a front page notice, surrounded by a black border, announcing that this would be the last issue. The interests in the paper were sold to the publishers of *Jacobs' Band Monthly* and *Jacobs' Orchestra Monthly*.

The publication dates of the three different Fillmore Brothers periodicals have confused music librarians and archivists for many years. A summary, based on actual issues located and studied in the course of research for this book, is therefore presented below.

The *Musical Messenger* was published in three periods. The first period ran from January, 1891 (Vol. I, No. 1) to January, 1897 (Volume VII, No. 1). The numbering system was started over again with the second period, which ran from October, 1899 (Volume I, No. 1) to December, 1902 (Volume IV, No. 4). The same numbering system was used again for the third period, which ran from sometime late in 1905 (Volume I, No. 1) until February, 1924 (Volume XX, No. 2). In the third period, issues were sometimes not published during one or two of the summer months.

The *Concert Quarterly for Sunday Schools* ran from sometime in 1896 to sometime in 1909.

The Choir ran from sometime in 1899 (Volume I, No. 1) to May, 1922 (Volume XXIII, No. ?).

31   REDS ROOTER

With business matters in the good hands of Herman Ritter and others, Henry found that he could devote more time to personal matters. Baseball, for instance. He was an avid fan of the Cincinnati Reds and had come to know several members of the team personally.

The player he was closest to was southpaw pitcher Eppa Rixie, whom he knew not only as a baseball player but also as a Shriner. Rixie was a member of Syrian Temple, and he was so fond of Henry's band that in one parade of 1923 he marched at the head of the band as drum major! He was one of the National League's finest pitchers, and long after his career ended he was elected to the Baseball Hall of Fame.

When the very first broadcast of a Cincinnati Reds baseball game was made, Henry Fillmore was there to assist. He was spotter for Powell Crosley, Jr., the owner of two pioneer Cincinnati radio stations. Crosley insisted on announcing the first part of the game before turning the microphone over to his sports commentator, Eugene Mittendorf. Since Henry knew the players so well, Crosley asked him to help with this historic broadcast, which took place on Tuesday, April 15, 1924.

Radio was in its infancy, and it was quite a popular novelty. Receivers were very expensive until Crosley entered the radio manufacturing industry. He is remembered today for the inexpensive automobiles, refrigerators—and radios—bearing his name. He was a manufacturing wizard, and it was his opinion that the high price of radio receivers in the early 1920's was a colossal rip-off. Applying his manufacturing expertise, he began to make radio sets which sold at a fraction of the going rate. He was highly successful, and others had to follow suit.

To generate interest in his products, he started broadcasting, using the call letters WLW and WSAI. Commercial broadcasting was brand new, with few stations and ever fewer regulations. The early receivers were crude, and it was difficult to pick up stations because few knew ahead of time when who was going to broadcast or on what frequency. Only a limited number of frequencies were being used, and several stations were often broadcasting at the same time on the same frequency.

By the time newspapers started publishing broadcast schedules, there was tremendous interest in radio. Thousands of people were constructing their own sets, often from wiring diagrams printed in newspapers. Newspaper people got caught up in the craze and carried advice columns, question-and-answer columns, and so forth. A typical question-and-answer entry might read like this:

Q. I have my aerial wire hooked up to my bed springs and a ground wire to the water pipe, but all I can receive is the two Cincinnati stations with my crystal receiver. But my neighbor can pick up KDKA in Pittsburgh. Could this be because he has a tube in his receiver?

A. Buy some good quality copper aerial wire and string it outside to the nearest telephone pole.

A tube! Perhaps this example will serve to illustrate what these pioneer days of radio were like. Advertising brought very little income. In fact, it was not until the 1930's that Crosley's stations sold enough advertising to cover his broadcast expenses. He was primarily interested in selling radio receivers.

Crosley's first "station" had been the living room of his home, but things happened so fast he had to build a professional studio. WLW operated on 309 meters (981 KHz) and WSAI on 423 meters (709 KHz), and to broadcast the first Reds game over both his stations he had to obtain government permission to use the 423 meter slot so as to avoid interference with other stations which might decide to use the same frequency that day. Incidentally, the 709 KHz frequency used for WSAI was very close to the eventual permanent operating frequency of WLW, 700 KHz.

There were other broadcasting stations in Cincinnati at the time, but on the day of the first Reds broadcast the Cincinnati papers listed only WLW and WSAI in their broadcast schedule. Things were still so informal in the world of commercial radio that one could fiddle with *both* tuning knobs on his radio and not know what to expect! (This was before the superheterodyne receiver was adopted as the standard; it uses only one dial for tuning.) Often, nothing could be picked up because nothing was being broadcast at that particular time.

To give notice of the intent to broadcast that first Reds game, which was to be played against the Pittsburgh Pirates, one of the Cincinnati papers carried a brief notice that WSAI would give a live verbal description at 2:45 p.m. Nothing was said about WLW, but

DRUM MAJOR FOR A DAY—Future Baseball Hall of Fame pitcher Eppa Rixie was an admirer of Henry's Shrine band and led the band once in a 1923 parade. He was a member of Syrian Temple and at the time was ace of the Cincinnati Reds pitching staff. After his baseball career ended in 1933, Rixie settled in Cincinnati and became a prosperous businessman.

Crosley carried the game over both stations. The notice created quite a bit of excitement. In Cincinnati's City Hall, there were two receivers: one in the City Clerk's office, and the other in the Department of Health. The latter was rigged up with a wire across the department ceiling and out the window to an electric wire beyond. A few employees brought headphones from home and took turns listening to accounts of the game. Across the river in Newport, Kentucky, the people in the Sheriff's office went first class—they had a loudspeaker.

Crosley had to overcome several obstacles to make the broadcast. First, he had to string a long, long transmission line from his studio across several city blocks to the ball park. Then, the only logical spot to sit with the microphone was atop the stadium. This was opening day, and the ball park was so crowded they had to share the rooftop with several hundred fans. The weather was nice, except it was so windy they thought they would be blown off the roof. When the game got exciting, the crowd noise completely drowned out the accounts of the game.

The following day, the *Cincinnati Enquirer* ran a feature article on the broadcast. The headline read "THOUSANDS TUNE IN TO OPENING GAME," and there were reports from four states—Ohio, Kentucky, West Virginia and Indiana. There were no reports of the broadcast being picked up in Pittsburgh. The fans there were not being deprived, however, because KDKA had been broadcasting home games of the Pirates for over a year.

Crosley certainly did his part to initiate baseball broadcasts in Cincinnati, and WLW, one of the stations he founded, today still boasts of being "the voice of the Cincinnati Reds." Henry Fillmore, who had known Crosley through their association with Syrian Temple, was proud of the fact that he had participated in that first broadcast. It was especially sweet for him, because the Reds won the game 6-5. And it was even more memorable because his friend Crosley later became owner of the Cincinnati Reds, and the stadium atop which they sat on that windy Tuesday afternoon broadcasting the game became known as Crosley Field.

32   PROHIBITION? WHAT'S THAT?

Syrian Temple officials decided not to present a Shrine circus in 1924, apparently because they had difficulty scheduling Music Hall for the time they wanted. Besides, they had enough money left over from the previous year to make substantial contributions to their charities and to send the band on its annual pilgrimage. This year, the Imperial Council was to be held in Kansas City, on June 2-5.

Syrian Temple had pledged to help pay for construction of a new Masonic Temple in Cincinnati. Since the circuses were not held to raise money for that, money would have to be raised another way. The day was saved by a wealthy Shriner, however. A large part of Syrian Temple's contribution came through the benevolence of newspaper magnate Charles Phelps Taft, half-brother of former President William Howard Taft. In recognition for his timely act of generosity, Henry dedicated one of his finest marches to him: "Man of the Hour."

The convention at Kansas City was another impressive event, with John Philip Sousa again leading the massed bands. And once again the Shriners did not come straight home. Rather, they made a long vacation of it by taking an extensive Great Lakes cruise. They lived like kings, with all the food and drink they could handle. Henry again saw to it that there was no shortage of booze, and he lived it up with the best of them. Mabel was the only one who could get him to go to bed. As if this was not enough luxurious living for one summer, Henry and Mabel later took another vacation in July up in the wilds of Canada.

Syrian Temple got back into the circus business in 1925, partly because the band had run out of money and had big plans for the 1925 pilgrimage. The circus, held March 30 through April 4, was another huge success. Although John Robinson engaged only eighteen acts instead of his usual twenty, the show still cleared twenty-five thousand dollars. This was the profit after admitting three thousand underprivileged and orphan children free and treating them with bags of candy and peanuts. William J. Howard and Ralph A. Tingle, two of the men to whom Henry had dedicated marches, both served on the advisory committee and made certain that the band received its share of the profits.

This year's pilgrimage, to Los Angeles, was the most extravagant of all the pilgrimages while Henry was director of the band. There was the usual revelry on the way to Los Angeles, with impromptu parades or concerts every time the train stopped for any length of time. The Syrian Temple Band again won top honors as the outstanding band at the convention and proudly brought home their trophy.

After the convention was over, the fun began. The band members first traveled down to Mexico, spending a day at Tijuana. Then they went northward up the Pacific coastline through Oregon and Washington and on into Canada. Traveling partly by train and partly by ship, they continued their northward path into Alaska, stopping at Hyder and then heading southward and eastward through British Columbia, Alberta, Saskatchewan and Manitoba before coming back into the United States. In Winnepeg, they paused just long enough to enter—and win—a band contest.

As usual, there was plenty to eat and drink. A commisary was opened up aboard the train, and at many of

Henry and his Shrine band lived high on the hog on their pilgrimages to the annual Shrine conventions (Imperial Councils). He was enough of a ham to pose for anyone with a camera. This snapshot was taken by Bill Schueler (of Sousa's Band) at the Kansas City convention in 1924.

the stops Henry purchased fresh fruit and other food. Despite the fact that these were prohibition days, Henry managed to find plenty of liquor. He consumed his share, of course. He was indulging more and more these days but had the good sense not to drink if it would interfere with the performance of his duties. Twice on this trip he became intoxicated, and Mabel prudently kept him out of sight until he was sober enough to navigate by himself.

There were a few non-drinkers in the band who thought Henry was a bad influence in this regard. For instance, he insisted that his good friend George Grau, a French horn player, drink a large glass of liquor. George knew he could not handle it, but Henry imposed on him. George began to fade away and finally passed out cold—in the room of one of the Shrine officials.

George's wife Marie could not arouse him and asked Henry what would happen when the official returned. "Phooey on him!" said Henry, finishing off a bottle. "Let the old fossil sleep someplace else."

And so it went. Some Shrine officials were of the opinion that the band was having too much fun and was being far too immoderate. It was their opinion that the money they used for self-indulgence should be applied to charitable causes. Henry argued that the band members had worked especially hard to raise the money and were entitled to a good time. Besides, he reasoned, there was still plenty left over for the charities. Nevertheless, it was apparent that there would be more and more resistance to his extravagances.

Henry was an exceedingly popular figure in the Shrine, but indeed there was trouble brewing.

33 MUTT

Henry Fillmore was a big-hearted fellow. He had many friends and was to remain faithful to all of them until his dying day. Most were musicians. This came about naturally; he was so popular around Cincinnati that he always found himself surrounded by those who made their living in music. The best friend he ever had was not a musician, however. He could not be, because he had no arms. He had four legs.

Henry's next door neighbor had a most unfriendly female coon hound, Joonie. Joonie was so vicious that if anyone leaned over her back yard fence he risked losing those parts which leaned over. She had only two friends: her owner and the chubby musician next door who always sweet-talked her and fed her leftovers from his table. Joonie got out one day and met a boy dog—a drifter who was believed to be a black-and-tan breed terrier. They got very friendly.

When Joonie had her litter of pups, the fifth and last was a runt. He was always being crowded out at feeding time, and it appeared that the scrawny little fellow would not survive. Henry and Mabel felt sorry for him and volunteered to care for and feed him until he got big enough to fend for himself. Henry would hold him in his arms while Mabel fed him with an eyedropper. Little did Henry know that the tiny pup he held in his arms would some day make radio history!

The veterinarian had predicted that the pup would not survive, but he did not take into account the loving care it was about to receive. The canine father did not live to see his five offspring; he was killed by an automobile about the time the litter was born. When it became evident that the pup was well and growing normally, Henry asked the neighbor if he was planning to find a home for it—whereupon the neighbor said it already had a home. Besides, every time anyone tried to take it away from Henry or Mabel, it would put its front paws around their necks and cling for dear life. It was almost as though they were meant for each other, so Henry and Mabel said they would adopt it in memory of the sire.

What could they name him? One day Henry was having lunch with a newspaper columnist who thought the pup should be named for something out of the ordinary. There were already enough Rovers and Fidos. They were talking about radio that day. Radio was so new at the time he thought that if Henry were to give the pup a name having to do with radio it would surely be a little-used name. Aerial? Loudspeaker? Tube? Condenser? Studio? Microphone. . .Mic. . .Mike. That would be a good name—Mike!

As it turned out, they could not possibly have picked a better name—as we will see in later chapters.

34 WHISTLING FARMER BOY

On Sunday, November 15, 1925, Fred A. Fillmore passed away. He was sixty-nine. Henry lost not only an uncle, but a dear friend as well, because Fred had exerted more of a positive influence on him than any male member of the Fillmore family. Also more than any other, he had sympathized with Henry in numerous periods of trial. They thought alike in many respects. The *Musical Messenger* printed mostly hymns, anthems and other religious music when it started up in 1891, but

Fred was giving it a degree of balance by contributing marches and waltzes to complement the religious pieces he also wrote.

Fred had been with the Fillmore Brothers Company since right after the very beginning but took leave shortly thereafter to attend college, working his way through by teaching vocal music. While still maintaining an association with the company, he then took to the road and taught singing school classes. For a period of three or four years he taught in Ohio, Indiana, Kentucky, Tennessee, Alabama, Missouri and Pennsylvania.

The "farmer musician" was listed in Cincinnati directories as a song writer, and his total output of songs and other pieces is estimated at something less than two hundred compositions. His most popular songs and hymns were "The Bible That My Mother Used to Have," "Are You Sowing the Seeds of the Kingdom?" and "Father In Need I Come to Thee." His most popular collections were *Songs of Rejoicing, Heart Songs* and *New Songs for the Sunday School.* His two books of anthems, *Triumphant Praise* and *Anthem Praise,* also were used widely. Along other lines, another of his most popular works was *The New Practical Organ Instructor.*

Fred had been Vice President of the Fillmore Brothers Company from 1910 until his death. The only logical successor was Henry, and this was made official at the next stockholders meeting. J.H. was still President, and even though he was seventy-six he was still very active. He was mostly a figurehead, however; Herman Ritter handled most business matters, and Henry was responsible for all music acquisition and publication activities.

It is perhaps fitting that the only piece of music Henry composed in 1925 was one which Uncle Fred would have loved, but he probably did not have the opportunity to hear it. It was a descriptive piece called "The Whistling Farmer Boy," and while the sheet music does not give details of the story or tell exactly what sound effects should be used, Henry never passed up a trick when performing it himself. His usual explanation to an audience went like this:

> "The farmer is asleep, and you hear the snores of all the family members—including the baby. The alarm clock goes off. The boy dresses and goes out whistling for his dog. You hear the sounds of chickens, cows, ducks, horses and pigs. There's a big fat crow disturbing the peace out in the chicken yard, because he's helping himself to the chicken feed. The boy gets his gun. The dog yelps and fetches the crow after it falls to the ground."

"The Whistling Farmer Boy" made its way in the music world and brought Henry quite a few pennies before this type of novelty piece faded into disuse. John Philip Sousa helped give it a good sendoff. On October 21, 1925, the Sousa Band was again in Cincinnati, and Henry had a chat with Sousa backstage at Music Hall. In their conversation, Sousa casually mentioned that "Military Escort," by a Harold Bennett, was making a big hit with his matinee audiences because so many of the school children were familiar with it. He wanted to know if Henry could tell him who this Harold Bennett was! Henry nearly fell off his chair with laughter, and when he revealed that Harold Bennett was just another of his pseudonyms, Sousa had a good laugh too. It was on this occasion that Sousa said to him "I wish that march had *my* name on it."

Sousa asked Henry if he had any good novelty pieces. It just so happened that he did; he gave him enough copies of "The Whistling Farmer Boy" for the band. They played it for the first time four days later at a Purdue University concert, and it went over so big it was used daily for the remainder of the tour.

For two reasons, it is rather significant that Sousa was using "Military Escort." First, he did not know that his friend Henry had written it; he was programming a march he believed to have been written by a person totally unknown to him. The second reason had to do with a law of show business whereby a performer does the specialty his public expects of him. All over the world, people flocked to Sousa Band concerts because they wanted to see the "March King" personally conduct his own marches. Consequently, Sousa usually programmed *only* his own marches because his manager said that was what people came to hear. But Sousa had a show business law of his own; he played *anything* people would like to hear. If he thought "Military Escort" would please his audiences, they would hear it.

The fact that the Sousa Band was playing a non-Sousa march every day for the greater part of the 1925-26 tour was a beautiful tribute from this legendary figure of American music. And Henry was highly flattered to know that Sousa was also using "The Whistling Farmer Boy." He was still using "Lassus Trombone" occasionally, too.

When Henry had composed "The Whistling Farmer Boy," he had specific sound effects in mind. Percussionists use their box of "traps" to accomplish these noises, but some "traps" are notoriously unreliable. The device that Henry's Shrine Band used to produce the barking malfunctioned so often that the percussionists usually ended up doing the barking themselves. Henry thought it would be nice if they could have a real dog bark. But the dog would have to be very intelligent and be trained to bark only at the right times. *Mike* was a very intelligent dog. . .

Mike did not get the idea at first. Henry just could not get him to bark on command. But on the other hand, he barked without fail when Henry threw a rubber ball for him to chase. It dawned on Henry that Mike was barking every time he swung his arms in an upward direction with the ball in his hand, whether he released the ball or not. He soon had Mike barking whenever he swung his arm upward *without* the ball, and since this always brought a reward of some kind, Mike learned to do it naturally. This was the trick Henry needed—an upbeat of his conducting hand. But would Mike do it in front of a band? Or in front of an audience? With music to distract him?

When Henry thought he and Mike had the stunt worked out pretty well, he took Mike to a Shrine Band practice and put "The Whistling Farmer Boy" on the music stands. Mike was situated on a chair just to Henry's right. Henry did not use a baton, since dogs are naturally afraid of sticks, so he conducted without one. It worked! Mike barked every time Henry gave him the upbeat signal. The band members were amazed. A dog that barked in time with the music—what an act! But this was just the beginning.

Henry's version of the Fillmore Brothers' slogan, "more fraternity," differed quite a bit from his father's. Even though it would have been appropriate, he never used the slogan with reference to the Shrine Band. Since some of its members tipped quite a few bottles of booze during the time Henry was director, J.H. would assuredly have raised a king-sized ruckus if the slogan would have been applied in any way. The Shrine Band was an extremely closely knit group, however; the slogan could have accurately described their bonds of friendship. In 1925, Henry found an even more fitting phrase, as we shall see momentarily.

The band held rehearsals in the Scottish Rite Cathedral downtown for many years. In May, 1925, the building was razed. For a while, they rehearsed in the basement of a downtown church and then moved to Charlie Jones' flower shop on East McMillan Street. Charlie Jones was a French horn player in the band and another of Henry's close friends, and by moving away from the church they could indulge in something other than chocolates and tea after rehearsals. The space available in the lower level back of Charlie's shop was very limited, but being crammed together was perhaps symbolic of their closeness. They were soon to demonstrate this closeness in a dramatic way.

The first public appearance of Mike was with the Shrine Band on Friday, January 15, 1926, at the annual election-of-officers meeting. He was an immediate sensation. His second appearance came a month later, at a ceremonial on February 27, when the band was presented a loving cup from Oleika Temple of Lexington, Kentucky, in appreciation for their earlier appearance there at the National Shrine Directors Association meeting. The presentation came as a surprise to Henry, and he became so choked up he asked the Acting Potentate to accept it for him. In the official minutes of this meeting, the recorder made a humorous entry which was obviously intended as a reference to the band's drinking reputation, and it was not appreciated. It read as follows:

> Band Leader Noble Fillmore was too full [of emotion] for utterance, and this beautiful gift was accepted on behalf of the band by Acting Potentate Meads.

The recorder, F. William Harte, was very much disliked by the band members. He would make complimentary entries in his recorded minutes but would then turn around and do everything in his power to block their plans for post-convention celebrations.

Mike's third public appearance was made at the 1926 Shrine circus. This was held March 15-20 and was the fourth and last of the Shrine circuses for Henry. It was the biggest and best ever, with the highlight of the show being an appearance of the celebrated Poodles Hannaford and his troupe of bareback riders. The emphasis was on clowns this year, forty-one in all, led by the renowned Art Adair. The elephants were there, as usual, with Tillie once again. Tillie was now a hundred and nine years old.

The 1926 Imperial Council was to be held June 1-3 in Philadelphia, and the band was making plans for another of their extended parties whereby they would take the long way home. But the plans ran into stiff opposition from a quartet of Shrine officials which the band contemptuously referred to as the "4 H's." This included Recorder F. William Harte, Potentate Dr. Willard D. Haines, Trustee Charles F. Hake, and a fourth man whose name has been forgotten by the few remaining members of the band.

The issue regarding the band's expenditures caused a split in Syrian Temple ranks. On one side stood the conservatives, and on the other side was the band and a few of its staunch supporters. The band members were far outnumbered. Few took an in-between position; it appeared that everyone in the five thousand-member Shrine body was on one side or the other. The issues were debated heatedly, and Henry was right in the middle. He did not have to say much; the band members, who had a good thing going, vigorously defended what they believed to be their rights.

The issue boiled down to this: lavish trips versus charity and building fund. On the conservative side, it was argued that the Shrine was trying to raise $150,000 to supplement their earlier pledge of $125,000 for construction of the new Masonic Temple which was to be completed in 1928. Too, the conservatives felt that money raised by the circuses should go almost entirely toward the crippled childrens' fund and other charities, and that only the band's expenses for travel straight to and from Philadelphia should be paid. The word was passed around that Henry was "spending them broke." In particular, they had come to dislike Henry's practice of hiring additional professional musicians to swell the ranks of the band at the conventions—even though this was a common practice in those days.

On the other side of the issue, the band had some convincing arguments. It had been Henry's idea to initiate the Shrine circuses in the first place, and it was necessary for the band to rehearse the circus music intensely for many weeks. Many members of the band were not union musicians and were donating their services. Without the fun trips, there would be no incentive and they would have to pay to hire outside musicians. Besides, the avowed purpose of the circus [as entered in the recorder's minutes of December 12, 1925] was "to defray the expenses of the band and the patrol to the Imperial Council."

The point of contention here was the definition of "expenses." According to Henry, expenses included elaborate post-convention trips as a reward for the men who made it all possible. There were those in Syrian Temple who were mighty proud of their band and wanted the whole world to see it; they felt the way Henry ran the band was not the business of Shrine officials. In their opinion, the band was an auxiliary unit of the Shrine and was entitled to spend the money they raised as they saw fit; there would still be plenty left over for charities.

As for Henry "spending them broke," this was a

farce. Shrine officials made a big issue about raising money for the new Masonic Temple, but the Shrine was not about to go broke by any stretch of the imagination. An audit dated December 31, 1925, showed that Syrian Temple had a surplus of $409,947.83. Henry and the band could not force themselves to be sympathetic with the officials' outcries. They asked why money could not be taken from this surplus to pay for their obligations. The lines were drawn, and the battle was on.

The band members took the offense by attempting to get Henry "started in the line," i.e., have him advanced in Syrian Temple ranks so that he would eventually become Potentate. That way, they reasoned, the band members would have enough clout to do as they pleased with the money they raised.

Their plans were thwarted, however, by those the band referred to as "the old guard." This, of course, included the "4 H's," and others who sided with them. They held a special meeting in a local theater, evidently not open to band members, at which Henry's petition was denied. This special meeting, incidentally, was not duly recorded in the official minutes of the recorder.

When the band members learned of the special meeting—and the outcome—they were infuriated. Henry was deeply hurt. After thinking it over for several days, he told the band he would resign as director effective after the Philadelphia convention. There would be no point in resigning before the convention, because they were already committed to make the trip. Besides, their budget for the trip had been begrudgingly approved with the understanding that there would be no more extravagant post-convention "paid vacations" after 1926.

To show their esteemed leader how they felt, every member of the Syrian Temple Shrine Band vowed to resign with him! On Thursday, May 13, Henry turned in his resignation, effective upon his return to Cincinnati after the Imperial Council in Philadelphia. Then, one by one, each band member followed suit. Henry's parting gesture was a march which he dedicated to the group of men he had grown to love dearly—"To the Members of Syrian Temple Shrine Band, Cincinnati, Ohio." The title told all: "Golden Friendships." Henry was approached by newsmen when the word got out, and the only reason he would give to them was "to devote more time to personal affairs and to the growth of my music publishing business."

Philadelphia was the ideal city for the 1926 convention; the city's sesquicentennial celebration had just commenced, and the Shrine parades and other revelry added to the general excitement. W. Freeland Kendrick, Mayor of Philadelphia, was a former Imperial Potentate of the Shrine in America, and Shriners went comfortably about their nonsensical activities knowing that City Hall might look the other way if they made too much whoopee. They certainly needed such indulgence, because late one afternoon they gave an impromptu concert in the street in front of their hotel, causing a monumental traffic jam.

After the convention, the band had its last fling. They went by train up to Quebec and then by boat down the St. Lawrence River, through Lake Ontario and Lake Erie. From Detroit, they returned to Cincinnati by train.

As the boat sailed toward Detroit, Henry sat in his cabin alone, reminiscing about the happy times he had seen with this glorious group of bandsmen during the past five-and-a-half years.

He remembered how he had taken a mediocre band and worked with it until it was recognized as the finest fraternal band anywhere. He remembered the many spectacular parades and the merrymaking at the annual conventions, as well as the wonderful post-convention trips which took them as far as Alaska and Mexico. He remembered the thrill of that first Shrine circus and the three that followed. He remembered playing "Men of Ohio" on the White House lawn for President Harding. He remembered supplying instruments at cost to his fellow musicians in the band.

He remembered many happy hours spent with the band manager, Charlie Jones, and his family; the many visits to Charlie's secluded summer home in Moscow, Ohio—and the good times the band had rehearsing in

THE JOLLY GOOD FELLOW—Henry led the Syrian Temple Shrine Band for five-and-a-half years, during which period it became the most highly regarded of all fraternal bands. He initiated Shrine circuses in Cincinnati, raising approximately $80,000 for charities. When he resigned after a dispute with Shrine officials, the entire band resigned with him.

Charlie's flower shop. He remembered the pleasant association with trombonist John Klohr, his long-time friend and fellow composer, whom he had asked to conduct his own music on numerous occasions. He remembered the many sparkling cornet solos by Augie Schaefer, his pal since childhood. He remembered entertaining these men in his home and being entertained in theirs. Yes, he would forever remember these friendships. These *golden* friendships.

He picked up his baton and made his way to the ship's ballroom, where he heard ragtime music being played on the piano. He was in search of his friend George Grau, and the music led him directly to George. There sat George at the piano, with a crowd of Shriners and their wives gathered around. Henry spotted Marie, George's wife, and kidded her as he had done many times before. "Say, Marie," he said, "where in the world did he learn to play ragtime like that? What house of ill repute did you meet him in? I never knew he could play that kind of music!" Marie just grinned and said, "Why Henry, he told me he learned all about that from *you!* Where did *you* learn it?"

When she asked Henry why he was carrying his baton, he said he would talk about it later—that he wanted to speak to George alone. When George finished his ragtime pieces and the crowd dissipated, Henry motioned for him to come over by the door. He put his arm around George and walked out onto the deck of the ship.

George was puzzled. A moment ago Henry was laughing and joking with the crowd, but now he had a look of solemn seriousness which he had never seen before. Henry placed the baton in George's hand and said, "I thought you'd like to keep this, old friend. This is the end." George was speechless. Henry said no more; he turned and walked slowly down the deck toward his cabin. George did not press him, for he noted that Henry's eyes were a bit watery. He knew what it meant. Good times were over—but golden friendships remained.

About fifty miles from Cincinnati, Henry made his way through the train with his pockets bulging. One by one he approached each band member, shook his hand, reached into one of his pockets and handed him something. It was a gift each man would remember for the rest of his life: a miniature gold plated pocket knife. It did not take them long to realize the symbology—they had severed the tie together.

As each member received his knife, he joined the crowd following Henry to the last man. When he had given out the last knife, they all broke into a lusty rendition of "He's a Jolly Good Fellow"—in harmony! Henry could do nothing more than look down at the floor. There were tears in his eyes.

Nearly three weeks passed. Henry was reading the paper on the back porch of his Harrison Avenue home one Saturday morning when he heard a band playing down the street. A very good band. He wondered what was going on, especially since they were playing his own "Men of Ohio." He had not heard of any parades to be held, and the Fourth of July was still a week away. The band seemed to be getting louder, so he decided to go out front and see what it was all about.

A band of about forty-five players was marching right up Harrison Avenue, and when it was half a block away he recognized some of the players. As it came closer and closer, he recognized all of them—they were former members of his Shrine Band! There was a delivery truck following the band, but he thought it was just part of the traffic which had been tied up.

"Men of Ohio" ended just before they reached the front of Henry's house, and the drums continued in a marching cadence. The band did a column-right maneuver and marched right up on Henry's front lawn! When the truck, bearing the name ALBERT & SEIFERT WHOLESALE JEWELERS, pulled up to the curbing and stopped right behind the band, Henry did not know what to think. He looked at Mabel. With a twinkle in her eye, she said, "I forgot to tell you, Hennie— we're having some company this morning." Just then, the band started into the final trio of "Golden Friendships." When this was finished, they all broke into song with "He's a Jolly Good Fellow," just as they had done aboard the train three weeks earlier. By this time, the whole neighborhood had gathered around, and they joined in too! Henry was at a loss for words.

He looked again at Mabel and said, "And you told me that big kettle of lemonade was for a neighbor's church dinner!" She just smiled. One of the neighbors yelled to Mabel, "You want me to bring that beer over now?" and she nodded. Henry realized that this had all been very carefully planned in advance, and he motioned for the band to come into the house.

The house was packed. Three delivery men, carrying a wooden crate over seven feet long, followed the band into the house, and Charlie Jones showed them where to set it down in the hallway. As the crate was being unpacked, Henry could see that it was a huge grandfather's clock. Soon the delivery men had the chimes and weights unpacked and the clock assembled.

The Shrine boys had gone first class; it was a Herschede-Hall, the prestige American grandfather's clock of that period, made right there in Cincinnati by the company Frank Herschede had founded half a century earlier. It was a marvelous eight-day timepiece, six-and-a-half feet tall and two feet wide, and the delicately engraved face was topped with a moving dial which indicated the phases of the moon. It had polished brass weights and seven nickel-plated tubular chimes. One of the delivery men showed Henry how to change the chimes from "Canterbury" to "Westminster." Fancy. Very fancy.

John Klohr then stepped to the front, asked for silence, opened a folder, and read a poem written by one of the boys in the band. It was not a literary masterpiece by any means, but it was so touching that once again Henry had tears in his eyes. John read it ever so slowly and deliberately, because the content was as meaningful and sincere as anything Henry would hear in his lifetime:

THE CLOCK SPEAKS TO HENRY [Author unknown]

I'm only a bit of metal and wood
Yet I speak to you, friend, as none other could.
For each time you hear the sound of my chimes,

76

Reminded you'll be of those happy times
You've had with friends by Time's process true,
Friends who love you because you are you.
And wherever you are, on sea or on land
I'll bring thought of your friends, the Boys of the Band.

The hours I'll work from day unto day,
Hours of labor and hours of play
And as my chimes ring out the hours
May Memory bring you her sweetest flowers,
And lay them gently at your feet
To fill your life with their fragrance sweet,
And let each tick—each move of my hand
Bring thoughts of your friends—the Boys of the Band

Since time began there has been here on earth
Much of real value and lasting worth,
But that which most to happiness tends
Is finding one's self surrounded by friends,
Of love and respect real friendships are made
And of't in our hearts are great harmonies played.
So I know from my words you must understand
Just what's in the hearts of the Boys of the Band.

Whenever hereafter you look upon me,
A symbol of Friendship to you may I be;
A friendship unselfish—devoted—sincere
A friendship you'll galdly forever hold dear;
For tho' but a bit of metal and wood
I bring you a message of ''Brotherhood.''
Of ''Golden Friendship''—and here is my hand,
It's a message of love from the Boys of the Band.

It was a beautiful, beautiful expression of affection. As soon as John finished, the men all applauded. Then he opened the big door of the clock and pointed to a brass plaque on the left hand side. Henry squatted down and looked intently at the plaque, and this is what he saw:

C. Asimus
O. Bachman
O. Bacon
E. Ball
R. Bellstedt
F. Burnhardt
C. Betzner
C. Bose
J. Boharer
R. Brand
R. Brinkman
W. Brinkman
A. Buck
W. Byrnes
G. Carr
B. Chaliff
L. Chaliff
E. Davis
H. Dhunau
E. Dill
L. Diserens
J. Elliot
G. Grau
F. Grau
H. Hafford
L. Hahn
C. Hapner
J. Hofer
V. Hofman
H. Hornung
A. Huston
G. Hynes

C. B. Jones
D. Jones
C. Joseph
H. Kabiesch
A. Kaiser
J. Klohr
W. Kopp
A. Kumler
O. Kunkel
C. Link
H. Lind
G. Martin
R. McDermott
T. Menge
E. Miller
D. Moore
M. Platt
W. Poysell
J. Rahm
G. Rickel
R. Rigio
W. Saatkamp
E. Schath
A. Schaefer
R. Schellhouse
A. Schirmer
F. Schopper
H. Schott
J. Sivgey
A. Siebler
W. Simon
C. Smith
C. Sonneman
H. Tiemeyer
R. Van Wye
J. Warington
W. Waterworth
M. Weiner
A. Witschger

It was a list of the seventy-one members of the band—seventy-one men whose friendship he would cherish for all eternity.

Again John asked for silence and said, ''Henry, we had planned to ask you to make a speech, but I can see that you're in no condition to make one!'' Some of the men chuckled, and this was followed by another round of applause. Henry simply stood there with tears streaming down both cheeks. He was so taken back that he could not have spoken if his life had depended upon it.

When the men left, Henry sat in his living room holding the poem in his hands. It was so true. . .so poignant . . .so profoundly meaningful. The words burned their way into his memory—''friends who love you because you are you. . . .finding one's self surrounded by friends. . . .may memories bring you her sweetest flowers. . . .reminded you'll be of those happy times. . . . what's in the hearts of the boys of the band. . . .golden friendships.'' Its meaning was so deep he had difficulty grasping it all.

It would take him quite some time to recover from all this.

Syrian Temple had no band for a while, but a new one eventually was formed. According to comments of numerous Cincinnati musicians who were a part of the scene at that time and have observed the band's progress over the years, it never achieved the degree of excellence for which it was noted when Henry was director.

The new director was Charles Esberger, and he was followed by his brother Walter. Both encountered many problems. The relationship with the Cincinnati Musicians Association was not the same, because Henry had been extremely cooperative and was highly regarded by union officials. The Esbergers had big shoes to fill. Whenever there was a dispute over union-sanctioned engagements involving the current and former directors of the Shrine Band, the current leader came out second best. The records of the Local 1 Board of Directors' meetings show several instances where Henry and the Esbergers were bidding against one another for engagements, and references to the Esbergers were sometimes less than flattering. It must be considered, however, that Henry Fillmore was a hard act to follow and these men were trying to do the same job with less experienced musicians. They did a very credible job under the circumstances.

The members of Henry's old band wanted to stay together, and they accomplished this two ways. First, they played numerous free concerts for orphanages, hospitals, homes for the elderly and so forth. All these were judged noncompetitive by the union, and Henry directed them. The band billed itself as either the *Golden Friendships Band* or the *Sunshine Band*.

The second way they kept together was by joining the band of another Masonic order. This was the Grotto, often humorously referred to as the "poor man's Shrine." Nearly all of the old group became members of the Oola Khan Grotto Band there in Cincinnati, and several who played in this band were of the opinion that it was an even better band than the old Syrian Temple Shrine Band had been. It had a higher percentage of professionals, at least, and many of the finest professional musicians in town were "franked" into the band, i.e., accepted without paying dues. Henry was not the director of this band, but he did appear as guest conductor numerous times, the most noteworthy event being a Grotto circus every bit as big as the old Shrine circuses. This was held November 19-24, 1928. He also guest-conducted the Kishmee Grotto Band of Covington, Kentucky, several times.

Mike, of course, performed in practically all of Henry's concerts; they were inseparable pals. Whenever Mike would sing, or bark, his song at an outdoor concert, other dogs in the area would invariably join in with a chorus of their own. The only problem was that the others did not keep time with the music. These uninvited guest artists sometimes stole the show, and audiences loved it. Henry always looked surprised, but this was just part of his act.

There were not, up until that time at least, many pieces of music written for or dedicated to dogs. Henry filled that void with a new march in the spring of 1927. He called it "Playfellow," and the dedication read, "To a dog. Our dog, Mike, a faithful playhound." This was the piece Mike could call his own, because Henry did not mark the published music with the barking spots. Whenever he played it at a concert, he would tell the musicians where to cut off and let the barks come through.

One day when Henry was eating lunch at a downtown restaurant, his friend Powell Crosley, Jr., came up to his table and sat down beside him. He asked Henry if he had ever thought about conducting a professional band for radio broadcasts. He replied that it would be a grand experience but that he had never explored the possibility. Crosley then asked him to go over to the WLW studio and talk to Ford Billings, his station manager, who had a proposition for him.

Sensing an opportunity, Henry went directly to the WLW studio. Billings explained that band music had proved to be quite popular on the radio and that sponsors often asked for band music to be played between their commercial messages. He said that Cincinnati boasted of some of the finest musicians in the nation and that in his opinion a professional band would be the most effective way to bring them to the attention of the radio audience.

Billings said that in searching for the right conductor Henry's name had come up repeatedly and that his showmanship and personal magnetism were the deciding factors. Then he pointed out something which had never occurred to Henry. "Listen to this," he said. "Hen. .ry Fill. .more. Hen. .ry Fill. .more. Hen. .ry Fill. .more and his band!" He tried to make it sound as though an announcer was putting zest into it. "Do you realize that your name has a natural ring to it? "Hen. .ry Fill. .more; that's classy sounding, don't you think? Think how this would come over on the radio! You're the man we want, and we want you to form the best darn studio band in the country. What do you say?"

No further selling was necessary; Henry had already been sold on the idea. Billings wanted a professional band on a "sustaining" basis. It would be an official studio band and perform as sponsors were acquired. He said he would try to attract regular sponsors but explained that most of them came and went according to immediate sales increases of their products and usually did not have the patience to wait and see if their advertising had any long term benefits. He added that radio advertising differed quite a bit from newspaper, magazine and handbill advertising and that much was yet to be learned. It would mean steady employment for the band, and if a constant stream of sponsors was not forthcoming, the band would still perform radio concerts anyway. The broadcasting schedule was to be very flexible.

They discussed the number of musicians required. Billings asked if eighteen would be sufficient, but after Henry worked up a list of essential instruments, they agreed that twenty-two would be an absolute minimum.

It would be a small but practical band: four cornets, three trombones, three French horns, one euphonium, two tubas, two flutes or piccolos, six clarinets and one percussionist. Henry would have liked more, but he was sure that with a stellar musician in each chair they could do the job. Billings explained that they would be broadcasting over both WLW and WSAI, since Crosley owned WLW and had a controlling interest in WSAI.

Crosley had come a long way since the first radio broadcasts in the living room of his home in 1921. At the beginning of 1923 he was broadcasting with only 100 watts, but this was increased to 500 the same year. In 1924 it was 1,000; 5,000 in 1925 and 50,000 in 1928.

Crosley did not sell his first radio commercial until 1926 or 1927. Before that, his commercials were mostly plugs for the Crosley Radio Corporation. This type of advertising worked wonders; his company's profit in 1928, for example, was 3.7 million dollars. But this was profit largely from the sale of radios, not the sale of commercials for others; his stations did not become self-sustaining until 1930. Crosley's stations were not unique in this regard; other radio stations were owned and operated by such establishments as railroads, banks, newspapers, and even churches. But WLW was unique in one respect; Crosley had started a policy of using almost all live talent, as opposed to recordings, and WLW was to broadcast more live entertainment than practically any other American radio station for the next fifty years.

Henry quickly got together a group of fine musicians for the radio band. About half were members of the Cincinnati Symphony Orchestra's wind section, and the broadcast schedule was arranged so there would be no conflict with the Symphony schedule. Cincinnatians were very proud of their orchestra, and neither Billings nor Henry would have done anything to create personnel problems for them or to upset their timetable.

The broadcasts began over WSAI, with regularly scheduled programs every Thursday and additional programs as needed. Mike did his specialty on the first broadcast, which was October 4, 1927. Just before the band broadcasts began, WSAI and WLW were picking up and relaying network programs. Both had broadcast the Dempsey-Tunney fight on September 22; shortly thereafter, WSAI went to the Columbia network and WLW went to the NBC Blue network.

There is no reliable public record of the exact number of broadcasts by Henry Fillmore's Band during this time period. Programs were not always listed in the newspapers, and the actual radio station logs have not survived. But the band had frequent broadcasts, as did an orchestra which was also sponsored by Crosley. Henry sometimes conducted this orchestra, as he did for a special Christmas Day broadcast in 1927 which went out over the NBC Red network (rather than the Blue network). For this occasion, Henry composed his "The Crosley March", and it was played for the first time on that broadcast.

There were many sponsors for Fillmore's Band on these early broadcasts. One of the first was the R.F. Johnson Paint Company, and another was Standard Oil of Ohio (Sohio). Mike, of course, was featured on a few

Mike, Henry's constant companion, was an unusually gifted dog— he barked in perfect time to music! When introduced to the radio audience with music written or arranged especially for him, he became a national celebrity.

of the programs, and when it became obvious that the public liked this kind of novelty he was used more frequently.

Henry was extremely busy, with the music business expanding and the broadcasts taking up what time was left. He became so fatigued that he asked Ford Billings for a three-week leave of absence in February of 1928. At this time, he made his first trip to Florida. He spent a week in DeLand with his friend John Heney, the noted Sousa Band percussionist, and then went on to Fort Lauderdale and Miami. In Miami he and Mike were celebrities; many people there had heard them on the radio. He was asked to conduct a few numbers at a band concert in Bayfront Park and was amazed when a man from the audience recognized Mike from the bark he had heard over the radio!

A strange thing happened in Caracas, Venezuela, in the autumn of 1928. In the ornate new bullfighting ring, the Muevo Circo, a scheduled battle between two unusual combatants did not take place. A chain of circumstances then led to two visiting Spaniards—who had nothing to do with bullfights—being sent to the United States. Confusing? Read on.

At the Muevo Circo, President Gomez of Venezuela and a huge crowd had gathered to see a battle between a bull and an alligator. Neither seemed the least bit interested in fighting, however, and the bloodthirsty crowd grew restless.

President Gomez uttered a sharp remark like "Somebody do something!"—or words to that effect. Somebody did something; they quickly arranged for an impromptu concert by Emita Ortiz and Francisco Fuentes, two vocalists from Spain who were making a recital tour of South America. They were highly regarded artists who were usually entertained by the heads of state and were being hosted by President Gomez at the time.

Ortiz, a lyric soprano, and Fuentes, a lyric baritone, apparently gave a marvelous concert that afternoon. President Gomez was so pleased that he wished to present them with a special gift. One of the most desirable gifts a Latin American could give at that time was an expense-paid trip to the United States. So Ortiz and Fuentes were put on a luxury liner bound for New York.

Charles Miller, Manager of the Cincinnati Zoo, happened to be in New York at the time Ortiz and Fuentes were there. He was impressed with a performance they gave and booked them for a two-week engagement at the zoo. Their appearance was set for August 26 through September 9, which coincided with the annual Pure Food and Health Show (Exposition).

During the weeks of the annual Pure Food and Health Shows, the Cincinnati Zoo was no ordinary zoo. There was entertainment galore. An attractive ice show was featured, plus several vaudeville acts, numerous musical groups and a fun house. For the children there was a merry-go-round, a kiddieland house, pony rides, a Punch and Judy show and numerous games and rides. All this was sponsored by the Cincinnati Retail Grocers' Association. The show was always a tremendous financial boost for the zoo, which normally operated in the red.

This was a banner year for the zoo, because Miller also booked a very fine twenty-four-piece professional band led by a popular bandmaster-composer named Henry Fillmore. There were actually twenty-five performers rather than twenty-four, because Mike the "radio hound" was written into the contract too! Henry and his band were to share the stage with Ortiz and Fuentes, presenting four concerts daily (actually two separate concerts of two-and-a-half hours each but with long intermissions). Henry was delighted to have these stellar artists sing with his band and made numerous special accompanying arrangements for them.

The band was at its very best. They drew enormous crowds; partly because of their radio fame, partly because Henry and Mike were there, and partly because of the attraction of the imported singers. The pavillion was a beautiful setting for these outdoor concerts, and all the programs were well attended.

Henry acted as master of ceremonies at the concerts, and after having been director of the Syrian Temple Shrine Band for several years he had turned into a first class ham. He was normally a modest man; but when it came to his music, he was a jolly extrovert who worked a crowd for all it was worth. His remarks introducing each number were perfect; he had a homespun way about his delivery, interspersing his stories with humor so that audiences were delighted. In introducing a number he would typically give some interesting background, tell how good the piece was going to be and convince the audience that they were going to enjoy it very much. His chats were informal, almost as if he was explaining something to a few close friends.

Resplendent in his new white uniform, Henry was a big hit at the 1928 Cincinnati Zoo concerts. Audiences loved him because of the informality—and excellence—of the programs he and his band presented. He narrated in his own inimitable, humorous way. He was truly a ham, playing his audience and revelling in their admiration. The hard work of the 1920's was taking its toll on him, however; note the dark circles under his eyes.

In his conducting, Henry did not use a musical score; he memorized everything. This way, he could better communicate with both musicians and audience. He was such a good communicator in this regard that his audiences felt as though they were part of the music. When nearing the end of a piece, he had a marvelous way of building up to a climax so that the audience would be ready to give an enthusiastic ovation.

There was enough variety in his programs to make them highly interesting, and everyone would find something he liked. There was absolutely no slow, boring music. He would commence with a lively march or two, then get to the more serious concert selections and follow up with something entertaining. Usually this was a novelty of some sort. The listeners would never get restless; rather, there was enough variety for them to feel as though they were attending a show rather than a concert. As encores, he would usually play marches or some of his trombone smears. All things considered, his philosophy seemed to be "Let's have some fun!" Quality was never sacrificed, however; everything had to be performed as perfectly as possible.

Mike, like his master, was turning into a ham. Audiences adored him, and he actually began to enjoy the audiences. Somehow, he considered all those people out there his personal friends. He was building up quite a repertoire of songs, because Henry arranged and composed new pieces tailored to his barks. One of these was a novelty piece incorporating several familiar tunes and called "The Contest," or "Who Wins?" Mike always won, of course, and he was rewarded with an ice cream cone at the end. One night he was given a basket of flowers instead, and the *Cincinnati Enquirer* reported that ". . .doubtless he would liked to have exchanged it for delicacies from the butcher shop."

Henry had come to the realization that Mike was an extraordinarily intelligent dog. He talked to him as if he were another human being, and Mike seemed to understand. One evening, a lady came backstage to request a number, and Henry had to check with the librarian to see if it was available. "Go get Louis," he said, and the woman asked who he was talking to. "Mike, of course," he said. She thought this was preposterous until Mike came back with Louis Hahn, the librarian.

When it came time for Mike's entry at a concert one night, Henry got their signals crossed. He stood at the center of the stage calling Mike and facing stage right. But no Mike. He got a stricken look on his face, but then Mike entered behind him from stage left. He waited patiently while Henry kept calling, then barked. Henry was startled, and the audience roared with laughter. From that time on, this little routine became part of their act.

It seemed that every friend and relative Henry ever had was attending the zoo concerts before the two weeks were up, and they all wanted to know more about Mike. When asked what kind of dog he was, Henry had a pat answer: "Don't you know? He's a hound dog. . .a *radio* hound!"

Another one of Mike's tricks was that of adding, subtracting, multiplying and dividing numbers. Henry would ask a question like "How much is two plus three, Mike?" Then he would turn so the audience could not see the index finger on his right hand flicking upward ever so subtly. Mike would bark the right number of times, and many people in the audience actually believed he was doing the arithmetic himself.

Among the new music Henry introduced at the zoo that year was a march which today is generally regarded as his best. He wanted to introduce it at the zoo, because some of the programs were broadcast over WLW and it would therefore get more exposure. Henry played it at every concert but could not decide on a title. Some days he would announce the piece as "The Cincinnati Zoo," and on other days as "Pure Food and Health." Neither title was used for publication, however. He realized it was one of his finest if not *the* finest, and he waited until just the right title entered his mind. When finally published in March, 1929, it was called "Americans We," dedicated simply "To all of us."

Henry had another ace up his sleeve for the concerts in the person of a pretty young teenage girl, Luise Reszke. Luise had received quite a bit of notoriety over WLW by being featured as the "phantom clarinetist."

One of Henry's soloists at the 1928 zoo concerts—and for many years thereafter—was the talented Luise Reszke. At the age of twelve she was performing over WLW Radio as the "phantom clarinetist." Henry composed two solos for her.

She had a faultless technique on the clarinet. After she had played a solo over WLW on December 5, 1926, the announcer encouraged the audience to guess who the artist was, whether it was male or female, how old, and so forth. Some of the letters which came in were hilarious. Henry wrote a special solo for her, featuring it at the zoo. He called it "The Phantom." "The Phantom" was never published, because he later wrote a similar solo for her and published it as "Lightning Fingers."

The band worked hard, because of the difficulty and amount of music Henry put before them, but they had fun too. The concerts were a huge success, and toward the end of the two weeks everyone was in a good humor. One night they played "Sally Trombone," and Henry had the two trombonists, John Klohr and Earl Miller, come to the front of the stage. He had brought his own trombone so he could play along with them, hamming it up a bit. After they got started, the two regulars laughed so hard they just quit and let Henry play the entire piece by himself. He went along with their gag and broke into laughter at the end. These were happy times.

The zoo audiences enjoyed Henry immensely, and he also enjoyed them. Between concerts he would mingle with the crowd, always willing to talk to anyone who approached him. He also enjoyed the animals. Much to the amusement of the band, he gave the animals names according to whom they reminded him of. There was a bear he called George (Grau), a cheetah he called Luise (Reszke), a tiger named John (Klohr), an ostrich named Mabel, and on and on. There was also a huge hippopotamus named Henry!

The Cincinnati newspapers were lavish in their praise of Henry's concerts. While acknowledging that they were different from the concerts previously played there by the Cincinnati Symphony Orchestra, they also acknowledged that the performances were all on a high plane. The critics were impressed by the band's great precision and noted that they played with considerable vitality. What they liked most, however, was Henry's showmanship and the freshness of his approach. They appreciated the way he projected his personality and set the mood.

It should be noted that this was Cincinnati—a city with a rich musical tradition. If Henry's concerts had not met critical standards, they might not have received as much as a mention in the papers. As it turned out, however, the papers were generous with their accolades. They ranked Henry's band, small as it was, with the finest in the country.

38   LIVING HIGH ON THE DOG

Mike Fillmore, the "radio hound," and Henry Fillmore, publicity hound, were approaching their prime years. Technically speaking, Mike was a musician; at least he had a union card saying he was! He made such a hit at the 1928 zoo concerts that Local 1 issued him an honorary membership card. Since he was a bona fide union member, there could be no outcries from two-legged musicians such as "Unfair to organized labor! He's putting us out of work!" No one complained, however, and Henry admitted that he had conspired with Local 1 officials to have the card issued as a publicity stunt.

New opportunities were opening fast for Henry and Mike. Within a month, they became involved in the world of phonograph records and the world of movies. The phonograph record activity came first, with a recording made for Columbia on October 1, 1928.

An executive of the Columbia Phonograph Company traveling in the Midwest heard one of Henry's broadcasts from the zoo which featured Mike in "The Whistling Farmer Boy." He was excited about a dog barking in time with music and sent Henry a telegram inviting him to bring Mike to their New York studio for a recording session. In subsequent correspondence they decided on the October 1 date and agreed to allow Henry to bring his solo cornetist Augie Schaefer and a percussionist, both of whom were familiar with Henry's interpretations. This way they would use a minimum of valuable studio time.

Three selections were recorded: Henry's "The Whistling Farmer Boy" and "Golden Friendships," and Arthur Pryor's "The Whistler and His Dog." The latter was subsequently eliminated[1], and only one record was produced. "The Whistling Farmer Boy" was recorded first, and it was necessary to do five "takes." During the first attempt, the musicians became so engrossed in Mike's performance they lost their places in the music and had to stop! After a pause so they could admire and pet Mike, they continued in a more relaxed manner.

On subsequent "takes," there was the usual re-positioning of microphones and musicians, which Henry was not accustomed to. After an apparently acceptable recording had been made, one of the Columbia executives listened to the playback and rejected it. Mike was too perfect, he said. He reasoned that people who listened to the record would not believe it was a real dog barking, so he asked Henry to do it again. This time, Henry had Mike bark slightly off the beat in a few spots. That was better, according to the executive, and the production record was pressed from that "take."

Henry was not happy about the production record with the off-beat barks, but he did not belabor the issue because he felt the executive knew what would sell and what would not. He did, however, register a mild complaint about the musicians, saying he wished he could have brought his own band from Cincinnati because they were better musicians. The record was to be released under the name "The Fillmore Band," implying that it was his own hand-picked band from Cincinnati. These recordings were the only commercial records ever made by Henry Fillmore and today are considered rare items by collectors of band records.

[1] "The Whistler and His Dog," paired with "The Whistling Farmer Boy," was released in England on the Regal label.

Henry shared the stage with Mike, the "radio hound," wherever he performed. Mike even had a union card naming him an honorary member of the Cincinnati Musicians Association, Local 1, and Henry charged $100 per day for his services. Henry composed or arranged numerous pieces of music for him, and all were heard on WLW broadcasts. Mike received thousands of fan letters from all over America and several foreign countries.

The movies were next for Henry and Mike. In the last week of October, they became the subject of a short news feature film, the Pathe *Audio Review*. It was not necessary for them to travel; Pathe sent a crew to Cincinnati, and the film was made in one of the WLW studios. Henry was apprehensive about how Mike would behave in front of movie cameras, but he came through in flying colors—or rather, in flying black and white. The only problems came with the bright lights and also with the flash bulbs used for still photos. These made Mike nervous at first. For this performance, Mike wore his best harness, and the band was attired in the standard black Local 1 uniforms. Bromley House, one of Crosley's staff announcers, did the narration.

The only selection performed was a new composition of Henry's, "An Old Time Political Parade." This was a descriptive piece requiring barking dogs, tin horns, the hoofbeats of horses, shouting and whatever else the band members could come up with to simulate the sounds of a political parade. According to the story which Henry often told when he performed the piece, participants in the parade included the brewery horses, a fife and drum corps, volunteer firemen, a Negro band,

and a farmers' band which was very, very bad.

The Pathe film had its first showing in Cincinnati at the Palace Theater in January of the following year, and then it was put into general distribution. The Palace Theater management did not allow pets in the theater, but an exception was made for the star of this show. Mike had the best seat in the house.

Once the Columbia record and the Pathe news short were released to the public, the Fillmore Band broadcasts over WLW became very popular indeed. By popular demand, Mike was featured every week. One day he accidentally bit his tongue, and Henry attempted to substitute for him that night on the broadcast. His poor imitation brought a stack of letters protesting the artificial barking.

There were few powerful radio stations in the 1920's, and when WLW increased its power to 50,000 watts, Mike inherited a host of new listeners. People were hungry for entertainment on long winter nights, and WLW now reached millions of people it had never reached before. There were a surprisingly large number of listeners in Canada. When Henry vacationed in Ontario in the summer of 1929, he and Mike were greeted as celebrities in every city they visited. Numer-

Mike was the featured soloist on Henry's only commercial records. A Columbia artist retouched the WLW publicity photo, reversing it so that Henry appeared left handed. "The Whistling Farmer Boy" was paired with "Golden Friendships" on this 78 rpm record released in November, 1928.

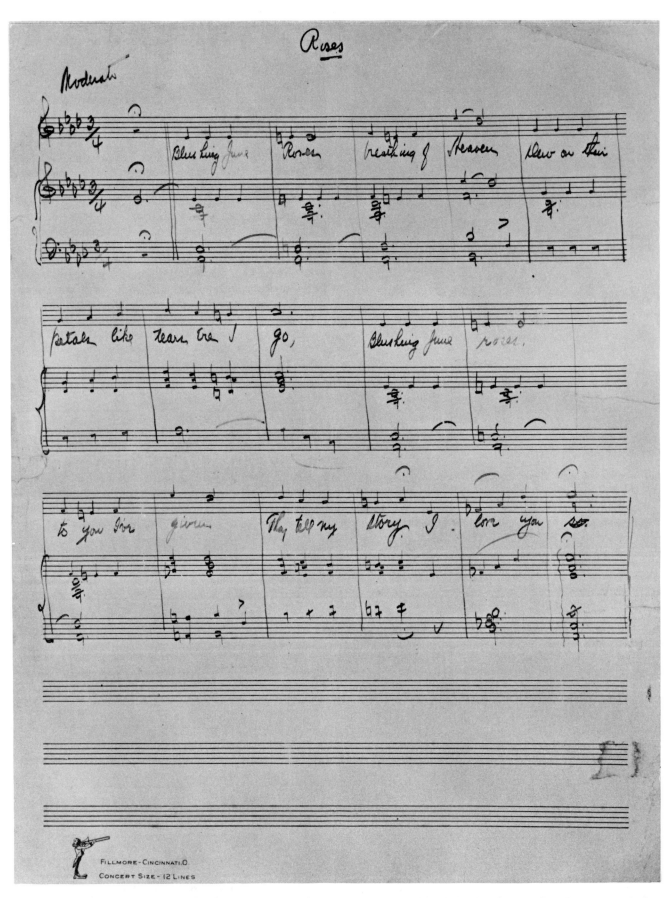

Henry had no children of his own—just Mike. But he loved the children of his sisters. When Mary's daughter Annie Emily had a poem to recite in a 1928 high school class play, she thought it would be nice if it could be sung instead. A few sweet words to Uncle Henry brought this pretty little song, "Roses." Note the Fillmore Brothers logo at the bottom of the manuscript.

84

ous people recognized Mike by his bark.

Fan letters for Mike poured in from all forty-eight states and several foreign countries. The excess mail was put in bushel baskets and stacked almost to the ceiling in a storage room. This put quite a burden on Henry, who not only read all the letters but personally answered all those requiring answers. Occasionally he would have Mike "sign" the letters with an inked paw-print.

There were many gimmicks used on those radio programs—such as the night Mike did a duet, "The Song I Love," with WLW staff announcer Richard Pavey. Henry also doctored up several well-known songs for Mike's exclusive use. The band members were delighted to be a part of these programs; they never knew what Henry was going to come up with next but knew that everyone in town would be talking about it the next morning.

Henry also wrote several original novelty pieces for Mike. None of these were ever published, however. Since Henry apparently destroyed them several years later, a complete listing will probably never be made. There were such pieces as "Chasing the Fox," "Mike at the Hog Calling Contest," "The Dog and the Music Box," "Giving Mike the Ha Ha," and "Mike Hunting Birds."

Around Cincinnati, Mike was the toast of the town. The newspapers referred to him as the "Rin Tin Tin of the airwaves," the "John McCormack of Dogdom,"

"Fillmore's unpedigreed artist," and of course the cognomen which everyone knew—Mike, the "radio hound." When people spoke or whistled to him on the street, Henry beamed with pride.

Mike and Henry were always seen together, fair weather or foul. One wintry day a snowstorm blew up while they were in the Fillmore Brothers' office, and when it came time for Henry's morning shave, Mike balked at walking in the snow to the barbershop. Henry then constructed a set of cardboard snowshoes for him and tied them to his legs with guitar strings. "Now you can go to the barbershop with me," he said. Out the door they went, with Mike prancing proudly through the snow.

At the barbershop, Henry said "Mike, show the men your snowshoes." Mike thrust his head high, pointed his ears outward and paraded back and forth past the four chairs as if he were putting on his own private fashion show! Then he curled up in his favorite chair atop his favorite cushion—Henry's three hundred dollar light gray alpaca overcoat.

When Henry, Mabel and Mike went for a ride in their Ford touring car, Mike hogged the front seat in such a way that Mabel often gave up and sat in the back seat. He disliked the wind blowing on him, you see. Some people thought Mike was terribly spoiled, but Henry looked at it differently. "I treat him with respect," he would say. He meant it; he dearly loved that dog.

39 PENNIES, HAMS, KLAXONS, ETC.

With the coming of the stock market crash of 1929, many Cincinnati businesses folded, and thousands were out of work. But still, Cincinnati was not hit nearly as hard as most other large American cities. Powell Crosley, Jr., for one, certainly did not roll over and play dead. WLW maintained normal operations, and Henry's band continued their weekly programs almost as though nothing had happened.

The American Rolling Mill Company (Armco) in Middletown, Ohio, sounded a positive note when they initiated weekly broadcasts by their own professional band, the Armco Band, led by Frank Simon. Henry had wrriten the march "Gifted Leadership" for his old friend Frank Simon two years earlier. Simon, incidentally, was a charter member of the American Bandmasters Association, which had been founded that year. The ABA was planning a convention in 1930. Henry was soon to become a part of this organization and was destined to play a vital role in the years ahead.

There were several new sponsors for Henry's WLW programs, including the Walgreen Company (the pharmacy chain) and the Crown Overall Manufacturing Company. The makers of Johnston's paint were still actively advertising, and their sponsorship continued until the spring of 1930. Henry had a special interest in the Johnston people, because his friend Charlie Jones was related to them. The Johnstons were idealists; they used Henry's band for advertising because they felt it

was in keeping with the great musical tradition of Cincinnati. They believed it was perhaps the finest band in the United States made up of musicians exclusively from any one city and hoped listeners would relate the quality of the music to the quality of their product.

Ironically, the sponsor who created the most lasting impression (other than Crosley) advertised for such a short time that no one can even remember who it was! This was the sponsor for whom Henry wrote his now famous march "The Footlifter." Some say it might have been a bank or a savings and loan; some say an insurance company. But the evidence strongly suggests a small Cincinnati insurance agency which carried the program for just a few weeks and then fell into hard times at the beginning of the depression.

The president of this agency was evidently a personal friend of Henry's. One night after a broadcast he asked Henry to compose a piece of music which would be suggestive of their new slogan. The slogan was "A penny a day," meaning that for the price of only a penny a day one could purchase their life insurance. Four days later, Henry had fulfilled the request; he had composed the piece, written out all the musicians' parts and had it ready for broadcast. He did not give the march a name at that time, referring to it only as the "Penny-a-Day March."

When the president of the agency heard the new piece the first time it was broadcast, he telephoned Henry to

The Fillmore Band, founded in 1927, was an extraordinarily fine 22-piece band made up of musicians from the Cincinnati Symphony Orchestra and other professional organizations. This portrait was made at Music Hall on the occasion of the 1930 Automobile Show. The band's popular canine soloist is on the chair beside Henry. The tuba player at far right in the second row is the legendary William J. Bell.

J.H. never thought he would live to see the day when his son's fame would eclipse his, but he did. His descendants and other relatives helped him celebrate his 80th birthday on June 1, 1929. He is center in the front row, with Henry behind him.

express his gratitude. He casually mentioned that it was certainly "a footlifter." This gave Henry the idea for the eventual title. Henry felt he should not use a business slogan as a published title because this would constitute an undue endorsement and would limit sales.

As it turned out, the piece was not published for another six years. Henry used "The Footlifter" title when he played it at concerts some months later, but he was apparently waiting to see if his sponsor would weather the depression.

By coincidence, the sponsor was not the only one who had suggested "The Footlifter" as a title. One of Henry's good friends was the music educator Phil Gates of Piqua, Ohio. Gates asked Henry to conduct the massed bands at his Miami Valley Festival held in Piqua May 15-17, 1930. Henry remarked that the marchers who made the best impression were those who lifted their knees high enough so one could see all of the bottoms of their feet. The term "footlifters" came up several times in the course of their discussion, and Gates suggested that "The Footlifter" might be a good name for the new march he had not yet titled.

Henry had great admiration for Phil Gates, who had been a pioneer high school band director in Ohio and had presented the state's first football game halftime show. He was a dynamo as a music educator and one of the early presidents of the Ohio Music Education Association. He was in charge of the entire Piqua public school music program, both vocal and instrumental, from the elementary schools up through high school. When Henry was about to publish new school-grade music, it was his policy to first try it out on a typical school band or orchestra. He would often drive up to Piqua and ask Gates to run through several new pieces. But first, he would have to find Gates—he was so busy flitting from school to school that Henry never knew where he would be.

1929 was another memorable year for Henry Fillmore compositions. Among others, there was "Americans We," "The Footlifter," "An Old Time Political Parade,"—and his final two trombone smears. The first of these was "Boss Trombone." The second was unofficially named for Henry himself: "Ham Trombone!" The ending of "Ham" is highly interesting in that it is a musical statement telling exactly how Henry felt when penning this, the last of his fifteen smears. In the very short ending there is a slow phrase, then a pause, and finally a brisk two-measure recapitulation of the main theme. This coda is another of Henry's subtle musical jokes. In effect, it says this: "The old man is very tired, and this is the end. . .but there's still a lot of life in him!"

With the release of "Boss" and "Ham" came this bit of enlightening advertising copy which plugged the entire series of smears:

AN ATTROUPEMENT UV UNPRECEDENTED DIATHYRAMB PREMONSTRATING DE JOCOSENESS UV DE PERAMBULATIN' TROMBONE

The interpretation of this literary gem is left to the reader's imagination.

After "Boss" and "Ham" were released, they were published with the others as a "family"—in a book en-

Henry was an overworked man in the late 1920's and early 1930's. He allowed so little time for recreation that he even sold the motorboat he used for evening cruises up and down the Ohio River. Financial rewards were finally coming his way—quite a contrast from the days when he worked equally hard and could not even afford furniture for his own cheap apartment.

titled *The Trombone Family—A Collection of 15 Original & Humorous Trombone Novelties.* Looking back at the advertising which heralded each of the fifteen smears as they were released, we see how Henry cleverly tied them all together:

"Miss Trombone" (1908) . . . . The soloist with the famous Colored Ladies' Band of America.

"Teddy Trombone" (1911). . . . . . . A brother to Miss Trombone. The first class colored band's trombonist shinin' before the Great Side Show.

"Lassus Trombone" (1915) . . . . The big, lanky, colored gentleman slidin' a rag with the minstrel band. De culled valet to Teddy Trombone.

"Pahson Trombone" (1916). . . . . . . Lassus Trombone's ole man, a colored preacher.

"Sally Trombone" (1917) . . . . Pahson Trombone's eldest gal— some crow. The long, shuffling, loose-jointed cullud sistah playing her favorite rag.

"Slim Trombone" (1918) . . . . Sally Trombone's city cousin, the jazzin' one-step kid.

"Mose Trombone" (1919) . . . . He's Slim Trombone's buddy.
"Shoutin' Liza Trombone" (1920) . Mose Trombone's ah-finity.
"Hot Trombone" (1921) . . . . He's jes a fren ob Shoutin'
Liza Trombone.
"Bones Trombone" (1922) . . . . He's just as warm as Hot
Trombone. He's the Big Dick,
or Number 10.
"Dusty Trombone" (1923) . . . . He's de next door neighbor to
Bones Trombone.
"Bull Trombone" (1924) . . . . Yas'ir. Dat's he. They say he's
a culled toreador.
"Lucky Trombone" (1926) . . . . He's de thirteenth member ov
de fambly.
"Boss Trombone" (1929) . . . . He's de head man.
"Ham Trombone" (1929) . . . . A cullud bahbaque.

Only two of the smears carried dedications, both to fellow musicians. "Teddy" was dedicated to Theodore Hahn, and "Mose" to John Klohr.

Still another popular Henry Fillmore composition—his loudest—was penned in 1929 (although not published until 1930) for use at the Cincinnati Automobile Show held in Music Hall the week beginning January 12, 1930. It was called "The Klaxon," or "March of the Automobiles" Automobile manufacturers sent copies of the sheet music to their dealers all over the United States in an effort to stimulate the economy.

Henry invented a new musical instrument for use at the show, and this created quite a bit of excitement. It was his klaxophone, which consisted of twelve automobile horns, or klaxons, mounted on a table and powered by an automobile battery. Delco Remy of Anderson, Indiana, built it to Henry's specifications.

Automobile warning horns were in the process of graduating from "aaaOOOOOgah" type devices, and Delco Remy was tooling up for production of an electric horn with a chrome plated trumpet bell affixed to it.

This unusual musical (?) instrument is the klaxophone, made from auto horn energizers and chrome plated trumpet bells. It was built exclusively for Henry by Delco Remy to be used in his march, "The Klaxon," at the 1930 Automobile Show in Cincinnati. Joe White, who built it, is left; Delco Remy Chief Engineer, R.M. Critchfield, is right.

These were to be sold for forty dollars a pair. There was a problem, however; these horns all sounded at approximately the same musical pitch. The Delco Remy people took care of that, however, by cementing combinations of pennies and dimes to the diaphragms until they sounded the desired notes of the musical scale.

Yes, the kaxophone made quite a racket! It was not a good idea to sit in the front row at a concert where this electrical monster was used.

40   MIKE IN FAST COMPANY

The 1930 automobile show in Cincinnati was the first of two automobile shows at which the Fillmore Band played; the second was in Dayton on February 2-6. These two events were very important to Henry professionally, but the most significant event of 1930 was one not involving his band: the first convention of the American Bandmasters Association.

On July 5, 1929, a group of nine distinguished bandmasters from the United States and Canada had met in New York City to organize the ABA, and since that time it has become the most influential band organization the world has ever known. These gentlemen came to New York at the invitation of Edwin Franko Goldman, conductor of the famed Goldman Band, who was promptly elected President. John Philip Sousa, who could not attend, was named Honorary Life President.

One of those present was Frank Simon, and at a later date he suggested that their first convention be held in Middletown, Ohio, where he was conductor of the Armco Band. The date was set for March 13-16, 1930. In the meantime, invitations were extended to a select list of bandmasters, and the wheels of organization were

turning. Henry Fillmore received one of the invitations because of his importance to the band movement not only as a bandmaster but also as a composer and as a publisher.

A total of thirty-eight bandmasters, instrument manufacturers and music dealers attended this historic event. Frank Simon was host, and his Middletown employer, the American Rolling Mill Company, financed the convention. John Philip Sousa arrived early the second day, and much to his surprise was met at the train depot by the sixty-piece Middletown High School Band and the entire ABA delegation. He was obliged to conduct his own "The Stars and Stripes Forever" there at the depot, and then they all paraded to the hotel where the meetings were being held.

Numerous professional papers were read at the meetings. One paper proposed the commissioning of military bandmasters, and Henry read the paper in the absence of the author, U.S. Army bandmaster Arthur S. Haynes. At the time, this was a matter of great concern to bandmasters in general, and Sousa had previously testified before Congress on the issue. Henry subse-

Henry Fillmore was elected to membership in the prestigious American Bandmasters Assn. just prior to the first convention at Middletown, Ohio, in March, 1930. Those in this historic photograph are: 1—Samuel Harris; 2—Henry Fillmore and Mike; 3—Karl B. Shinkman; 4—A.A. Harding; 5—Harry J. Charlton; 6—J.F. Boyer; 7—J.J. Gagnier; 8—Peter Buys; 9—Lt. Philip Enger; 10—Lt. Charles Benter; 11—Edwin Franko Goldman; 12—John Philip Sousa; 13—Charles O'Neill; 14—Sam H. Treloar; 15—Karl L. King; 16—Ernest Glover; 17—R.B. Hayward; 18—C.D. Pierce; 19—George O. Frey; 20—Albertus L. Meyers; 21—Richard J. Dunn; 22—Eugene S. LaBarre; 23—Walter M. Smith; 24—Everett McCracken; 25—Frank Simon.

quently followed up with letters to legislators and military authorities.

The highlight of the convention came on Sunday afternoon, the final day, with a concert by the Armco Band at which each selection was conducted by a different bandmaster. One hour of this concert was broadcast over WLW. Henry and Mike performed after the broadcast portion of the program, and his perfect timing delighted the bandmasters.

Mike and Henry almost missed the convention, because they had been involved in an automobile accident three days earlier. Another car struck Henry's from behind while he was waiting at a red light, and Mike was thrown against the dashboard. He did not bark for several days but came through like the veteran performer he was when seated on the stage before the large crowd at the concert. He hammed it up after the concert, shaking paws with Sousa and all the other famous bandmasters.

On the first night of the convention, which was Thursday, March 13, the delegates gathered around a radio in the hotel to hear one of the weekly WLW broadcasts of the Fillmore Band. They liked what they heard. Unfortunately, WLW was obliged to discontinue the band's broadcasts in May of 1930 in favor of less expensive programming. Listeners objected vigorously, but the effects of the depression were finally being felt. This decision, coupled with cutbacks in other areas and an increase in advertising rates, enabled WLW to operate in the black for the first time. The Fillmore Band broadcasts were reinstated for a short period two years later, however.

Although the Fillmore Band was no longer needed for regular radio broadcasts, Henry did keep the men together by performing at numerous civic and private events, and even some chautauqua, in the Ohio, Kentucky and Indiana area. For example, they played engagements at Coney Island (Cincinnati's), the Blue Grass Fair (Lexington) and for the laying of the cornerstone at the new Cincinnati Union Terminal. Wherever they appeared, they were greeted enthusiastically.

After a vacation at Lake Muskoka, north of Toronto, Henry returned to Cincinnati by way of New York. On July 30, 1930, Edwin Franko Goldman held a special ABA concert on the Mall at Central Park. He invited fifteen ABA men to conduct that evening. Despite all the famous names on the program, the one with the shortest name stole the show—Mike. Goldman marveled at his performance, noting that he even barked on cue at one spot when Henry was distracted and looking away from him.

The Fillmore Band played its second series of Cincinnati Zoo concerts, an engagement lasting for two weeks starting August 24, 1930. Henry's concerts were remarkably popular, and the pavillion was packed for nearly every performance. One reason was that his type of entertainment was ideal for depression days. He projected happiness and optimism, both of which were desperately needed.

Mike certainly did his part to keep people smiling. He seemed to understand; many of Henry's friends told him that Mike was the smartest dog they had ever seen. He did just about everything but talk, and some said it was not necessary for him to talk because Henry read his thoughts. Mabel or Luise Reszke would stay backstage between concerts to make sure Mike was ready to go onstage when needed. But usually he needed no prompting. One day Henry said to him, "Mike, we're going to play 'The Whistling Farmer Boy' this afternoon, so be ready." During the previous number, Mike ambled out on the stage, surveyed his audience, then walked over and sat beside his pal George Grau in the French horn section. At the proper time, he came over to Henry's right, jumped up on his chair and positioned himself sideways so the audience could see his new blue jacket with "MIKE" on the side!

Luise Reszke, incidentally, was Henry's prop girl for "The Whistling Farmer Boy," and George Grau was his prop man. Where a shot was called for at the end of the piece, George fired a shotgun. Mike barked several times, Luise threw the crow (actually one of Henry's black stockings stuffed with rags and tied in a knot) from the wings, Mike retrieved the crow and took it to

Henry.

Mike always received some tasty morsels after every performance, and at that time he was eating better than many of the people who saw him perform. But if he was spoiled, perhaps he deserved to be. He showed his contempt for scraps one afternoon when a boy behind the bandstand threw him some unshelled peanuts. He sniffed them, then lifted his leg and sprinkled them.

Mike was Henry's star performer, but there were many others; variety was his watchword. He invited numerous talented school musicians to play solos with the band, and anytime it was possible to squeeze in a guest conductor he would do so. He was literally smothered with requests and played as many as possible. His concerts were highly entertaining, and it is understandable that people came from all directions when the band began to play. Many people had little else to do during the depression days, and in lifting their spirits Henry's concerts served an admirable purpose.

Another feature of Henry's zoo concerts was the appearance of Bill Bell, the virtuoso tubist of the Cincinnati Symphony Orchestra and formerly of Sousa's Band. He had invented a double tuba, appropriately called the Bellophone, which was played simultaneously by two players. Bell had acquired a following as soloist on Henry's broadcasts, and when he played his novel instrument at the zoo where people could see it, there was standing room only.

Another treat for the zoo audiences that year was a hilarious novelty piece which Henry called "Watch the Traffic Lights." This was a parody on traffic jams, narrated by Henry and featuring original music with slowdowns, speedups and pauses, according to the situations he would describe. The focal point was a battery-powered traffic light which was usually operated by Charlie Jones, one of the two French horn players. Henry described the crazy antics of both drivers and pedestrains, with emphasis on an unpredictable woman driver. It was all punctuated with auto horns, police whistles, breaking glass, sirens and any kind of verbal assaults the bandsmen (and Mike) could dream up. Needless to say, the piece was never the same way twice. "Traffic," as it was sometimes called, became one of Henry's most requested numbers and was inspired by a member of the band, Grover C. Smith, whose regular job was that of Safety Director for the City of Cincinnati.

People around Cincinnati were not the only ones who came to the zoo concerts. A group of famous musicians showed up at a concert on Sunday, August 24: the United States Marine Band. They were in town to perform at the Grand Army of the Republic's encampment and came to the zoo en masse to see Henry and Mike perform. Henry was highly flattered and took time to greet each member personally. So did Mike, naturally.

Another distinguished visitor was Edwin Franko Goldman, who was passing through Cincinnati on his way to Tulsa to judge the national high school band contest. Henry had him conduct the band, of course. After the concert, Goldman had an interview with a reporter of the *Cincinnati Times Star*. Part of his interview, which appeared in the August 28 paper, was a beautiful tribute to Henry and read as follows:

> "I know of no marches better than those written by Henry Fillmore. I wish I had written them. With Mr. Fillmore, it is a fine art, and invariably perfect. Every part is snappy and thoroughly harmonized with every other part. You ought to be very proud that you have him here in Cincinnati."

After the concert that night, Henry threw a party for Goldman, the band members and their families. Goldman was still amazed at Mike and asked Henry if he knew "The Whistling Farmer Boy" well enough to bark at the right places with music other than band music to accompany him. "Sure!" Henry said, and he asked the men from the band to whistle the tune. They did, and sure enough—Mike barked at exactly the right spots, with no cues from Henry!

Perhaps Edwin Franko Goldman, the noted bandmaster-composer and founder of the Goldman Band, explained the phenomenon of Mike best when he said (as quoted in the *New York Times* of August 1, 1930): "Mike is art. He is art because he is nature." The photograph above was the soft-hearted Henry Fillmore's favorite; he had thousands printed to pass out to fans.

With the Fillmore Band not playing regular engagements after the 1930 zoo season, Henry began to take life more leisurely. He went to Florida for an extended vacation shortly after his forty-ninth birthday on December 3, and during the winter months of 1930-31 he rented an apartment in Miami Beach at 2437 Northwest Third Avenue. The only time he ventured north during that winter was to attend the second annual A.B.A. convention in Boston during the second week of February. He was liking the sunshine of Florida more and more.

In 1931 and 1932, Henry was much less active as a composer and arranger. Only four of his pieces were published during that time; he wrote several others, but these were unpublished arrangements for concerts of the Fillmore Band at the zoo in 1932. In a sense, he was feeling "played out." A clue to this attitude is found in a letter he had written earlier to his contemporary composer-bandmaster Karl L. King (dated July 22, 1929) in which he said "It's getting awfully hard for me to write new numbers. Maybe it's old age creeping on."

Henry and Karl were to become fast friends in the years ahead. Karl had published a few of his pieces with the Fillmore Brothers, as well as with several other publishers, but now he had his own publishing house in Fort Dodge, Iowa, where he also directed the Fort Dodge Municipal Band. He had much in common with Henry. Both were popular march writers, ranking close to Sousa. Each was also publishing his own music and was the conductor of a professional band. They had their own private mutual admiration society, exchanging letters telling how much they liked each other's latest march.

Karl King was not the only famous march writer who published with the Fillmore Brothers. At one time or another, most all those who could be considered the "march kings of America," except for John Philip Sousa, Edwin Franko Goldman and Robert Browne Hall, published with the company. Their catalog read like a "who's who" of march writers and included names such as these:

Karl L. King	Hale A. VanderCook
Fred Jewell	J.J. Richards
Russell Alexander	Frank Losey
John Klohr	Charles Sanglear
Harry Alford	Frank Panella
John C. Heed	Harry Hughes
Charles Duble	James M. Fulton
Harold J. Crosby	Herman Bellstedt

This is just a partial list, but it is impressive indeed. March buffs recognize these names as being among the greatest march writers of all time, and it is rather amazing that all of them published with one house, even though not exclusively. The attraction of the Fillmore Brothers was Henry himself, plus the company's outstanding reputation for fairness.

An example of this fairness is seen in the way Henry personally dealt with a promising young band composer named Leon Metcalf when the company first published one of his compositions. Metcalf was just getting situated in the Cincinnati area and had asked if he might have an outright payment of twenty-five dollars for the piece. Henry recognized an outstanding talent and instead put him on a royalty basis and gave him an advance of a hundred-and-fifty dollars. Metcalf eventually became one of the company's best selling composers. His *Transition Band Book* (1930) filled a gap between beginning instruction books and more serious compositions and for many years was used widely in schools.

Because of the popularity of the music being published by the Fillmore Brothers, and because of the variety of musical instruments and accessories, the store at 528 Elm Street became quite a hangout for musicians and music teachers. It was the fashionable place to be seen and an excellent place to meet one's colleagues; one could often walk in and be introduced to a famous person of the music world. The *Fillmore Advertiser* was now a regular monthly publication, and musicians could find just about any kind of music they needed at the Fillmore Music House, including that published by dozens of publishers other than the Fillmore Brothers. The instrument trade, both new and second hand, was brisk, partly due to a liberal trade-in policy. There were other Cincinnati music stores in competition, but the Fillmore Music House was the prestige store and had the most complete stock of music items in that part of the country.

The Buescher line of instruments, used exclusively by the Fillmore Band, was carried (until May, 1935, at which time the coveted Conn franchise was acquired). Also on the shelves were prestigious lines of other instruments, such as Haynes flutes, Ludwig drums,

Perhaps Mike did not belong in a picture with ABA brass, but Henry had a principle he adhered to: where he went, Mike went. Mike was a star performer at the annual convention held in Boston, April 9-12, 1931. Standing, left to right, are Frank Simon, Herbert L. Clarke, Edwin Franko Goldman, Henry Fillmore and Lt. Charles Benter; seated. . .Mike Fillmore.

Deagon orchestra bells and so forth. The number of in-house accessories had been increased, and now there were such items as the Fillmore coiled-wire drum snares, the Fillmore "Fawn" snare drum heads, Fillmore "Presto" polish cloths and the Al Hayes cork and joint grease.

Still competing with the brand name instruments were several Fillmore lines. This included the "Solo" lines of clarinets, saxophones and cornets (all of which were American made), a complete line of "National" brass instruments, the imported "Princess" cornet, the "Marvel" cornet, the "Sterling" trombone, and several others which were carried for a short time. And the cheap Japanese violins (which had been used for the vaudeville head-bashing exercises) were replaced by a Fillmore "Stradivarius" model from Italy, which earned a respectable reputation. The manufacturers of the various Fillmore instruments were never revealed to the public.

The instrument repair shop on the fourth floor was well equipped and was a very busy shop, especially on Saturdays. In all, there were five floors in the building, the fifth being used for storage of both instruments and music. The upper two floors were connected via fire doors to an adjoining building, and those areas were rented for storage of the Otto Zimmerman printing plates. The third floor was another storage space except for several small rooms used for teaching. All the offices were located on the second floor, and this was where Henry spent much of his time when in the building.

The retail store, which was the spot most familiar to visitors, was on the ground floor. One got his exercise going to the upper floors, because there were no elevators and the stairs were steep. The old red brick Fillmore Brothers landmark between Fifth and Sixth is gone today; the row of buildings in the area where it once stood was razed to make way for a hotel across from the Convention Center.

There were between eighteen and twenty-eight employees of the business all during the 1930's, and since they managed the business so well Henry continued to do most of his work at home. He did not wait on customers when in the store, leaving this to the others.

The employees considered him an especially kind employer and used to joke that even the Board of Directors would have scrubbed the floor if he would have asked them to. Henry disliked selling, but occasionally he was obliged to accompany others from the store to outlying areas for instrument demonstrations. It was good for business when Henry came along.

Much of the work Henry formerly did himself to prepare music for publication, such as extracting, editing and arranging, was now being done by Louis Hahn and Augie Schaefer. With a lessened work load, Henry seldom came into the store before 11:00 a.m. After a break for lunch, he would come back to the store for only a short time and then leave to indulge in one of his favorite pastimes—sports.

Henry could usually be seen at a Cincinnati Reds' game, often with Frank Simon, who was just as much of an ardent baseball fan as he. When the Reds were not in town, Henry would often frequent River Downs for the horse races. He was not a compulsive gambler, but he would never go to the track without placing heavy bets. His favorite was the daily double, and he won often enough to break even. Another of his loves was football, and he attended University of Cincinnati home games regardless of the weather. Since Mabel did not care for football, he usually went with his friend Max Reszke and his charming daughter Luise, who also happened to be Henry's favorite clarinet player.

One of the main reasons for the change in Henry's lifestyle in the early 1930's was failing health. This is something he seldom mentioned. His doctor advised him to slow down and also to lose weight. He was not what one would call grossly overweight, but he tired easily and was short of breath. It is not known whether or not he had a heart problem at this time, but the facts would seem to indicate that he did and that the doctor had warned him.

Whatever the problem, it resulted in the Fillmore name being used in an unusual way. For lunch every day he had a special salad made up at Kirchner's Restaurant above the Palace Theater on Sixth Street, where he, George Carr and often Luise Reszke went together. The item was soon added to Kirchner's menu as the "Fillmore salad."

42   TRAGEDY

In looking at Henry's schedule for the spring and summer of 1932, one could easily conclude that he was ignoring his doctor's advice to keep a more relaxed schedule. He was not doing much composing, but he was busy with the baton.

The half-hour WLW programs of the Fillmore Band were reinstated as of April 25 and were broadcast weekly until July 14. The broadcast times varied; sometimes it was Monday, sometimes Tuesday or Thursday, and after the first broadcast in June the beginning time was changed from 9:00 to 10:00 p.m.

The band was engaged for its third series of concerts at the Cincinnati Zoo starting Sunday, August 21, and running through Labor Day. Mike was written into the contract—but this had to be changed.

On Sunday, July 17, Mike was not feeling well. He got steadily worse, and on Wednesday, Henry took him to the Townley Veterinary Hospital on Montana Avenue, about a mile from the Harrison Avenue home. Dr. Henry D. Townley diagnosed the problem as poisoning and advised Henry to leave Mike there at the hospital. He said it would take several hours to determine the type of poison and that he would not know about Mike's chances of recovery until the type of poison was known.

Henry was much distressed and upset. This would be the first time in seven-and-a-half years he would be without Mike at his side. Even on trips, he had not checked into hotels without assurance that Mike was an acceptable guest—he was adamant about that.

How could Mike have been poisoned? Henry had always exercised extreme caution and had fed him the same food that he and Mabel ate. *They* had not suffered any ill effects from food. To his knowledge, no one else had given him anything out of the ordinary.

The next day, Dr. Townley called to say the poison was a phosphorous compound. Henry asked where this could have come from, and the doctor said it was commonly found in rat poisons. Then it dawned on him! In one of his neighbor's yards he had seen several dead sparrows the same day Mike had become ill. When he asked the doctor about Mike's condition, the doctor said it was worse than before and that he could not predict the outcome—but that his chances were not good. Henry pleaded with him to do everything possible to help him recover, regardless of the cost.

Henry had been letting Mike out for a few minutes each night just before bedtime, and he was free to roam around the neighborhood. He must have picked up the poison the previous Saturday night. But how? He was so well trained that he never ate anything he found before first bringing it to Henry to see if it was all right! Either he had found something which was so temptingly seasoned that it was irresistible—or he was coaxed. Coaxed? Why would anyone want to kill Mike, the "radio hound"? Henry had no enemies. Mike certainly had none. This was unthinkable. With all his might, he wanted to believe that the poisoning was not deliberate. Still, he had not heard of other dogs in the neighborhood being sick. . .

He rushed over to the veterinary hospital to visit Mike, and what he saw saddened him terribly. There was nothing he could do that the doctor was not already doing except provide love and affection. But even this did not turn the tide, for Mike was getting progressively worse.

On the following Sunday night, Mike was extremely weak. He opened his little brown eyes part of the way, looked pitifully at Henry and feebly attempted to wag his tail. It was more than Henry could bear. Dr. Townley assured Henry he was doing all he could possibly do and suggested that Mike have no visitors the following day.

The phone rang in Henry's home at approximately 9:10 a.m. on the morning of Tuesday, July 26. It was Dr. Townley. "I have some bad news for you, Henry," he said. "An attendant was with Mike all night, and Mike had three severe hemorrhages. I am very sorry to tell you that he did not make it through the night."

Henry thanked him and hung up. Mabel was just coming down the stairs and asked who had called, but Henry did not answer; he merely buried his head in his hands. She knew.

Only one who has great compassion for animals can understand the heaviness in the heart of Henry Fillmore at that moment. He had not lost a pet—he had lost the dearest friend he ever had.

There have been many stories about the unspoken communion between a dog and its master. If ever such a communion existed, it existed between Mike and Henry. Henry's sorrow was more profound than most anyone can imagine. It had been seven-and-a-half years since he and Mabel had weaned a whining, scrawny little puppy with an eyedropper, and those years had brought a million happy memories. But it would take many times that number of years to erase the indescribable anguish of that moment.

Henry decided to bury Mike in the country, at the Harrison, Ohio, farm of his friends Harry and Norma Schott. Harry had been a cymbal player in the Shrine Band. Henry and Mabel had left the hot city on many summer nights to visit the Schotts at their farm, and this seemed to be an appropriate final resting place for Mike, who had also enjoyed those visits.

Henry and Mabel picked up Mike's body at Dr. Townley's and drove over to Harrison. In the meantime, Harry hired a local carpenter, Arthur Montgomery, to build a casket. Mike's body was wrapped in Mabel's finest blanket. The carpenter took measurements and spent the afternoon constructing a small casket there in Harry's garage.

Jim and John Yeager, nephews of Harry's, had known Henry only as a happy, jovial friend of their Uncle Harry's. But when they saw Henry with the horribly

Mike died of phosphorous poisoning in July of 1932, and Henry was so broken up he could scarcely communicate with friends. He buried Mike with his jewel-studded collar and several medals on a farm in Harrison, Ohio. The upper part of the grave marker is now kept in a separate location so the grave cannot be identified by potential grave-robbers.

solemn, grief-ridden look on his face they knew that something terrible had happened.

By the time the casket was finished, Harry and Henry had dug a grave on the side of the hill on the east end of the farm. Henry put Mike's bejeweled collar on him, laid his medals beside him, wrapped him snugly in the blanket and placed him in the casket. The carpenter secured the lid, and the casket was lowered into the grave facing the east.

Henry had a Harrison monument maker cut a tombstone, with "MIKE THE RADIO HOUND 1925-1932" engraved on the top. On the base was an epitaph of five lines, four of which have since been gouged out, apparently by vandals. All that can be read of Henry's final tribute to his beloved four-legged companion is as follows:

God called our loved
_____ _____ not wholly
_____
_____
_____

Among the mementos found among Henry's personal belongings when he died twenty-four years later was a poem by Elizabeth Newport Hepburn which appeared in the March, 1933, issue of *Good Housekeeping*. Because it so touchingly—and accurately—echoed the thoughts of his own heart, he preserved it. The only friends he ever showed it to were those he thought would understand his reason for keeping it. It read as follows:

SAVE ME, SAVE MY DOG

If We live on when Death has closed a door,
How shall the dog who loves us live no more?
For if "soul" is the force we love with, say,
Then who loves more than dogs in their brief day?
And if God's Heaven harbors righteousness
And love and faith and courage, I confess
I find these virtues thriving royally
In dogs, who serve their gods so loyally.

And so, my little friend, I feel that you,
Somewhere out there beyond the sky's cool blue,
Are waiting for me to take you to the park,
The biggest park in Heaven; that your bark
Will wildly welcome me upon that day
When I arrive at last and we two stray
Through shady uplands or along the shore,
Where you may race, unleashed, forevermore!

43   FEET IN FLORIDA, HEART IN OHIO

After the 1932 zoo engagement, Henry finally gave in to the dictates of reason and settled down to a less strenuous life. His spirit was broken, at least for several weeks, because of the loss of Mike. Some of his friends said he was so embittered that he even considered moving away from Cincinnati. In all probability, he learned who had been responsible for Mike's death. But all he would say was, "It was some maniac." While hinting that the poisoning was accidental, he also hinted that it could have been prevented. There was no sense belaboring the subject, he said, because nothing could bring Mike back to life.

He and Mabel took a longer vacation in Florida that winter, driving down in his new Franklin touring car. One might say that Henry burned up the road, for he was always a fast driver when he could get away with it. On straight stretches of road, he would push a car to its limit.

Once again they stopped in DeLand for a lengthy visit with John and Margaret Heney. When they reached warmer weather, Henry removed the side flaps and retracted the top, an arrangement Mabel did not care for because she feared a snake would drop down from a tree into the open car. She had seen comic post cards from Florida showing trees crowded with snakes and was sure that every tree in Florida was full of snakes just waiting to drop on open-top cars. John and Margaret teased her about that for years.

Miami was again their destination. This winter, as well as the next three, they rented a nicely furnished suite of rooms at the Durant Apartments located at Twelfth Avenue and Flagler Street, not far from the ocean. It was above a pharmacy operated by Rucker Haley, with whom they became good friends.

Upon returning to Cincinnati in the spring of 1933 for the annual Fillmore Brothers Board of Directors meeting, Henry was elected President. J.H. had finally decided to retire. He was not in the best of health, and the trusted employees of the company had proven that the business was so efficiently organized that it practically operated itself; there was no need for J.H. or Henry to be present most of the time.

J.H. was now living in the home of his cousin, L. Challen Fillmore, who was still the company's treasurer. J.H. fostered a dream of publishing one more hymnal—one which would be the grandest in the company's history—but he got absolutely no cooperation from Henry. Ralph Van Wye, one of the musicians of the Fillmore Band, remembered one heated discussion on the subject between J.H. and Henry, after which J.H. stormed out of the store. "Those hymns just don't sell worth a doggone!" Henry said to Ralph, and promptly forgot the matter. By and large Henry was more congenial than ever to his father but seldom visited with him.

Henry had very few engagements lined up for the Fillmore Band during 1933 except for the fourth appearance at the Cincinnati Zoo. And in keeping with his intent to work less, he composed very little this year. The most noteworthy composition was "His Honor," a pretty march he dedicated to Mayor Russell Wilson of Cincinnati. The Mayor had impressed Henry with his executive excellence and also with his delightful sense of humor. The piece was premiered at the zoo on August

22, 1933, and has subsequently become one of his most widely known pieces. The Mayor was obliged to be out of town on the night of the premiere, but he wrote Henry a letter of sincere appreciation. Henry was to find use for "His Honor" many times in later years to pay tribute to dignitaries.

With the winter of 1934-35 came another extended vacation in Miami, more enjoyable than ever. Florida was beginning to seem like a second home because so many friends were there. Some had moved down from Cincinnati permanently. Billy Kopp, for example, in whose band Henry had played many years back, was now director of the Mahi Temple Shrine Band in Miami. There were many reunions with friends from up north, and these get-togethers were very enjoyable because of the absence of business and professional pressures. Henry invited Luise Reszke down to visit them and insisted that she bring her clarinet so she could play solos with the local bands. Both he and Mabel were fond of Luise and affectionately referred to her as "little daughter."

As much as Henry enjoyed Florida, he missed Ohio more. He missed his band, because conducting a professional band was more satisfying than anything else he did. There were fewer and fewer engagements available for professional bands, but he thought one possible way of keeping his band active would be to play some of the summer park concerts in Cincinnati. He had not previously made application to conduct any of these, because he had been very busy in radio and felt the park concerts should be left for other bandmasters. But now that his own band was inactive, he let Local 1 officials know it did not deserve this fate.

Cincinnati was a city of many scenic parks. Free concerts were presented several nights each week, held alternately in parks which had suitable bandshells or bandstands. These were financed mostly by private endowments such as the Schmidlapp Concert Fund or the Groesbeck Endowment Fund, with additional assistance from the City of Cincinnati.

When Henry made application with Local 1, he learned that these concerts were much sought after by local directors. Because of his great popularity, however, they gave him special consideration; they knew he would definitely bring more prestige and larger crowds to the concerts. He was awarded fourteen concerts for the summer of 1934 and was promised many more for 1935. The 1934 series started June 21 and ran until July 15. Fifty-one concerts were assigned to him in 1935, running from June 20 through August 17. In these two series, the band performed in Burnet Woods, Turkey Ridge, and in Eden, Lytle, Washington, Ault, Northside, McKinley, Mt. Echo, South Fairmont, and Inwood Parks.

For the park series, the band was expanded from twenty-two to thirty-two players, and it did not take the public long to discover that Henry Fillmore was on the scene. The crowds were huge. It is perhaps poetic justice that many of the concerts which Henry conducted would ordinarily have been conducted by Walter or Charles Esberger, his successors as leader of the Syrian Temple Shrine Band, and with whom there previously had been unpleasant relations. Walter Esberger was also a composer of marches, and a study of his programs shows that he almost never played any of Henry's music. Henry's friends who played in Esberger's band resented this. On the other hand, Henry showed his magnanimity by programming Esberger's. He was not a believer in professional jealousy and tried his best to present what he thought the public would like.

The thirty-two piece band was made up of the finest professional musicians he could find, and those who had not previously worked for him learned that his concerts were fun to play because the audiences were more receptive. Sousa had died in 1932, and Henry was often referred to as his successor. While this might have been overstating, Henry was exceedingly popular, and people flocked to see him. He knew that audiences liked a good show, not only in performance but in appearance, so he insisted that the band members keep their uniforms neat and clean. The uniforms were the standard Local 1 black uniforms with black velvet cuffs and Local 1 emblems on the collars. Henry loved a sporty uniform, so he wore white. To match the white uniform, he used a long white baton.

In addition to the park concerts of 1934 and 1935, Henry made his last two appearances—his fifth and sixth—at the Cincinnati Zoo. These concerts proved to be as popular as ever. He played some additional concerts in 1935 for a completely different type of audience—at Cincinnati Reds baseball games. Cincinnati introduced night baseball to the major leagues with a game on May 24, 1935. President Roosevelt gave the signal for the lights to be turned on, and Henry Fillmore's band provided the music. The band played all seven of the night games that year.

Henry continued to narrate his concerts, except for those at the ball park. He was as much of an avowed ham as ever, and crowds adored him. There were no gimmicks; his pleasant and highly interesting style of narrating was a product of his own personality and resourcefulness. He seldom repeated himself, even when using the same piece of music at a later date. His flow of speech was homey and clever, and his ad libbing kept the audience relaxed and in good humor at all times.

He used no notes and, to the amazement of both musicians and audience, he used no music. His memory was so incredible that he conducted every piece on his programs without referring to a score. This was his way of communicating, and it was very effective. His relationship with an audience was so close that they sometimes shouted comments back to him. One night in Washington Park, for instance, a group of youths started a disturbance when he announced Suppe's Overture to *Poet and Peasant.* He suddenly realized that "peasant" was an unpopular word to be using during the depression days, so he quickly acknowledged their sentiments and offered an alternate title.

It was Henry's practice, much like John Philip Sousa's had been, to treat each piece of music with respect, whether it be a masterpiece or an insignificant little song. But some pieces of music could be handled humorously, and he had fun with these. The programs had extreme changes of pace, sometimes even within a given piece of music. One of his favorite devices was to make the most of contrasts between loudness and softness, so as to hold the attention of the listeners.

Henry never played his own music exactly as it was published, adding accents and massaging it in many ways so it would sound different from the way others played it. His marches stirred people because he played them at vigorous tempos. He also had a curious practice of omitting the usual four-bar introductions of his marches.

One way Henry teased his audiences was by renaming a piece of music or crediting it to some fictitious composer. For example, if the audience was familiar with one of his pieces, he would say it was composed by someone like "James" (as in James Henry Fillmore, Jr.), or by "Phil Mohr." He would make many outlandish remarks just to spice up a concert, and since he had a fantastically large library of music at his disposal (anything in the Fillmore Music House's stock, in fact) there was no limit to his bag of puns and witticisms. And if he had just composed a new piece and had not yet given it a title, he would call it by perhaps a dozen different names—anything that came to his mind befitting the occasion.

To create local interest, Henry programmed his own pieces and those of numerous other Cincinnati composers. He played quite a few of Stephen Foster's songs, partly because they were well liked, but also because people knew that Foster had spent time in Cincinnati and had met his wife there. Now and then he would toss in a piece for his own amusement; he played "Meet Me in St. Louis" quite a bit just because he had met Mabel there.

He continued his generous practice of inviting guest conductors, much to the delight of concert goers. Dr. Charles Benter was one of his favorites. Benter was Director of the U.S. Navy Band in Washington and had been one of the ABA founders. He was a close friend of Henry's and made it a point to pass through Cincinnati while on vacation each year. They were also drinking buddies down through the years, and it was an old ABA convention story that "Fillmore and Benter held up lampposts all over the United States."

This was the period of history when professional bands were fast disappearing. Their function was, in many ways, taken up by school bands. There were many other reasons for the demise of the professional band, such as the introduction of radio, sound movies and the general mobility of the population which was made possible by the automobile. But Henry had still another reason: too much tradition and not enough showmanship. This, he said, was why dance bands were becoming so popular; at least they offered individuality.

Henry Fillmore's concerts were not commonplace, however; there was standing-room-only when he made an appearance. In fact, people would be seated in the grass and on every available bench within hearing range. If a person wanted a good seat at one of Henry's concerts, it was necessary to arrive at least half an hour early. He had that individuality he spoke of, as well as a winning personality, and long before the word "charisma" was so widely used, Henry had it.

44   FOUNDER'S END

Henry's 1935-36 winter vacation in Florida was shorter than the year before because of several interruptions. First, he came back north to judge at the National High School Band Contest on the campus of the University of Illinois early in January, 1936. He made arrangements for the annual Board of Directors meeting of the Fillmore Brothers Company to be held as he passed through Cincinnati on his way back to Florida to avoid making another trip in that direction.

But he made another trip in that direction anyway. He had been back in Miami for only two weeks when he received a letter from sister Fred saying that Papa had been admitted to Bethesda Hospital in Cincinnati because of internal problems. He had been rather weak at the time of the Board of Directors' meeting, having just recovered from penumonia, but he was able to attend. In another letter several days later, Fred said his condition was serious. Then a telegram came saying that Papa had died at 10:00 p.m. on the night of Friday, February 7, 1936. He was eighty-six years of age.

Henry caught the next train back to Cincinnati so he could be there in time to help make funeral arrangements. Mabel could not make the trip because of illness. Papa was laid to rest at Cincinnati's beautiful Spring Grove Cemetery in a grave beside his beloved Annie, who had preceded him in death by nearly twenty-three years.

Henry's simple explanation of the cause of his father's death was perhaps as accurate as a non-medical person could make: "His innards gave out." He died of internal complications caused by blood clotting, and the technical statement on his death certificate read: "Thrombus of mesentery involving transverse colon and thrombus of right kidney, with enlarged prostate as a contributory cause." No doubt this detailed statement was made possible by the autopsy which was performed.

James Henry Fillmore, Sr., was the first man of the Disciples of Christ denomination to bring it distinction through music. It would be safe to say that during the peak years of his career, a church service of that denomination would not have been complete without a few strains of his music.

Although an accurate catalog of all J.H.'s works has never been compiled, a somewhat complex search at the Copyright Division of the Library of Congress revealed that he composed approximately two thousand gospel hymns, songs and other church works. On over twelve hundred of these, he collaborated with Palmer Hartsough. Additionally, he edited several thousand works of other composers in processing them for publication.

By way of comparison, the number of his original works was approximately three times the combined output of his brothers Charles M. and Fred A. Fillmore.

J.H. composed church music of nearly every category: gospel hymns, anthems, vocal solos, duets, quartets, juvenile cantatas and recitations, pageants and so forth. In addition, he wrote a considerable amount of music for temperance and prohibition causes, such as "Father, Sign the Pledge Tonight." Also numerous patriotic songs. His most famous gospel hymn, still sung in some churches, was "The Beautiful Garden of Prayer." Some of his other popular gospel hymns were "Purer in Heart, O God," "If I Could But Tell All the Glory," "What Is Thy Will for Me?" "Tell It Today," "Only Waiting," "Calling Me Over the Tide" and "I Know That My Redeemer Liveth." He was actively composing in his eighties, and at the time of his death he was still working on the hymnal which Henry had refused to publish some three years earlier!

J.H.'s composing process was quite a bit different from Henry's. Whereas Henry did not use a musical instrument as a composing aid, J.H. would sit down at the piano and start a trial-and-error process of writing as soon as an idea would come to him. Evidently he always composed under his own name, never using a pseudonym. On many of his gospel hymns, just the initials "J.H.F." are given.

Although J.H. and his son Henry were different in many ways, not the least of which was their basic philosophies of life, it is amazing how much they still had in common. Both were honest and possessed unquestioned personal integrity. They were both mild-mannered and inordinately reluctant to be openly critical of others.

Both were generous, often in the extreme; it was an old family story that J.H. would contribute as much as twenty-five hundred dollars a year to Billy Sunday's ministry even if it meant he would have to stop eating!

Both J.H. and Henry were devoted husbands and lovers of children. Both had tremendous drive and were determined to do well at whatever endeavor they undertook. But perhaps the most striking similarities between them were their love of music, the ability to compose fluently and the desire for simplicity and directness in their compositions.

J.H. had always been active in church work. He was an elder first at the Richmond Street Christian Church, then the Norwood Christian Church and finally at the Evanston Christian Church. He was a member of an endless number of committees and held positions on several missionary boards. Although not politically oriented, he was a strong backer. . .yes, a very strong backer. . .of the Prohibition Party. Perhaps his only vice, if it could be called that, was smoking an occasional cigar. This he gave up at the age of sixty, however, after a group of young people at his church debated the issue with him and other church leaders.

Although the gospel hymns of James Henry Fillmore, Sr., are probably more widely used today in denominations other than the one in which he was active all his life, he left it a considerable musical legacy. He was truly a man of God—one who not only professed his religion but lived it as well—and it may conservatively be said that those who were privileged to pass within his sphere of influence received no small amount of inspiration and enlightenment.

45   A CHANGE OF ATTITUDE

Henry had been negotiating with the owners of a home at 3481 Epworth Avenue in Cincinnati just before his father's death, and the sale was consummated in early March, 1936. It was a lovely, spacious three-story house with brick facing, about a mile west of the Harrison Avenue home but still in the Westwood section. Henry and Mabel were destined not to live in the house long, however.

When the terms of J.H.'s will were read, Henry received one of the greatest shocks of his entire life. He had expected that the Fillmore Brothers Company, which constituted the bulk of the estate, would become his sole responsibility, but the will divided it equally among his three sisters and himself. The section of the will pertaining to this read as follows:

> ITEM 3. I give, devise and bequeath all the residue of my estate, real and personal, to my four children, James Henry Fillmore, Jr., Mrs. Mary Fillmore Shipley, Mrs. Fred Fillmore Toll and Mrs. Anna Fillmore Shedd, to be divided among them in equal portions, share and share alike.

The appraised value of J.H.'s estate, at the time of his death, was $21,220.81. This included five hundred and eighty shares of Fillmore Brothers stock.

If J.H. had died thirty years earlier, Henry would have thought nothing of an equal distribution of the estate. But in 1936, the situation was quite different; had it not been for Henry's published music, the company would have collapsed many years earlier. Getting into the band and orchestra field had been his idea, and his theory about the advisability of diversifying and making a transition into this more profitable line of business had proved to be correct. Without Henry, his concept and his creations, there would have been no company to divide.

No matter what line of reasoning he applied, he could not understand his father's rationale; of course his sisters were entitled to equal shares of his money and personal property. But equal shares of the business too? He wondered why his father would have wanted the sisters to be owners of an establishment they had never become involved with.

Henry was more than baffled; he was embittered. He tried to conceal his feelings, but friends who knew him well realized that the situation preyed upon his mind; he kept bringing up the subject at unexpected times. And he frequently used strong descriptives, such as "cheated out of my inheritance." It was as though he was hoping someone would explain it all to him. No one could, however, and there was very definitely some coolness in family circles at that time.

The will had been drawn up nearly seven years earlier, but conditions had not changed much since that time except that business was slightly better. Henry was named sole executor, and this upset him even more. What irritated him most of all, however, was a second will which had somehow been invalidated. Although he spoke of this often, it is nowhere to be found today. No one knows what the terms of that will might have been, exactly when it had been drawn, or what happened to it.

The immediate—and permanent—result of his disillusionment was that he practically lost interest in the business and spent less time in the store than ever before. He was, however, concerned about providing steady employment for the employees who had been so faithful for so many years. He collected royalties on his music just the same as all the other composers on the list, and since the business was in good hands why should he interfere? His sisters owned three-fourths of the business and were not required to be present, so why should he?

Henry was still president of the company and as such had an obligation to keep it intact. He would do whatever was necessary to assure that.

SIX MONTHS TO LIVE

Henry conducted the last of his Cincinnati park concerts in the summer of 1936, after which the famous Fillmore Band was no more. There were only thirteen concerts, starting July 16 and ending August 9. To fulfill these engagements it was necessary to miss the annual ABA convention, which conflicted with the schedule. He preferred not to travel, because he was feeling exceptionally tired.

There were the usual Fillmore attractions, such as the guest conductors and soloists. The popular Ruth Best normally sang most of the vocal solos, but this year Henry invited his cousin Annette Fillmore Manning to sing with the band on two occasions. Annette drew enormous crowds, partly because of the popularity she enjoyed through her regular WLW radio programs. Henry was quite proud of Annette, who had a silky lyric soprano voice and later sang regularly over WOR in New York. She subsequently achieved considerable distinction as a music educator. Henry was also proud of Annette's older sister, Hildegarde Fillmore Smith, Associate Editor of McCall's magazine and a lecturer on beauty and fashion. Chalma, the younger sister of Annette and Hildegarde, was the inspiration for Henry's "Chalma" waltz. Their father was L. Challen Fillmore, treasurer of the Fillmore Brothers Company.

The only other concerts Henry conducted before leaving for Florida in October were guest appearances in Columbus, Ohio, on August 17, and Lawrenceburg, Kentucky, on September 19. For both of these concerts he utilized the talents of Luise Reszke and other soloists of the Fillmore Band.

Henry and Mabel came back north for the eighth annual ABA convention, held in Milwaukee March 5-7, 1937, after which they returned to Cincinnati. Henry then completed work on some new Harold Bennett pieces so that another collection, the Bennett Band Book No. 4, could be released in time for the next school year. There were sixteen pieces in this book, most of which were composed in the spring of 1937. These Bennett pieces constituted Henry's final period of concentrated composition; for the remainder of his life he did not compose more than three pieces in any one year.

The Bennett Band Book No. 4 was the last of the Harold Bennett music.

Looking back on the Harold Bennett music, we see the typical Henry Fillmore humor coming through. "Have a Little Fun" is a good example; in this piece all the instruments get in some clever licks, with instructions for the comedians of the band to do their thing. "Don-a-Do-Dat" is another, inspired by Mabel and a meddlesome little neighbor girl; it has rhythm suggestive of an adult pointing an admonishing finger and saying, "No, no, no, no. . .don' a do dat!" "Put and Take" was arranged so that the predominant sections of the band or orchestra drop out, exposing the weaker sections. "Eels" features some easy trombone smears and was described as a "trombone zipper."

Henry tried to make the titles interesting, appropriate and sometimes descriptive. "The Little Gray Church" was intended to sound organ-like; "Little Arab" uses a tom-tom and has a Near East flavor, while "Havana" is definitely Latin; "Little Rastus" is a rag; the trio of "Sola" was built around the notes "sol" and "la"; "Military Escort" makes use of bugle calls; "Proclar" projects the clarinets, and so forth.

Some have general titles without specific meaning, such as "Normal," "Success," "Courage," "Advance" and the tongue-in-cheek "Bliss Eternal." Others have definite purposes, such as "At Sight," which was intended for sight reading at contests. Three were named for relatives: "Annette," "Chalma," and "Aunt Hannah." Others were named for friends: "Marie" (Grau) and "Vera" (Marie's daughter). "Norma's Dream" was Henry's joke on Norma Schott, who was frequently telling about the interesting dreams she had. There were also some enigmatic titles which Henry did not explain, such as "Delmar," "Biga" and "Sabo."

When Mabel and Henry went south in the fall of 1937 for their annual winter vacation, they leased an apartment in Miami Beach rather than in Miami, at 8920 Byron Avenue. This was in the Surfside section, just two blocks from the ocean.

They were finding more and more of their friends

from the north in the Miami area, one being a young man by the name of Stan Dulimba, whom Henry had met in Cincinnati. Stan was a professional musician but had given up his job for a music scholarship at the University of Miami. He was quite a Henry Fillmore devotee and was responsible for a very important event in Henry's life.

Stan sang Henry's praises to Walter Schaeffer, director of the University of Miami Band, but with little apparent effect. Schaeffer was such a lover of Sousa's marches that he looked upon most other march writers as imitators. Further, he did not have a broad knowledge of Henry's trombone smears, thinking they were just junk music. As a whole, he believed Henry's music was the type which would soon be forgotten.

Stan's father was a good friend of Schaeffer's, so Stan felt free to offer some polite corrections. He told Schaeffer that his concept of Henry's music was ill-founded and that he was missing a wonderful opportunity by not having Henry guest-conduct the University of Miami Band. He pointed out that Henry vacationed every winter in the Miami area and that there would be no travel expenses.

Schaeffer listened but did not act immediately. Stan was most insistent, and Schaeffer reluctantly invited Henry to come work with the band at a rehearsal and consider the possibility of conducting at one of their concerts. Henry was aware of the situation and brought along some of his best music. At the first rehearsal, Schaeffer got the surprise of his life; after half an hour, Henry had the students playing with greater enthusiasm than ever before!

Henry enjoyed this rehearsal as much as anyone, and a concert appearance was arranged. The concert was a delight to the audience, and Henry was invited back at a later date. Stan Dulimba quietly told his friends, ''I knew it would happen exactly that way.'' Meanwhile, Henry was itching for more of the same. The University of Miami Band members were somehow different from those of the few college bands he had led up north.

This was the first of three incidents which convinced Henry that Miami might be a nice place to make his permanent home. The second came when his friend John Heney invited him to attend a meeting of the newly formed Florida Bandmasters Association over the Thanksgiving weekend in 1937. Henry accepted and conducted a "clinic" band which was a two-day all-star band organized to read through and study new music. He enjoyed this very much, noting that the Florida school directors were the most cordial lot of directors with whom he had ever been associated. Henry's unassuming manner and the way he inspired the students led several of them to tell him they wished he could be in Florida all the time. John Heney, in particular, was especially grateful and asked Henry to be a judge in the upcoming state high school band contest.

The third incident suggesting that Florida might be a nice place to live came in the summer of 1938 after Henry and Mabel returned to Cincinnati. This was a most unpleasant incident, and it came in the form of a gloomy, moribund prediction.

Henry had caught a nasty cold when he returned from the ABA convention at the University of Illinois on March 21-24. He recovered from the cold but continued to feel run down. His doctor suggested that any man fifty-six years old with this type of problem should have a complete physical examination.

The results of the examination, conducted at a local clinic, were grim indeed. Henry had a serious heart problem and was advised to see a specialist immediately. The name of the clinic and the specialist are not known today, because Henry kept all this to himself. The specialist told him that he had six months, or possibly as long as a year, to live.

He was told that he was now paying the price for having lived under such severe stress most of his life. If all sources of further stress were removed, he could possibly live longer than the predicted time. It was not likely, however. At any rate, he was advised to change his pattern of living completely and to take immediate retirement.

The doctor said that cold weather was especially hard on people with his condition and told him bluntly that moving to a warm climate was the only thing which would offer any hope. Henry had just the place in mind.

There would have been no point in beating around the bush, so Henry went directly home and broke the news to Mabel. He said it was probable that she would soon be a widow and that they needed to talk over several things.

Henry wanted to know if she could be happy living in Florida for the rest of her life, or at least until he died. She assured him that she could. She had made new friends there and knew others from the North who had settled there. She liked the climate, and although they had not been there during the hot summer months she believed she could adjust.

As for Henry, he also liked the climate, the people, the University of Miami Band, the Florida bandmasters, the horse races, the dog races and the general relaxed atmosphere. But he believed he would not live long enough to enjoy much of this, so Mabel's happiness was foremost in his mind. He would miss the cultural atmosphere of Cincinnati, but then again he could think of a few things about Cincinnati which brought unhappy memories—such as the heartbreak of giving up his Shrine Band, Mike's tragic death, and the disappointment of his father's will.

It was settled. They would move to Florida with the hope that Henry could live longer than six months.

The Epworth Avenue home in Cincinnati was sold, and the furniture was put into storage. Henry bought a new Ford coupe. There was no sense buying an expensive car, because it would be harder for Mabel to sell when he died; she did not drive. They bade friends farewell, telling them absolutely nothing about Henry's short life expectancy.

Again they moved into the furnished apartment at 8920 Byron Avenue in Miami Beach. This time, they leased rather than rented, apparently with an option for sixty-day renewals. Henry wanted to eliminate the possibility of having to move out when he became terminally ill.

With only a short time to live—supposedly—Henry thought he would compose one last march. He wanted to salute the city of so many fine acquaintances where he and Mabel had spent most of their winters during the past decade. The piece was called "Miami" and dedicated "To the Folks of Greater Miami, Florida." It did not have a drab air of finality, as one might expect; it was actually one of his more melodious and dynamic marches!

With the Fillmore business in the good hands of such stalwart gentlemen as Herman Ritter, Bill Jung, Louis Hahn and Charles Martin, with no band concerts to prepare for, and with no future plans for composing, Henry was more relaxed than at any other time in his entire adult life. After having been in Florida for three months, he was feeling better, not worse. Mabel was the one who was suffering, not Henry. She had a lingering cold and a terrible cough, aggravated by the many cigarettes she smoked in her nervousness. Henry knew that the thought of being a widow weighed heavily on her mind, and the only thing he could do about it was to be optimistic. He tried to comfort her by declaring that he would surely prove the doctor's prediction to be false.

Miami appealed to him more than it had before. He resigned himself to the fact that it would be his home for the rest of his short life and took a greater interest in local affairs. The Miami of the late 1930's was much different from the Maimi we know today. It was surrounded by wilderness, with few railroads and no four-lane highways connecting it with other parts of the state. It was rapidly outgrowing its small city image, however.

There had been a dramatic boom in the 1920's, only to be quelled by the tragic hurricane of 1926, but still Miami's population doubled in the 1930's (and doubled again in the 1940's). One way the city differed from Cincinnati was that it grew in an outward direction, not upward. It had grown so fast that in some sparsely settled areas there were still numerous wild animals—including some sizable rattlesnakes.

Business was good in Miami; it was a city of many luxurious hotels, occupied seasonally, and the effects of the depression had hardly been felt. It is amusing that one very small part of the business community was shaken when Henry Fillmore moved to town: the music stores. A rumor had gotten started that he had come to Miami to open a huge new music store which would surely put all the others out of business. He quickly put an end to that rumor.

The only business Henry was concerned with was the race track business! Parimutuel betting had been legalized in 1931, and Hialeah Race Track was one of his favorite spots. He frequented Hialeah two or three times a week during the racing season. The race track at Tropical Park was another of his favorite spots. He saw sport in gambling on the horses—one day he won over five thousand dollars—but he steered clear of the gambling casinos. He also enjoyed the greyhound races. Everyone heard about his winnings, but he was reticent and sometimes sullen when he lost. Often he would place bets as high as a hundred dollars.

Toward the end of the 1938-39 winter, Henry was feeling quite well. He had already lived longer than his allotted lower limit of six months and certainly did not feel like a dying man. He even planned to attend the ABA convention at Fort Dodge, Iowa, in February, but after hearing on the radio that Iowa had been the victim of a heavy snowstorm, he decided against it.

Henry missed his music activities so much he could restrain himself no longer. He accepted John Heney's invitation to judge at the state high school band contest in Orlando the first week of April, 1939. At the insistence of an old friend, Ernie Pechin, he stayed at his home in Orlando. Ernie, another former cornet soloist of Sousa's Band, was to conduct the All State Band that year.

Ernie had a fine sense of humor, and Henry put it to the test after everyone went to bed the night before the All State Band rehearsal. He opened the window on his second floor bedroom and bellowed like a cow. Ernie's window flew open, and he shouted, "Ethel! There's a cow in our back yard!" After the window closed, Henry cut loose again. "MooOOOOooo!" Again Ernie's window opened, and he could find no cow anywhere with his flashlight. Henry did it a third time and then retired for the night.

The next day, when Ernie was rehearsing the band in "The Whistling Farmer Boy," Henry ambled back to the percussion section and came out with his "Moo-OOOOooo!" at an opportune time. Ernie got an enlightened look on his face, stopped the band, and stared back at the chuckling Henry. The band members were puzzled when Ernie said, "If you kids think that's realistic, you ought to hear it in the middle of the night!"

While in Orlando, John Heney told Henry that the DeLand High School Band would be playing in the Orange Bowl Stadium the following November. He explained that the Orange Bowl was getting to be quite a popular football center and that someone needed to compose a first-rate piece of music with "Orange Bowl" in the title. Henry got the hint; his pen had been idle long enough, he decided. He promised to fulfill that need within the next couple of weeks, because John's band had scheduled a concert about then.

Henry's "Orange Bowl" march was played in manuscript form by the DeLand band, first at the May concert and then in the Orange Bowl on November 19, 1939. Three days later it was published, and it has since become one of the most popular of all the Fillmore marches. Like the "Miami" march, it is one of his happiest and most spirited—not bad for a man who was supposed to be on his deathbed!

Henry and Mabel had not been able to attend the first performance of the "Orange Bowl" march at the May concert, because they had driven back to Cincinnati for the annual meeting of the Fillmore Brothers Board of Directors. While there, Henry caught a severe cold and wound up in bed for two days with his chest plastered. "That'll teach me not to leave Florida!" he told friends. Thereafter, it became a habit with him to catch a cold every year when he went north for the business meetings—almost without fail.

They stopped in the mountains of North Carolina for several days on the way back to Florida, just to break up the trip. After returning to Miami they wished they could have stayed in North Carolina, because they both suffered from the heat. If it had not been for the sea breezes and an occasional refreshing swim in the ocean, they might have returned to the mountains for the entire summer. They had done enough driving around for a retired couple, however; their new Ford coupe already had nine thousand miles on it.

On Thanksgiving Day, 1939, four days after John Heney's DeLand band had performed in the Orange Bowl, he presented a concert in DeLand. Henry drove up to conduct a few numbers, and he was welcomed royally—John was very good at making flowery introductions. At the end of the concert, Henry was presented a toy piano as a token of the band's appreciation. This piano was to become quite a conversation piece in the years ahead.

Toy or not, the piano was put to good use; it was utilized as a Christmas card every year! Ernie and Ethel Pechin were visiting the Fillmores in Miami during the 1939 Christmas season. On Christmas morning, Henry arose early and started playing "Jingle Bells" on the toy piano. Ernie had his cornet with him, so he joined in. Mabel and Ethel could not sleep with all this going on, so they got up and sang along with them. After playing it a few times, Henry said, "Say, Ernie, that's pretty good. What do you say we serenade the neighbors?" Ernie was game, so they put on their clothes and went out the door.

Henry and Ernie went all around the neighborhood playing "Jingle Bells." Henry would set down the piano, ring a doorbell, then get down on his knees and start playing, with Ernie joining in. Some of the neighbors thought this was a bit nutty at first, but they soon got in the spirit of things.

This was so much fun they went back to the apartment and started calling friends around town—Billy Kopp and some of the local high school band directors. As soon as they would get an answer, they played "Jingle Bells" and hung up without saying a word! Then they called people long distance—John Heney and then several people back in Cincinnati.

This quaint way of saying "Merry Christmas" became a tradition with Henry. Every Christmas morning he would telephone several of his friends, play "Jingle Bells" and hang up without ever identifying himself. When word finally got out about who was doing it, people would eagerly await a call. It became quite an honor to receive the call because only his closest friends received his unique "Christmas card." Some might not have appreciated it as much as others, however, because sometimes he started out as early as 5:00 a.m.!

When the end of 1939 rolled around, Henry had already lived several months longer than the specialist back in Cincinnati had predicted. And he was still going strong.

48 UNCLE HENRY, THE CLEANUP MAN

At fifty-seven, Old Man Fillmore concluded that he would somehow live to be even older, so he moved three blocks away to a more spacious apartment at 8801 Emerson Avenue. This was in the summer of 1939. He and Mabel lived there for nine months and then moved back to a still nicer apartment just two blocks up the street from where they had lived before, to 9124 Byron Avenue. This second-floor apartment was more luxurious than the others he had occupied in the past, with a balcony all around and a garage and storage area below.

Henry was cultivating several lasting friendships among the five high school band directors in the Greater Miami area. His friend Stan Dulimba had graduated from the University of Miami and accepted the position as director at Miami Jackson High School. Stan invited him to be guest conductor at one of his concerts, and he was such a hit with the students that they began to call him "Uncle Henry." The name stuck like glue.

Stan was probably Henry's best friend in the Miami area until entering military service in the spring of 1942, at which time Henry threw a wingding of a party for him. He had accompanied Henry on many trips to the race track, acting as his page boy and making regular visits to the hundred-dollar window.

At Stan's going-away party, one of those who enjoyed the liquid refreshments so much he never figured out how he got home was Fred McCall, the highly effective and personable band director at Miami Edison High School. Henry and Fred had met at the Thanksgiving weekend meeting of the Florida Bandmasters Association in 1937 and became fast friends. Fred invited Henry to conduct his band, and this was just the beginning of a very close relationship. Henry was in constant touch with Fred each football season, because Fred was in charge of all high school band activities at the Orange Bowl.

Uncle Henry, as he was lovingly called by school musicians, became a legendary figure in Florida. He was often called the "patron saint of Florida school bands"—and with good reason.

Ringling Brothers and Barnum & Bailey Circus for two years; percussionist with the Sells-Floto Circus for three years; and percussionist with numerous other professional groups. He was a fabulous musician and expected perfection from his students. He was so dedicated to this end that he gave private instruction to every member of his school band at no cost. When Henry conducted John's ninety-piece band he remarked that it was so well trained there were a hundred-and-eighty eyes glued to him and that he had better not make any mistakes himself!

John Heney was an energetic man who never held just one job at a time. He also directed the band at Stetson University in DeLand and edited all the percussion music published by the Fillmore Brothers. He was also active in numerous professional organizations and was President of the Florida Bandmasters Association from 1938 to 1941.

John insisted that Henry attend all FBA meetings, and Henry became so enthusiastic about the organization that he advanced money to help finance the early state high school band contests. He noted that the contests were different from those up north because there was less back-biting and dog-eat-dog activity; everyone seemed to be pulling for everyone else.

At the time Henry came to Florida, many towns had no music programs. Henry and John had discussed this

Still another bandmaster friend whom Henry found in the Miami area was Al Wright, the brilliant, innovative, young music educator at Miami Senior High School. Henry adopted his band too, so to speak, and over the years Henry was called upon to conduct at many of their concerts.

Al was one of the participants at an important meeting Henry held with the Florida Superintendent of Schools in which high school band improvements were discussed. Al and several others made presentations telling how marching band served the same purpose as physical training. As a result of this meeting, students were given physical training credit for marching band rehearsals. With the regular band periods added to this, students could then have two band rehearsals a day rather than one. This was, without a doubt, one of the best things that ever happened to the high school music program in the state of Florida.

By far the most significant association Henry had with any Florida bandmaster between the time he moved to Florida and America's entry into World War II was with John J. Heney of DeLand. John was one of the most remarkable music educators this country has ever known and never ceased to amaze Henry with his achievements. Henry was extremely pleased to align himself with a man of this caliber, and what these two men accomplished together during this period borders on the miraculous.

John carried the excellence of his professional musician's experience into the classroom. His credentials were impressive: percussionist and xylophone soloist with Sousa's Band for six years; percussionist with the

John Heney (right) is seen here with his "cleanup man" (Henry, left), who appeared gratis as guest conductor at the schools where he and John helped get bands started. Center is Herman Ritter, Henry's colleague at the Fillmore Bros. Co. for 45 years and a frequent visitor at Henry's home in Miami.

at length when Henry was in DeLand for the Thanksgiving concert of 1939. Henry was familiar with the dynamic high school band programs of some of the northern states and said he would like to do something to help the new bands of Florida. That was music to John's ears! As if John did not have enough to do, he said that if he could have Henry's help he would do anything possible to initiate music programs in towns within reasonable driving distances from DeLand. Henry agreed to help him, and the rest is history.

John Heney and Henry Fillmore had much in common, not the least of which was a birthday; they were both born on December 3, John being twenty-one years the younger. They made quite a team. They would go to a town and talk to the city fathers and school administrators about the advantages of a school music program.

Henry was a potent salesman in this regard, because he knew he was preaching the truth. Bands bred discipline, because music required that in abundance; bands instilled school spirit and pride; they livened things at football games and other sporting events; they brought goodwill and an undeniable community pride; they created public interest in school welfare; and bands were good for business. What kind of parades could they have without a school band? And did they now know that a community's music program was a measure of its culture and civic standing?

Henry had contacts all over the United States, and he offered to help find qualified directors. Not only that, but he offered to conduct at some of their concerts—without a fee. Every kid loved a band, he explained. All they needed was the opportunity to participate. He also pointed out that small towns sometimes had better bands than those in big cities because the kids worked harder at it; there were fewer competing activities. "Just look what John Heney has done in DeLand, and he started with absolutely nothing!"—that was his clincher.

These were the days before superhighways, and travel was tedious and slow through the many small towns of Florida. Sometimes John would go by himself, and sometimes Henry would accompany him. But eventually Henry would follow up, and he referred to himself as "Heney's cleanup man." A typical town sequence would start with a display of instruments in a drug store window appealing for local support and end up with Henry Fillmore in town working with the band at rehearsals for a day or two and then appearing as guest conductor.

Henry lived up to his promises, and when the word was spread that a famous composer would be in town to conduct the newly formed high school band, it had an electrifying effect. He would often make a short speech appealing for money to help the music program, and he had such a compelling manner that when the money and pledges were counted the bandmaster was usually very pleasantly surprised.

Audiences in these towns fell in love with Henry, but not nearly as much as the students did. They caught on to him fast. He had a way with high school musicians. He was jovial and fun-loving; he was friendly and so very approachable; he was. . .Uncle Henry! The rapport he had was, to say the least, astonishing. He worked the students hard but always stopped long enough to tell some interesting stories. They were cognizant of his stature in the music world and were fascinated. He gave many good words of advice, always using the most positive of approaches, and he usually wound up by saying, "Always listen to your bandmaster!" He encouraged them on to greater things, and a band would receive such an uplift that things would not be the same for months afterward.

One might wonder how Henry Fillmore, after having been conductor of a superb professional band for so many years, could acclimate himself to the amateurish sounds of the high school bands he led. The answer lies in the fact that he too had humble beginnings and realized that they were doing their best. In his own youth he had many belittling experiences. Whereas some conductors become so remote they do not remember or understand, Henry *did* remember and *did* understand. He related to the youthful band members, and it was thrilling for him. He inspired them, and they inspired him.

Henry actually risked sudden death many times while conducting these high school bands. They, of course, did not know of his heart condition, and he simply pretended not to have a problem. When he stepped up on the podium and looked into the faces of young people, he seemed to forget the heart trouble. It was the consensus of those who knew him best that he fully realized the risks but secretly felt that this might be an appropriate way to end his career. Knowing that each trip to a podium might well be his last, he lovingly breathed new life into the music; he put an entirely new meaning into every piece he conducted. These were thrilling moments for the students—experiences they would never forget.

Henry advised John, who in his enthusiasm was also performing xylophone solos whenever asked, to stop performing gratis so much—that it would only sweeten his doctor's pot. But look who was talking!

A study of the record shows that these two spark plugs caused a revolution of sorts in the central and northwestern sections of Florida. Between 1939 and 1942, John Heney and his "cleanup man" actually started thirty-two high school music programs! Pensacola, Panama City, Defuniak Springs and Madison were just a few of the towns benefitting from their combined efforts, and it is noteworthy that nearly every one of the towns still has a thriving school band.

Henry enjoyed all of this immensely. One of his favorite stories was about how the students loved their music so much they would march with their band in a parade even if they did not have shoes to wear. This story originated at a parade in one of the northwestern cities where the members were resting in a park when the bandmaster unexpectedly blew his whistle; they hurriedly tied their shoestrings together, slung their shoes over their shoulders and marched off barefooted. Henry loved to tell that story to audiences. The youngsters went barefooted at home, so why not in a parade? Somehow, these lovable kids reminded him of his

tion of being able to eat her fried shrimp as fast as she could prepare them.

Despite the fact that John continually had his nose to the grindstone, he kept on an even keel with his sense of humor. He delighted in teasing Henry, and of course Henry loved it. Once John wrote back to Herman Ritter at the Fillmore Brothers asking him for a copy of the worst-sounding, most obscure march Henry had ever written. Herman sent back "Lord Baltimore," and John had his band memorize it for a football game Henry was to attend. When they marched down the field playing "Lord Baltimore," Henry said, "Gee, John, that's familiar. Isn't that one of mine?" John replied, "No, Henry, that's a fine march. It couldn't be one of yours!"

There was never a dull moment around John and Margaret's house with Henry there, and he kept the children occupied with funny stories. Other visitors also found him interesting, like a representative of the C.G. Conn Company who once stayed overnight enroute to Miami. Henry knew he was deathly afraid of snakes and made up a story about how the cottonmouths climbed the vines outside John's country home and sometimes slithered in bedroom windows. The Conn man nearly suffocated in the heat that night because he refused to open his window. The next morning they were all sitting on the front porch when a tiny chameleon came up the steps and Henry nearly sent the Conn man into a state of hysteria by yelling, "Look out! There's one of those baby snakes!"

The beauty of Henry's association with the school bands which he helped get off on the right foot was that he was invited back time and again. He enjoyed mixing with the students he had met earlier and never failed to tell them how proud he was of their progress. He enjoyed meeting the younger ones as they came along, and it is not surprising that they seemed to know all about Uncle Henry long before he got there.

Uncle Henry was becoming somewhat of a legend. His grandfather, Augustus Dameron Fillmore, would surely have been proud of him; like A.D., Henry was sowing some seeds of kindness.

John Heney (center) was a dynamo as a music educator, who with Henry started thirty-two music programs in Florida schools. John and his two brothers were charter members of the Florida Bandmasters Assn. All three had been associated with Sousa's Band: Ed (left) as saxophone soloist, John as percussionist and xylophone soloist, and Bill (right) as Sousa's valet.

boyhood days.

One of the fringe benefits of Henry's work with John was that he could always count on the marvelous cooking of John's lovely wife Margaret. Her biscuits and gravy were a special weakness of his, to say nothing of her Southern fried chicken. He also had the reputa-

49   PRESIDENT FILLMORE, KING HENRY

For a man with a serious heart condition who had been advised that he did not have long to live, Henry Fillmore certainly flirted with death more times than reason would normally allow. Not only was he running all over the upper part of Florida with John Heney; he also became involved with schools in the southern part of the state, volunteered to adjudicate high school band contests and allowed himself to be elected President of the American Bandmasters Association.

His doctor in Miami told him he had absolutely no business doing these things. But, as he told John Heney in confidence, if he ever entertained any thoughts of giving up his music activities he would only be fooling him-

self. One who has a great love of music might understand his predicament, but his doctor could not.

As an example of how little he heeded his doctor's advice, consider this: In August of 1941, the doctor told him "Absolutely no more conducting!"—and less than a month later he was back at it again, conducting pep assemblies at Miami Edison High School to teach the students the new pep song he had written for them. This was "Go Raiders Go," dedicated to Fred McCall (unpublished until 1946).

The friendship between Henry and Fred McCall had grown steadily stronger ever since they had met back in 1937. Fred was a pleasant, soft-spoken man who was consistently effective as a music educator. In his own quiet way, he inspired students to achieve great heights through self-discipline. The Edison school complex was a large one, encompassing all twelve grades, and Henry spent a lot of time following Fred around. All the while, he marveled at how smoothly the entire music program was administered.

Fred looked upon Henry as a famous bandmaster and composer, but he also saw in him a father image. He made certain that all his students were exposed to him as much as possible. Henry did not mind this a bit and soon knew every one of Fred's students by name. Fred's wife, Betty, also taught at Edison and enjoyed his company as much as Fred did.

Fred succeeded John Heney as President of the Florida Bandmasters Association, and he encouraged Henry to adjudicate at the state high school band contests because a large number of students could benefit from his knowledge of music. Henry not only obliged but eventually became the coordinator of judges. One of the first things he did was recommend that the FBA hire only the top bandmasters in the country as judges—meaning, of course, men from the ABA. This met with some opposition, because a few thought these high-powered conductors would be too tough on them. But Henry stood his ground, and in the end this paid off handsomely.

Henry was an excellent judge, because he heard things through the ears of a composer as well as through the ears of a conductor. He could detect the tiniest flaw. Although a personal friend of all the school band directors, he played no favorites and was honest, straightforward and fair. If anything he was tougher on those who knew him best because they had easier access to his advice and guidance. After each contest was over, it was his practice to take all the judges out to dinner at his own expense.

Henry's appointment as President of the ABA came in two steps; the President always served a year first as Vice President. He had been elected Vice President at the 1940 convention in Hagerstown, Maryland, and was then elected President at the convention held in Madison, Wisconsin, from February 27 to March 2, 1941. The United States was dangerously close to war as the 1941 convention was held, and there was some concern over whether or not the organization could hold itself together if war came.

The 1941 meeting was important for several reasons, among the most important being the crisis looming ahead if many of its members entered military service. Another threat came in the form of a potential degradation of military bands after military leaders had taken so many years to arrive at a standard instrumentation. This came about because the renowned symphony orchestra conductor Leopold Stokowski had suggested to government officials that radical changes be made in Army band instrumentation.

Henry had profound respect for Stokowski, who was at one time conductor of the Cincinnati Symphony Orchestra, but he was outspoken over Stokowski's ideas. After several lengthy discussions, the ABA drafted a strongly worded letter to Congressional committees and to the Secretary of War. They challenged Stokowski's credentials, saying he was completely out of his element, not being either a bandsman or a military man. They pulled no punches, picking his theories apart and calling them destructive, pointless, unworkable and retrogressive. None of Mr. Stokowski's suggestions were ever adopted.

Being President of the ABA could have been Henry's downfall, because he would have been obliged to make preparations for the next convention in a relatively short period of time. But the next convention was not held until after the war, and Henry's erstwhile duties consisted mainly of writing several hundred letters. An ABA president serves only one year, but since activities were suspended all during the war years, Henry served for six. The 1942 convention was to have been held in Miami, and Henry had grandiose ideas. He even had planned an "ABA day" at the Hialeah Race Track.

ABA President Fillmore was honored by his colleague Karl King, who dedicated one of his marches to him: "King Henry." It was a dandy, and Karl admitted to having spent more time on it than on any of his others, adding that ". . .it was good enough to have been written by Henry himself." Despite his extraordinary efforts, the march was not regarded as his best; nothing would ever replace his "Purple Pageant" or "Barnum and Bailey's Favorite." Henry was a bit slow in returning the compliment; his march dedicated to Karl was published posthumously. Karl's wife, Ruth, incidentally, was one of Henry's favorite ladies; she had been a circus calliope player.

At the Madison convention, Henry asked one of the ABA members, Otto Kraushaar, who had left the music education field to become a representative of the C.G. Conn Company, if he missed being away from school music. Otto said he had and inquired as to Henry's reason for asking. Henry then told him that an experienced school band director was needed for Lake Wales, a nice little Florida town. Otto was definitely interested and said he would think it over.

Henry knew from talking to school officials and others at Lake Wales that they would provide adequate community support, or else he would not have approached a man of Otto's stature. With Otto's diversified background, he would be the ideal man for the position. As a professional musician, he had played bassoon with Sousa's Band for four years, and it was a fact of the music world at that time that anyone who was good enough to have played with Sousa's Band would qualify for a job almost anywhere.

Otto had also played with numerous other professional organizations. In addition, he had a wealth of experience as a music educator in Wisconsin and Indiana and had been ranked (by the *School Musician* magazine) as one of America's ten top school bandmasters. Otto liked the town and its people, so he accepted the position in August of 1941. Thus began another one of Henry's beautiful relationships with school bandmasters, and we shall learn more of Otto Kraushaar in later chapters.

1941 was an unforgettable year for Henry as far as his professional activities were concerned, but his friends in Miami remembered it as the year he was almost lost at sea. One summer night the heat was too much for him, and he left the apartment alone to spend the night on the houseboat of a friend who was vacationing up north. Somehow, the boat broke loose from its mooring during the night, and Henry drifted out to sea while soundly asleep. Mabel went to call him for breakfast the next morning, but the boat was somewhere out over the horizon! She was frantic and called the Coast Guard. They found him about nine miles out. He was thankful for being rescued, and he told his rescuers, "I didn't mind so much not having a radio, but I was out there all that time with no gin!"

Henry was certain, by the summer of 1941, that he would live to a ripe old age. The lease was running out on his apartment, so he elected to buy a house. He chose a house which was being built not far from the center of Miami, next to the James Deering estate; the address was 3110 Miami Court. The new house was charming and very solidly constructed but was not presumptuous by any means.

While he was moving in during early October, Mabel went to Cincinnati to take their furniture out of storage and arrange for shipment to Miami. Henry said he did not care what she sent down or left behind as long as his prized grandfather's clock was on the truck. Most everything was shipped except for his baby grand piano, a Kurtzman with a player piano attachment, which he sold to his cousin Annette Fillmore Manning. While Mabel was away, Henry drove up to Lake Wales and dropped in on Otto Kraushaar to see if he was happy in his new position.

Henry and Mabel bought their last home in 1941, an attractive but modest home in Miami next to "Vizcava," the James Deering estate. Behind the house was a wilderness, where Henry made friends with numerous wild animals.

Henry's last adventure of 1941 was playing Santa Claus at a Christmas party in Billy Kopp's home. Kopp chose him because of the similarity between his figure and Santa Claus', of course. He was in his costume when he stopped at a gas station and was quickly surrounded by about thirty boys and girls. He did not want to leave them without a treat, so he got out of his car, opened the trunk where his toy piano was, played "Jingle Bells" for them, and left.

50   WAVES TO LADIES, IRKS F.D.R.

Henry was seeing quite a bit of his long-time friend Augie Schaefer, who had moved to Miami after an unfortunate series of financial reverses and professional setbacks in Cincinnati. Henry felt obligated to find him a school bandmaster's position in or near Miami, because he had encouraged him to make the move. He felt further obligated because he had been partially responsible for shortening Augie's career as a trumpet and cornet player. At one of Henry's last concerts in Cincinnati, he had swung his long baton around and cracked Augie across the upper lip. Augie was never able to play as well after that.

Henry had painted a rosy picture of Florida. But after Augie relocated, the bottom nearly fell out of his already troubled world. Although he had a wealth of professional experience and had taught trumpet pedagogy on the college level, he could not obtain a high school band director's job for the simple reason that he lacked a degree in music! He was further frustrated to learn that there would be a delay before he could perform as a professional musician in the Miami area because of a union requirement on the length of residency.

It seemed ridiculous that a man with Augie's credentials could not find immediate employment anywhere he wished. He had taught at the Cincinnati Conservatory of Music, the College of Music of Cincinnati and Miami University (of Ohio); he had been associated with the Cincinnati Symphony Orchestra for twenty-five years, part of the time as principal trumpeter; he had been a staff conductor at WLW, solo cornetist of Fillmore's Band, and had performed with or conducted many other professional organizations. In addition, he had numerous published works to his credit. Henry helped the situation somewhat by engaging him to edit and arrange music for Fillmore Brothers publications, and by helping him to get established as a private teacher. The war soon caused a shortage of school band directors, however, and Augie eventually found his way back into the music education field; he taught in the Miami school system and also at the University of Miami.

Henry was also instrumental in Augie's appointment as conductor of the Mahi Temple Shrine Band of Miami in 1941, a position he held until his death fourteen years later. Henry had not transferred his Shrine membership from Cincinnati, but after Augie was appointed leader of the band he often came to rehearsals and concerts to conduct a few numbers. Henry was, however, active in the fun-loving Jesters, another Shrine auxiliary unit.

He enjoyed the company of the Jesters so much he gave his teeth for them! Not willingly, however. At the initiation ceremony, members poured liquor all over him. On his way home, he was (mostly) sober, and his car was struck by another. The impact knocked him unconscious, and he lost seven teeth. Because of the strong aroma of liquor, he had some explaining to do when the police responded to the emergency call! This was one incident Henry never discussed with anyone. It was necessary to have the remainder of his teeth pulled, and he was fitted with dentures.

Henry would have loved to have traveled more for guest conducting appearances, but his health would not permit it. Had it not been for the advent of airline travel, he would not have made the few out-of-state trips he did make before all travel was restricted because of the war. The three most noteworthy trips of the early 1940's were festivals he conducted in Fort Thomas, Kentucky (May, 1941), Winona Lake, Indiana (July, 1941) and Enid, Oklahoma (April, 1942). He also made a short trip to Cuba with Fred McCall's Edison High School Band in March, 1942. At the Winona Lake festival, he had a reunion with his old friend Homer Rodeheaver. Rodeheaver led the singing and also preached at one of the church services.

After the United States entered World War II in December of 1941, travel was severely limited. Henry's travel was confined mostly to the southern and central sections of Florida and to Cincinnati for the annual Board of Directors meetings of the Fillmore Brothers Company. As a substitute for being where the action was, he spent more time listening to the radio. To his delight, there were many broadcasts by various bands of the armed forces. One program he particularly liked was that of the Philadelphia Navy Yard Band, which often featured the phenomenal cornet soloist Leonard B. Smith. Many times he telephoned Smith to compliment him on the programs. This was a magnificent band, made up of some of the finest musicians in the country and sometimes conducted by Eugene Ormandy, Conductor of the Philadelphia Orchestra. Henry once commented to Smith, "You're so perfect you'll ruin it for the rest of us!"

Although sixty years old, quite a bit overweight and handicapped by a serious heart disorder, Henry attempted to enlist in the Army in the summer of 1942! Howard Bronson, the noted bandmaster and former Sousa Band clarinetist, had an important administrative post in Washington and was recruiting bandmasters for Army bands. He requested an official waiver on Henry's health and had tentatively offered him a captaincy at a salary of $3800 per year plus travel expenses.

It was first necessary for Henry to undergo a physical examination in Miami, and, as might be expected, the doctor put an end to his dream. Henry explained that he would be serving in a soft administrative position, but the doctor was totally unsympathetic. The results of the physical examination were so bad that Henry voluntarily wrote to Bronson asking him to forget the matter. He remarked in letters to John Heney that many of his friends had strongly suggested that he not enlist. In one letter, dated August 16, 1942, he said, "When you play a Fillmore march, think of Old Hen wanting to do something in the emergency but has to be content with watching the parade go by."

If by some miracle Henry had been accepted by the Army, he would surely have ended up in an Army hospital; his physical condition became complicated by a chronic congestive lung problem. The doctor had detected it at the physical examination and had advised him to seek treatment, but he did nothing about it until he had no other choice. Late in October, 1942, he was admitted to Phillip's Hospital in Miami, where he was bedridden for a few days and then put on outpatient status for another three weeks.

It was not necessary for Henry to become a military figure to stir things up; his music spoke for him. His marches were used all over the world by bands of the armed forces, particularly "Americans We," "Men of Ohio," and "Military Escort." His new "U.S. of A. Armed Forces" (1942), however, which was written for parade reviews, did not find the mark. He deliberately sacrificed melody in favor of mechanical rhythm, and the piece was regarded as very ordinary and decidedly not one of his better efforts.

One of his arrangements became the subject of controversy: the 1934 version of "The Star Spangled Banner." He had spiced it up by inserting trumpet flourishes in the part that goes, ". . .and the rocket's red glare," and tradition-minded military bandmasters declined to adopt this arrangement. Most people might be inclined to consider this a trivial matter, but leaders of the premier service bands in Washington have always been touchy on the subject; for the most part, they have abstained from any frills. In fact, they are so conscientious about the performance of the national anthem they assume an almost possessive stand.

The new director of the U.S. Navy Band (Charles Brendler, who succeeded Charles Benter, Henry's close friend), however, happened to like Henry's arrangement. When the band played it at the White House on the occasion of a visit by Queen Wilhelmina of the Netherlands in August of 1942, President Roosevelt was displeased. He later heard it played by another Navy band and subsequently issued an order that all bands of the U.S. Navy use more conservative versions. The President might not have paid much attention to the matter had he not been urged by bandmasters of other branches of the service.

Henry's final musical contribution to the war effort came in the fall of 1942 in the form of a march called "Waves," which was based on the song "Sobre las Olas" ("Over the Waves"). This was inspired by four Waves (Women Accepted for Volunteer Emergency Service) of the U.S. Navy who were temporarily living in the bungalow next door to him. They were stationed in Miami as office workers, and the Navy leased the bungalow for the summer because of a shortage of military housing facilities.

The march received its first public hearing in early October at a concert by the Norfolk (Virginia) Navy Yard Band. Their new assistant was John Heney. John had enlisted in the Seabees, but when Navy officials in Washington discovered this, he was involuntarily transferred to the Navy as a bandmaster! John invited Henry up to Norfolk to conduct the premiere of "Waves," but

Henry could not get a train ticket because of wartime travel regulations. When John learned of this he spoke to his commanding officer, an admiral, and Henry was shortly on his way. True to form, Henry not only paid his own expenses but also made a short speech about how the Waves were helping to win the war.

51   KEEPING THE HOME FIRES BURNING

On New Year's Day, 1943, Henry was master of ceremonies at the annual Orange Bowl game. This was the first of several years he was to act in this capacity. He led the bands in his "Orange Bowl" and "Americans We" marches and "The Star Spangled Banner" (the version with the trumpet flourishes, naturally, since President Roosevelt was not in attendance).

1943 was a year Henry would long remember, because it was during this year that:

a) The mosquitoes in Miami were the worst in history.
b) He experienced his first hurricane.
c) He dug out an ingrown toenail with a razor, making a bloody mess and causing Mabel to become sick to her stomach.
d) Mabel had a nervous breakdown.
e) (c) and (d) brought him many sleepless nights.
f) A four-foot diamondback rattler was run over by a car and crawled to his back yard to die.
g) The Fillmore Brothers building caught fire.

The store fire, in January, was minor; Herman Ritter was working late one evening and caught it before much damage was done. It caused Henry to entertain thoughts of moving the company to a safer, more modern building—at least one with an elevator. At the annual Board of Directors meeting, however, it was decided that business was too bad to warrant the expense.

One of the problems with the business was that new musical instruments could not be obtained because of metal shortages. Used instruments were also scarce, so the Fillmore Music House shelves were nearly bare. But there were many tons of metal music engraving plates on the upper two floors, so Henry looked into the possibility of salvaging some of it to help in the war effort. He, Louis Hahn and Bill Jung took an inventory of all the music and disposed of the plates for music which had not been selling. He remarked afterward that the company made more money from the sale of the zinc plates than they ever made from the music!

Music sales were also down. The government had made heavy purchases of Fillmore Brothers publications at the beginning of the war, but nearly all of the existing military bands were now well stocked with music. Paper was scarce, and new music had to be printed on paper so thin that it did not stand up by itself on music stands. Still another problem was a shortage of qualified employees. In general, the country's labor force was shifting to defense work. The Fillmore Brothers company felt the effects of this, and their staff shrank to fifteen.

As soon as Henry recovered from the usual cold which he caught when returning to Cincinnati, he was back in the swing of things as a guest conductor. When high school band contest time came, the procedures were much different. There was insufficient fuel for the bands to travel to contests, so Henry appointed judges to travel from school to school. This way, the yearly contests were stretched out over a period of several weeks instead of being held on one or two days. This method of adjudicating was used in several states, but in numerous others the contests were suspended for the duration of the war.

The itinerant judge method of adjudicating was a unique experience for student musicians. They prepared as usual, but instead of playing to a live audience they played to empty auditoriums. The only audiences were the judges.

Henry was busy as one of the judges. Part of his 1943 schedule read as follows:

April 13	Ft. Pierce
14	Daytona Beach
15	Orlando
16	Lake Wales
17	Sebring
22	Miami Edison
23	Miami Senior

He was obliged to cancel several other engagements because of Mabel's health, which then improved. She worried more about him than herself.

Mabel was feeling much better by May. Henry provided the incentive by promising to take her to Lake Wales for Otto Kraushaar's spring concert. She had greatly enjoyed the visit with Otto and Fern in the spring of 1942, and this year marked the end of Otto's second year with his "Highlander" Band. The band was coming along very nicely, and Otto was everything the people of Lake Wales had hoped for.

For the first two years, and all succeeding years, Otto's spring concerts were held on Friday nights. Henry and Mabel always showed up early in the week, however. Henry would often visit the classrooms because he enjoyed being with the students. Then after band practice, he would go watch practices of the baseball team or the football team.

By being confined to Miami most of the time, Henry and Mabel began to appreciate the comforts of their new home. The screened-in patio was used often, as was the tiled concrete lawn table under a big umbrella in the back yard. The back yard was very attractive, with several royal palms, four orange, one lemon and two grapefruit trees. Eventually, Henry had a masonry wall built around the periphery.

The focal point of the house, which came as no surprise to anyone who knew Henry well, was the grandfather's clock situated in the living room where everyone entering the front door would see it. The Fillmores

Henry recommended former Sousa Bandsman Otto Kraushaar as band director for the Lake Wales, Fla., High School. The band became one of the South's finest. Henry had profound respect for Otto, referring to him as "the pro" and conducting each year at his band's spring concert.

had no fancy furniture or decorations; they were not the type to make a show of opulence. Their treasures were instead the mementos of Henry's illustrious career, and he loved to show people the various plaques, scrolls and gifts he had been presented by bands all over America.

Mabel did her own housework and cooking, but she had a cleaning lady, Sarah, to help with the heavy work one day a week. Henry did not care for her; he mentioned from time to time that ". . .all she ever did was crab about anything that came to her mind!" Sarah was called in more often as Mabel grew older, despite Henry's objections. She was eventually replaced by Anabelle, who was much more pleasant and industrious.

The neighborhood was peaceful and quiet, but to prevent burglaries and vandalism the residents engaged a security man who made nightly rounds to check windows and doors, unfamiliar automobiles and so forth. In the years they lived at 3110 Miami Court, the home was never broken into, despite their being gone quite a bit.

The huge lot behind the Fillmore house was totally undeveloped, somewhat resembling a jungle and abounding with wildlife. This delighted Henry, who still loved animals, and he fed them regularly. He even gave them names and would talk to them, and one by one they learned to trust him: parrots, rabbits, squirrels,

possum and many others. Some said he even fed a rattlesnake! He also had a bird feeder and would watch the birds for hours from the patio.

The way in which Henry made friends with one particular rabbit, which he named Alphonse, epitomized his patience. He tied carrots to a long string, ran the string to a clothesline pulley on the house and back out toward the wilderness. As Alphonse got closer to the carrots, Henry would pull slowly on the string, drawing the carrots closer to him. Every day Alphonse got a little bit closer, and eventually he was eating right out of Henry's hand.

Henry and Mabel loved to entertain company and also took pleasure in dining out, but they also enjoyed a certain amount of quiet. Anniversaries, for instance, were special moments when they often had their simple bean dinner by candlelight. Al Wright told the touching story of how he happened to attend one of these dinners. He dropped in one afternoon after school, and Henry invited him to stay for dinner. Al was more than a little surprised when Mabel set the table for three and then opened a can of beans!

Henry explained that they now considered themselves very fortunate and that the bean dinner was to remind them of the days when they were terribly poor. When they were married in St. Louis back in 1905, their honeymoon had consisted partly of riding a streetcar across town to a small restaurant. When they had paid their streetcar fare, all they could afford was a platter of beans. The sincere act of humility Henry and Mabel displayed that day made a lasting impression on Al—as well as numerous others who had dropped in on them over the years while they were having their anniversary dinner.

Another of Al's favorite stories of this era was about what happened at his Miami Senior High School Band's 1943 spring concert. Henry conducted "Military Escort," and a soldier in the audience came up to him after the concert and said he had been wanting to meet the composer of that famous piece. But then he added, "I don't know whether to kiss you or kill you; every morning at 5:30 I'm blasted out of the sack with that _____ _____thing!"

It was not surprising to see servicemen at high school band concerts—or any other type of entertainment—in Miami in those days. Miami was overrun by armed forces personnel; all the hotels were packed, and even private homes were being rented for housing. Miami was a major naval and aviation center, and both the Army and Navy established training facilities there. What hotel space was not being used for living quarters was being used for classrooms.

During the World War II period, Miami was by no means a typical American city, being much closer to the war than most. It was sobering to know that German submarines were sinking ships rights off the coast, sometimes within sight of the shoreline. Miamians often dashed out in their private boats to rescue survivors of a torpedoed vessel.

There was rationing of all sorts. The 35 miles per hour speed limit forced people to drive slower and save gasoline, oil and rubber. With an allotment of only three gallons of gasoline per week, one could drive so little that getting license plates was hardly worth the investment. Tires were almost impossible to find, and Henry's were bald.

Henry and Mabel walked around town a lot, and because shoes were also scarce they often went barefoot around the house. Buses were sometimes so crowded that awaiting passengers were passed up. It seemed that anything not rationed was hard to get anyway, including many foodstuffs, cigarettes, beer and so forth. What really cramped Henry's style, however, was that the race tracks were closed!

In addition to the war woes, Miami had natural disasters. The hurricane of 1943 was bad, but it was mild compared to the one of 1944. The latter stripped Henry's trees, blew water in on the rug and knocked sixty-five tiles off the roof.

Henry suffered a mild heart attack shortly after Thanksgiving. Recovery came quickly, however. Through all of this, he was heard to complain very, very little. He was enough of a patriot to be concerned for others, profoundly remorseful over the thousands of gallant servicemen who were dying in defense of their country—his country.

52   PAHOKEE PRANCER

Reinholdt Schmidt moved in with Henry and Mabel in January, 1945. No one knew what his real name was, but to Henry he was Reinholdt Schmidt. With a name like that he should have come from Cincinnati, but he was just another Miami beagle hound of no particular distinction except that he was yellow, knock-kneed and a fine watchdog.

Reinholdt was not invited; he merely showed up at the Fillmore front door one day and wanted in. Mabel insisted that Henry give him away, which he did, but Reinholdt returned the next day. His visit lasted for a year, at which time he was run over by a car.

After Mike had been poisoned back in 1932, Henry had said he never wanted another dog. But the fact of the matter is that he would have taken in every stray dog or cat in southwestern Miami if Mabel would have let him. After Reinholdt, the only other animal which might be called Henry's was Walter, a rather wild cat, which never came into the house. No one in the neighborhood could get close enough to feed him but Henry. Walter disappeared in a few months, however, right after the 1945 hurricane.

The hurricane of 1945 was not quite as bad for Miami as the one in 1944, but it was worse south of the city. Navy hangars at Richland Field, which had supposedly been designed for winds of 250 miles per hour, fell apart at 150. Water was once again forced into the Fillmore home, and the roof was again minus some tiles. Miami had now been hit by hurricanes for three consecutive years.

The war was drawing to a close by the spring of 1945, and things were slowly returning to normal. Henry had not conducted for several months, and after leading the Miami Jackson High School Band in May he had severe chest pains and broke out into a cold sweat. For several hours he thought the end had come, but two days later he had recovered. Undaunted, he was ready to put himself to the test again two weeks later.

Two Miami high school bands were emerging as Henry's favorites—Al Wright's Miami Senior High and Fred McCall's Miami Edison. There was a tremendous rivalry between those two schools. Miami Senior had such a powerful football team that it went unbeaten for twenty-eight years! When Al's and Fred's bands put on their halftime shows at a game between their two

schools, it was a sight to behold, with the most interested spectator in the stadium being Henry Fillmore. Al and Fred were, in many ways, students of Henry Fillmore. But when it came to football halftime shows, Henry was a student of theirs. They were both extremely clever and original with their colorful shows. Henry made sure that he advised his bandmaster friends up north to come to one of their games if they wanted to see the ultimate in gridiron pageantry.

Just after the Orange Bowl game on New Year's Day, 1946, Henry suffered from gallstones. But he continued to forge ahead, clearly overextending himself. Two weeks after the gallstone attack, he drove Al and Fred to Sarasota for an FBA meeting and was forced to bed for three days. After exhausting himself at a University of Miami Band concert in March, he was bedfast for two more days. He simply refused to quit, and his heart could take just so much. As he told John Heney (in a letter dated February 6, 1946): "I have some pain there, and no foolin.' "

Airline travel shortened the trips back to Cincinnati for the annual business meetings, and this allowed him more time to spend with his Florida bands. This year, however, he stayed in Cincinnati long enough to be guest of honor at a dinner and concert held by the Syrian Temple Shrine Band. Over thirty members of his 1921-26 band had come back into the fold, and Henry remarked that it was one of the finest Shrine bands he had heard in recent years. He conducted "Golden Friendships" and "Men of Ohio" (what else?) and was given many presents. Just like old times.

Back in Florida, Henry managed to keep himself occupied as a guest conductor, driving around the state in his new Mercury coupe (he had temporarily graduated from Fords). One of the high school bands he added to his list of most interesting bands was Bob Lampi's at Pahokee. Bob was badly in need of more public support. He suggested to his principal and PTA president that he might be able to obtain the services of Henry Fillmore as guest conductor, but they laughed at him. "You must be joking, Bob," they said. "Why would a big name musician like that want to come to a small town like Pahokee?" But Bob had worked with Henry on numerous FBA committees and knew more about Henry than they did.

Of course he would come to Pahokee! All Bob had to do was ask. What could be more fun than making music with young musicians? He and Mabel came to town the day before the concert and stayed at the Lampi household. Characteristically, Henry removed his shoes, made himself at home and benefited from the typical Florida small town hospitality. The townspeople brought in chicken, vegetables, pies, cakes and other foodstuffs. Bob's wife Ilimae prepared what some would classify a feast. Henry made good use of his appetite, as always, having several helpings of Ilimae's biscuits and gravy.

At the first rehearsal, Bob's band had trouble getting into the spirit of the music from *The Student Prince,* but Henry quickly solved that problem. He said, "No, not like *that;* like *this!*" Then he sang the melody and pranced around in front of the band and down the aisle like a chorus girl! They got the idea and tore into the piece with an enthusiasm they had never displayed before.

There was standing room only at the concert the next night. The students had spread the word, and the whole town came out to see the famous composer who had the youngsters so excited. Henry put on quite a show for them, and at the end of the concert he told the audience how wonderful those kids were—and how nice it was going to be when the town supported them. In his speech, he let all the stops out and proved to be irresistible. When the collection was counted, the band had fifteen hundred dollars in cash, checks and pledges. Bob was absolutely flabbergasted. Uncle Henry, the pied piper of Florida bands, had struck again—all for free. In the process, he had gained another lifelong friend.

Among the other bands Henry conducted that spring were Ernie Pechin's in Orlando and Otto Kraushaar's in Lake Wales. Otto's band, incidentally, purchased the chimes Henry had used with the Fillmore Band many years earlier, making him feel quite at home when he conducted the "Highlander" Band—as if he did not already feel at home with Otto around.

Feeling footloose, Henry and Mabel would often start out in their car and drive around Florida with no pre-planned itinerary. The purpose of these jaunts was to call on high school bands—completely unannounced. Henry would listen, conduct a few numbers and offer friendly advice. He became the subject of much talk among Florida bandmasters because of these surprise visits. They were much flattered, to say the least, and after Uncle Henry left, their bands played with more vigor and enjoyed their music more.

It was usually late winter or early spring when Henry did his informal visiting. The students were normally quite serious at this time of the year, more attentive and eager to learn things which would help them do better at the contests. And who knows—the jolly old fat man who was offering them advice might turn out to be the same jolly old fat man who would be judging them at the contest. Yes, Uncle Henry was always very welcome.

Henry not only visited; he had visitors. The summer of 1946 was an especially hectic time at 3110 Miami Court. Relatives and friends from Cincinnati literally descended upon the Fillmores. Henry remarked afterward that his home had seemed like Grand Central Station. He enjoyed company, but there was simply too much that summer. He could not understand why anyone in his right mind would want to come to Miami for a vacation during the hot summer months, but in they came. One possible explanation for the rush was that these people had been unable to travel all during the war and simply had to go someplace. After they had all left, Henry and Mabel fled to the mountains to escape—the mountains of North Carolina, where they stayed for over four weeks. This year, as in most other years, they rented a cottage in the Fontana Dam area.

With the approach of football season, Henry was eager to head for the nearest stadium to see the marriage of his two great loves, sports and music. He was spending more time with Fred McCall, and in the fall of 1946 he wrote the second of his two pieces for Edison High School, a marching song called "Hail! Hail to Edison." This came about after Fred had first tried his hand at composing such a piece himself. He was unhappy with his creation and asked Henry what he might do to improve it. After playing it on the piano, Henry said, "Fred, let's start from the beginning; put that one aside and I'll write you one." The result was "Hail! Hail to Edison," and it became a fine side partner for "Go Raiders Go," which was already being used several times each game.

There was more football in Miami that fall than ever before, because the city now had the Sea Hawks, a professional team in the new All American League. Henry was very enthusiastic over having a professional team in town and even flew to Chicago to see one of the "away" games. He composed a pep song for the team, "Sea Hawks," but it died a natural death at the end of the season; the Sea Hawks lost some $100,000, and the franchise was moved to another city. The problem evidently was lack of interest; there was so much good college and high school football in the Miami area that the professionals had to take a back seat.

Mabel did not share Henry's enthusiasm for football. It bored her terribly, and she never went to a game unless Henry was scheduled to conduct. No doubt she enjoyed his conducting more than anyone in any of his crowds—she was a Henry Fillmore fan through and through. She enjoyed his conducting so much, in fact, that at home when he would be listening to a band play over the radio or on a record, she would say, "Conduct for me, Henry!" He would then pick up his baton and lead an imaginary band—even if there was a house full of company.

"Lassus Trombone" made a surprising comeback after the war, and strangely enough, dance bands were responsible. Some composers are indignant when others take liberties with their music, but Henry was not. These special out-of-character arrangements simply delighted him. The wilder the better. His favorite was the version recorded by that granddaddy of all musical slapstick artists, Spike Jones. Henry had a collection of "Lassus" records, but the one he played most often was, by far, the one by Spike Jones. Like Henry Fillmore, Spike Jones believed in putting humor in music.

111

Henry was fond of his three sisters, who were pleasant ladies indeed: Mary Shipley, Fred Toll and Annie Louise Shedd. Mabel loved them too, despite the fact that many years earlier they had not approved of her marriage to Henry. She had always been a bit uneasy around them. This was only natural, because the sisters had graduated from institutions of higher learning, and her own education had ended before graduation from high school. They really had little in common.

By Henry being the only boy in the family, the sisters had a tendency to be possessive of him. He and Mabel kept to themselves at family get-togethers, and Mabel was not talkative. The sisters were quite the opposite; they were warm and open and felt that Mabel was unfriendly. Over the years, however, the barriers of misunderstanding broke down. Mabel realized that the sisters were made of the same stuff as Henry. On the other hand, the sisters came to realize that Mabel was as devoted to Henry as a wife could possibly be and that he was supremely happy with her. Thus in later years when the sisters visited Henry and Mabel, or vice versa, they were all more open with one another. Mary and her husband Carl later moved to Vero Beach, Florida, only 140 miles from Miami.

Mary was visiting Henry and Mabel in the spring of 1947 and had planned to return to Cincinnati with them when it came time for the annual business meeting. They would first stop in DeLand, where Henry was to judge at a high school band contest.

Because Henry was involved in some urgent last minute preparations with Fred McCall's Edison High School Band, Mary decided to go on to DeLand and let Henry come up later on the train. Mabel was having foot problems, so she did not make this trip. Mary flew to Orlando, and John and Margaret Heney met her at the airport. As she stepped off the plane, John presented her with a bouquet of red roses with a fancy ribbon marked "SISTER OF HENRY FILLMORE." John was taken back by her response: "Well! Henry finally did get important!" John said later he had to bite his tongue, for he wanted to say, "Finally? For gosh sakes, Mary, where have you been for the past thirty years?"

Henry arrived at the New Smyrna Beach train depot twenty-five miles to the east of DeLand, where John had planned quite a welcome for him. The DeLand High School Band drove over in a motorcade, accompanied by the Mayor of DeLand, and they were joined at the depot by New Smyrna Beach's mayor and his entourage. Henry stepped off the train, and the band struck up his "Miami." When John handed him the baton, he had never seen a happier look on Henry's face.

One the way back to DeLand in the car, Mary repeated the remark which had earlier caused John to raise his eyebrows, only this time she was addressing Henry: "Well, Henry, I see you finally did get important!" John just shook his head and drove onward.

Henry countered John's surprise with one of his own. John had been urging him to compose a new fight song

for the DeLand High School, because he thought the current one was outmoded. Henry had suggested he try using "Go Raiders Go" and substitute the word "Bulldogs" for "Raiders." The band tried it at several school assemblies, but it did not work out. So Henry brought John a new manuscript, "Bull Bull Bulldogs," and said, "Here's a little something for you to try out after the contest." Unfortunately, Henry's new piece did not work out either; the students preferred their old fight song, so "Bull Bull Bulldogs" was put on the school shelves and was never published.

The contest this year was actually a regional, or district contest. In previous years there had been just one contest for bands from the entire state, but there were now so many new bands that the state was divided into six districts. The top rated bands from each district would then advance to a state contest.

Henry was relieved that the contests were being held by districts; this way he would not have to judge the bands in the Miami area. A few of the bandmasters had raised the issue of possible favoritism, but Henry had a ready answer for this. He said he had actually been tougher on the Miami bands because they had greater access to his counsel. He had coached several of the bandmasters on conducting and had advised others to study with professionals who were available only in the Miami area, and he expected more from them than from bandmasters of other parts of the state. Because of the criticism, he took the opportunity to do less adjudicating. It required too much concentration for too long a period, and the press of the crowds was very tiring.

He told his colleagues in the FBA that there were many other highly qualified judges and that they should avail themselves of their services. One he introduced to them was the popular composer Paul Yoder. Paul, another of Henry's revered friends of the ABA, was indeed prolific as a composer and arranger (his output, numbering over fourteen hundred works, exceeded Henry's). Paul judged at the Florida state band contest every year until several years after Henry's death.

Since Henry was to be judging in John Heney's district that year, he was free to coach bands around Miami if he wished. This is how he happened to be working with Fred McCall's band. The Sunday rehearsal at Edison was preceded by a bit of typical Fillmore comedy. Henry met the band members secretly as they came in for the rehearsal and briefed them on a prank he wanted to play on their esteemed leader. Fred was normally a very serious man, and Henry thought a little humor might help relax the band at this critical rehearsal.

Fred took his place on the podium and explained the importance of the afternoon's rehearsal. He noticed that the students were a bit fidgety and apprehensive about something but gave it little thought. But there stood Henry behind him, shaking his fist and making menacing gestures at the students to remind them of his instructions. Down came the baton, and instead of the warmup piece it was the "Orange Bowl" march by

Henry Fillmore.

Fred's urgent concert preparations came about because of a last minute substitution of music. The band was scheduled to play on Wednesday, and their final rehearsal was to have been that Sunday afternoon. Fred asked Henry to come listen to their performance of the most difficult piece, the Finale of Dvorak's *New World Symphony.* After they had played it through once, Henry yelled down from the balcony, "Take a break, Fred; I need to talk to you."

Henry took him aside and was blunt and to the point. "They're clobbering it!" he said. "The players you have on those exposed woodwind solos will never handle it, and the French horn section is in water over its head. I suggest you use the alternate." Fred nearly panicked, because the band had never played the alternate piece, *Raymond* Overture by Thomas.

After much deliberation, they pulled *Raymond* from the library and worked on it for nearly four hours. Fred arranged to have the band members excused from classes Monday and Tuesday, and they continued to work on *Raymond* for two solid days. Fred and Henry took turns working with different sections and with the band as a whole. Their labors paid off; Edison won top honors at the contest.

After the contest, Henry and Mary went on to Cincinnati. Henry caught his expected annual cold there and was obliged to return a day early. He seemed weaker than usual and had another complete physical examination. This time he went to a different doctor, who thought he had "discovered" a heart condition and advised him to give up smoking. No problem—he seldom smoked. But the doctor said he should relax more and not partake of any stimulants such as coffee and alcohol. *That* was a problem!

As was his custom, Henry ignored the doctor's advice, point by point. In the next few weeks he conducted bands at Lake Wales, Miami Senior High and Miami Jackson, and presided at the ABA convention in Elkhart, Indiana. For the Lake Wales concert, he composed "The Chimes of Iron Mountain," featuring the tubular chimes of the old Fillmore Band, which Otto had purchased earlier. So the band could have exclusive use of the piece, Henry did not publish it until Otto moved on to another school eight years later.

54   KISS OF DEATH

Henry went to a revival meeting in June, 1947. It was not the usual kind of revival, however. Souls were not saved, but an eminent organization was. An American Bandmasters Association convention had not been held since Henry had been elected President in 1941.

There had been serious doubts about the ABA continuing its existence through the war years, but thanks to the tireless efforts of Lynn Sams, a musical instrument manufacturer's representative, the organization survived. Lynn was editor of the highly interesting *ABA Newsletter,* which served the vital purpose of keeping members informed of one another's activities.

After an unsuccessful attempt in 1946 to organize a convention in Chicago, Lynn persuaded his company, C.G. Conn, and eleven other musical instrument manufacturers in Elkhart, Indiana, to foot the bill for the 1947 convention there. His reasoning made sense; the ABA represented the cream of American bandmasters, and the horn makers needed their support as much as the ABA men needed the support of the industry.

Henry aptly called this convention, held June 13-15, the "revival" convention. At the general meeting, he spoke for a full fifteen minutes about how Lynn Sams had almost singlehandedly saved the ABA. From that moment on, the ABA never faltered. Henry was happy for Lynn, because they were close friends. Lynn, like Henry, had a wonderful sense of humor, and his newsletters were eagerly awaited—as was his presence at the conventions.

Henry conducted two numbers at the convention: "Man Among Men" and "Lassus Trombone." His presentation of "Lassus" brought down the house, as always. When he directed one of his smears at an ABA concert, he was invariably the hit of the program, and no one wanted to follow him. His colleagues were heard time and again to say, "What an act to follow!" or "It's the kiss of death to be the next conductor after Henry Fillmore!"

It became an ABA tradition to have Henry conduct the last number just before intermission. This was good crowd psychology—the crowd would have a few minutes to recover before the next conductor appeared, and fewer comparisons would be made. Even then, there was an acute shortage of volunteers to be next in

The ABA, inactive during the World War II years when Henry was President, had its "revival" convention in 1947, thanks to the extraordinary efforts of the affable Lynn L. Sams (left). He, Henry and Mabel are shown here with Maj. George W. Landers, bandmaster of the Spanish-American War era and founder of the Iowa Band Law.

line!

The only man who would dare to follow Henry was his friend Karl King, who was a famous man in his own right and always a crowd pleaser. Karl complained, but he did it good naturedly. After the 1947 concert at which they both appeared, Karl said, "I'm going to have a talk with the so-and-so who scheduled me after the Shah of Miami!"

While it might seem odd to the layman, Henry Fillmore had his detractors. They were a very small minority, however. Granted, he had no formal conducting training and was by no means a dignified, polished conductor. Nevertheless, formal training does not necessarily make one a good conductor. It has been demonstrated many times that musical genius is a great compensator. Case in point: John Philip Sousa, whom some authorities regard as one of the greatest conductors of all time, had no formal training as a conductor.

In Henry Fillmore's amazingly retentive mind were stored the impressions of countless performances of great conductors whom he observed very, very carefully. This, combined with the considerable musical ability Nature had given him, enabled him to reach the level of conducting proficiency he desired. If there is any doubt about his musical genius, consider the following: How many conductors—of any medium—have conducted practically every concert of their careers without a musical score? How many composers have perceived the exact pitch of every note of every chord in their heads and have written their music without the aid of a piano or musical instrument of any kind?

If Henry Fillmore would have wished to become a composer or conductor of weighty music, he certainly had the tools with which he could have accomplished precisely that. But instead, he leaned toward the world of entertainment.

It was Henry's opinion that many ABA members took themselves too seriously. He felt that nearly every audience should be loosened up, and when he appeared on a program it always worked out that way.

One of the ABA's primary objectives has always been to upgrade band music. While none can question that Henry was a party to that goal, he also served to balance the organization's temperament. He deliberately refrained from conducting music which was not entertaining, because the ABA was supposed to be representative of *all* types of bands and their convention audiences expected more variety than his few detractors would have presented by themselves. Although Henry did not use the term "professional jealousy" with regard to his critics, no doubt it applied in some instances.

The ABA needed Henry Fillmore because he was a stabilizing influence and because of his popularity as a composer and bandmaster. They also needed him because he had no small influence and expertise as a publisher. None would have wanted to have done without him, despite his choreographic podium antics. A handful of his more serious minded colleagues did not approve of the theatrics, but the crowds loved him. Oh, how they loved him!

55   FLORIDIAN, TEXAN, CUBAN. . .WHATEVER

Henry had been President of the American Bandmasters Association for six years, and for the greater part of those six years he had earnestly longed for a successor. The ABA traditionally elected its president for a term of only one year, but because the organization was in limbo during the war years, Henry was in office longer than any other president before or after him.

It was sweet relief. His plan for the future was simple: to spend more time with school bands, mostly in Florida. This was more pleasure than work, and he wished to do this as long as he was physically able. He had no way of looking into the future—no way of knowing if his last breath would be drawn tomorrow or twenty years from tomorrow. He was supposed to have been dead in his fifty-seventh year, but he was now in his sixty-fifth.

He broke a barrier of sorts at a football game in the Orange Bowl on December 6, 1947, by conducting the all-Negro band from Florida A & M. There was much talk about the excellent work of Dr. William Foster, who was in his second year as bandmaster there, and Henry had to see for himself. Foster telephoned Henry the morning of the game and asked if he would come to the bandstand after the halftime show so the band members could meet the composer of "Lassus Trombone" and all those familiar marches. "Sure!" said Henry.

Why should he wait until after halftime? Shortly after the game started, Foster looked up, and there was Henry to tell him how nice the band sounded and how much he appreciated the fine work he was doing. When asked if he would like to conduct a number, Henry chose Sousa's "The Washington Post." Would he like to conduct "Americans We" at halftime while the band was in block formation? "Sure!"

This was the largest crowd, up until that time, to see an all-Black team play in the United States. These were the days of segregation, with half the stadium Black and the other half White—except for the jolly fat White man on the Black bandstand who had always been a little bit color blind in this regard. After the halftime show, he complimented Foster and many of the individual band members on their performance. Later, he told his bandmaster friends that the A & M band sounded more crisp and clean than most other college bands and that this Bill Foster would go places. (He did.)

Henry led a king-sized band on New Year's Day, 1948—the massed bands of fifty-five schools. This was his sixth year as master of ceremonies at the annual Orange Bowl classic. Uncle Henry was not a stranger to many of the student musicians, however, because most of the bands were from Florida.

This appearance served to make Henry more widely known than ever before, and he received more invitations to guest conduct than he could handle. A trip to Havana with the University of Miami Band that January was cancelled, but he went there the following month with the combined bands of Miami Senior, Edison and Jackson. He also conducted several other high school bands before contest time in April and still others in the spring concerts which followed.

Henry watched Fred McCall's activities with great interest, because he seemed to be going off on a political tangent. Fred was disenchanted over the way Miami schools were being run, and he campaigned for Superintendent of Schools. The incumbent Superintendent viewed this as an uprising, and when Fred lost the election he was in a somewhat precarious position.

He was saved from embarrassment and possible retribution, however, because in July of 1948 he was selected as the new director of the University of Miami Band. Henry was elated with this development because he knew Fred would be just the man to mould the band into one of the nation's finest college bands and that this would undoubtedly have a positive impact on the band situation around the state. He celebrated by having a lavish dinner in Fred's honor and inviting all the school band directors in the Miami area.

The complexion of the University of Miami campus changed rapidly after the war. With the replacement of temporary military barracks built for wartime use and the move to a new location, it was no longer referred to as "Cardboard University." Thus Fred's appointment took place at a time of considerable change. He wasted no time in persuading university officials to increase the number of music scholarships available, and for several years a high percentage of the band members were scholarship students.

Fred took a genuine interest in his students' welfare, just as he had done at Edison High School. The bonds of friendship between Fred and his students were very real indeed. Henry greatly admired him for this, and in the few remaining years of Henry's life, Fred McCall was to become his closest friend.

Fred's halftime shows were described by his colleagues as "spectacular." He was a tireless worker and was a showman—Henry's kind of man. It would be difficult to say whether Henry adopted the University of Miami Band or if the band adopted Henry. He was around the rehearsal room so much that in practically no time he was on a first name basis with every member of the band. Fred bestowed a title upon him to show his appreciation for the enthusiasm which he generated: Permanent Guest Conductor.

The University of Miami Band is today known as the "Band of the Hour," thanks to a clever public address system announcement at one of the home football games that year. Al Freehling, the band's narrator, had a flamboyant style, and on the spur of the moment he said, "Henry Fillmore's stirring march, 'The *Man* of the Hour,' will now be played by the University of Miami *'Band* of the Hour.' " Fred thought that was

For several years, Henry was master of ceremonies at the annual Orange Bowl classic on New Year's Day. Typically, he led the combined bands in "The Star Spangled Banner" and his own "Americans We."

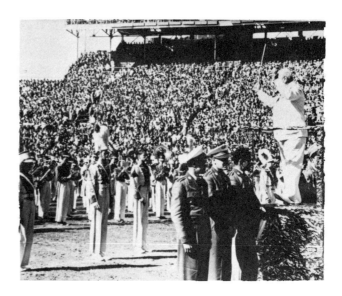

Henry Fillmore will be remembered by countless thousands as the man in the white suit who led bands at the Orange Bowl. But to the student musicians in those bands, he was *Uncle Henry*.

catchy, so the band acquired a nickname.

Fred's move to the University of Miami was not the only development which was destined to add prestige to Florida bands, however. Simultaneously, Col. Harold

115

Bachman was appointed bandmaster at the University of Florida in Gainesville. Bachman had been the conductor of professional bands for many years, including the famous Million Dollar Band, and was leaving his position at the University of Chicago.

Bachman was another of Henry's ABA associates and also a personal friend of many years, and Henry wrote to several school band directors around the state to inform them of the development. With Foster, McCall and Bachman assuming prominent positions in Florida at approximately the same time, things were looking up for Florida bands.

It became a tradition for Henry to conduct pre-game ceremonies whenever the football teams of the University of Miami and the University of Florida played one another, whether in Miami or in Gainesville. On the first occasion, in Gainesville, Bachman—resplendent in his new white uniform—slipped off his podium and landed in the mud. He made a terrible mistake by having such an accident in the presence of Henry Fillmore, who would never let him live it down. Henry gleefully described the incident, with great embellishment, to their fellow bandmasters. Each time he told the story, Bachman fell in a more unceremonious manner and into deeper mud.

On this occasion, Bachman asked Henry to compose a march for his band. Henry explained that he would love to but that his allegiance was with Fred McCall's band. He did, however, later compose the march "Men of Florida," complete with words. Although the dedication reads, "To all Floridians," he privately let Bachman know that this one was for him. It was published the following year.

One of the most memorable moments of Henry's career came on the night of Friday, November 5, 1948. The occasion was a football game between his two favorite schools, the University of Cincinnati and University of Miami. The national convention of the American Legion was also being held in Miami, and there was a sellout crowd at the Orange Bowl.

It was "Fillmore night" at the Orange Bowl. Henry led the combined bands of the five Miami high schools in his new arrangement of the University of Miami's alma mater. The stadium lights were turned out, and spotlights of various colors fell on the gold podium and Henry in his white suit. The bands played "Men of Ohio" and "Shoutin' Liza Trombone," and the applause lasted for over five minutes. The game was broadcast over both Miami and Cincinnati stations, and

At the Orange Bowl game of January 1, 1949, Henry was presented a ten-gallon hat and a certificate signed by the Governor of Texas naming him an honorary Texas citizen. He enjoyed this immensely, and for months he signed his letters "Tex."

Henry was on the telephone constantly for two days receiving congratulatory messages.

The next time Henry conducted in the Orange Bowl was on New Year's Day, 1949, for the game between the University of Georgia and the University of Texas. He led the combined bands at the pre-game ceremony, and at halftime he was awarded an honorary Texas citizenship. The ten-gallon hat presented to him became one of his prized possessions, and for over a year he wore it everywhere he went except to church. The only reason he did not wear it to church. . .was because he seldom attended.

56   HO, HO, HO!

The winter of 1949 was another busy time at the Fillmore home because of a surge of visitors from the North. Henry and Mabel did quite a bit of entertaining up until the last part of March, the only break being the annual trip to Cincinnati for the business meeting. All this activity tired them, and Henry had to decline a trip to Havana with the Miami Jackson band. Shortly after

the last of the visitors had gone, Henry had another mild heart attack. A week later, however, he was back in the swing of things.

He made no apologies for making statements to the effect that the high school bands around Miami were the finest high school bands in the country, especially when it came to marching. Friends and relatives back in Ohio

The high school bands of Florida were clearly among the nation's best in the late 1940's. One of the reasons for their prominence was the influence of Henry Fillmore. His colorful and informal conducting endeared him to all.

One of the pieces he used frequently was an audience-participation piece called "Ha Ha Ha." In this, the audience would answer the band. If the band sang, "Ha, ha, ha," so would the audience. Then it would be, "Ho, ho, ho," "Hee, hee, hee," "Hay, hay, hay," "Hoo, hoo, hoo," or complete silence—in time with the music. Whatever the band did, the audience would mimic. He would slow down to a complete stop, then accelerate, and in the process there would be such a mixup that everyone would be roaring with laughter. It worked every time.

Another of his favorites was "Military Escort in 5 Ways," where the theme of his popular march, "Military Escort," would first be played as written and then played in the style of an Italian opera, a Viennese waltz, a jazz band, and finally as a parade march. Another favorite was his humoresque of "Comin' Round the Mountain," which featured the traditional old tune played in several styles—amidst a variety of sound effects. These two pieces are more or less considered passe' by today's sophisticated audiences, but Henry certainly had a lot of fun with them.

Henry's good deeds were bringing expressions of appreciation in the form of scrolls, certificates, plaques

interpreted this as so much boasting, but it was certainly not just his opinion alone. Judges from other sections of the country who had adjudicated at contests and festivals agreed with him. He quoted them as saying they had heard all of the country's finest high school bands and that even the best bands from the North were no match. As Henry put it, they "could not put up the music stands for the Miami bands."

Al Wright's Miami Senior High School Band was the most impressive of all, and in letters to friends Henry told how surprised the judges were to find a band of this caliber south of the Mason-Dixon Line. He was extremely proud of Al and his accomplishments.

One night Henry substituted for Al on the last half of a program, because Al had to leave for Tampa to attend a directors' clinic. So that he too could slip out early, Henry made the following short speech just before the last number:

> "Al is not the only one who has to leave early. My wife needs me at home, so for this last selection I am turning the baton over to a man well known by every student in the school—your beloved janitor, Herman!"

There was really a love affair between Al's band and Uncle Henry. One of Al's students later made him a beautiful white tie with four big red roses on it. He wore it to practically every concert he conducted for nearly two years and delighted in telling how it had been handcrafted by one of Al's students, adding, "This is my Four Roses tie—my favorite brand of liq...uh, tie."

At one time or another, it is probable that Henry visited every high school band in Florida. At least there was not a single one he missed in Southern or Central Florida. When he came to conduct, an entire school would benefit because of the enthusiasm which always resulted. The importance of humor to his acceptance everywhere must not be underestimated. This came partly from his narrating and partly from the music itself.

One of many expressions of appreciation for Henry's contribution to the advancement of school bands was an engraved gold plaque presented to him jointly by the Florida Bandmasters Assn. and the American Bandmasters Assn. in May, 1949.

117

Each summer, Henry (fifth from left) was Honorary Guest Conductor at the University of Miami's Summer Band Camp, founded by Fred McCall (fourth from left). To keep student tuition down, Henry set his fee at $1.00 per year.

and the like. One of his treasures was a plaque presented him in the Gator Bowl at Jacksonville, jointly by the FBA and the ABA at a state high school band contest. It read as follows:

In Appreciation of
His Great Contribution to the Advancement
of Florida School Bands and
In Recognition of
His National Prominence as a Band Conductor and
His International Prominence as a
Composer of Band Music
This Plaque is Presented
On Behalf of His Many Friends and Co-Workers in
The Florida Bandmasters Association
The American Bandmasters Association
May 12, 1949

For Henry's appearances as guest conductor, he never accepted a fee unless school administrators insisted. He sometimes accepted travel expenses, but rarely.

A different situation existed, however, when Fred McCall organized the band camp at the University of Miami in the summer of 1949. University administrators issued a policy that all the faculty members, consultants and guest conductors were to be paid. Fred wanted Henry above all others, but the budget was tight. Henry solved the problem neatly by offering to serve for a dollar a year. He carried his annual check in his wallet, and whenever the subject of the band camp came up he would pull it out and say, "See how much this university thinks I'm worth!"

Fred started the band camp at the suggestion of the U of M President, and an excellent staff was organized. It included such highly regarded Florida band directors as Al Wright, Major James O'Neal, Paul Gustat, Logan Turrentine, Vernon Hooker, John Coleman and Paul Cremaschi. Otto Kraushaar joined the faculty at a later date. Henry's function was that of Honorary Guest

Conductor. He came and went as he pleased but was always on hand when needed, and he conducted at many of the Sunday concerts as well as the grand finale at the end of the five-week period. The students lived in dormitories, and the faculty members were housed in cabins. The cabins all had numbers—except for Henry's, which was marked "X."

Henry was excused from summer band camp for a few days in July so he could accompany the Miami Jackson High School Band to New York. They were competing with fifty other bands in the Lions International marching band contest. Stephan Jones was the bandmaster and another of Henry's understudies. Henry beamed with pride as they high-stepped down Fifth Avenue and won first prize. Later, the band performed in Madison Square Garden and also in the Polo Grounds. Henry appreciated the latter, because the Giants were playing the Cincinnati Reds. While in New York, he guest-conducted the Goldman Band once again and attended a broadcast of the recently organized Cities Service Band of America.

On the way home, Henry stopped in Washington to visit George Howard of the U.S. Air Force Band and Charles Brendler of the U.S. Navy Band to discuss future appearances of their bands in Miami. He was involved with both as guest conductor, first with the Air Force Band at the Veterans of Foreign Wars convention on August 22 and then with the Navy Band on October 11. At the October concert he conducted the premiere of his new "Men of Florida" march, which had been in various stages of preparation for several months.

After numerous other conducting engagements, including the New Year's Day Orange Bowl extravaganza, Henry suffered still another mild heart attack. He had to cancel at least two engagements in mid-January, 1950, but three weeks later he was at it once again. Same old story.

The Belasco Theater in New York City was the scene of many an exciting program for lovers of good old-fashioned, hard-hitting band music—the kind that gives you goose bumps on top of goose bumps and makes you want to jump up and wave a flag.

Every Monday night for nearly eight years, starting June 4, 1948, Americans heard a thrilling program over NBC Radio that began: "Forty-eight states. . .forty-eight stars. . .forty-eight men. . .marching down the main street of everybody's home town! Here comes the Cities Service Band of America, conducted by Paul Lavalle!" It was one of the most stirring series of broadcasts in the history of radio, and the devoted audiences were always emotionally aroused.

Among the Band of America's most enthusiastic listeners was Henry Fillmore, whose music was often featured on the program. When Henry attended one of the broadcasts on the trip to New York with the Miami Jackson band, he made the acquaintance of Paul Lavalle.

Here were two birds of a feather; each was a dynamic conductor and a tremendous showman, and their philosophies of entertainment were strikingly similar. When they met, it was as though they had known one another for a lifetime. The band's style was intense and aggressive, and Lavalle employed an unorthodox seating arrangement and special microphoning techniques to give it a big, bold sound. Henry was beside himself over that sound.

He arranged for Paul Lavalle to judge at one of the Florida high school band contests, and Lavalle reciprocated by inviting Henry to appear on a Band of America broadcast. As such he would be their first guest conductor. Henry accepted; he told Lavalle to set any date he wished and he would be there regardless of what other activity might have to be cancelled. The date was set for July 24, 1950.

At the rehearsal, Henry was introduced by the legendary euphonium soloist Simone Mantia, formerly of Sousa's Band and Pryor's Band, and Henry let it be known that he went by "Henry," not "Mr. Fillmore." He related some interesting anecdotes and told how much the band was admired by amateur and professional musicians alike—and what a marvelous example it was setting for the thousands of school bands around the country.

After Lavalle had rehearsed the band in three numbers, Henry had his turn. "Americans We" was on the stands, and they really opened up for him. He did not try to hide his excitement; in the first section he yelled, "Hot dog!!!" Several times during the rehearsal he shouted, "Wow-eee!!!" Needless to say, the band responded. They were all top professionals who, as a general rule, are hard to impress. But they enjoyed Henry immensely. When he finished, the band gave him a loud, standing ovation.

As the announcer was introducing Henry at the broadcast that night, Henry turned toward the band and whispered, "Come on, boys, let's really put it on."

Judging from the pile of letters and telegrams he received, the band really did "put it on!"

Paul Lavalle had not had a vacation for two years because of the demands of the weekly broadcasts and other commitments. But if he could persuade Henry to conduct one entire program, he could have a brief holiday. Henry needed no persuading whatever. As before, he told Lavalle to pick his time and he would make himself available.

In the annals of band music lovers, the night of Monday, August 5, 1951, ranks high on the list of "most thrilling moments in music." The audience warmed up to Henry immediately. The first number was Karl King's rousing march, "Purple Pageant." Henry took it at a brisk tempo, and the band played with a spirit and

The dynamic conductor of the Cities Service Band of America (1948-1956) was Paul Lavalle, and he invited Henry to be its first guest conductor. Henry was overjoyed and said it was the best band he had ever conducted, ". . .like driving a team of spirited horses rarin' to go!" He appeared on Lavalle's popular Monday night NBC radio program three times.

conviction which is rare among professionals.

Ford Bond, the narrator, then gave this brief announcment, which brought down the house: "Our guest on the podium tonight, for our own bandmaster, Paul Lavalle, is the brilliant guest conductor, Miami's own, the famous bandmaster and composer, Henry Fillmore!" Henry stepped to the microphone and spoke to Paul Lavalle, who was listening from a fishing camp in Canada: "It's a thrill, Paul, to be here on your bandstand. . ." That was an understatement!

Broadcasting was nothing new to Henry, but this great new band was over twice the size of the Fillmore Band which had broadcast over WLW Radio twenty years earlier. And since the Band of America programs were carried over that same station, many of his old friends were listening. Henry was in the height of his glory. The band knew it. The audience knew it. The atmosphere was truly charged.

Arthur Marotti's toe-tapping xylophone solo, "Twelfth Street Rag," was next, and this was followed by Sousa's "Semper Fidelis," both of which were played with gusto. The surprise of the evening came next, Henry's "Pahson Trombone," in a cleverly harmonized arrangement by Band of America trombonist Harris Hubbell. From the look of ecstasy on Henry's face, the Belasco Theater audience knew his mind was somewhere up in the clouds.

He was able to catch his breath while the Cities Service Green and White Quartet sang a medley of "moon" songs, but the band was back with a driving, unrestrained performance of Julius Fucik's time-honored old march, "The Florentiner." As the program moved on, there were more and more shouts and whistles of approval.

The finale was a pair of Henry's marches, "The Footlifter" and "Americans We." After this, the audience was so enthusiastic that Henry had to raise both hands so Ford Bond could make his closeout announcement. To end the program, Henry led the band in its theme song, Paul Lavalle's own "Band of America March." At the final chord, the audience fairly raised the roof; they let loose with cheering, foot stomping and whistles such as Henry had seldom before experienced.

Forty-eight states. . .forty-eight stars. . .no, that night there were forty-*nine* stars.

58   HENRY BURNS HIS MANUSCRIPTS

Clever and resourceful as he was, Al Wright could not be in two places at the same time. In February of 1951, he was committed to a guest conducting appearance in Tampa when his Miami Senior High Band received a last minute invitation from the Cuban government to perform in Havana at a festival. Uncle Henry came to his rescue with a solution: he could not stand to see Al's students disappointed, so he volunteered to be Al's substitute for the Havana trip. With a minimum of preparation, the band and its temporary assistant conductor made a splendid showing.

Henry made numerous other appearances in Florida that year, plus out-of-state appearances in Pennsylvania, Iowa, New York, Illinois and Washington, D.C. After the Band of America broadcast in August, however, he declined most engagements because it was necessary to make several trips back to Cincinnati for the purpose of negotiating a very important business matter: he and his sisters were selling the Fillmore Brothers Company to Carl Fischer, a much larger music publisher with offices in both New York and Chicago.

Whose idea it was to sell the business is not known, but more than likely it was Henry's. He was nearly seventy years of age, and since stiff competition had caused a rapid decline in the musical instrument business, he probably convinced the sisters that it would be better to sell at that time rather than later. The situation would undoubtedly have been different if Henry had tended the business himself, but that was out of the question. The staff was down to thirteen.

Fischer was interested mostly in Henry's music, and since they had worldwide distribution, they could no doubt pay him more royalties on his music. It was a wise business decision all around; the sisters could only lose by keeping the business longer, and Henry could only gain by selling. Additionally, Fischer put him on a limited expense account so he could "advertise his music" at the conventions he would normally be attending.

The situation was precarious as far as the employees were concerned, however. Although Henry insisted that all the employees be retained at their prevailing salaries, there was no way of knowing how long Fischer would keep the business in Cincinnati. They gave the impression that they would not move, but this was evidently not written into the contract. The older employees would probably not be willing to relocate. Herman Ritter and Charles Martin, for example, had lived in Cincinnati all their lives and had been with the company forty-five years. All the employees agreed to stay on except for Ritter, who retired.

The sale of the business came as a shock to the employees, but it was not totally unexpected. Henry and Herman Ritter had held occasional discussions with various publishers for over six years. Henry went back to Cincinnati for conferences with Fischer representatives beginning in mid-September. The sale was consummated on October 5, 1951, and was effective November 1.

Fischer agreed to keep the Fillmore music catalog intact; that is, the music which the Fillmore Brothers had published would retain its identity indefinitely as the *Fillmore Catalog*. Further, no new music would be added to that catalog unless it was composed or arranged by Henry Fillmore.

The Fischer people were not interested in the huge stock of band and orchestra music of other publishers,

Henry greatly admired Al Wright, the exceptionally talented and enterprising bandmaster at Miami Senior High School. Wright introduced the art of Swiss flag swinging to American audiences in 1939 and was using black light techniques in his football halftime extravaganzas at about the same time. Miami was just the beginning of his remarkable career.

but there were literally tons of it in storage on the upper floors. Several times Henry had advised his employees against such a buildup, but he made the most of the situation by holding out for an additional $50,000. Fischer used a more modern printing process, so they had no use for the metal printing plates. These were later sold for scrap.

All of the printed music which had not sold well was set aside to be destroyed. At this time, Henry did something which, to music scholars and nearly everyone else, has seemed simply incredible. To this rather large pile of old music he added nearly all of his own manuscripts and personally supervised the burning of every last page!

To understand this somewhat shocking course of action, it is necessary to think of Henry's manuscripts as being of two distinct classes. The first class included the manuscripts of both his original music and the arrangements of the music of others which *were published*. He saw no need to preserve these manuscripts because he felt they were made obsolete by the published editions.

The second class of his manuscripts consisted of the music of other composers which he arranged specifically for the private use of the Fillmore Band and which *was not published*. This included the pieces he adapted in his own ingenious way for a small concert band, among them many tailored to vocalists such as Ruth Best. These were unauthorized arrangements, in a sense, all made before Henry was elected to ASCAP (American Society of Composers, Authors and Publishers) in 1937. In burning these manuscripts, he eliminated the possibility of their falling into the hands of someone who might later put them into wide use and not pay ASCAP royalties.

The Fischer men were greatly pleased with the records which the business had kept over the years, saying they were the best they had ever seen. They were also pleased with the caliber of the employees, but the feeling was certainly not mutual. Those who remained disliked Fischer's way of doing business, and one by one they either retired or resigned. Fischer offered some of them positions in New York, but they resented receiving orders from outsiders. For many years they had run the business as though it was their own, with the kindly Henry Fillmore being little more than a figurehead.

The Fillmore Music House continued in operation under that name as an affiliate of Carl Fischer, but not for long. For some time, Fischer had wanted to acquire the music published by the Willis Music Company in

"If you'd like to know what Florida is *really* like. . ." Newsmen arranged this publicity photo when Uncle Henry accompanied the Miami Senior High School Band to Chicago for the National Band Clinic in December, 1951. He also took this band to Cuba earlier that year, substituting for Al Wright.

Cincinnati, while Willis in turn had wanted the Conn musical instrument franchise held by the Fillmore Music House. A trade was arranged. On April 23, 1952—less than six months after the Fischer takeover—trucks came to haul away the remaining stock at 528 Elm Street. The Fillmore Brothers Company and the Fillmore Music House were no more.

Henry regretted seeing the end of the institution his father and Uncle Frank had established seventy-seven years earlier, but such was the course of business. He looked back with amusement, however, at an incident which took place one Sunday morning when two of the Fischer representatives went into the store alone. They inadvertently set off the burglar alarm, not having been informed that the store had one. The police soon burst into the store with revolvers drawn. The Fischer men raised their hands above their heads, and one explained that they were from Chicago and were going to take over the business.

"Chicago!" shouted one of the policemen. "Reach higher!"

The Fillmore Brothers Co. was sold to Carl Fischer, the New York-Chicago music publisher, in November, 1951. It had been founded 77 years earlier, in 1874. Herman Ritter (front) and Charles Martin (behind Ritter) had been with the company 45 years; also shown are Jack Kiefer, a 14-year employee, and Joseph G. Powell, of Fischer (rear).

59   GIANTS AT ODDS

The beautiful friendship between Henry Fillmore and Edwin Franko Goldman came to an abrupt end in March, 1952, at the ABA convention held in Columbus, Ohio. Henry proposed Paul Lavalle for ABA membership, but Goldman let it be known in no uncertain terms that he was strongly opposed to extending the invitation. A polite exchange of words developed, and President Earl Irons interrupted to ask that the associate members adjourn so that the regular members could "wash their dirty linen." (Up until this time, both regular and associate members participated in membership discussions. Since the 1952 meeting, however, the associate members have been asked to excuse themselves when membership matters come up.)

Henry was much impressed with Paul Lavalle and his work with the Band of America, but certain of the ABA men had reasons for keeping him out of the ABA. Since this became such a delicate issue, not once but at four different ABA conventions, it is best to take a look at both sides of the argument.

Lavalle was an energetic, gymnastic conductor, given to showy displays of podium pyrotechnics. Some jokingly referred to him as a "cheerleader." This impressed an audience, but to a certain extent it diverted attention from the music being performed. Some ABA men disliked this, but Lavalle was an emotional man, and it cannot be denied that when a high point of music was

reached he certainly made an audience aware of it. But this was a minor objection. Slightly more serious was the fact tht Lavalle had made several appearances where ABA men had also appeared—and had stolen the show.

Paul Lavalle was also a sensational clarinetist and saxophonist. He had played several years in the NBC Symphony Orchestra under Arturo Toscanini and was once regarded as the finest lead sax man in New York. For several years he conducted the string orchestra on the NBC *Highways of Melody* radio program. Since he was not noted as a conductor of bands until the Band of America was formed in 1948, some of the ABA men regarded him as an orchestra man who was only temporarily involved with band work while the money lasted— that he was therefore not a bandmaster at heart.

His selection as conductor of the Band of America was another factor. ABA stalwart Frank Simon also had entertained hopes of capturing that prize. When it became known that Cities Service was planning a band program, Simon proposed a program similar to his Armco Band program of the 1920's and 1930's. In fact, he even produced three pilot programs but lost out to Lavalle because Lavalle's program was judged to be more appealing to modern radio audiences—it had shorter pieces, sometimes abridged, and the pace was more lively overall. Simon thought Lavalle's approach was bad and resented the fact that he had lost out to a

Johnny-come-lately bandmaster. Goldman now had an ally.

Goldman also resented the fact that Lavalle had never invited him to appear on a Band of America broadcast, as he had Henry. Goldman's Central Park Mall programs were high level performances; he was a purist who presented many masterful transcriptions of classical literature (his own in many instances) and intensely disliked Lavalle's style of programming.

The esteemed A.A. Harding, Director of Bands at the University of Illinois and another giant in the band world, also disliked Lavalle's programming. With Goldman, Simon and Harding—three of the ABA founding fathers and former presidents—all firmly opposed to having Lavalle become a part of their organization, Henry had formidable adversaries.

What is "good" programming? What is a "bandmaster"? By virtue of the tremendous popularity of the Band of America radio programs, Paul Lavalle was actually doing more to focus public attention on bands than any member of the ABA was doing at the time. While his programs did not satisfy band purists, they certainly satisfied the public. Even people who were not lovers of band music found the programs entertaining and stimulating.

Paul Lavalle was obviously good for bands, arguments against his broadcast format notwithstanding. It was evident that Henry's theory about showmanship making friends was correct. It was proved not only in the popularity of Lavalle's broadcasts but also in the popularity of his recordings for RCA, which far outsold those of the Goldman Band and all others as well.

Henry did not stand alone in his fight to gain ABA membership for Lavalle. There were others who felt that if Lavalle was not eligible, neither were many of those who were already members. Henry thought that denying Lavalle membership would be a gross miscarriage of justice, and he said so. He pointed out that the ABA was supposed to be an organization representative of all types of bands, not just those which were academically oriented or tradition-bound. He said the members should "let their hair down."

It would seem that an organization which could have benefitted by having Paul Lavalle in its ranks would have welcomed him with open arms. But Goldman, Harding and Simon held their ground and won by a very slim margin—partly because of the large number who abstained from the voting. It is a known fact that it is extremely difficult to elect someone to the ABA if the top brass is in opposition; other members, for professional reasons, do not wish to alienate them.

Today, there are still a few of the older ABA men who grumble about what they considered an injustice. Indeed, they were more than a little upset. They argue that the achievements of many of the present members do not compare to Paul Lavalle's. Before Henry passed away, he proposed Lavalle's name four times and was defeated all four times. This appears to be one of those arguments which will continue, even though the principals who started the argument have been dead for many years.

60   ALMOST A MOVIE

The Big Brass Band was to have been the name of an MGM movie produced by Jesse Lasky, but it was never made.

Lasky attended the 1952 ABA convention in Columbus and made a formal announcement. He had made a similar announcement five years earlier at the 1947 "revival" convention, after much encouragement from Lynn Sams of C.G. Conn, who was arranging to have part of the footage taken inside a musical instrument factory (C.G. Conn, naturally) to show how musical instruments were manufactured.

The proposed film had its roots much earlier, however. Sams had suggested such a movie to Lasky in 1936, but it was shelved until 1947 when Lasky thought the time was right. By this time, Sams had done considerable background research. The movie would salute student musicians, and hopefully it would broaden America's appreciation of music and win support for school music programs.

The Big Brass Band was to be Hollywood all the way, but as authentic as possible with a brief history of bands somehow squeezed in. Stereo sound was to be used, and of course it would be in technicolor.

There were to be many spectacular scenes, such as the "Ballet of the Batons," featuring twenty-four twirlers with a special effects background. Another scene was to take place at the annual Chicagoland Music Festival at Soldiers' Field, with all the pageantry for which the festival was famous and with the huge crowd adding to the excitement. Lasky was counting on the support of the *Chicago Tribune,* which sponsored the festival as a charity project, since one of his relatives was on the editorial staff.

Part of the supporting cast was to be an All-American high school band of over a hundred members, led by Clarence Sawhill of the University of California at Los Angeles. Henry Fillmore and Edwin Franko Goldman were both to have parts, and Henry was to conduct his "Shoutin' Liza Trombone." Lasky wanted one colorful, flamboyant conductor in the picture, and he was convinced that Henry was his man.

The story revolved around a typical musically inclined American family, showing the childrens' progress from the time of their first music lessons until they became accomplished musicians. A high school faculty love triangle was the basis of the plot. Involved are a sexy vocal teacher, the band director and the football coach. Tragedy strikes when the band director dies just two weeks before the band goes off to a contest—one they have a good chance of winning.

As the plot continues, a low class circus happens to be passing through town, and Henry is leader of the band.

At the 1952 convention, ABA bigwigs posed for a publicity picture to promote Jesse Lasky's proposed movie, *The Big Brass Band*. Seated are A.A. Harding and William Santelmann. Standing are Charles Brendler, Edwin Franko Goldman, Herbert Johnston, William Revelli, Barry Drewes, Jesse Lasky (of MGM), Earl Irons, Henry Fillmore and Harold Bachman. Except for Lasky (not affiliated with the ABA) and Drewes, all these men served as ABA Presidents at one time or another.

He is a rough and tough character but has a soft spot in his heart for youngsters. Since the school is desperate for a bandmaster, he takes leave of the circus and fills in for the bandmaster. In just two weeks, he brings the band around to a new level of excellence and wins the contest—as well as the hearts of everyone in town.

All does not end happily, however; the movie ends in another tragedy. The old bandleader returns to the circus but perishes shortly thereafter when the tent blows down and catches fire in a terrible storm.

A composer for the movie's background music had not been named, but one spirited march was to be included. When this was announced, Henry and numerous other ABA men immediately went to work. Henry's march, called "The Big Brass Band," was the one selected.

Lasky's would-be-spectacular movie never got beyond the planning stage, however. The most damaging blow came right after the 1952 convention when a rival studio, Twentieth-Century-Fox, produced *Stars and Stripes Forever,* the popular movie about John Philip Sousa's life which featured Clifton Webb. Then the script of *The Big Brass Band* was attached by the Internal Revenue Service because of back taxes owed on profits from the movie *Sergeant York,* but Lasky later won a U.S. Supreme Court decision on this.

Also, MGM officials complained of too much documentary material in the script. Another delay resulted when MGM considered using the "3-D" process. Then it was learned that Paul Lavalle had coincidentally written a new march entitled "The Big Brass Band." The final blow came when Meredith Willson's *The Music Man* was announced as a forthcoming Broadway musical, also on the general subject of bands. The night Lasky learned of this he suffered a fatal heart attack.

Henry's march was not published in his lifetime. He told Fred McCall that if he should die and the movie was never produced, the march should be re-titled and dedicated to his good friend and colleague Karl L. King. "The Big Brass Band" was published posthumously as "King Karl King." He informed Karl of his plans and said he hoped the new march would cause him to gnash his teeth. Karl's reply was that it would not bother him because he had dentures just the same as Henry.

Henry's Uncle Charlie died in an Indianapolis nursing home, at the age of ninety-two, on September 18, 1952. When he was lowered into the ground, Henry was not present; Henry himself came close to being lowered into the ground at the same time.

He conducted several bands at a Shrine convention in Miami that summer and then took a vacation in North Carolina. After returning, he suffered another of his heart attacks. He and Mabel were thus represented at Uncle Charlie's funeral by the flowers he sent.

Next to Uncle Fred, Charles Millard Fillmore was Henry's favorite uncle. He had a sparkling sense of humor and no beard. Henry disliked beards, and any uncle of his who did not sport one just had to be a regular fellow.

Henry overlooked Uncle Charlie's Prohibition Party leanings because of his views on patriotism. When he was quoted as saying, at the outbreak of World War II, "I would rather live in America for eighty years than anywhere else for eight hundred years!", he could have been speaking for Henry as well. His most famous patriotic song, "Thank God for America" (1940), was his answer to "God Bless America"; America had already been blessed, he explained.

Henry admired Uncle Charlie for his wonderful warmth of personality, his fortitude, his determination and optimism. He was a self-made man who had lost an eye in childhood due to scarlet fever but overcame his handicap with grace and was indefatigable in pursuit of his objectives. After taking advantage of a one-year scholarship at the College of Music of Cincinnati, he continued to work his way through college, first as a traveling singing school teacher and then by giving private music lessons. He graduated from Butler University in Indianapolis in 1890.

Charlie was a minister in the Disciples of Christ Church for over fifty years, and for all practical purposes he did not retire. He was an extremely industrious man, doing much charity work after stepping down from the pulpit. He wrote on the subject of the psychology of old age, that is, how to live happily and gracefully despite old age.

His contribution to Fillmore Brothers music publications was considerable, and he was a contributing editor of the *Musical Messenger* for many years. At one time, he also edited the *Clean Life Educator*. He wrote poetry, too, but this talent was not developed to any great extent.

In his twilight years, he had the quaint custom of composing a new gospel hymn on his birthdays. He will be remembered mostly for the gospel hymns and other songs he composed in earlier years, however. They totaled over five hundred. One would think he had a mother fixation, because among his most popular pieces were such titles as "Tell Mother I'll Be There," "Home and Mother," "A White Flower for You, Mother," "I'll Wear a White Flower for You, Mother Dear," "My Good Old Mother's Religion" and "There Is No

Henry was inspired by the perseverance and industry of the remarkable Charles Millard Fillmore (1860-1952). Uncle Charlie was a minister for over fifty years and composed over five hundred pieces of music. Henry never understood his passion for prohibition causes.

Love Like a Mother's Love."

Charlie was also a Sunday School teacher, but not all his pupils were numbered among the pious. A particularly errant one was John Dillinger, the notorious gangster, who was in his class at the Hillside Christian Church in Indianapolis. When Dillinger was gunned down by law enforcement officers in 1934, the Reverend Charles Millard Fillmore was called upon to preach the funeral.

He began the funeral oration with the words, "We believe in a God of forgiveness. . ." One might wonder if he felt that way about his nephew Henry and his social drinking. Charlie was such a strict prohibitionist that he refused to visit his niece Fred Fillmore Toll in Lawrenceburg, Kentucky—too much liquor was manufactured in Lawrenceburg!

The heart attack Henry suffered at the time Uncle Charlie died was serious enough for him to tell friends that ''Gabriel was calling me!'' It kept him in bed for over a week, and only after a series of shots did he begin to regain his strength.

When Fred McCall took his University of Miami Band on a tour, Henry was always invited. But on their trip to El Salvador in December of 1952, it was necessary for him to decline because he had not fully recovered from the heart attack. He was growing restless, however, and it was just a matter of time until he would grab his baton and try Gabriel's patience once again.

The first appearance after his recovery was at the annual North-South All Star game in the Orange Bowl on Christmas evening, 1952. This game was sponsored by the Mahi Temple Shrine of Miami to raise money for crippled children. Henry composed his ''North-South College All Stars'' march for the event, but only after being prodded by Logan Turrentine, bandmaster at Coral Gables High School.

Fred McCall was in charge of music for the North-South game, and he asked Henry to make an appearance. Henry, in turn, asked Logan Turrentine if he would have his fine Coral Gables band perform at the game.

Logan knew that Henry had not composed anything for over two years, and since he had been a lover of Henry's music for many years he felt he would be doing the music world a favor if he could stir him back into action once again. So he said his band would provide the entertainment only if Henry would compose a new march for the occasion.

The finest college football players were invited to play, and this year they were honored to have eight All Americans in the game. The game ended in a 21-21 tie. There were winners, however: the crippled children in Shrine-supported hospitals around the country.

Logan and his 160-piece Coral Gables band gave Henry's new march a fitting premiere. The band members had lights affixed to their hats, and with the stadium blacked out, the band converged on the center of the field with one half playing ''Dixie'' and the other half playing ''Yankee Doodle.'' When they met, a spotlight fell on dead center, and there was Henry perched atop a shining podium to conduct the new march. Another highlight of the show was the appearance of the Mahi Temple Shrine Band—and Augie Schaefer—and a row of Shriners dressed in red, white and blue holding placards which pretty much told the whole story. They read: ''STRONG LEGS RUN THAT WEAK MAY WALK.''

There were numerous guest conducting appearances and therefore several opportunities for Henry to conduct the new march after it was printed in March, 1953. One was in Medford, Massachusetts, where he led the Catholic Youth Organization Band at St. Joseph's Rectory on the occasion of the twenty-fifth anniversary of the CYO. Another came when he appeared at Otto Kraushaar's spring concert in Lake Wales.

In the course of his involvement with Masonic music organizations, such as the Mahi Temple Shrine Band of Miami, Henry came in contact with many celebrities of the music world. He is shown here in 1952 with Leonard B. Smith, whose Moslem Temple Shrine Band of Detroit he led many times at Shrine conventions. Smith was regarded as the world's premiere cornet soloist and had just founded the renowned Detroit Concert Band (then known as the Leonard Smith Band).

Students all over the state of Florida had a name they affectionately applied to Henry. It was *not* ''Mr. Fillmore.''

"Ho!!!" Henry enjoyed conducting school bands so much that his enthusiasm was felt by everyone in the house. Countless thousands of students could never forget "the night Uncle Henry came." Note the expressions on the faces of the flute players.

The spring concerts at Lake Wales were always enjoyable to everyone, particularly Henry and Mabel, who had become very fond of the Kraushaars. Henry was such a familiar sight around town that even the swans knew him! One of his delights was feeding the swans and then coaxing them all the way back to the Kraushaars' with morsels of food. They would have followed him right into the house had Fern and Mabel allowed it. Even after Henry left, the swans would come to Otto's house looking for Henry!

The Lake Wales youngsters were so much fun that Henry reached deep into his bag of tricks to spice up their concerts. One time Otto invited the school principal to conduct a number, and Henry conspired with the band to give offstage directions just out of sight of the principal. Henry would speed up or slow down the tempo, and the principal had no choice but to follow the band instead of leading it.

On another occasion, when Henry conducted the second half of a concert, he explained that they were to be honored by the presence of another guest conductor, the great Russian composer, Dr. Alexander Smirnakovski. If no one was familiar with that name, it was because it was a figment of Henry's imagination.

According to the story Henry told the crowd, Dr. Smirnakovski was in Lake Wales with a Russian delegation to make a comprehensive study of the Bok Tower, and he had consented to come conduct the band in one of his own compositions. The composition was actually a little known piece by Leon Metcalf, and Henry gave it

a fictitious name. Dr. Smirnakovski spoke no English, Henry explained, but the band would be able to follow his direction since music was the universal language.

What the audience did not know—and never found out—was that Dr. Smirnakovski was actually Otto Kraushaar dressed in tails, a frilly white shirt, white tie and vest. He wore a wig and a beard. It was all such a well-kept secret by every band member that the only ones who knew of the prank were Henry, the teacher who applied Otto's makeup and several high school actors who were taking part. Even Fern and Mabel did not know.

Dr. Smirnakovski was introduced by Henry, and the fun started. The piece began with a soft clarinet solo, and just then two of the actors came out with hammers and nails and proceeded to repair the podium! As the solo ended, there was more pounding, sawing and other commotion from backstage. Meanwhile, more of the actors came down the aisle selling peanuts and popcorn. Henry had previously explained to the Principal that this was a custom in the great Doctor's native country.

Such a fiasco it was! All the while, the band continued straight-faced as though nothing out of the ordinary was happening until Dr. Smirnakovski stopped the band and refused to continue. Henry tried, with much

Henry demanded a guest conducting fee of $0.00 in Florida. He was almost always presented a gift, however. Sometimes individual students would show their appreciation, such as the girl at Miami Senior High School who made his treasured "four roses" tie.

127

gesticulating, to make excuses, telling how thrilled the band was to be playing under the direction of such a great composer. So he continued. In a flair of frustration and showmanship, Dr. Smirnakovski leaped high into the air and came down on the podium precisely on the beat, trying to keep the band together. All the while, there were more interruptions, and Henry was still attempting to apologize.

Dr. Smirnakovski left the stage after his number; Henry apologized for the constant interruptions and continued his program. Otto reappeared at the end of the concert, minus his formal attire and makeup, no one being the wiser. The whole spoof was so well executed that people thought it was for real. The father of the girl who played the clarinet solo at the beginning had been trying to signal her to stop and walk off the stage in protest. And one of the school officials remarked that it was amazing how Mr. Fillmore could persuade this great Russian composer to take part in a high school program.

Yes, sir. That Henry Fillmore really knew how to swing his considerable weight around!

63   NOT JUST A TIME-BEATER

Judging from Henry's conducting schedule for the year 1953, it would appear that he was slowing down and was concentrating on quality rather than quantity. He accepted fewer engagements, but they were important ones. Since this was the year which marked his steady decline, let us review some of the more notable engagements.

The first engagement of the year was the Orange Bowl game on New Year's Day, when he again led the massed bands. In March, he helped host the ABA convention in Miami, and this grand event was followed by a band festival in Chattanooga. The concerts in Medford, Massachusetts, and Lake Wales, have been discussed previously. On March 16, he conducted the Cities Service Band of America for the third and last time in a special St. Patrick's Day broadcast, again in Paul Lavalle's absence.

On Saturday, August 22, he was a guest of honor at the massive Chicagoland Music Festival at Soldier's Field, sharing the spotlight with Victor Borge. He directed a band of two thousand players in a program which had as its theme "Salute to Hollywood." At this festival, ASCAP presented Henry with a certificate of appreciation for "His outstanding achievement as a composer, author and broadcaster."

In September, he conducted the massed bands at the *Miami Herald's* annual football clinic in the Orange Bowl, and in October he conducted more massed bands on Band Day at a Florida State football game in Tallahassee. Other significant appearances of 1953 were with the University of Miami Band, and these will be discussed in the next chapter.

The year ended as it started, with a performance in the Orange Bowl, this time at a game between Miami Senior High and Edison. On this occasion, the Mayor of Miami presented Henry a certificate of merit in appreciation of his being such a splendid musical ambassador for the city. Self-appointed and without remuneration, no less!

The lasting impression Henry made on the members of school bands he conducted was partly due to a practice which is unique among conductors. Henry's podium antics have been described elsewhere in this book, but there has been little mention of his verbal contact while conducting. He was different in that he talked to the players not only during rehearsals but during performances as well! Few do this, because it is a taboo among conductors with any degree of polish. Henry, however, could never be accused of being a polished conductor. He was as informal as they come. Tradition be hanged; he was in the entertainment business!

At rehearsals, student musicians were immediately put at ease when Uncle Henry stepped up on the podium. When they played incorrectly or not in the proper style, his comments were always made in a positive manner. Rather than make derogatory remarks, he would tell a funny story or poke fun at an errant player in such a humorous manner that everyone would try harder to please him. He had an uncanny knack of knowing a band's limitations and how to bring out the best in every player.

To add a little humor to rehearsals, he would give nicknames or abbreviated titles to some of the music. For instance, "We" was "Americans We"; "Under Arms" became the "B.O. March"; and the overture to *William Tell* became "Bill the Squealer."

Tension and stagefright disappeared when Henry conducted at a concert. When he ascended the podium and lifted his baton for the first number, he would

Abe Aronovitz, Mayor of Miami, presented Henry a certificate of merit for the fine publicity he had brought the city since moving there in 1938. The ceremony took place during halftime at a game between Miami Senior and Miami Edison High Schools on December 30, 1953, and Al Wright's Senior High band saluted Henry on the field.

usually say something relaxing to the performers privately and then make a remark like, "O.K., let's give 'em the works!" or "Shoot it!"

If something was especially pleasing during a number, he would shout out such encouraging words as "Fine!", "That's it!", "Beautiful!", "Yeah!", "Swell!", "Gooooooooood!", or "All right!" When he wanted something played with gusto, it would be "Ho!!!" He intended for the audience to hear these remarks, not just the band members, so it mattered not if microphones were near him. He had to use a certain amount of restraint, however, because occasionally he would get so excited that his false teeth would come loose!

The importance of the bass drum beat in rhythmic music, such as marches, was emphasized. One of the first things he would do at a rehearsal would be to get the bass drummer aside and explain why a dependable beat was essential. He had certain gestures he used just for the benefit of the bass drummers when he wanted to throw in accents that were not marked in the music.

A bass drummer who did not follow the conductor's beat was the cardinal sinner as far as he was concerned. He had this story which he often told to questionable bass drummers:

"When I die, I just might end up in hell. Not an ordinary hell, mind you, but a very special place. 'Way down beneath all the fire and brimstone there'll be a cavern, and deep down inside that cavern will be the torment of torments designed just for me. I'll be chained to a throne, and that throne will be surrounded by a bunch of lousy bass drummers who can't keep the beat. Don't *you* be one of those bass drummers!"

Much to the amusement of youthful musicians, Henry shouted encouraging words during a performance. They would hear exclamations such as "Swell!" or "Beautiful!", and immediately after finishing, he was likely to shout "Good enough!" Audiences loved it.

64 THEIR BUDDY

The final two musical compositions of Henry Fillmore were written during the University of Miami summer band camps. "The Big Brass Band" was written in 1953 (published posthumously as "King Karl King"). When it appeared that Jesse Lasky's grand movie would not be produced, Henry apparently decided to change the name to "The Presidents March" and dedicate it to the current and former presidents of the University of Miami. At least this is the indication given by the twice-altered title on the manuscript. He decided against this, however, and composed a new march by that title in the summer of 1954. It was his last composition.

Henry made the most of the initials of "The Big Brass Band." To add humor to U of M Band programs when he appeared as guest conductor on one of their tours, he announced it as the "3B's March." The audience would be told that two of the B's stood for Beethoven and Bach, and then he would turn to the band and ask what the third one stood for. "Budweiser!" they would shout. Once they spoiled his act by shouting, "Booze!" He used some rather sharp language to express his lack of appreciation to the band that night.

That was one of the few times the band members ever saw Henry in anything but a happy frame of mind. The

ad lib remarks he used at concerts were usually thought out long in advance, and ever since his circus days he had followed his sequences right down to the last detail.

There were other instances when the band conspired to add variations to his routines, but he let them know in no uncertain terms that he did not like surprises of this nature; if they wanted to alter the performance he would be happy to consider it, providing he had an opportunity to talk things over well in advance.

Henry's relationship with Fred and Betty McCall was a very close one. His professional life more or less revolved around the U of M Band, and his and Mabel's social life more or less revolved around the McCalls. Betty was the picture of dignity, but she also had a charming sense of humor which Henry loved. He also loved her cooking and bragged about it to others. In turn, Fred and Betty dined at the Fillmore's at least once a week. Henry treated Fred almost as though he were a son.

Whether the U of M Band went on tour, had a concert or played at a football game, Henry was expected to be there. If not as a participant, at least as a spectator. It was a custom for him to conduct one of his smears at each home game, and when they played "Lassus Trombone'' they used a special arrangement which featured a trombone "pyramid."

Henry might drop in on a band rehearsal at any time—and stir things up. He also loved to watch the football team practice, and he attended so many practices that coach Andy Gustafson issued him a special employee's pass. He came to know several of the players personally and read the newspapers carefully so he could bolster their morale by bragging about their news coverage.

Henry was not held in awe as a famous man by the students; he was their buddy! He derived a considerable amount of pleasure from this personal relationship and was genuinely flattered when a student would ask him for an autographed picture. He was elated when Allene Bushong, one of the pretty majorettes he loved to be surrounded by, knitted him a pair of green and orange (school colors) sox with trombone figures on the sides. Everywhere he went he had to lift his trousers and display his "trombone sox."

Whereas university faculty members normally have reservations about fraternizing with students, Henry had absolutely none. He wanted to know them better so he could give them the benefit of his broad experience in the music world.

Henry and Mabel welcomed students into their home on many occasions. Anyone in the U of M Band who wanted to know Uncle Henry better could easily do just that. He sometimes singled out lonesome students and went out of his way to make them happy. Often he would drop by the band office and say, "Anyone for hamburgers?" Usually they would all end up in a swank restaurant rather than a sandwich shop, eating steak dinners.

Although Henry knew every single band member by name, those closest to him were the ones who were studying to become music educators. In many respects he was an excellent teacher, because they learned practical things from him they would never have learned in the classroom. He had hundreds of fascinating stories about people and events in the real life world of professional music, and conversations naturally gravitated to music, performers and others involved with music.

Students came to Henry for advice concerning career possibilities and music matters of all nature. Even personal matters. For those who would become future band directors, he advised them on dealing with school administrators, becoming a part of a community, how to deal with students' problems, and so forth. Mabel entered into the discussions too, offering such timely advice as "The successful band director always treats the girls with respect—and keeps his hands off."

Above all, he taught students the importance of being well organized. He cited the examples set by circuses and spoke with authority. He never spoke of the conditions under which he entered circus life, however; he did not want them to know of his rebellious nature as a youth. In particular, he did not want them to know he had been with the Lemon Brothers Circus, because some of them might have heard of that circus' bad reputation.

Henry drank with the students, too; in fact, he encouraged social drinking. He would not tolerate drun-

kenness, however. Many times he would stay up until the wee hours of the morning discussing various music situations with a group of students. If at his home, the drinks were on him; if in a tavern, he always picked up the tab. He had a great capacity for liquor, and students told many stories about how "Uncle Henry could drink us all right under the table and stay as sober as a judge." Then he would sometimes turn their stomachs by having a chocolate soda as a nightcap!

When on tour, one night was always unofficially designated "Uncle Henry's night." On these nights, he would pay for the food and drink of any student, male or female, who chose to join him. Drinking was against university rules, but somehow he always got away with it. Once Fred walked into a tavern after hours and caught a group of students drinking with Henry. He said, "For gosh sakes, Henry! Don't you realize that these students have to be loaded and on the bus by 9:00 o'clock tomorrow morning?" Henry's predictable answer was, "Don't worry about a thing, Fred; we'll all be *loaded* long before that!"

The amazing thing about the drinking relationship with the students was that all of them managed to stay out of trouble. One of the reasons, obviously, was that they missed so much sleep they were too tired to get into

Henry was so close to the University of Miami Band members that, for all practical purposes, he was one of them. He accompanied them on their tours, including three trips to Central America. In Guatemala, he was awarded an honorary Doctor of Music degree. It was the first of two he was to receive.

130

trouble. Fred was much annoyed with the drinking, but he looked the other way.

On one occasion, Henry devilishly helped himself to a student's fifth of whiskey. The band was on its way home from Gainesville by train, and one of the students had a bottle hidden in his euphonium case so he could go with his girl to an empty stateroom and enjoy himself. Henry learned of his plans, however. The couple ducked into the stateroom just as he came down the aisle, leaving the euphonium case in the aisle. Henry pretended not to see them; he stopped right in front of the door and sent for several of his favorite students. "I hear a couple of the band members hid a bottle in this case here," he said in a loud voice. "You all know that's against the rules, so don't you think we'd better relieve them of it?" They (names omitted to protect the guilty) then proceeded to assist Henry in consuming the whole bottle, while the couple in the stateroom listened helplessly from behind the door.

Henry's drinking with the students was insignificant compared to what they all experienced when the band went to New York for a football game with Fordham. Drinking was strictly forbidden at home in the Orange Bowl, so they were shocked to see many bottles being tipped at the stadium in New York. Fordham won the game, 20-0, knocking the U of M team out of their previously held national ranking. The crowd was so jubilant they confiscated the band's paper mache palm trees and other props which had been used in the halftime show, and then they started a general riot.

Fred stopped the riot by playing "The Star Spangled Banner," but over Henry's objections. Henry stood by and yelled, "What's the use, Fred? Why not just let the idiots kill one another?" (As a footnote to this story,

The genial Fred McCall, bandmaster at the University of Miami, was Henry's closest friend in the last years of Henry's life. Under Fred's leadership, the U of M "Band of the Hour" became one of the nation's finest university bands. Through Henry's influence, many famous bandmasters appeared as guest conductors of the band.

the U of M avenged their loss in Miami the next season, by the score of 75-7. The following year, Fordham dropped football.)

The band members thought Henry was so much fun they went along with any gag he wanted to pull. One time on a tour they passed through Vero Beach where his sister Mary lived. He persuaded the bus drivers to make a detour through the residential section, and they all stopped for a surprise visit—two bus loads of students!

An outstanding flute player, Harold Supank, was featured as soloist on one of the tours. Harold was a very serious minded student—too serious, Henry thought. So he arranged to have a small girl in the audience at Arcadia, Florida, bring Harold a bouquet of flowers immediately after he finished his solo. As Harold went to the edge of the stage to accept the bouquet, one of the band members slipped a bird's nest in his chair and placed a big glass egg in the nest. When Harold sat down, he arose rather quickly with a loud shriek. "My goodness, Harold!" Henry exclaimed, "You really laid an egg that time!"

With regard to the U of M's rule against drinking, a peculiar problem arose when the band made its second trip to El Salvador in December of 1953. (Henry had not made the first trip). The El Salvador government bought the drinks! At the hotel where the band stayed, the members were furnished any kind of beverage they wanted. Since those making the trip had been instructed not to drink the water, many of them used this as an excuse to pay frequent trips to the bar. Fred had reason for concern.

Henry gave Fred some anxious moments on that trip, but it was all in fun. One of the first things Fred did upon arriving was to get the men students aside and give them a serious talk about personal behavior—about how they should consider themselves representatives of the United States and set good examples.

He had just started his briefing when Henry burst excitedly through the door. "Hey, fellows!" he exclaimed, "Have I got something to tell you!" His message concerned the toilets, which were built very close to the floor and had a rather high water level. He had just used one of them, and. . . For the sake of propriety, the nature of his unpleasant surprise must be left to the reader's imagination. So much for the mood of Fred's serious meeting.

Fred established a curfew, too. The girls were housed in a private school, and one night at 2:00 a.m. he heard a group of young men serenading them outside their windows. He rushed out to see who was so boldly violating the curfew, and there was Henry leading an all-male chorus. Fred did not recognize a single student, however—they were not from the U of M! Since the U of M men were observing the curfew, Henry had gone to a nearby medical college and recruited his own chorus!

This trip, requested by the El Salvador government, was full of adventure. They had asked for a band of mostly women, or, if possible, an all-female band, so the people could see for themselves that women actually did become involved in cultural activities in other countries. Consequently, not many of the U of M Band men

131

made the trip.

The male population of El Salvador looked forward to the U of M Band's appearance. Rumors had even been spread about the Hurricanettes to the effect that there were sixteen naked white-skinned majorettes in white high top boots who would lead the parade! This naturally brought hordes of people, and the press of the crowd was so great that the band was flanked by national guard troops with clubs and fixed bayonets. A row of government officials, with arms locked, brought up the rear.

Even so, the crowds pushed and shoved until there was scarcely room for the band to march, and it was reduced to a single file and eventually broken into three separate sections. One section ended up at the police station, where the government brought in a marimba band to entertain them and served free beer! As for the other two sections, who knew? After one of the majorettes fainted, a news service reported that half of the U of M band had been lost in a riot. Fred learned of this and quickly phoned the editor of the *Miami Herald* before it got into print in the Miami area.

After the confusion ended, security was tightened. Government officials proved to be gracious hosts, and great hospitality was shown at all times. Henry was treated as a celebrity, and of course he made the most of it; he knew how to go first class when there was an opportunity.

The government of Guatemala was not to be outdone by El Salvador. It too invited the U of M Band for a similar visit, in September of 1954, the occasion being the 133rd anniversary of Guatemala's independence from Spain. The band played to enormous crowds—one of their concerts, for example, was attended by 100,000 people. And "El distinguido Maestro Henry Fillmore" was awarded an honorary doctorate—the first of his career.

The band's visit was a tremendous boost to diplomatic relations between the United States and Central America. This could not have come at a better time,

because American popularity in Latin America was on a serious decline. The band members proved to be worthy ambassadors. One government official told Fred McCall that if they had their choice between the U of M Band and jet fighters, they would choose the U of M Band.

Three months after the U of M's trip to Guatemala, in December of 1954, Henry made his third visit to Central America, this time again to El Salvador. The Central American trips were memorable indeed, but just as enjoyable were many trips he made with the band around Florida on the annual spring tours. The band played in both large and small towns, and in many instances the small rural towns were anything but culturally minded. If a concert seemed tedious, however, a dramatic change came when Henry was introduced as guest conductor; he quickly brought things to life with one of his trombone smears.

The audience in one small town was particularly unresponsive, and the band became discouraged. During intermission, Henry was surrounded by students who told him of their displeasure. He said, "Just you wait. I'm going to liven them up!" But they did not believe that even Henry Fillmore could do anything with this impossible audience.

There was a polite applause after the first number, and then Henry was introduced. He strode to the center of the stage, grinning at the audience as he usually did, and then went into a deep bow. Deeper and deeper he went, and he did not come up! The applause grew louder. The band members wondered if something was wrong. He stayed in that position until finally the applause turned to shouts and whistles. When he came out of the bow he continued to flash his smile all around the auditorium as if he were thanking each person individually. Then "Shoutin' Liza Trombone" did indeed "liven them up!" For the remainder of the program, the band played to an enthusiastic, appreciative audience.

Showmanship. . .

65   AND THEN THERE WAS ONE

Casual acquaintances of Henry Fillmore were sometimes confused about his real name. After all, he had composed music under eight names. They would have been even more confused if they had had access to his personal letters (all handwritten, incidentally), because he ended them by using such names as "Phil Mohr" or any of the seven pseudonyms which suited his mood of the moment. For letters from both he and Mabel, it might be "Trom and Bone," "Tex and Texaco," or some other amusing combination.

Casual acquaintances were also confused about his religious preference. He signed many of his letters using Jewish names such as "Abe Cohan," "Moe Ginsberg," "Oscar Greenburg" or "Abie Silverberg." He and Mabel were "Sol and Rheba," "Levi and Becky," "Mose and Rose," and other such combinations. He

applied the same to friends. The John Heneys were often addressed as "Mr. and Mrs. Honus Hockenstool"; the Otto Kraushaars were often "Moe and Mary Bloomberg" or "Lou and Sylvia Humberger." Paul Yoder was "Moritz," Herman Ritter was "Cincinnati Moe," and so forth. He also used these names freely in public.

The Jewish names were a joke with him. "I look Jewish because of my big nose," he explained. There were many Jewish people in Miami, especially during the winter months, and he felt perfectly at home with them.

The plain fact of the matter was that Henry was not a religious person himself, and another person's religion did not concern him in the least. He seldom darkened the door of a church in his adult life, so it is little

One of Henry's idiosyncrasies was celebrating his birthdays on the 2nd of December, whereas his birthday was actually December 3rd. His reason was that since Mabel's was on the 2nd day of the month (November), his should be also. He is cutting his 72nd birthday cake here in 1953, the last he would share with his beloved Mabel. The cake was baked by Al Wright's wife, Gladys, also a distinguished band director, and she decorated it with bars of Henry's "Military Escort."

wonder that people were curious about his religion. He had no strong preference, although on the rare occasions when he attended church in Miami he went to the First Christian Church.

Henry's religious beliefs were simple. To him, no one was evil; there were merely different degrees of goodness. He thought of himself as God's little boy and that if he was bad he would be punished in some way but not permanently hurt. He believed in an afterlife but that there certainly was no such place as hell as it is usually envisioned. He did not subscribe to the theory that a person must attend church regularly to earn peace in that afterlife.

Henry earnestly believed that his purpose in life was to make others happy and that his good deeds would outnumber the bad when judgment day came for him. Even when near death several times, he did not call for a minister.

He did not go out of his way to cultivate the friendship of clergymen. He knew Mabel would acquire the service of one when he died, because among her circle of

friends were many women who were heavily involved in church work. But what if Mabel died before he did? He was not prepared for that. He was not prepared for what happened on Tuesday, April 13, 1954.

On the evening of April 12, he was to treat a group of U of M students to a dinner at the El Bolero Steak House in Miami. At the predetermined time of 7:15, everyone was present except Henry and Mabel. It was not like their Uncle Henry to be late, because he had always set a good example of punctuality. Shortly after 7:30, the restaurant manager came outside looking for the dinner party and informed them that they should go on in and order their dinners; that Mr. Fillmore had called and left the message that he would be detained.

Henry and Mabel were dressing for the dinner when one of the U of M Band members, Lillian Meyer, dropped in. Lillian was sitting in the living room when Mabel suddenly staggered out of the bathroom and shrieked, "Oh, Henry! I have a terrible pain in my head!" Henry and Lillian helped her to a chair, and she complained that the pain had extended to her shoulder. He immediately called for an ambulance, and she was rushed to Mercy Hospital. The hospital attendants wheeled her into the emergency care room, and this is when Henry called the restaurant.

A doctor came out and informed him that Mabel had

Mabel May Fillmore died of a stroke on April 13, 1954, at the age of 72. She and Henry had celebrated their 49th wedding anniversary just eight days earlier.

133

suffered a massive cerebral hemorrhage. By this time she was unconscious, and she was never to awaken; she passed away at 6:30 the next morning.

The funeral service for Mabel May Fillmore, aged seventy-three, was held at the Ben Lanier Funeral Home on Thursday morning at 10:30. After the service, her body was taken to the Grove Park Crematorium, and her ashes were placed in a crypt at Woodlawn Park Cemetery in Miami.

Henry was severely shaken and was so despondent that he believed he could live only a short while longer. The first thing he did after Mabel's cremation was to go to the Ben Lanier Funeral Home and make arrangements for his own funeral, writing a check for full payment in advance.

He received hundreds of letters and cards of condolence. Of all these, he kept only one. It was a letter from Father James P. Ryan of St. Joseph's Rectory in Medford, Massachusetts, where Henry had conducted the Catholic Youth Organization Band a year earlier. In the short time Henry had been there, Father Ryan gained some keen insights into Henry's character. His special delivery letter, which touched Henry deeply, was a fine tribute to both Mabel and Henry. It read, in part, as follows:

I wish to express my sympathy at this time of your bereavement because of your dear wife's death. Let me hasten to say that she is with Our Blessed Glorified and Resurrected Lord in Heaven.

That Joy and happiness which she so richly deserves calls for the most joyous and triumphant music of rejoicing such as one in your grand angelic profession can realize. To say that you will miss her is to belabor the obvious.

Whenever you spoke of her during your most memorable visit here, just a year ago, we could feel the love and devotion you had for each other. I noted too the rapt attention and satisfaction of your listeners, the band boys and their friends, when by means of those simple and sincere words of yours about your dear wife, of being away from her, of talking to her on the phone, of getting back home soon, etc., all unwittingly perhaps, looked through the unlocked doors of your innermost thoughts and saw there in all its richness the mutual love, the understanding, the years of joy, happiness, understanding, admiration and encouragement.

And particularly they saw there the greatness of your noble soul, great in humility, great in love of everything that is good and true, noble and beautiful. All these wonderful Christ-like things you have shared with each other and with everyone whom you could help.

66   TWILIGHT

There was a time when the Fillmore household at 3110 Miami Court was noisy. Mabel contributed very little of the noise, however. Henry would have a football game on the television set, another game on a radio and perhaps a horse race on still another radio. Meanwhile, he might be talking to some students or perhaps working on some music.

But now, it was quiet, Henry was sullen. No doubt his memories brought him happy flashes of the past, accompanied by the tick-tock, tick-tock of the grandfather's clock which had meant so very much to him over the years.

The clock put him in a pensive mood, reminding him of the happiest years of his life—his early forties—the heyday of his Syrian Temple Shrine Band. Yes, the clock reminded him of those happy times; it had said it would!

"...For each time you hear the sound of my chimes
Reminded you'll be of those happy times..."

Yes, he reminisced quite a bit about those golden friendship years...

"Whenever hereafter you look upon me,
A symbol of friendship to you I may be;
A freindship unselfish—devoted—sincere,
A friendship you'll gladly forever hold dear..."

But why spend time mourning in the few remaining days? Why live in the past? He had been an optimist all his life, so why change at such a late date? Eventually, Henry emerged from his shell and began to circulate among associates and friends. However, he was never again to have the old spark and spirit; not quite.

His first step toward returning to a normal life was judging a district band contest in Tampa on May 6, 7 and 8 (1954), and then on May 13, 14 and 15 he judged in Tallahassee. The following weekend he was at Lake Wales for Otto Kraushaar's spring concert.

While at Lake Wales, he passed along some privileged information to Otto. Al Wright was leaving Miami Senior High School to take another step upward in his professional career; he had been appointed Director of Bands at Purdue University.

Henry felt Otto should know this because he wanted him to apply for Al's position. He would certainly get the job because of his impressive record and because Henry would strongly recommend that the school officials hire no one else. But Henry had another reason for suggesting the move: he wanted Otto and Fern to live at 3110 Miami Court.

Otto promised to think it over. But he did not think fast enough for Henry, who telephoned at least twice a week. Otto came to Miami, talked at length with school officials and discussed the situation with his colleagues in the Miami area. Henry continued his calling at regular intervals, and in August, Otto yielded to Henry's pressuring and accepted the position.

It was a difficult decision to make, because he had been at Lake Wales for thirteen years and would have been happy to have spent the remainder of his career there. He and Fern owned their home in Lake Wales and were respected members of the community.

When Al Wright went to Purdue, he took with him

When Otto Kraushaar left Lake Wales to be bandmaster at Miami Senior High School, he and Fern lived with the widowed Henry for nearly two years. Henry is seen here conducting the Miami Senior band at its spring, 1955, concert.

many ideas about football halftime presentations which were in wide use in the Miami area. His brand of pageantry was new to Indiana audiences, and they loved it. Other band directors of the Big Ten took notice, and the spirit of friendly competition took on a new dimension.

Henry had long preached to Al that there were two ingredients for success as a school band director. "First," he said, "you should have a good band. Second, you should always answer your mail!" Simple, but thoughtworthy. To this day, Al Wright has followed those principles religiously.

In August of 1954, Henry revised his will, making drastic changes. He removed the provision for Mabel's younger brother Clarence, of Hawaii, perhaps because there had been very little contact in recent years. The most important change, however, was his generous gift to the University of Miami Band, which will be discussed in the next chapter. Fred McCall had been unsuccessful in attempts to obtain an adequate band building, and Henry assured him that some day soon they would have one.

Henry's health was definitely fading. The lung congestion problem recurred just before Otto and Fern moved in with him in August, and then again just after he returned from the trip to Guatemala with the U of M Band in October. The latter caused him to decline Al Wright's invitation to lead the massed bands at Band Day in West Lafayette—Al's first big splash at Purdue.

Henry was able to make an appearance with the Purdue Band, however, in February of 1955. This trip was planned to coincide with the ABA convention in Elkhart. But it wore him down. In his own words (letter to Al Wright dated March 12, 1955): "I was knocked out for a few days after Purdue, Elkhart. . .Too much, no sleep, liquor, etc."

At this period of Henry's life, he was revealing more of his intimate thoughts to friends. He spoke more freely of his philosophy of life, but only to those who were close to him. At the ABA convention in Elkart, for example, he made a rather amazing statement to Al

Wright: "I moved to Miami thinking I'd die drunk, but here I am alive and kicking around sixteen years later!"

Perhaps the most revealing statement of his outlook came in a letter to Harold Bachman, dated June 24, 1955:

When I was young and ambitious, I worked hard and Mabel and me just knew that some day we'd be able to put away the pen and paper and business worries and spend the rest of our days just doing what we wanted to do. That day came about a year before she passed away, and we had started our dream. She didn't live long enough to enjoy it, but the time she did live— no cares, no financial worries—she certainly did enjoy it.

Now, I have no future responsibilities, no heirs, so am care free. My royalties since Fischer took over have doubled, and the bigger the check to me the happier they seem.

No, I haven't gone to a rocking chair and fly swatter, but I'm enjoying life at 73 with no thought of getting married.

Bachman asked him to compose a march, "Gator Growl," similar to his "Orange Bowl," but he responded that he felt "written out" and that he was "getting lazier every day."

Two legends of the band world pose for a photographer at Tampa on January 15, 1956, where each conducted the Florida All-State Band. William D. Revelli, left, was well on his way to becoming one of the most revered music educators of all time.

The letter to Bachman was written just as the U of M summer band camp had started, and while he was with Fred McCall and Otto Kraushaar one evening he spoke quietly of his obsession with music. He said it was extremely difficult to stay away from the podium and even more difficult to restrain himself when he began to conduct. He said that some day he just might drop dead on a podium. While he hoped that would not happen, it would be preferable to a slow, painful death.

Several days later, Henry suffered still another heart attack. He was in the hospital for twelve days and was released just in time to attend the final concert at the band camp—as a spectator.

His troubles were far from over. Two weeks later he was again taken to the hospital, this time to be treated for asthma. Again he was confined to a hospital bed for twelve days. When released, his weight had fallen to 159 pounds; he had not weighed so little in forty years. He was too weak to drive and was thoroughly disgusted with the turn of events.

He was in good hands at home, with Fern and Otto there to take care of him. It was fortunate that he was able to care for himself by the time school started, because Fern also taught school and was away during the daytime. She was very kind to him, and he appreciated this very much. He tried to express his gratitude by taking them out to dinner frequently. His schedule often made theirs complicated, because he had become a night person and would sleep all day if he felt the urge. During some days he would catch catnaps of five to ten minutes and then go right about his business.

Fern was an immaculate housekeeper, and although Henry did not always cooperate, she cheerfully accepted his informality. As an example of that informality, she and Otto came home from school one day and found him lying beneath the dining room table. That was the coolest place in the house, he explained; he had learned this from Mike twenty-five years earlier!

Living with the Kraushaars was convenient for all. Otto was President of the FBA in 1955 and 1956, and it was nice to have a walking encyclopedia of FBA history within easy reach!

Henry visited Otto at school with regularity. He frequently took his noon meal at school as Otto's guest. Of course he had to tease Otto about the cafeteria food. "That cheap guy!" he would tell friends. "I treated him to a five-dollar steak dinner last night, and all I ever get from him is a thirty-five cent lunch!"

Henry had a small air conditioner installed in the house because of his asthma problem, and this helped make him more comfortable. He was cooled off outside, too, with his new automatic sprinkler system. It was activated by a timer, and he got soaked several times when it malfunctioned. This provoked him, since the system had cost over four thousand dollars, and he remarked that he would have gotten further in the world by spending the money entertaining business acquaintances and friends.

After the last two illnesses, Henry did not bounce back as quickly as he had done in the past. But he *did* bounce back. He conducted a few times in the last months of 1955, but in each instance it was for just one

or two numbers.

The happiest moment in the last year of Henry's life came on February 6, 1956. On that date he was presented an honorary doctorate by the University of Miami. He was now Henry Fillmore, Doctor of Music.

Two others received honorary doctorates that day: Judge William E. Walsh of Miami and Harold B. Maynard, an international management consultant. Dr. Maynard delivered the commencement address, but it was Dr. Fillmore who received the most applause. He was much closer to the hearts of Miamians. The prolonged applause he received when his name was read brought back fond memories of the times he had raised his baton on that campus, in the Orange Bowl, in the high schools and for numerous other gatherings of appreciative Miamians.

The next month, Henry attended his final ABA convention, at Sante Fe, New Mexico. His doctor advised him not to attend, but he was wasting words. At this convention, Henry was commissioned a "Colonel and Aide de Camp" on the staff of the Governor of New Mexico.

Perhaps because his spirits were high, he did not suffer ill effects from the trip to New Mexico. Still, he was but a shell of his former self. He had little energy and could not accept conducting engagements. In May, he caught pneumonia and was out of action for several weeks.

On February 6, 1956, the University of Miami presented Henry with an honorary doctorate. At left is U of M President Jay F. W. Pearson, for whom Henry had composed his last piece of music, "The Presidents March," in 1954.

136

OFF IN ANOTHER WORLD! Henry conducts the U.S. Air Force Band at the ABA convention in Santa Fe, New Mexico, in March, 1956. After several illnesses, his weight dropped to the lowest in forty years.

At 74, Henry had not lost his magic touch. His conducting amused even the professionals, as can be seen by the expressions on the faces of Air Force Band musicians.

The various illnesses slowed him down physically but not mentally. And certainly not when he was behind the wheel of an automobile. He purchased a new Lincoln in June of 1956 and put it through the paces on a vacation trip to North Carolina. He bragged about how the 285 horsepower engine enabled him to travel as fast as 115 miles per hour! On one stretch of straight Florida road he averaged slightly less than ninety miles per hour. Shades of the old Henry Fillmore!

When Otto and Fern moved in with Henry in July of 1954, it had been with the understanding that it would be only until they could find a suitable home of their own. They found one to their liking in April of 1956 and moved into it in June. They invited Henry to sell his house and come live with them, but he declined.

Fred Toll, Henry's sister, came for a lengthy visit shortly after Otto and Fern had moved away. She was widowed now and just as footloose as Henry. Now he had two Freds looking after his welfare: Fred Toll and Fred McCall.

It was a blessing that she came at this particular time, because Henry's health was deteriorating steadily. His heart weakened, and the asthma added to his misery.

Conducting was out of the question. He was able to attend a few football games but sat in the lower level because he could not climb the ramps. By the end of October, he was so frail that most of his time was spent in bed. His diet consisted of salt-free crackers and orange juice, much to his displeasure.

He rallied somewhat when cooler weather set in and he was able to drive around town. The most exciting things he did were to attend U of M Band rehearsals and watch the football team practice. Coach Andy Gustafson had recently named him Honorary Coach because of his enthusiasm for the team, and he tried to make as many appearances at the practice field as possible.

He was receiving two shots a week for the asthma, and by the end of November another complication came with fluid on his lungs. The doctor prescribed a diuretic, and this left him looking more emaciated than ever. Otto and Fern suggested that he be admitted to the hospital, but he had come to dislike hospitals very much and said he would consider that only as a last resort.

On Sunday, December 2, Otto and Fern had a birthday dinner for him at their new home. They noticed that he was breathing especially hard. He was lethargic but was in reasonably good spirits, and he managed a weary smile so Otto could take a snapshot of him and sister Fred. It was his last photograph.

On Tuesday afternoon, he went to the practice field to watch the team in their daily workout. While sitting on a sideline bench, he mentioned to one of the stadium workers that he suddenly felt very ill. He drove home, went straight to the telephone and called for an ambulance to take him to Mercy Hospital.

For three days he lay in the hospital bed in an extremely weakened condition. He complained little, however, and tried to be as cheerful as possible when there were visitors. But it was very, very difficult.

On Friday morning at 9:00 o'clock, Fred McCall stopped off to see him on the way to the university. He was under an oxygen tent and was reading the sports

Henry shared his last photograph with his sister Fred and the new Lincoln sedan which he drove at speeds up to 115 mph! The date was Sunday, December 2, 1956. He was celebrating his 75th birthday (actually December 3rd) at Otto Kraushaar's new home.

page of the *Miami Herald*. He had little to say except, "I see my boy made All American," referring to Don Bosseler, halfback of the U of M team. After that, he dropped off to sleep. Fred left quietly, not knowing that he would be the last person ever to converse with Henry Fillmore.

At 10:30 p.m. on Friday, December 7, 1956, Henry Fillmore passed away in his sleep.

The heart that kept time with some of the happiest music ever heard on the concert stage had finally lost its beat.

How did Henry Fillmore die? Of congestive heart failure, with the contributing causes being myocardial insufficiency, bronchial pneumonia and pulmonary emphysema.

How did Henry Fillmore live? As one eager to bring happiness to others through his music—and his everyday life.

The funeral was dignified and simple, held at 6:30 on the evening of Sunday, December 9, 1956, in the Ben Lanier Funeral home. The parlor and hallway outside were literally filled with flowers—several thousand dollars worth. The minister's oration was short. Only a few hymn tunes were played by the organist; strangely, none were ones written by Henry, his father or his uncles.

The last person to leave was Fred McCall, who knelt in a pew to offer a final prayer. He wept bitterly. He had lost his dearest friend.

The next day, Henry's body was cremated at the Grove Park Crematorium, and his ashes were placed in the vault with Mabel's at the Woodland Park Cemetery in Miami. In the same mausoleum are the remains of August Schaefer and Billy Kopp—significant in that the

The ashes of Henry and Mabel Fillmore are in this vault at the Woodlawn Park Cemetery in Miami. A potted plant (removed for this photograph) is maintained by the University of Miami Band in honor of their memory.

three Cincinattians are close in death as they were in life.

Henry was to have conducted the pre-game festivities at the U of M-Pittsburgh football game in the Orange Bowl on Saturday, December 8, so this portion of the band's presentation was dedicated to his memory. A moment of silence preceded the playing of "The Star Spangled Banner." It was a sad moment for those who had known Henry, but the strains of his arrangement of "The Star Spangled Banner" served as a reminder that his music lives on.

News of Henry's death stunned the band world, because few knew he was seriously ill and because the end had come so quickly. For many, who were accustomed to the happiness and humor for which he will always be remembered, it was indeed a profound shock.

The Midwest National Band Clinic was in session in Chicago, and the leaders hurriedly planned a tribute. At the concert of the Joliet (Illinois) High School Band on Saturday evening, Henry's last composition, "The Presidents March," was performed. This was followed by a roll of muffled drums and a moment of silence. Three thousand of the nation's finest school band directors rose as "Taps" was played, some with tears in their eyes. As a final gesture, the band played Wagner's "Liebestod."

On the day of Henry's funeral, the Music Selection Committee of the Florida Bandmasters Association was meeting, and they, too, quickly arranged for a tribute to Henry's memory. A select band of one hundred students made up the band which performed the music at the clinic session that afternoon. Harold Bachman attempted to speak, but he became so emotional he could not continue. Alton Rine, of Haines City, took over and presented a brief but moving testimonial about how Uncle Henry had influenced so many of their lives. There was not a dry eye in the house. The band then played "Military Escort" without a director, the empty podium symbolizing that no one could ever take Henry Fillmore's place. It was a fitting requiem for a man who was truly one of a kind.

Henry had named Fred McCall as executor of his will, the provisions of which jolted the family. Neither of Henry's sisters received a penny. This was a direct result of his dissatisfaction with his father's will some twenty-one years earlier. Sister Fred took it philosophically, but sister Mary was visibly shaken. Mary's husband was even more upset; he had tied up his savings in lifetime annuities because he was sure Henry would leave money to Mary.

During sister Fred's visit just before he died, Henry had definitely been planning to change his will; he discussed it with her. The new will would have included Fred and Mary and also Otto Kraushaar, but he never got around to changing it.

The will left the sisters only a set of Haviland China which had belonged to their mother. Fred McCall received $10,000 and Herman Ritter $5,000. The University of Miami Band was given the Herschede Hall clock, and the remainder of the estate went to the University of Miami with the stipulation that the money be allocated to the band and used for equipment, maintenance and the promotion and maintenance of a hall for the band's accommodation.

The estate included future royalties from Henry's music and from ASCAP, which were substantial. In the first quarter of 1958, for example, the ASCAP royalties were $3,815.14. The appraised value of the entire estate was as follows:

House	$22,500.00
Government savings bonds and stock in CarlFischer/Fillmore Brothers	33,064.62
Checking and other accounts	43,170.05
Insurance policies and Social Security death benefit payment	6,880.86
Misc. personal property and royalties from music and ASCAP	56,475.00
Total	$162,090.53

Fred McCall was busy for quite some time taking an inventory of Henry's belongings and making plans for the proposed band building. Many of the mementos having to do with Henry's career were earmarked for a museum of some sort. As for personal items of no historical value—such as the girdles he sometimes wore in a rather futile attempt to keep his midsection from making so many excursions while he was conducting—these were distributed among relatives and friends. Some of the music manuscripts were left for the museum, and Fred delivered the remainder to the Carl Fischer office in New York. For technical reasons, Fred was temporarily named a member of ASCAP so the royalties could be collected for the university.

There have been numerous tributes and memorials to Henry Fillmore, such as football halftime shows highlighting his music, memorial concerts, his election to the Hall of Fame of Distinguished Band Conductors, and the Henry Fillmore Composition Contest sponsored by the Florida Bandmasters Association. And there have been numerous pieces of music dedicated to him, such as "King Henry" by Karl King, "Heads Up" by John Klohr, "Fillmore's Triumphal" and "The Melody King" by S.B. Stambaugh (all marches), and "The Bard of Buckeye" overture by Richard Raymond.

The most lasting memorial of all, however, is Henry Fillmore Hall at the University of Maimi, of which the Fillmore Museum is part. Fred McCall worked diligently to create a band building which would have pleased Henry. The entire building was paid for by money from the estate. Fillmore Hall was the third structure in the School of Music complex, which now consists of nine buildings.

The building is very functional, all air conditioned. It includes a rehearsal hall with recording facilities, a music library, a dehumidified uniform room and five dehumidified storage rooms, two offices and the Fillmore Museum. The building is adjacent to Student Lake and also the football practice fields—just as Henry would have wanted it. Fred McCall thought of everything.

Photographs fill several glass cases, and others are hung elsewhere in the museum. There are dozens of items which Henry collected over the years: certificates, diplomas, medals, trophies, plaques, batons, Masonic gear and much other memorabilia. There are also a few of his manuscripts and two career scrapbooks. One of the scrapbooks contains additional photographs.

The building was dedicated at 2:00 o'clock in the afternoon of Friday, March 6, 1959, during the annual American Bandmasters Association convention. The convention was originally to have been held in Madison,

Henry Fillmore Band Hall, on the University of Miami campus at Coral Gables, was dedicated in 1959. This photograph shows the building before others in the School of Music complex were joined to it. The Fillmore Museum is on the second floor, extreme left.

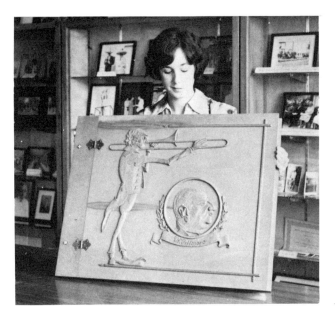

Student assistant Debbie Richey displays one of Henry's two career scrapbooks. The hand carved cover depicts the Fillmore Brothers Co. emblem and a caricature of Henry.

Wisconsin, but the location was changed so that the ABA could participate in the dedication of the hall. The ABA men were very much pleased to see such an elaborate structure named for one of their fellow bandsmen.

The traditional ABA banquet was held on Thursday night, with the Hurricanette twirlers, in their new gold and creme costumes, providing the entertainment. Among the guests of honor were the Graus and Ritters of Cincinnati and Henry's two sisters. Both sisters were presented bouquets, and when their names were mentioned, the ABA membership arose as a body. More than ever before, sister Mary was convinced that, in her her own words of nine years earlier, "Henry finally did get important."

The dedication ceremony was held on the football practice field nearest the building, with the U of M Band furnishing the music. Fred McCall led the band in Henry's "King Karl King" march, which was to be published as soon as the estate was completely probated, and he made a beautiful gesture by stepping down and away from the podium as the band played "His Honor" and "Lassus Trombone." After University of Miami President Jay F. W. Pearson made the formal dedication, Fred McCall gave a short but touching address. Straight from the heart. He climaxed his talk by saying, "There must be a trombone in Heaven."

Fred then introduced sister Fred Toll, and it started to ιain just as she began her speech. Everyone fled to the band rehearsal room for the remainder of the ceremony.

Henry's treasured clock stands proudly in the Fillmore Museum. Because of the clock's historical importance, it was completely rebuilt after this picture was taken in 1980—thanks to the generosity of the Herschede Hall Clock Co., which had manufactured it in 1926.

141

Glass cases in the Fillmore Museum house photographs and memorabilia of Henry's illustrious career. Another large case contains smaller items and a few manuscripts. His two career scrapbooks are seen on the table.

One of many salutes on the occasion of Henry Fillmore's centennial was Band Day at the Orange Bowl on October 3, 1981. The event was sponsored by the University of Miami Band, with many Florida high school bands participating.

Fred continued her fine talk, telling stories of Henry's youth and of the early days of the Fillmore Brothers Company.

Herbert N. Johnston, the ABA President, then presented words of appreciation in behalf of Henry's many colleagues in the ABA. After the benediction, the U of M Band closed the ceremony with the Henry Fillmore arrangement of their alma mater.

Nothing could have been more fitting than an event on Saturday afternoon. The ABA convention committee arranged for the sixth race at Gulfstream Park Race Track to be called "Henry Fillmore race." Several of the ABA men placed bets on a horse named *Best Brother*—and he won!

1981, the centennial of Henry's birth, brought about many tributes in the form of concerts exclusively of Fillmore's music, radio programs, new recordings, articles and the like. Fittingly, the program at the American Bandmasters Association annual convention in Washington, D.C., was dedicated to his memory.

Perhaps the most appropriate centennial salute took place at the university he loved so dearly. The University of Miami "Band of the Hour" sponsored a Band Day program at one of the home football games in the Orange Bowl, and high school bands from around the state fairly filled the playing field in a huge block formation which spelled out "FILLMORE."

68   MUSIC IS FOR ENJOYMENT

> Whatever touches the heart is
> better than what is merely
> addressed to the ear.
> Walt Whitman

How will Henry Fillmore be remembered? He will be remembered for the music he composed, for being one of the finest showmen who ever mounted a podium, for his positive influence on thousands of musicians—both professional and amateur—and for his humor.

His music has stood the test of time. It is happy, buoyant and toe-tapping, and if one understands that music is for enjoyment, he is well on his way to understanding Henry Fillmore.

Numerous writers have said that Henry Fillmore was the successor to John Philip Sousa, but this is perhaps not a fair appraisal. Although some comparisons of the two men are valid, their styles of both composing and conducting were quite different, mostly because Henry's humor was more predominant.

As do his flashy trombone rags, Henry's marches have, in general, a minstrel flavor. They are pretty. They are listenable. It is interesting to know which he considered his favorites, and for the record, his choices were "Americans We," "Men of Ohio," "His Honor," "His Excellency," "Golden Friendships," "The Crosley March," "The Footlifter," "Noble Men" and "Military Escort."

His favorite trombone rags, judging from the frequency with which they appeared on his programs, were "Lassus Trombone" and "Shoutin' Liza Trombone."

Henry was reluctant to evaluate his own music. In some respects he was a trifle egotistical about what he had written, because he believed in it. But on the other hand, he was so modest that he was genuinely flattered when he heard it played in places where he had not expected to hear it. By and large, he took a modest view of its worth and of his own importance to America's musical heritage. Had he not burned his own manuscripts?

Whether Henry was conducting his own works or the works of others, he enjoyed making music so much that his audiences could not help but enjoy it with him. Perhaps Fred McCall best described this phenomenon: "It was as if he reached out and grasped the music, tasted it, and then passed it on to others."

Henry Fillmore, like his distant cousin Millard Fillmore, is proof that even men of modest means can rise to prominence in a democracy. He certainly did not ride into the music world on his father's coattails. He had an enormous talent, the eventual blossoming of which was inevitable. Being shackled to his father's music publishing business perhaps worked to his disadvantage. Others would surely have discovered his genius, and if his music had been published elsewhere he would not have expended so much of his energy on non-creative efforts.

When the final page of the history of music is written, somewhere in that volume will be the account of a minor musical genius by the name of Henry Fillmore, who was as unpretentious in the music he gave to the world as he was in his personal life.

There will no doubt be a few sentences in that volume about his importance as a publisher and a few paragraphs about how he inspired youthful musicians and helped raise the level of music education in America.

But the chapter which tells of his contribution as a composer and as an entertainer will be a long chapter indeed.

Good enough!

APPENDIX I
THE MUSICAL COMPOSITIONS OF HENRY FILLMORE

The catalog of compositions below is a catalog of the original music of Henry Fillmore. His arrangements and transcriptions of the music of other composers are not included. For a complete listing of his musical works, the reader is advised to refer to *The Music of Henry Fillmore and Will Huff*, by Paul E. Bierley (Integrity Press, 1982). That volume also includes publishing and copyright information.

MUSIC COMPOSED UNDER THE NAME OF HENRY FILLMORE

"All Day"
"Americans We"
"Better Be Good"
"Bones Trombone"
"Boss Trombone"
"Bull Bull Bulldogs"
"Bull Trombone"
"Celtic"
"Chasing the Fox"
"Chasing a Pig"
"The Chimes of Iron Mountain"
"Christmas Dollies"
The Christmas Spirit
"The Circus Bee"
"Comin' Round the Mountain"
"The Contest"
"The Crosley March"
Crowned with Light
"The Cuckoo"
"Deep Bass"
"The Dog and the Music Box"
"Dusty Trombone"
"An Earl"
Easter Bells
Easter Joy-Bells
"Five Ways to Play America Exultant"
"The Footlifter"
"Gifted Leadership"
"Giving Mike the Ha Ha"
"Glory to God on High"
"Go Raiders Go"
"Golden Friendships"
"Ha Ha Ha"
"Hail! Hail to Edison"
Hail! Hail Joyful Morning
"Ham Trombone"
Happy Children's Day
"The Hikers"
"His Excellency"
"His Honor"
"Honor and Glory"
"Hot Trombone"
"How Do You Do!"
"I Have Found the Fount of Gladness"
"In Uniform"
"Jackson Pep"
"King Karl King"
"The Kingdom of the Lord"
"The Klaxon"
"Lassus Trombone"
Life and Glory
"Lightning Fingers"
"Lord Baltimore"

"A Loyal Gideon Band"
"Lucky Trombone"
"The Man Among Men"
"The Man of the Hour"
"The Marvel"
"Men of Florida"
"Men of Ohio"
"Miami"
"Miami U-How-Dee-Doo"
"Mike Hunting Birds"
"Military Escort in 5 Ways"
"Miss Trombone"
"More Fraternity"
"Mose Trombone"
"My Master Was a Worker"
"The National Press Club"
"Noble Men"
"North-South College All Stars"
"O Santa Please Come Down My Chimney"
"O You Christmas Candy"
"An Old Time Political Parade"
"On the Wings of the Wind"
"Orange Bowl"
"Our Happy Land"
"Our Own Red, White and Blue"
"Pahson Trombone"
"Paths of Pleasantness and Peace"
"The Phantom"
"Playfellow"
"The Poet, Peasant and Light Cavalryman"
"The Presidents March"
"Ring Out the Old Ring In the New"
"Rolling Thunder"
"Roses"
"Safe in the Arms of Jesus"
"St. Edmund"
"Sally Trombone"
"Sea Hawks"
"Shall We Gather at the River"
"Shoutin' Liza Trombone"
"Slim Trombone"
"Spirit Divine"
The Star-Lit Way
"Sugar"
"The Sunbeams Shining Brightly"
"Teddy Trombone"
"Tell Mother I'll Be There"
"Tosti's Goodbye March"
"Troopers Tribunal"
"The Trumpet Call of God"
"The U.S. of A. Armed Forces"
"Vashti"
"The Victorious First"
"Watch the Traffic Lights"
"Waves"
"We Will Be True"

"When Our Dear Old Santa Comes"
"Whistling Farmer Boy"
"The Wireless S.O.S."
"136th U.S.A. Field Artillery"

MUSIC COMPOSED BY HENRY FILLMORE UNDER THE PSEUDONYM GUS BEANS

"Mt. Healthy"
"Nut Stuff"

MUSIC COMPOSED BY HENRY FILLMORE UNDER THE PSEUDONYM HAROLD BENNETT

"Activity"
"Advance"
"Al and Hal"
"Aline"
"Ambition"
"Annette"
"Anona"
"At Sight"
"Aunt Hannah"
"Biga"
"Bliss Eternal"
"Bright Star"
"The Buglers"
"Chalma"
"College Boy"
"Concord"
"Courage"
"Dawn"
"Delmar"
"Dōn A Do Dat"
"Eels"
"Energy"
"Genius"
"Gyral"
"Havana"
"Have a Little Fun"
"Headway"
"High Tower"
"Hiland"
"Idle Fancy"
"Improvement"
"Indian Boy"
"Janet"
"Knighthood"
"Laurel"
"Little Arab"
"The Little Grey Church"
"Little Marie"
"Little Rastus"
"Maybell"
"Military Escort"
"Mister Joe"
"Mutual"
"Normal"
"Norma's Dream"
"Pivot Man"
"Power"
"Precision"
"Proclar"
"Progress"
"Project"
"Put and Take"
"Sabo"
"Safety"
"Service"
"Sola"
"Stop"

"Success"
"Summit"
"System"
"Vera"
"Village Chimes"
"Welcome"
"Yare"
"Zenith"

MUSIC COMPOSED BY HENRY FILLMORE UNDER THE PSEUDONYM RAY HALL

"Cupid's Dart"
"The Merry Makers"
"Our Waving Colors"

MUSIC COMPOSED BY HENRY FILLMORE UNDER THE PSEUDONYM HARRY HARTLEY

"Gaiety Polka"
"Mabel Polka"
"Polka Militaire"
"Triumph Polka"
"Valse Fantastic"
"Whirlpool Polka"

MUSIC COMPOSED BY HENRY FILLMORE UNDER THE PSEUDONYM AL HAYES

"Altos to the Front"
"America Exultant"
"The American"
"Banner of Democracy"
"The Black Mask"
"Clovernook"
"The Courier"
"Cradle of Liberty"
"Determination"
"Dew Drops"
"Duke Street"
"Emerald Waltzes"
"Empyrean"
"Evening Breezes"
"Extempore"
"Exuberance"
"Fall Roses"
"Flag of Humanity"
"Los Flores"
"Fraternity"
"Gibraltar"
"The Glencoe"
"Go To It"
"Good Citizenship"
"The Gypsy Festival"
"The Herald"
"Inspiration"
"Joyful Greeting"
"Juliet"
"A Little Bit of Pop"
"Longtone"
"March of the Mighty"
"Mariana"
"The Merrimac"
"The Monitor"
"Necoid"
"The North Pole"
"Old Kentucky Home"
"The Old Oaken Bucket"
"The Only Tune the Band Could Play Was Auld Lang Syne"
"Onward Christian Soldiers"
"Organ Echoes"

"Peace and Prosperity"
"The Pirate"
"Pond Lilies"
"Queen of May"
"Rocked in the Cradle of the Deep"
"Sinfonia"
"Softly Peals the Organ"
"Solo Pomposo"
"Southern Pastime"
"Spirit of the Age"
"Under Arms"
"United Service"
"The Universe"
"Visions"
"Vivian"

**MUSIC COMPOSED BY HENRY FILLMORE
UNDER THE PSEUDONYM WILL HUFF**

"Alamo"
"La Albuera"
"La Cascade"
"Dynamic"
"Go"
"Golden Plume"
"Higham March"
"March of the Blue Brigade"

**MUSIC COMPOSED BY HENRY FILLMORE
UNDER THE PSEUDONYM HENRIETTA MOORE**

"Twilight Song"

APPENDIX II
THE RESIDENCES OF HENRY FILLMORE

The residences listed below are Henry Fillmore's *permanent* residences and do not include temporary residences during the following periods:

a) His three school years at the Miami Military Institute in Germantown, Ohio, between 1898 and 1901.

b) The summers of 1898 and 1903 when he ran off with circuses for short periods.

c) Lengthy winter vacations spent in Florida. During the early 1920s he vacationed in Ft. Lauderdale; each winter between 1928 and 1937, he leased apartments in Miami or Miami Beach.

d) Shorter summer vacations spent at his father's rented camp at Crooked Lake, Michigan, between 1915 and 1932, or his own rented camp at Gaylord, Michigan, between 1932 and 1938.

The months listed are approximate in some cases.

December, 1881 to July, 1882:	105 Broadway, Cincinnati, Ohio.
July, 1882 to March, 1887:	Farm at Terrace Park (Cincinnati).
March, 1887 to July, 1888:	66 Betts Street, Cincinnati.
July, 1888 to August, 1891:	52 Clinton Street, Cincinnati.
August, 1891 to September, 1894:	368 West 7th Street, Cincinnati.
September, 1894 to September, 1900:	647 Forest Avenue, Avondale (Cincinnati).
September, 1900 to April, 1905:	4228 Floral Avenue, Norwood (Cincinnati).
April, 1905 to September, 1905:	(with Lemon Brothers Circus).
September, 1905 to March, 1907:	631 West 4th Street, Cincinnati.
March, 1907 to June, 1915:	2 View Court (earlier known as Eastview Court), Mt. Auburn (Cincinnati).
June, 1915 to September, 1923:	2900 Vine Street, Cincinnati.
September, 1923 to March, 1936:	2458 Harrison Avenue, Cincinnati.
March, 1936 to October, 1938:	3481 Epworth Avenue, Cincinnati.
October, 1938 to August, 1939:	8920 Byron Avenue, Miami Beach, Florida.
August, 1939 to July, 1940:	8801 Emerson Avenue, Miami Beach.
July, 1940 to October, 1941:	9124 Byron Avenue, Miami Beach.
October, 1941 to December, 1956:	3110 Miami Court, Miami, Florida.

APPENDIX III
HENRY FILLMORE'S MASONIC AFFILIATIONS
AND DATES OF SIGNIFICANT EVENTS

22 March 1912	Entered Apprentice (First Degree) Enoch T. Carson Lodge, Cincinnati.
19 April 1912	Fellow Craft (Second Degree) Enoch T. Carson Lodge.
31 May 1912	Master Mason (Third Degree) Enoch T. Carson Lodge.
3 November 1916	Petitions for membership in High Noon Lodge, Cincinnati.
23 November 1916	Charter membership in High Noon Lodge.
17 April 1919	Fourteenth Degree, Scottish Rite, Cincinnati.
24 April 1919	Sixteenth Degree, Scottish Rite.
25 April 1919	Eighteenth Degree, Scottish Rite.
22 May 1919	Thirty-second Degree, Scottish Rite.
24 May 1919	Petitions for membership and initiated in Syrian Temple Shrine, Cincinnati.
8 January 1921	Elected director of Syrian Temple Shrine Band.
8 January 1921	Elected director of Syrian Temple Shrine Band.
10 May 1921	Petitions for membership in Oola Khan Grotto, Cincinnati.
18 May 1921	Initiated, Ooola Khan Grotto.
14-17 June 1921	Leads Syrian Temple Shrine Band at national convention (47th Imperial Council Session), Des Moines, Iowa.
27 February- 4 March 1922	Leads Syrian Temple Shrine Band in first Cincinnati Shrine circus.
13-15 June 1922	Leads Syrian Temple Shrine Band at national convention (48th Imperial Council Session), San Francisco.
26 February- 3 March 1923	Leads Syrian Temple Shrine Band in Shrine circus, Cincinnati.
4-7 June 1923	Leads Syrian Temple Shrine Band at national convention (49th Imperial Council Session), Washington, D.C. Private concert for President Harding on White House lawn.
10 June 1923	Leads Syrian Temple Shrine Band at Yankee Stadium, New York.
10 June 1923	Leads Syrian Temple Shrine Band at Yankee Stadium, New York.
2-5 June 1924	Leads Syrian Temple Shrine Band at national convention (50th Imperial Council Session), Kansas City, Missouri.
30 March-4 April 1925	Leads Syrian Temple Shrine Band in Shrine Circus, Cincinnati.
2-5 June 1925	Leads Syrian Temple Shrine Band at national convention (51st Imperial Council Session), Los Angeles.
15-20 March 1926	Leads Syrian Temple Shrine Band in Shrine Circus, Cincinnati.
14 May 1926	Gives notice of resignation as director of Syrian Temple Shrine Band, effective 4 June 1926.
1-3 June 1926	Leads Syrian Temple Shrine Band at national convention (52nd Imperial Council Session), Philadelphia.
2 February 1927	Honorary membership in Lu Lu Temple Shrine, Philadelphia.
August, 1927	Guest conductor of Kishmee Grotto Band, Covington, Kentucky, on trip to East Coast.
September, 1927	Organizes informal splinter group from Syrian Temple Shrine Band for performances at hospitals, etc. Called "Golden Friendships Band" or "Sunshine Band."
19-24 November 1928	Guest conductor of Oola Khan Grotto Band in first Cincinnati Grotto circus.
15 November 1930	Elected to Court 7, Royal Order of Jesters, Cincinnati.
28 March 1931	Initiated (created) in Court 7, Jesters.
20 November 1939	Demitted from Syrian Temple Shrine.
December, 1939	Affiliated with Mahi Temple Shrine, Miami.
January, 1940	Affiliated with Court 88, Royal Order of Jesters, Miami.
12 October 1950	Life membership in Scottish Rite, Cincinnati.
7 December 1950	Honorary life membership in Mahi Temple Shrine.

BIBLIOGRAPHY

BOOKS

Bachman, Harold B. *The Biggest Boom in Dixie.* Gainesville, Fla.: Author, 1968.

Berger, Kenneth. *Band Encyclopedia.* Evanston, Ind.: Band Associates, 1960.

Bierley, Paul E. *The Music of Henry Fillmore and Will Huff.* Columbus: Integrity Press, 1982.

Bierley, Paul E. *John Philip Sousa: American Phenomenon.* Englewood Cliffs: Prentice-Hall, 1973.

Bierley, Paul E. *John Philip Sousa: A Descriptive Catalog of His Works.* Urbana: University of Illinois Press, 1973.

Bridges, Glenn D. *Pioneers in Brass.* Detroit: Sherwood Publications, 1975.

Chipman, Bert J. *"Hey, Rube".* Hollywood: Author, 1933.

Edgerton, Joseph S. *The Pilgrimage 1923.* Washington, D.C.: James William Bryan Press, 1923.

Fillmore, Charles L. *Genealogy of the Fillmore Family.* Unpublished.

Fillmore, John. *A Narrative of the Sufferings of John Fillmore and Others On Board Capt. Phillips' Pirate Vessel: With an Account of Their Daring Enterprise.* Cincinnati: A.D. Fillmore, 1849.

Hall, J.H. *Biography of Gospel Song and Hymn Writers.* New York: Revell, 1914.

Severance, Henry O. *Palmer Hartsough.* Columbia, Mo.: Author, 1937.

Various writers. *Twenty Years.* [Published on the occasion of the twentieth wedding anniversary of James Henry and Annie Eliza Fillmore] Cincinnati: Armstrong & Fillmore Printing House, 1900.

ARTICLES

Bachman, Harold B. "Henry Fillmore: A Tribute to a Bandsman." *Music Journal,* December, 1968 (Part 1); January, 1969 (Part 2).

Benton, Elizabeth Gates. "Fillmore Music Marches On." *Selmer Bandwagon,* Fall, 1968.

Benton, Elizabeth Gates. "He Made America March." *Miami Herald,* April 9, 1961.

Benton, Elizabeth Gates. "Henry Fillmore, All-American Bandmaster." *The Instrumentalist,* December, 1960.

Benton, Elizabeth Gates. "Henry Fillmore's Tunes Keep America Marching." *Cincinnati Enquirer,* June 4, 1961.

Bierley, Paul E. "A Bit of Intrigue." On record jacket, *Heritage of the March, Vol. 45.* Produced privately by Robert Hoe, Jr., Poughkeepsie, N.Y.

Bierley, Paul E. "The Case of the Duplicate Composer." *The Instrumentalist,* October, 1979.

Bierley, Paul E. "Dedication—the Story of John J. Heney." *The School Musician/Director & Teacher,* April, 1979.

Bierley, Paul E. "Henry Fillmore (1881-1956)." On record jacket, *Heritage of the March, Vol. 47.* Produced privately by Robert Hoe, Jr., Poughkeepsie, N.Y.

Bierley, Paul E. "Pryor, Arthur W." In *Dictionary of American Biography, Supplement Three.* New York: Charles Scribner's Sons, 1973.

Bierley, Paul E. "Will Huff (1875-1942)." On record jacket, *Heritage of the March, Vol. 46.* Produced privately by Robert Hoe, Jr., Poughkeepsie, N.Y.

Braathen, Sverre O. "Circus Windjammers." *Bandwagon,* May-June, 1971.

Braathen, Sverre O. and Faye O. "The Parallel Development of Circuses and Bands in America." *Bandwagon,* November-December, 1972.

Chindahl, George L. "Lemon Bros. Circus." *The White Tops,* September-October, 1955.

Kalfs, Barbara B. "Famed Composer Was Part of Early Adelphi Band." *Chillicothe* (Ohio) *Gazette,* October 13, 1973.

Manning, Annette Fillmore. "My Grandfather, Phonetics and Music." *Bulletin of the Cincinnati Historical Society,* 1965.

Toll, Fred Fillmore. "Annie Eliza McKrell." Unpublished. No date.

Toll, Fred Fillmore. "James Henry Fillmore." Unpublished. No date.

Toll, Fred Fillmore. "James Henry Lockwood." Unpublished. No date.

Toll, Fred Fillmore. "The Old Rockaway." Unpublished. No date.

Toll, Fred Fillmore. "Our Heritage" (incomplete). Unpublished. ca. 1968.

Toll, Fred Fillmore. "The Red Carpet." Unpublished. ca. 1959.

Toll, Fred Fillmore. "Tea for Two Thousand." Unpublished. No date.

Yoder, Paul. "The Early History of the American Bandmasters Association." *Journal of Band Research,* Vol. I, Autumn, 1964 (Part I); Volume I, Winter, 1965 (Part II); Volume II, Spring, 1966 (Part III); Volume III, Autumn, 1966 (Part IV).

Autobiographical article by Will Huff. Unpublished.

"Henry Fillmore Band Hall Dedication To Be March 6." *Alumni Bulletin* (University of Miami), February, 1959.

"James Henry Fillmore." Chapter in *Cincinnati, the Queen City, Volume 4.* Chicago and Cincinnati: S.J. Clark Publishing Co., 1912.

"Remember the Florodora Band?" *Wellston* (Ohio) *Sentry,* February 15, 1972.

"Will Huff, an Appreciation." *Musical Messenger,* ca. May, 1913.

MISCELLANEOUS

ABA (American Bandmasters Association) *Newsletters,* various issues, 1944-1957.

Career scrapbooks of Henry Fillmore (2). Fillmore Museum, University of Miami.

Correspondence between Henry Fillmore and John J. Heney, 1942-1953.

Correspondence between Henry Fillmore and Otto J. Kraushaar, 1939-1956.

Correspondence between Henry Fillmore and Luise Reszke, 1934-1935.

Correspondence between Henry Fillmore and Al G. Wright, 1954-1956.

Correspondence between Henry Fillmore and others, mostly Harold B. Bachman and John J. Henery. Florida Bandmasters Association files, Gainesville.

Correspondence between Will or Eleanor Huff and the Fillmore Brothers Co., 1938-1945. Also various royalty sheets and royalty cancellation agreement.

Diaries of James Henry Fillmore and Fred Evans Fillmore, 1921-1922.

Miami Military Institute brochure, 1896.

Minutes of Syrian Temple Shrine (Cincinnati) meetings, 1921-1928.

Musical Messenger, various issues, 1891-1924. Cincinnati: Fillmore Brothers Co.

Wake, Arthur Norrie. ''Henry Fillmore.'' Term paper. Unpublished. March 13, 1961.

INDEX

Ironton, Ohio, 52
Israel, 64
Italy, 64, 92
Jackson High School, see Miami Jackson High School
Jackson, Ohio, 52
Jacksonville, Florida, 118
Jacobs' Band Monthly, 69
Jacobs' Orchestra Monthly, 69
James, 96
Japan, 64
Jennie (elephant), 39
Jergens, Andrew Nicholas, Jr., 23
Jergen's lotion, 23
Jesters, 106
Jesus of Nazareth, 5
Jewell, Fred, 46, 91
"Jingle Bells," 101, 106
Johnson Paint Company, 79, 85
Johnson, T.C., 32
Johnston, Herbert N., 124, 143
Joliet High School Band, 139
Jones, Charles B. (Charlie), 74, 75, 76, 77, 85, 90
Jones, Clarence, 135
Jones, D., 77
Jones, Jesse, 35
Jones, Mabel May, see Fillmore, Mabel May
Jones, Mary, 35
Jones, Spike, 111
Jones, Stephan, 118
Jones, Toots or Tootsie, see Whitford, Hanna
Joonie (dog), 72
Joseph, C., 77
"Joyful Greeting," 59, 66
Jung, William (Bill), 55, 100, 108
KDKA Radio, 70
Kabiesch, H., 77
Kaiser, A., 77
Kalamazoo College, 14
Kansas City, Kansas, 37
Kansas City, Missouri, 71
Kendrick, W. Freeland, 75
Kentucky, 5, 7, 8, 24, 50, 55, 64, 70, 73, 89
"Kid's Band," 52
Kiefer, Jack, 122
"King Henry," 105, 140
"King Karl King," 124, 129, 141
King, Karl L., 89, 91, 105, 114, 119, 124, 140
King, Ruth, 105
Kirchner's Restaurant, 92
"Klaxon, The," 88
Klaxophone, 88
Klohr, John, 45, 46, 50, 76, 77, 82, 88, 91, 140
Knights of Columbus Hall, 55
Kohlman, Charles, 30
Kopp, William J. (Billy), 34, 47, 77, 95, 101, 106, 139
Kopp's Military Band, 34
Kraushaar, Fern, 108, 127, 134, 135, 136, 138
Kraushaar, Otto, 105, 106, 108, 109, 111, 113, 118, 126, 127, 128, 134, 135, 136, 138, 139
Kumler, A., 77
Kunkel, O., 77
LaBarre, Eugene S., 89
Lahairoi herd of camels, 38
Lake Erie, 75
Lake Huron, 35
Lake Muskoka, 89
Lake Ontario, 75
Lake Wales, Florida, 105, 106, 108, 111, 113, 126, 127, 128, 134, 135
Lake Wales High School, 109
Lampi, Bob, 110, 111

Lampi, Ilimae, 111
Landers, George W., 113
Lanier, Ben, Funeral Home, 134, 139
Lasky, Jesse, 123, 124, 129
"Lassus Trombone," 1, 49, 60, 66, 73, 87, 111, 113, 114, 129, 141, 143
Latin America, 132
Lavalle, Paul, 119, 120, 122, 123, 128
Lawrenceburg, Kentucky, 63, 98, 125
Lemen Brothers World's Monster Shows, 38
Lemon Brothers Circus, 36, 37, 38, 39, 40, 41, 42, 43, 47, 130
Lemon, Colvin, 39
Lemon, Ed, 37
Lemon, Fay, 37
Lemon (also Lemen), Frank V., 37, 39, 40, 42
Lemon, Frost (Frostie), see Lemon, James
Lemon, James (Frost, or Frostie), 39
Lexington Fair, 30, 34, 47
Lexington, Kentucky, 30, 74, 89
Library of Congress, 61, 96
"Liebestod," 139
Lighthouse Mission, 36
"Lightning Fingers," 82
Lima, 50
"Lincoln," 55
Lincoln, President Abraham, 55
Lind, H., 77
Link, C., 77
Lions International, 118
Liszt, Franz, 49
"Little Arab," 98
"Little Gray Church, The," 98
"Little Rastus," 98
Littleton, John, 59, 66
Liverpool, England, 64
Local 1, see Cincinnati Musicians Association
Lockwood, Anna, 24
Lockwood, Ezekial, 6
Lockwood, Hannah, see Fillmore, Hannah
Lockwood, James Henry, 6, 24
Lockwood, Sarah, 24
London (Ohio) *Times,* 41
Longview Hospital, 48
"Lord Baltimore," 33, 104
Los Angeles, California, 18, 71
Losey, Frank, 46, 91
Louisiana Purchase Exposition, 34
Louisiana Territory, 35
"Lucky Trombone," 88
Ludwig instruments, 91
Lyon, Finley, 15
Lytle Park, 95
MGM, 123, 124
McCall, Betty, 105, 129
McCall, Fred, 101, 104, 105, 107, 110, 111, 112, 113, 115, 116, 118, 124, 126, 129, 131, 132, 135, 136, 138, 139, 140, 141, 143
McCall's, 98
"McCormack, John, of Dogdom," 85
McCracken, Everett, 89
McDermott, R., 77
McKinley Park, 95
McKinley, President William, 18
McKrell, Abraham, 7
McKrell, Annie, see Fillmore, Anna
McKrell, Molly, 16, 20
McKrell, Nancy Ryan, 7, 8, 16, 17, 18
McKrell, Solomon, 7
Madison, Florida, 103
Madison Square Garden, 118
Madison, Wisconsin, 105, 140, 141
Mahi Temple Shrine Band, 95, 106, 126
Malta, 64
"Man Among Men, The," 67, 113

Manchu, China, 64
Manhattan Band, 52
Manitoba, Canada, 71
Manning, Annette Fillmore, 98, 106
"Man of the Hour, The," 71, 115
Mantia, Simone, 119
"March of the Automobiles," 88
"March of the Blue Brigade," 33
Marconi, Guglielmo, 55
"Margaret," 55
"Marie," 98
Marotti, Arthur, 120
Martin, Charles, 100, 120, 122
Martin, G., 77
Mason-Dixon Line, 117
Masonic Temple, 71, 74, 75
Massieville, Ohio, 52
Maynard, Harold B., 136
Mays Lick, Kentucky, 7
"Meaco Overture," 55
"Meaco Waltz," 55
Mead Pulp and Paper Company, 53, 54, 55
Meads, 74
Medford, Massachusetts, 126, 128, 134
Medina Temple, A.A.O.N.M.S., 62
"Meditation, A," 48
"Meet Me in St. Louis," 96
"Melody King, The," 140
Menge, T., 77
"Men of Florida," 116, 118
"Men of Ohio," 1, 62, 67, 68, 75, 76, 107, 110, 116, 143
Mercy Hospital, 133, 138
Messiah, 2, 61
Metcalf, Leon, 91, 127
Methodist Book Concern, 7
Mexico, 71, 75
Meyer, Lillian, 133
Meyers, Albertus L., 89
"Miami," 100, 101
Miami Beach, Florida, 91, 98, 100
Miami Business College, 24
Miami Edison High School, 101, 104, 105, 108, 111, 113, 115, 128
Miami Edison High School Band, 107, 110, 112
Miami-Erie Canal, 10, 30
Miami, Florida, 79, 95, 96, 98, 99, 100, 101, 102, 104, 105, 106, 107, 108, 109, 110, 111, 112, 115, 116, 117, 118, 120, 121, 125, 128, 132, 133, 134, 135, 139
Miami Herald, 128, 132, 138
Miami Jackson High School, 101, 113
Miami Jackson High School Band, 110, 115, 116, 118, 119
Miami Military Institute, 20, 21, 22, 23, 24, 25, 26, 27, 28, 29, 34
Miami Senior High School, 102, 108, 113, 127, 128, 134, 135
Miami Senior High School Band, 109, 110, 115, 117, 120, 128, 135
Miami University (of Ohio), 106
Miami Valley Festival, 87
Miamisburg, Ohio, 43
Michigan, 14, 18, 20, 31, 35, 40, 56, 57
Michigan State Normal College, 14
Middletown High School Band, 88
Middletown, Ohio, 59, 60, 85, 88
Midwest National Band Clinic, 139
Mike the "radio hound," 72, 73, 74, 78, 79, 80, 81, 82, 83, 85, 86, 89, 90, 91, 92, 93, 94, 99, 110, 136
Milford, Ohio, 10
"Military Escort," 65, 66, 73, 98, 107, 109, 117, 133, 139, 143
"Military Escort in 5 Ways," 117

154